Patrons, Partisans, and Palace Intrigues

LATIN AMERICAN AND CARIBBEAN SERIES

Christon I. Archer, General Editor

ISSN 1498-2366

This series sheds light on historical and cultural topics in Latin America and the Caribbean by publishing works that challenge the canon in history, literature, and postcolonial studies. It seeks to print cutting-edge studies and research that redefine our understanding of historical and current issues in Latin America and the Caribbean.

No. 1 · **Waking the Dictator: Veracruz, the Struggle for Federalism and the Mexican Revolution** Karl B. Koth

No. 2 · **The Spirit of Hidalgo: The Mexican Revolution in Coahuila** Suzanne B. Pasztor · Copublished with Michigan State University Press

No. 3 · **Clerical Ideology in a Revolutionary Age: The Guadalajara Church and the Idea of the Mexican Nation 1788–1853** Brian F. Connaughton, translated by Mark Allan Healey · Copublished with University Press of Colorado

No. 4 · **Monuments of Progress: Modernization and Public Health in Mexico City, 1876–1910** Claudia Agostoni · Copublished with University Press of Colorado

No. 5 · **Madness in Buenos Aires: Patients, Psychiatrists, and the Argentine State, 1880–1983** Jonathan Ablard · Copublished with Ohio University Press

No. 6 · **Patrons, Partisans, and Palace Intrigues: The Court Society of Colonial Mexico, 1702–1710** Christoph Rosenmüller

Patrons, Partisans, and Palace Intrigues

The Court Society of
Colonial Mexico,
1702–1710

UNIVERSITY OF
CALGARY
PRESS

Christoph Rosenmüller

© 2008 Christoph Rosenmüller

University of Calgary Press
2500 University Drive NW
Calgary, Alberta
Canada T2N 1N4
www.uofcpress.com

No part of this publication may be reproduced, stored in a retrieval system or transmitted, in any form or by any means, without the prior written consent of the publisher or a license from The Canadian Copyright Licensing Agency (Access Copyright). For an Access Copyright license, visit www.accesscopyright.ca or call toll free 1-800-893-5777.

LIBRARY AND ARCHIVES CANADA CATALOGUING IN PUBLICATION

Rosenmüller, Christoph, 1969–
    Patrons, partisans, and palace intrigues : the court society of colonial Mexico, 1702–1710 / Christoph Rosenmüller.

(Latin American and Caribbean series, ISSN 1498-2366 ; 6)
Includes bibliographical references and index.
ISBN 978-1-55238-234-9

1. Alburquerque, Dukes of. 2. Patronage, Political—Mexico—History—18th century. 3. Viceroys—Mexico—History—18th century. 4. Political culture—Mexico—History—18th century. 5. Mexico—Politics and government—1540-1810. 6. Spain—Politics and government—1700-1746. 7. Spain—Colonies—America—Administration—History—18th century. I. Title. II. Series.

F1231.R74 2008   972'.02   C2007-907473-1

The University of Calgary Press acknowledges the support of the Alberta Foundation for the Arts for our publications. We acknowledge the financial support of the Government of Canada through the Book Publishing Industry Development Program (BPIDP) for our publishing activities. We acknowledge the financial support of the Canada Council for the Arts for our publishing program.

Cover design, page design and typesetting by Melina Cusano

Front and back cover illustration: Detail, Fransisco Férnandez de la Cueva Enríquez, tenth Duke of Alburquerque. Courtesy Museo Nacional de Historia, Mexico City.

Table of Contents

Acknowledgments   VII
Abbreviations   IX
List of Figures and Tables   X

1. Introduction   1
2. The Political and Economic Culture of Spain's
    Early-Eighteenth-Century Empire   11
3. Court and Corruption in Colonial Mexico   29
4. Clients and Creatures: Alburquerque's Pervasive Patronage   53
5. The Clash over Contraband Commerce and the *Consulado*   79
6. Fighting the Faux Habsburg Conspiracy, 1706–1708   101
7. Alburquerque Resists Royal Reforms   127
8. Reform and Revenge: The Fall of Alburquerque, 1711–1715   143
9. Conclusion   163

Appendices
    1. Glossary   170
    2. Biographical Information   175
    3. Prosopography of Mexican Audiencia Ministers in
        Relation to the Viceroy   180
    4. The Mexican Consulado and the Alcaldes Ordinarios of
        Mexico City's Cabildo Civil   188
    5. Index of Albuquerque's Appointments of Alcaldes Mayores,
        Corregidores, and Governors   191
    6. Alburquerque's Appointments in the Military   218

Notes   221
Bibliography   259
Index   273

Figure 1: Francisco Férnandez de la Cueva Enríquez, tenth Duke of Alburquerque (1666–1733)

Source: Museo Nacional de Historia, Mexico City

Acknowledgments

In the first place, I would like to thank my former advisor at Tulane University, Colin MacLachlan, for his support and substantial advice on the topic. I also wish to express my gratitude to Susan Schroeder and James Boyden, who helped me with their vast knowledge of early modern New Spain and Spain. Horst Pietschmann, who read my master's thesis at the University of Hamburg, Germany, continued to give me many thoughtful suggestions. The editor of the Latin American and Caribbean series at the University of Calgary Press, Christon Archer, has greatly aided me in many ways in bringing the book to publication. Mark Burkholder, K. C. Johnson, Guillermo Náñez Falcón, Caterina Pizzigoni, and Michael Polushin read earlier drafts of this manuscript. Many improvements are owed to their critique and historical knowledge. Javier Sanchiz at the Institute of Historical Studies of the National Autonomous University (UNAM) in Mexico freely shared data from his forthcoming monumental social history and genealogy of the Mexican nobility and the knights of the military orders. Linda Arnold counselled many times and gave access to her unpublished guides to Mexican archives.

I also profited from advice and conversations with William Beezley, Michel Bertrand, Alejandro Cañeque, Bill Connel, José Enrique Covarrubias, Linda Curcio-von Nagy, Mark Eagle, James Garza, Kenneth Harl, Renzo Honores, Sherry Johnson, Alan Kuethe, Murdo MacLeod, José Hernández Palomo, Julia Krause, Magnus Lundberg, Fritz Schwaller, María del Carmen Vázquez Mantecón, Enriqueta Vila Vilar, and Charles Walker.

A grant from the Selley foundation made research overseas possible. Middle Tennessee State University supported completion of the book with two Faculty Creative Arts and Research grants. I am most indebted to the staff of the Archivo General de la Nación in Mexico City for all their kind help. I also have fond memories of my research in the Archivo del Arzobispado, the Archivo Histórico del Distrito Federal, the CONDUMEX, the Biblioteca Nacional and the Instituto de Investigaciones Históricas at the UNAM as well as the Archivo del Cabildo de la Catedral Metropolitana. In Spain, I owe my gratitude to the Escuela de Estudios Hispano-Americanos in Seville for receiving me as their guest. The *jefes de sala* at the AGI proved helpful as well as the staff at the Archivo Histórico Nacional and the Biblioteca Nacional. My special thanks also to the Archivo Histórico Casa Ducal de Alburquerque located in a medieval tower overlooking the splendid town of Cuéllar. Editors Peter Enman and John King at the University of Calgary Press have spotted many errors and considerably polished the manuscript. Angela Smith at MTSU professionally drew up the map and scanned images. ¡*A todos mil gracias*! My parents Birgit and Joachim Rosenmüller supported me all along. Without their help, this book would not have been possible. *Vielen herzlichen Dank!*

Abbreviations

AEA	Anuario de Estudios Americanos, Seville, Spain
AGI	Archivo General de las Indias, Seville, Spain
AGN	Archivo General de la Nación, Mexico City
EEHA	Escuela de Estudios Hispano-Americanos, Seville, Spain
JbLA	*Jahrbuch für Geschichte Lateinamerikas*, formerly *Jahr buch für die Geschichte von Staat, Wirtschaft und Gesell schaft Lateinamerikas*, Cologne, Germany
RLRI	Recopilación de leyes de los reinos de las Indias, 1680

List of Figures and Tables

Figure 1   Francisco Fernández de la Cueva Enríquez, tenth Duke of Alburquerque (1666–1733)

Figure 2   Map of New Spain in the early eighteenth century

Figure 3   Plan from 1709 for the reconstruction of the first, second, and third floor of the viceregal palace

Figure 4   Fernando Brambila, Plaza Mayor of Mexico City

Table 1   The viceregal court of the tenth Duke of Alburquerque

Table 2   Appointments of criados to alcaldías mayores

Table 3   Appointments in the real hacienda

Table 4   Criados remaining in New Spain

Table 5   The alliances of Alburquerque and Luis Sánchez de Tagle in 1703

Table 6   Regional background and membership in the military orders among the feuding mercantile networks, 1703–1706

Table 7   Defendants in the conspiracy trials, 1706–1708

Table 8   The Mexican audiencia during the clash with the trustees of the Sevillian consulado, 1702–1703

Table 9   The Mexican audiencia during the conspiracy trials, 1706–1708

Table 10   The cathedral chapter of Mexico City in 1706

1

INTRODUCTION

Palace intrigues, patrons, and clients – these themes are not usually associated with the colonial state in Spanish America. Yet, increasingly analysts have acknowledged the power of Mexican mandarins' social ties to their friends and minions.[1] At the same time, social scientists again are putting more emphasis on institution building as a key to safeguarding successful democratization in Latin America.[2] The demise of the political monopoly of Mexico's Institutional Revolutionary Party (PRI) in 2000 heralded a new epoch in this regard.[3] The change of government poses the question of how to mediate the personal interests of the incoming politicians and their followers with the desire to build more effective institutions to continue the successful modernization of the country.

Under these circumstances, a historical investigation into the links between the bureaucracy and clientele politics in Mexico moves to centre stage – especially since recent historiography has almost completely ignored this subject. In this book, I therefore trace the interaction of power elites and their clientage with the most powerful office in colonial Mexico: the viceroy.[4] Elites and retainers met at the viceregal court to negotiate the imperial and their personal agenda, shaped the course of Mexican politics and society, and plotted against their enemies.

The traditional institutional historiography of Hispanic America has overestimated the power of the state to mould society.[5] Subsequently, historians have begun more fully to appreciate the gap between the legal intentions of the crown and the functioning of overseas institutions. The imperial administration turned out to have been less efficient and more influenced by American society. Scholars such as John Leddy Phelan helped forge a historiographical consensus, positing that Creole elites were firmly in control of Spanish America by the seventeenth century, a facet of empire typically linked to a weak Habsburg monarchy.[6] Following this explanation, Jonathan Israel postulated that the crown had a tight grip on colonial Mexico under King Philip II (1556-1598) and that its control slipped in the seventeenth century. According to Israel, the overthrow of the Marquis of Gelves in 1624 and the widespread corruption under his successor, the eighth Duke of Alburquerque (in office 1653-1660) characterized the decay of royal power in colonial Mexico.[7]

Previously, David Brading had advanced the thesis of a revival of royal authority over America under the Bourbon king Charles III (1759-1788).[8] Brading characterized the reforms in Spanish America initiated by the inspection tour (*visita*) of José de Gálvez (1765-1773) and his subsequent term as secretary of state of the Indies (1776-1787) as a "revolution in government."[9] According to Brading, Gálvez assaulted the Creole establishment with the introduction of intendants (regional royal governors) in 1786, the expansion of the bureaucracy with mostly peninsular, salaried officials, and the breaking up of monopoly trade.[10] Historian Colin MacLachlan has supported this thesis insofar as he argues that the monarchy breached the traditional contract of negotiating political issues between the centre and the colonies.[11] Soon, however, John Tutino entirely rejected the effectiveness of the reforms in New Spain, as colonial Mexico was then known. Having "encountered no evidence of altered social and economic structures caused principally by the reform movement," Tutino argued that the reforms left the Creoles' power untouched.[12] German historian Horst Pietschmann repudiated the "revolution in government" on the grounds that the establishment of provincial intendants resulted in enduring changes but fell short of Madrid's expectations.[13] Pietschmann argued that while officials took on Creole oligarchies, "the introduction of the intendancy system in New Spain did neither raise the effectiveness of the administration nor did it realize the general political intentions."[14] Pietschmann also viewed Gálvez's reforms not as a political sea change, but rather as the continuation of a long struggle between crown and feudal tendencies that went back at least to the Catholic kings, with their policy of appointing royal officials (*corregidores*) in Castilian town halls.[15] John Lynch had cast doubt on the novel character of the reforms under Charles III by tying them to the political program of the Count of Oropesa, sole prime minister since 1685 and dismissed in 1691. According to Lynch, this Habsburg statesman attempted to tighten control over the financial administration and the Church.[16]

While historians have illuminated the political conflicts and administrative changes for the pre-independence period (and the Conquest), we still know only the bare outlines of Mexican political culture from the late seventeenth to the mid-eighteenth century.[17] In comparison to European and United States history, where an abundance of monographs have tracked political, social, and economic changes through the centuries, this is even more disconcerting. Reflecting the trends in the national historiographies, the Spanish handbook *Rialp Historia General* includes the most comprehensive narrative on imperial politics and a short sketch of viceregal governance in New Spain, while the Anglophone manual *Cambridge History* does not have a chapter on the colonial state at all.[18]

In this book I focus on the conflict between expanding state power and the opposition it met in colonial Mexico prior to the well-known reforms of the later eighteenth century. Researchers have long sought to explain the rise of state power over its competitors in a wider framework of the Western world. Max Weber envisioned the formation of the modern state as the culmination of a process of centralization and rationalization where the prince progressively removed all financial or political competitors from power. Relying on an increasingly predictable interpretation of the law, Weber argued, a social caste of trained bureaucrats and jurists allied with the prince took over politics and subjected the individual to the tight bonds of modern discipline.[19] The process of modernization, Weber contended, confined man within the boundaries of the "iron cage."[20] Although perhaps somewhat faulty in detail, Weber's analysis of modernization has had significant impact on scholarship. Gerhard Oestreich, who subscribed to the idea of rationalization, pointed out that Weber had overlooked how little power the crown in the *ancien régime* exercised on the local level. Instead, Oestreich argued for a wider mental process based on the rising influence of neo-stoic thought in the seventeenth century.[21] Humanists during that era of great religious strife in Europe called for a strengthening and de-sacralization of the state to allow it to separate and pacify the feuding parties. These scholars and statesmen had recourse to Roman stoicism that praised values of will, strict education, and discipline to restore the state – a state as powerful as the scholars envisioned the classical empire to have been. While it gained legitimacy as arbiter between the warring parties, the state pursued the inculcation of its populace with a more rigid morale. Oestreich coined for this process the phrase "social disciplining."[22] Over time, the absolutist state extended these values into the military, the bureaucracy, the Church, and the economy. Oestreich argued further that the state slowly gained control, so that by the nineteenth century it was able to supervise humans even on the local level through instruments such as schools, hospitals, and statistical surveys.[23]

More recently, historian Wolfgang Reinhard added that the rising costs of modern warfare, with standing armies and mounting firepower, forced the centre to mobilize additional resources. In the urgencies of war, the monarch could legitimately divest power contenders such as the Church and aristocrats of their resources and subject them to his will. While disciplining the administration and the army, the monarchs cast the foundations of the rational state.[24]

Although the neo-stoic discourse itself did not notably affect the intellectual horizon proper in New Spain, the process marked debates and politics in Spain. These currents affected the crown's policies towards New Spain, reflected in an increasing attempt to enforce standards of conduct in the administration, the military, and the Church.[25] Symptoms of the conflicts between power elites and the monarch must be visible at the Mexican viceregal court even in the period before Gálvez's reforms. Thus, this analysis is a contribution to the larger debate about modernization and Brading's argument of the "revolution in government."

Since the 1960s, anthropologists and sociologists have increasingly stressed the importance of social networks for explaining social structures and the growth of state power.[26] Scholars hold that members of an immediate family have extended their network through collateral relations with aunts, uncles, cousins, and nieces. Godparenthood and coparenthood, or as they are known in the Hispanic world, *padrinazgo* and *compadrazgo*, also created an emotive bond that expanded the relationship of blood and marriage.[27] The terms have separate meanings: By sponsoring someone else's child at a baptism, godparents or *padrinos* usually establish a lasting, sometimes affective, and initially hierarchical bond to the baptizee. By sharing familial obligations, godparents also reinforce a tie to the natural parents, their *compadres*. Taken together, historians label this complex *spiritual kinship* or *compadrinazgo*.[28] Additionally, patronage, friendship, and economic ties enlarged these social webs. Patronage is defined as a dyadic and asymmetric tie between humans entailing the exchange of resources or services according to the social level of the participants.[29] Friendship (*amistad*) resembled patronage in the pre-industrial age but was symmetric in character.

Historians of the classical period have studied these phenomena since the nineteenth century. Yet scholars of early modern Europe have only recently begun to combine the systematic analysis of social networks with the study of the state.[30] For example, Sharon Kettering examined the social ties of provincial nobles to the central court in Paris. She contributed to the re-evaluation of French absolutism that historians initiated decades ago. Rather than seeing France under Louis XIV as a country under the complete control of a despot, scholars came to understand his royal rhetoric as a claim to power over territories largely ruled by traditional regional and local lords and corporations. Kettering argued that the seventeenth-century crown gradually built up a system of competing provincial clients who collaborated with the royal intendants. This way the centre expanded its reach into the provinces, incrementally replacing the traditional local powers.[31]

Within the context of Spanish America, John Phelan grasped the power of social networks in his book on the *audiencia* (high court) of Quito, although he did not pursue this subject in a systematic fashion.[32] Tamar Herzog reveals in a recent and detailed study on Quito from 1650 to 1750 that ties between ministers, attorneys, and aides determined the functioning of the *audiencia* rather than the laws. The judiciary – far from guaranteeing a neutral scrutiny of facts – acted as an "open system" where social groups manipulated the trial outcomes.[33] Michel Bertrand employed the prosopographic method to discuss the role of financial officials of New Spain in roughly the same period. The French historian assembled serial biographies of members of this clearly defined social group in order to discuss changing patterns of origin, marriage, and career.[34] Bertrand systematically reconstructed kinship ties by using litigation and notarial records. He postulated that in the seventeenth century the crown had begun inspecting the colonies and imposed structural reforms of the financial institutions. Bertrand concluded that the colonial society co-opted the financial officers through marriage and patronage and foiled most of these changes.[35]

Despite these advances in our understanding of royal authority in the *ancien régime*, few works address the viceroys and their courts in a similar fashion. Studies usually approach viceroys in the institutional framework, giving minute narratives of their activities.[36] A study incorporating recent methodological advances could, however, alter our view of colonial governance, since the viceregal apparatus was at the apex of society. Tracing viceregal social and political alliances will describe a key function of the viceregal court, a topic historians have addressed previously but only in a preliminary manner.[37]

In his landmark discussion of the French court society under Louis XIV, Norbert Elias departed from the liberal-bourgeois view that ridiculed overly embellished courtly conduct. The sociologist envisioned the court as a tool for subjecting the aristocracy to the will of the monarch.[38] According to Elias, the king summoned the nobles to the capital, tethering their autonomy and subjecting them to the rigidities of courtly etiquette. The king imposed with this instrument the political centre's authority on power contenders such as noblemen and clergy, thus laying the foundation for the modern state. If applied to the Mexican court, several problems arise from Elias's study. Historian Ronald Asch remarked that the court operated in different ways under different circumstances.[39] According to Geoffrey Elton, the court served not only as a tool to discipline the nobility but also as a place to negotiate politics between ruler and court factions.[40] Rather than being forced to join the court, French eighteenth-century nobles flocked to the capital uncoerced, seeking access to the money and marriage market to buttress their prestige and wealth.[41] In the process, the aristocrats lost power on the provincial level while gaining influence on the centre.

Elias's definition of the French court suggests other incompatibilities with the Mexican case. He states, "[w]hat we describe as the 'court' of the ancien régime is, to begin with, nothing other than the vastly expanded house and household of the French kings and their dependents with all people belonging to them."[42] The court of the viceroys, however, consisted only in small part of the personal household of the king's alter ego. Instead, a wider and at the same time more specific definition of the court is necessary. Wealthy merchants and clerics among others gained access to the viceroy. Most royal officials and ministers laboured in their offices within the palace and located in proximity to the viceroy. Everybody in the colony with physical access to the viceroy or to the living quarters and royal offices within the palace belonged to the court. In contrast, for example, the prison located in the southeast patio of the palace, the adjacent municipal council (*cabildo civil*) on the main square (*plaza mayor*) or the archbishopric with its own court did not constitute part of the viceregal court.

Admittedly, such a definition poses problems for drawing conclusions about the social profile of the courtiers, clients, and allies of the viceroy. Because of the shifting character of the court, historians will find it hard to deliver a clear-cut delimitation of the personnel of the viceregal court. Embarkation lists and documents from the *juicio de residencia* (the inquiry into the conduct of an official at the end of his tenure) provide an approximation of the number of retainers who travelled with the viceroy from Spain.[43] The distinction of these retainers from others who became viceregal clients in New Spain, however, became increasingly fluid over time. Additionally, other individuals enjoyed a less asymmetric position in relation to the viceroy because they held offices or professions independently of the official. For example, royal treasury officials may have benefited from patronage, but the viceroy could not oust them arbitrarily. Drawing a line between these mid-level clients and members of the upper social echelon is likewise difficult.[44] Relationships of elite members with the viceroy could entail an equal exchange of power and resources. Finally, viceroys themselves frequently relied through an asymmetric relationship upon patrons at the court in Madrid. Notwithstanding these blurred delimitations, I analyze prosopographic patterns among the viceroy's clients and allies. I distinguish between viceregal *criados*, that is, those retainers who travelled with the viceroy from Europe to New Spain, and other collaborators, termed here *clients* or *allies*.[45] Likewise, serial biographies of members of the important corporations such as the ecclesiastical chapter, the *audiencia*, and the *consulado* (the corporation representing wholesale traders that also served as a court for mercantile litigation) offer information about their relationships with the viceroy. This way, the constitution and behaviour of groups in the corporations in regard to the viceroy can be traced. These institutions were often less homogenous than has been assumed. Upon scrutiny they reveal tensions and conflicts between opposing factions and their social networks. An examination of the extension of the viceregal court also shows that the networks of the viceroy cut across social strata and were not limited to elite circles. Although the definition of *elite* as a clearly delimited social or occupational group often remains vague in research on colonial Hispanic America, the idea of networks expands these boundaries.[46] These networks bound together members of different social groups. Clients of patrons of a high social stratum acted as patrons towards persons of lower standing, thus bridging the social divide. Many locals who called upon the viceroy belonged to the higher echelon; others did not. Certainly not all of the viceroy's *criados* belonged to the elite, although they contributed to the operations of the court.[47]

By analyzing the functions of viceregal court and politics in the early eighteenth century, we can monitor change and continuity in the shift from the outgoing Habsburg monarchy to the new Bourbon regime. In the early eighteenth century, the viceregal court still performed a vital role in bringing together elites and entourage. In contrast, towards the end of the eighteenth century, the court probably ceded some of its functions to the expanding bureaucracy.[48] After the first Bourbon king, Philip V, acceded to the thrones of Castile and Aragon in 1700, he appointed the tenth Duke of Alburquerque as his first non-interim viceroy of New Spain. Alburquerque governed from 27 November 1702 to 13 November 1710.[49] Significant changes occurred after 1722, when Bourbon statesmen began appointing viceroys who came from the lower nobility (*hidalguía*) and had a military background. In contrast, Alburquerque belonged to a long tradition of viceroys chosen from the established titled aristocracy. Despite the lending of his ducal name to the city in New Mexico as a continuing legacy, historians have paid little attention to the term of Alburquerque, grandson of the viceroy with the same name in the seventeenth century.[50] In 1872 the Mexican erudite Manuel Rivera described the eighteenth-century viceroy as a moderate governor working for a "good end, although not always in accordance with the laws of European civilization."[51] In contrast to this rather balanced view, Spanish genealogical scholarship has tended to eulogize Alburquerque's competence and loyalty to Philip V. For example, Francisco Fernández de Bethencourt claimed that the duke exercised the viceroyalty "with utmost tact and discretion, skilfully overcoming many difficulties which that country traversed in moments of so much confusion for all the dominions."[52] More recently, Luis Navarro García has argued that Alburquerque and the *audiencia* persecuted Habsburg conspirators and sympathizers in New Spain. Additionally, Navarro García has revisited the crown's prosecution of the duke that forced Alburquerque to pay a tremendous fine for his transgressions.[53] Navarro García's research is careful and thorough, but he is perhaps a bit hesitant to formulate analytical conclusions on his subject.

Placing Alburquerque's tenure within a framework of patronage at court is one of the guiding aims of this inquiry. How did the viceroy ally with local networks and how did this affect politics? What were the major conflicts between members of these social networks and the viceroy? How did the viceroy comport himself amidst these conflicts as a representative of the crown? A combination of conflict analysis with an investigation into patronage patterns provides answers to these questions. Royal reform policies usually resulted in local resistance, and the episodes under analysis demonstrate the major conflict issues of this period. The quarrels of the viceroys indicate how far the incumbent collaborated with the nascent royal reformism or allied with particular local interests. The conflicts expose the constitution and interaction of social networks and allow us to grasp their responses to change.

Chapter 2 provides an overview of the economical and political culture as well as the demography of Spain's empire in this period. The third chapter examines the problem of corruption as well as patronage and palace activities and its use for the execution and display of viceregal power. The next chapter explores viceregal appointments in the military, financial, and district administration as well as promotions of clergymen. Through a serial analysis of colonial biographies, I can identify viceregal clients and *criados*, many of them beyond those officially recognized, and the trajectories of their careers. This chapter is also concerned with the question of the importance of patronage for the formulation of viceregal and royal politics in New Spain. The prosopography of *audiencia* ministers in their relations to the viceroy and the register of viceregal appointments can be verified in Appendix 3.

A complete discussion of all of Alburquerque's activities would be beyond the scope of this book. Instead, I concentrate on those issues that precede the later Bourbon reforms. As mentioned, the historiography has identified major conflicts of the later eighteenth century as revolving around the rising control of the state over traditional corporations such as the religious orders or the Indian communities, the structural reforms of the bureaucracy, and the development of contraband trade. These parameters guide the selection of symptomatic conflicts, which are discussed in Chapters 5 through 8. Chapter 5 deals with the clash between the representatives of the Seville *consulado* and contraband traders. Chapter 6 probes the problem of a Habsburg conspiracy against the new Bourbon dynasty. The shock waves of dynastic strife in the peninsula possibly reveal a nascent nativism and Mexican resentment towards the new dynasty and the metropolis – again, conceivably a precursor of later tensions. Chapter 7 explores how Viceroy Alburquerque resisted measures to strengthen the colonial state. The next chapter revisits the fall of Alburquerque after his return to the peninsula.[54] With this combination of approaches, I hope to provide a novel political and social analysis of a period and topic that historians have largely ignored.

2

THE POLITICAL AND ECONOMIC CULTURE OF SPAIN'S EARLY-EIGHTEENTH-CENTURY EMPIRE

Castile, the heartland of Spain, underwent a profound economic crisis in the seventeenth century, caused largely by epidemics and currency fluctuations, which lasted until about 1685. Around this time, agricultural production recovered, and the centre of the peninsula entered a period of modest expansion. Cantabria, in the north, and the Mediterranean provinces proved more resilient in this century, and commercial expansion in Catalonia and the Basque country was well underway a generation before the Castilian resurgence.[1] With the context of a general seventeenth-century depression in Europe in mind, Woodrow Borah has argued that the massive drop in indigenous population after 1580 also induced a great economic depression in New Spain. Based on an analysis of trade between colonial Mexico and Spain, Pierre and Huguette Chaunu have supported Borah in his thesis, although postulating that the crisis began after 1620.[2]

Recent research has refined our understanding of demography and depression in New Spain. After the conquest, the indigenous population collapsed to a catastrophic degree, from about twelve million before the conquest to ca. 0.9 million in 1650. Yet, starting in the middle of the seventeenth century, the native population began growing again, especially in the southeast of colonial Mexico. So impressive was the growth rate that it rivalled that of nineteenth-century Europe in the era of industrialization. Immigration from Spain and forced migration from Africa further boosted the population of New Spain.[3] After the great silver strikes in Zacatecas, San Luís Potosí, and Guanajuato in the sixteenth century, the north of Mexico became more densely settled than before and settlers continued to push out the frontier.

The mining sector of Mexico lagged somewhat after ca. 1640 but rebounded around 1670 to enter a phase of rapid growth in the early eighteenth century, producing annually about 10.2 million silver pesos. Admittedly, the slump in production in the mid-seventeenth century had serious consequences for those economic sectors directly linked to mining. Nonetheless, the impact on the overall economic performance of the realm was modest, since the Mexican economy did not rely exclusively on the extraction of precious metals. Once the settlements in the north were established, trade, agriculture, and the crafts continued to thrive even when mining output declined. The amount of silver shipped to Spain in the seventeenth century decreased, but with the effect that more of the precious metal remained in New Spain, boosting currency supply, improving infrastructure as well as supporting a larger and more differentiated administration and military apparatus.

In addition, the production of textiles in New Spain continued to expand. At the beginning of the seventeenth century, Puebla's textile industry increasingly supplanted Spanish imports and from the 1640s, new *obrajes* (workshops) opened in the basin of Mexico and in Querétaro. The estimated value of *obraje* textile production in the colony in this period fluctuated annually around 670,000 pesos. While also supplying fine material from Puebla, the viceroyalty produced chiefly low-priced cloth of a lesser quality. These products competed with finer textiles from northern Europe and from China.[4] Overall, while Spain suffered economic decay, the colony showed vigour, and it has been argued that Spain's recession induced America's growth.[5]

Spain's reduced role in the world became manifest again at the end of the Habsburg reign in 1700. The childless king, Charles II (1665–1700), ruled with the help of the secretary of the *despacho universal* and the various councils of Spain, after the last prime minister, the Count of Oropesa, had fallen into disgrace in 1691. Originally, the secretary of the *despacho* only relayed messages within the administration and dispatched orders, yet with the absence of a royal favourite, Secretary Antonio de Ubilla y Medina rose in stature. Along with most of the public and the nobility, among them the powerful Cardinal Portocarrero, the secretary supported the accession of a prince of the French House of Bourbon.[6] The opposing party at court around the Duke of Medinaceli and the Count of Oropesa demanded the continuance of the Habsburgs. Although these magnates had the ear of Queen Maria von Neuburg, they had by then fallen out of favour with the king. Medinaceli served as viceroy in Naples, removed from the political centre, and Oropesa was banned from the palace. The pro-Bourbon party ultimately prevailed. After an opportune recommendation by the Council of Castile backed by important aristocrats, the moribund king changed his testament and named as his successor Philip of Anjou, grandson of the French king Louis XIV. With the arrival of the French prince, the circle around Medinaceli suffered another serious setback.[7]

The European powers Great Britain, the Netherlands, and the Holy Roman Empire did not approve of the change in succession and the incipient alliance between Spain and France. Supporting the claim of the Habsburg pretender, Archduke Charles, the Allies declared war on France and Spain in May 1702. Britain struck against Cadiz, sacked the Spanish silver fleet at Vigo, and took Gibraltar in 1704.

After Philip's investiture, the dominant clique at court around the French ambassador and the *camarera mayor* (head of the queen's household), Princess des Ursins, strove to make the Spanish administration more effective, raising the peninsular contribution to France's military effort. Their program, monitored by Louis XIV, entailed an open attack on the various political councils of Spain, bastions of grandee power. Consequently, the French clique transformed the *despacho universal* into a government cabinet, which made most political decisions, while the French ambassador virtually acted as the prime minister of Philip V.

The grandees of Spain, accustomed to a supreme influence on matters of state, resented the new direction. From 1703 onward, Alburquerque's brother-in-law, the Duke of Medinaceli, secretly met with other nobles at their private residencies to grumble at length about their diminished role at court.[8] In the same year, Medinaceli clashed with the French ambassador, Cardinal César d'Estrées, and relinquished the presidency of the Council of the Indies.[9] Another brother-in-law of Alburquerque, the Admiral of Castile, foremost grandee of Spain, had already defected to the Habsburg camp in 1702.[10]

The advent of the new French ambassador, Michel-Jean Amelot, in 1705 and the fall of Barcelona to the archduke polarized the court factions even further. Even prominent Spanish pro-Bourbon politicians ran afoul of the dominant party. The king removed Antonio de Ubilla y Medina from the *despacho universal* to a position in the Council of the Indies and suspended him in 1706. Cardinal Portocarrera opened a meeting of the Council of State packed with irate nobles who angrily protested that the king had not consulted the conciliar body on the siege of Barcelona.[11]

At the time of the advance of the archducal forces on Madrid in 1706, the loyalty of several aristocrats to the Bourbon cause had been tested to the utmost. A number of nobles defected to the Habsburg pretender, among them the Count of Oropesa, former minister under Charles II, who had complained that the new prince no longer needed his services. The political reforms of the Bourbon king improved the effectiveness of the state, but it came at a price. In 1706 four of the twelve grandees of the first class had been disgraced because of their dealings with the archduke. By the end of the war, about one-third of Spain's nobles had fallen out of favour or defected.[12] Disaffection also ran strong in the Council of the Indies. The body convened during the summer of 1706 and collaborated with archducal forces that occupied the capital. When Philip's forces recovered Madrid in the fall of 1706, the king had the conduct of several councillors investigated. The proceedings resulted in a veritable purge of the body and the appointment of up to eight new councillors in 1707 and 1708. The new appointees remained loyal to the regime for the remainder of the conflict.[13]

By 1709 the undisputed dominance of the French cabal at the Spanish court ended, when Louis XIV pondered peace negotiations with the Allies. Madrid feared that the French king could sacrifice Spain's interests in exchange for a settlement and refused to make territorial concessions. Consequently, Paris began withdrawing troops from the peninsula and recalled the ambassador. Although the Princess des Ursins remained in Madrid, Philip's choice of ministers more clearly articulated Spanish interests.[14] As an immediate result of the Franco-Hispanic disengagement, Philip's forces now faced the Alliance on their own and suffered a number of military reverses. In the fall of 1710, the archduke's troops again occupied Madrid. As the Bourbon monarchy in Spain stood to collapse, Louis XIV changed course and sent the Duke of Vendôme with a sizable detachment of soldiers to the peninsula. The renewed French intervention in September forced the Allies out of Castile and by January of the following year after the battle of Villaviciosa, the Bourbon forces drove back their enemy to the territory around Barcelona.

Peace with the allies came when Emperor Joseph died in April 1711, bequeathing the imperial crown to his brother, the archduke. Charles left Spain in September, and on 11 April 1713 the representatives of Britain, the Netherlands, Spain, and France signed the treaty of Utrecht, concluding hostilities. The Empire joined the peace with France in the treaty of Rastatt in 1714.[15]

Jean Orry, who as *veedor general de la real hacienda* supervised the financial administration,[16] returned in April 1713 to Madrid, from where he had been expelled in 1706. He practically ran the Spanish government, implementing wide-ranging changes in the various councils. As a result of the growing hostility between France and Spain over the conduct of the war, the so-called Italian faction had slowly risen in power since 1711. Manifested in the appointment of Cardinal Francesco del Giudice as Inquisitor General, the political transformation reached its culmination in the king's wedding to Elizabeth Farnese on 16 September 1714 after the death of Philip's Savoyard wife Marie Louise on 14 February 1714. The new queen from Parma immediately dismissed the powerful Princess des Ursins, confidante of Louis XIV, and the French clique at court. A royal decree of 7 February 1715 removed the most prominent ministers, among them Counsellor Jean Orry. Several of his allies left the court, among them the secretary of state of the Navy and the Indies and the king's confessor.[17] Madrid had cast off the political control of the French monarchy.

After the fall of Ursins and Orry, a number of provisional ministers headed the administration. Cardinal Giudice obtained the portfolio for judicial and Church matters, while the Count of Frigiliana supervised the navy and the Indies. Frigiliana's career reflected the shifting alignments of the political constellation in Madrid. Around 1706 he joined the aristocrats in their secret discussions against the Bourbon regime and did not play a major role in that government. When the opposing court faction strengthened its influence with the departure of the French ambassador Amelot in 1709, Frigiliana gained the governorship of the Council of the Indies.[18] Nevertheless, the elevation of this noble did not herald a return to grandee power in Madrid. The secretaries of state retained the power over the most important political decisions.

The changing fortunes at court had significant bearings on the viceroyship of Alburquerque. As noble power waned, support for the viceroy in Madrid dwindled as well. The newly appointed members of the Council of the Indies were to take a less forgiving stance on a Spanish grandee than their predecessors. Politics therefore also played a crucial role in Philip's selection of his first non-interim viceroy for New Spain. Although the Council of the Indies nominated any of its members for the office, the king instead chose Francisco Fernández de la Cueva, the tenth Duke of Alburquerque.[19] Born in Genoa on 17 November 1666,[20] his ancestors had a tradition of serving the crown in important administrative posts, such as viceroys of Naples, Aragon, and Navarre. Alburquerque's – possibly better-known – grandfather, the eighth duke of Alburquerque, administered New Spain as viceroy from 1653–1660. The dukes of Alburquerque belonged to the top echelon of Castilian nobility, the *grandeza* (grandeeship) of the first class. King Charles V had legally confirmed the grandee status of the family in 1520. Aligning with one of the most powerful families in Spain, the tenth Duke of Alburquerque married the sister of the ninth Duke of Medinaceli, son of the former prime minister under Charles II.[21] In order to gain the support of this faction, Philip V appointed Medinaceli on 29 November 1701 to the presidency of the Council of the Indies. Medinaceli held the position until 8 May 1703,[22] allowing him to influence the choice of the new viceroy of New Spain.

Alburquerque's social background and family ties already indicate that he would not favour an expansion of royal power in Spain and overseas at the expense of the traditional prerogatives of dignitaries and corporations. Additionally, Alburquerque had only limited military and administrative experience, although he had served as captain general of the Andalusian coast.[23] Therefore, when Philip and his French advisors chose the grandee for the lucrative office of viceroy, they intended less to recruit an efficient administrator than to bind the power circle around

Medinaceli to the Bourbon cause. They also conveniently removed a powerful magnate and potential threat from influence at court. On 25 April 1702 the Council of the Indies communicated the decision to Alburquerque.[24]

At this time, British naval forces hovered on Spain's coast hindering the duke's voyage to America. Alburquerque and his entourage endured the embarrassment of embarking in La Coruña on a French man-of-war, since only Spain's new ally could safeguard the viceroy's conduct to the New World. Departing from Galicia on 30 June 1702, the duke arrived on 6 October in Veracruz after a dangerous voyage. On 27 November 1702 he took possession of the viceroyalty of New Spain.[25] On 13 November 1710 the duke handed over power to his successor, the Duke of Linares.[26] Alburquerque then remained in the colony for more than two years, an unusually long stay for an outgoing viceroy. On 26 November 1712 Alburquerque drew up a power of attorney in Mexico City to represent his interests there and stated his intention to embark in the fleet anchored in Veracruz.[27] This convoy departed New Spain in early January and reached Cadiz on 30 March 1713.[28]

The War of the Spanish Succession (1702–1713/14) laid bare Spain's weakness and the military dependence on her northern neighbor. Spaniards had debated the cause of their empire's decay ever since the final decades of the sixteenth century. The school of late scholasticism, including philosophers such as Francisco de Vitoria, Domingo de Soto, and Martín de Azpilcueta Navarro, gave important impulses to this debate. These scholars attributed the decline to, among other reasons, monetary inflation caused by the massive influx of silver into the peninsular economy. Other political theorists published a stream of memoranda while suggesting concrete solutions for the economic malaise. Among these *arbitristas*, Luis Ortiz, an accountant of the royal treasury, pointed out in 1558 that Spain only appeared wealthy, its prosperity obscuring a feeble industrial sector. With exports consisting principally of raw materials, the importation of manufactured goods drained silver from the realm. In his comprehensive plan to stabilize the country, he advised the monarch to encourage Spaniards to resume working. Ortiz called upon the crown to support the crafts, introduce foreign technology in textile production, foster agriculture, and improve transportation.

Then, cheaper Castilian products would be able to compete with foreign goods shipped in by coastal trade. He also suggested revising taxation by shifting some of the burden to the wealthy. Several other seventeenth-century *arbitristas* agreed with Ortiz's criticism. While some focused on a revival of agriculture, others such as Sancho de Moncada and Miguel Alvarez Osorio stressed the importance of modernizing industry and manufacturing. Some of the recommendations, such as levying a tax on all social groups proportional to their income (the so-called *única contribución*), seem very advanced for their time.[29]

The Spanish Enlightenment of the eighteenth century continued the debate about the causes of economic malaise. In contrast to the rather cosmopolitan and secular tendencies in France, the Spanish currents affirmed Catholic and patriotic ideals. Spanish writers of both the seventeenth and eighteenth centuries recognized the interdependence of economic problems, but the representatives of the Enlightenment increasingly grasped this in a more systematic fashion. Under the Bourbon dynasty, more and more statesmen in influential positions participated in the debate. The Marquis of la Ensenada, the Count of Aranda, and the Count of Campomanes, among others, addressed the question of how to cure the economic and political crisis of the empire.[30] Melchor de Macanaz, first intendant in Aragon, called upon the king to set an example for his subjects by becoming the country's first businessman. In 1724 Jerónimo de Uztariz, secretary of the *junta de comercio* (the junta dealing with commerce), followed mercantilist ideas in proposing an active crown policy to improve the economy. At the same time, he contributed to the development of proto-liberal thought by calling for a dismantling of oligopolistic trading companies and a reduction of tariffs and regulations within the empire. Bernardo de Ulloa argued along similar lines, calling for a liberalization of trade between Spanish ports and the Philippines. Philip V's secretary of state and the Indies, José del Campillo y Cossío (in office 1741–1743), outlined a comprehensive plan of change in his *Nuevo Sistema*. Campillo suggested a series of inspections of the colonial bureaucracy, the introduction of intendants to improve royal government in the provinces, and the development of Spain as an industrial power. Both he and Bernardo Ward called for a strengthening of monarchic rule in America.[31] In the 1760s the Count of Aranda supported José de Gálvez' program of reform in America. Aranda argued that Americans, regardless of race and social origins, should be eligible for crown appointments in the Indies, as long as they had the ability to serve. These ideas anticipated the concept of the equality before the law independent of one's origin.

Spaniards were familiar with many ideas of liberalism before Adam Smith formulated them in a systematic manner. Precursors of the nineteenth-century liberal state, the reformers abandoned the ideal of a society of estates. The radical reformers around Gálvez believed in a strong monarchic state able to foster the well being of the individual and free the economy from unnecessary restraints.[32]

The origins of the implementation of reform policies therefore go back to at least the sixteenth century. On a political level, the crown had traditionally quarreled with the nobility, the Church, and municipal corporations about power and attempted to tighten its control over society. By placing *corregidores* (royally appointed magistrates) in Iberian cities, the Catholic Monarchs had increased their supervision over urban life. The early Habsburg rulers then used the infighting among conquistadors in America to curb their power and replace their rule with that of royal officials.

Philip II ruled his empire with the help of his most trusted advisor, Ruy Gómez de Silva. Under Philip's heirs, however, the royal favourites (the *valido* or *privado*) such as the Duke of Lerma (1598–1618) reduced the sovereign to the role of a shadow-king. The crown lost momentum. Then the Count-Duke of Olivares (1622–1643) tried to assert royal supremacy over Spanish magnates and the colonial bureaucracy.[33] By 1621 Olivares had already secured the appointment of the Marquis of Gelves as viceroy of New Spain. The Marquis challenged the local oligarchy and tried to reduce corruption in the royal exchequer, that is, the financial administration. In his quest Gelves met the resistance of entrenched local interest groups who were able to secure his dismissal, putting an end to his turbulent term. The crown also prematurely aborted the inspection tour conducted by Juan de Palafox to improve royal oversight.[34] After the failure of these reform efforts, attempts by the crown to discipline the colony faltered.

Only the appointment of the Duke of Medinaceli, and subsequently the Count of Oropesa, as prime ministers in 1680 and 1685 put the reform program slowly back on track. The nobles tried to raise revenue by cutting bureaucracy and excessive pensions. Oropesa also ordered a suspension of the ordination of new clergy, to reduce the number of priests, as well as a halt to new religious foundations. His program included an outright attack on the powers of the Inquisition, especially its jurisdiction in civil and criminal cases – although many of his policies collapsed under the pressure of the opposition at court.[35]

During the War of the Succession, the Bourbons continued some administrative practices inherited from the late Habsburg regime, such as the sale of offices. In accordance with the laws of the Indies, the crown had offered since the seventeenth century offices such as notaries and *regidores* (town councilmen) for a lifespan of the official (*en propriedad*). The purchasers kept their post until their death and often bequeathed them to relatives for an additional fee paid to the monarch. The crown, however, did not sell any offices endowed with jurisdiction until the end of the seventeenth century. Then, under the demands of the treasury, the crown reverted to accepting donations in exchange for appointments (*beneficio de empleos*). Under the cloak of law, then, Madrid could offer appointments ranging from *alcaldes mayores* or *corregidores* (both district officials) to *audiencia* ministers to, allegedly, even the viceroyalty of Peru. Nevertheless, the offices obtained through *beneficio* were of limited tenure. The crown could also dismiss these appointees, as opposed to those who had purchased their office for a lifespan. The monarch did not sell *beneficio* offices in a public auction. Yet, since the Council of the Indies publicly posted the positions and effectively awarded offices to the highest bid, the differences in practice were minor.[36]

With victory in the War of the Succession near, Philip V and his court continued to move, albeit erratically, towards disciplining Spain and the colonies. Within the peninsula, the crown abolished the special privileges of the crown of Aragon and subjected the eastern realm to Castilian law. The Bourbons also introduced the intendancy system in the peninsula in 1711, only to revoke it in 1715, except for the provinces of the crown of Aragon. The instructions (*ordenanza*) of 4 July 1718 finally established the provincial intendants in all of Spain on a permanent footing with jurisdiction over the four areas of justice, *policía* (government), treasury, and war. In 1717 the House of Trade moved from Seville to Cadiz. In the 1740s the annual convoy gave way to independently sailing ships, so-called registered ships. These ships could travel to America anytime and did not have to wait in the port until the convoy departed.[37]

In America the crown began establishing new monopolies and levying the sales tax (*alcabala*) in the provinces. Charles II already had appointed a new type of superintendent in Puebla de los Angeles and Guadalajara to tackle specific tasks of the royal exchequer, such as the levy of the sales tax. While local corporations such as the *consulado* had long rented the administration of this tax, the crown now had royal officials collect taxes directly in some of the major cities. The superintendent of the *alcabala* in Puebla, a precursor to the permanent intendancy system introduced in 1786, increased the yield spectacularly. The local oligarchy, however, felt the pinch of this increased effort and responded with violence. Then, starting in 1710, a series of general inspections (*visitas generales*) and specific inquiries (*visitas* and *pesquisas*) of the royal treasuries and the *audiencia* put the colony under closer scrutiny of the state.[38] The crown terminated the sale of offices in the 1750s. In 1765 the monarchy also stationed regular army units in New Spain and reorganized the militias. The crown intended these policies to strengthen royal control. During his inspection tour, José de Gálvez, however, also applied some proto-liberal measures. In 1770–71 he broke up the control of oligarchic circles over the *cabildos* by creating elected offices such as honorary councilmen (*regidores honorarios*) and attorneys of the people (*síndicos personeros del común*). Social groups hitherto sparsely represented, above all merchants, entered municipal politics in Mexico City.[39] Following these crown measures to rein in the colonial oligarchy, the Gálvez *visita* and the ensuing introduction of the intendancy system must be considered as a continuation of a long-standing policy. This effort can be divided into phases. First, the Count-Duke of Olivares actively tried to increase tax revenue and fight corruption from 1621 to 1643. Then the momentum slowed down when control passed to the ensuing *validos* (the king's favourites). Thirdly, the Duke of Medinaceli and the Count of Oropesa resumed the pace of reform from 1680 to

1691. Even during the War of the Succession, the crown attempted to increase revenue from America and heighten control over the regular orders, such the Dominican friars. Fourthly, after their victory, the early Bourbons stepped up the program of cutting back waste in the financial administration. For example, the Marquis of la Ensenada, from 1743 to 1754 secretary of the treasury, the navy, and the Indies, put the financial administration of overseas colonies on a new footing. The Marquis of Esquilache, Charles III's minister of finance from 1759 through 1766, examined every branch of government and threatened a complete overhaul of metropolitan administration.[40] The fifth phase is marked by the promotion of José de Gálvez's to the position of secretary of state of the Indies in 1776 ushering in imperial efforts to restructure administrative power in the Americas. Finally, with his death in 1787, the pace of bureaucratic reforms once again slowed down. Apprehensive after the triumph of the French revolution and facing resistance from the traditional colonial bureaucracy and oligarchies, Madrid reversed course and dismantled many of the initiatives.[41]

The change in royal policy also affected the choice of viceroys of New Spain. In the seventeenth century the Habsburg monarchs usually appointed younger sons of the high nobility to this position. There were some notable exceptions to this pattern. The grandfather of the tenth Duke of Alburquerque held a grandee title at the time of his appointment. On the opposite of the spectrum, the parents of the Count of Montezuma, the last Habsburg viceroy, belonged to the *hidalguía*. The count rose into the titled nobility by marrying a descendant of the last Aztec ruler. With the appointment of Alburquerque, the Bourbons again picked a magnate. His successors followed the previous pattern as second-born sons of Spanish grandees.[42]

In 1722, with the selection of the Marquis of Casafuerte, a new type of official appeared in New Spain. Born in the Americas, Casafuerte became the first Bourbon viceroy drawn from the *hidalguía*. His father had served in several district officialdoms in Peru. Casafuerte rose through the ranks through his loyal military services to the Bourbons in the War of the Succession. As a reward, Philip created the marquisate in 1708. Casafuerte served as viceroy for the unusually long period of twelve years. Among his successors, the Duke of la Conquista and the Count of Revillagigedo both resemble Casafuerte in their career paths, earning their appointments through a record of proven accomplishments.[43] In contrast, the appointment of the tenth Duke of Alburquerque in 1702 saw the crown choose a viceroy for reasons of political expediency. In naming Alburquerque, the monarch did not yet intend to implement a novel reform program.

The Legal Dimension

The viceroy was intended to be the "alter ego" or "living image" of the king, hence the position wielded considerable power over New Spain. The crown granted the viceroy powers to act as if he himself were king and promised to uphold his judgment. The monarch ordered the *audiencias*, governors, judges, ecclesiastics, and vassals to treat the viceroy with the same level of respect as they would show to the king and to execute all his orders without delay. In this way, the monarch elevated the viceroy above any colonial administrator.[44] The viceroy enjoyed special symbols of power, such as a personal guard, reserved only for the king in the peninsula.[45] The salary of the viceroy exceeded that of any other crown official in America. In the seventeenth and early eighteenth centuries, the viceroy earned annually 30,000 ducats in Peru and 20,000 ducats in New Spain. The Mexican salary corresponded to 27,573 pesos 4 *reales* and 3 *granos*. By contrast, an *oidor* (judge) of the Mexican *audiencia* received 2,941 pesos, not even a ninth of the viceroy's official income but far above that of an *alguacil executor*, a constable at the tribunal of accounts, who earned 220 pesos annually. A soldier of the palace guard received about the same amount.[46]

    The responsibilities of the viceroy included the defence of the Catholic religion, good government, the administration of justice, and the collection of taxes for the royal exchequer in the colony as well as the protection of the indigenous peoples.[47] This broad outline of authority sketched in the laws of the Indies evolved over time as a stream of royal orders expanded or limited viceregal jurisdiction. As captain general, the viceroy controlled the entire military defence of New Spain's territory and supervised other captains general in the viceroyalty. The viceroy served as president of the *audiencia* of New Spain, although he could not intervene in the administration of justice. The *audiencia* reviewed civil and criminal cases as the highest appellate court in the colony and held some political functions. The *audiencias* in the viceregal capitals consisted of three chambers: Two *salas civiles* staffed with senior judges (*oidores*) and a crown attorney (*fiscal de lo civil*) heard civil cases and settled political disputes, while another chamber (*sala del crimen*) dealt exclusively with criminal affairs. The magistrates of the criminal chamber, the *alcaldes del crimen*, and a crown prosecutor called *fiscal del crimen* did not attend the *real acuerdo*, the joint meeting of viceroy and *oidores*, who discussed matters of political importance.[48]

The viceroy also monitored the royal institutions, such as the tribunal of accounts, and as governor (*gobernador*) of his territory regulated all aspects of public life, the economy, and traffic. He supervised subordinates and appointed interim officials in the districts and the treasury. The viceroy monitored the royal treasury but had no power to order expenditures save in cases of military urgency. Since the monarch and the Church guarded their prerogatives zealously, the vice-patronage over the Church was limited largely to supervision. Occasionally, the viceroy might appoint a priest to a parish who was not placed on top of the ranking (*terna*) submitted by the secular clergy. Yet even this limited role often irritated the Church considerably.[49]

The crown restrained the powers of the viceroy through several means. The viceroy had to report all matters to Madrid and await key decisions from the Council of the Indies. On important issues demanding immediate attention, the viceroy was required to consult with the *oidores* in the *real acuerdo*. The viceroy also usually conferred with an *asesor letrado*, a lawyer who frequently sat as judge on the *audiencia*. In matters of military jurisdiction, the viceroy referred to an *auditor de guerra*, also a lawyer. When suspicions arose about viceregal misconduct, the crown could send an inspector (*visitador*) to examine the status of the colonial administration. Finally, at the end of his term, the viceroy had to justify his actions in a process called the *juicio de residencia* or simply *residencia*. This routine assessment was required of all outgoing officials of the imperial administration. It consisted of a formal investigation in which an official questioned witnesses and listened to any charges that the crown or the public in New Spain might bring forth.[50]

The crown never clearly spelled out the exact geographical boundaries of the viceroy's jurisdiction. The term *New Spain* (*Nueva España*) was used in three different senses. First, it referred to the entire northern and far eastern part of the Spanish colonial empire, including the Caribbean and the Philippines. This definition applied to the Council of the Indies, where one secretariat (*secretaría*) dealt with either viceroyalty, Peru or New Spain. The Council allotted cases correspondingly.[51] Notwithstanding, the viceroy did not have any jurisdiction over many of the far-flung parts of this region such as Guatemala, the Caribbean, and the Philippines.[52] The viceroy merely received information on the major occurrences in these parts, weighing in only to assert his moral authority. The dependence of the fortresses in the Caribbean and in the Philippines on funds sent from New Spain, however, gave the viceroy some influence over these provinces.[53]

A second definition referred to the *reino de la Nueva España* (the realm of New Spain), also called the *gobierno* of New Spain. In this territory the viceroy acted as governor (*gobernador*) and captain general. This jurisdiction extended as far south as present-day Guatemala (excluding Chiapas and Yucatan) and in the north to borders that included the cities of Pánuco, San Luís Potosí, Guanajuato, and Puerto de la Navidad. North of this line a governor and the *audiencia* of Guadalajara administered a separate province (*gobierno*) called New Galicia. Here, the *audiencia* administered justice and the governor most aspects of government, such as the appointments of *alcaldes mayores* and financial officers. In that province the viceroy only controlled the captaincy general, that is, military affairs, and the treasury as its superintendent (*superintendente general de la real hacienda*). New Galicia and New Spain contained the territories lost to the United States in the nineteenth century (California, the original New Mexico, and Texas).[54] When speaking of New Spain or Mexico I refer in this book to both New Spain and New Galicia, unless I refer specifically to the *gobierno* of New Spain. To distinguish the capital from this realm, I usually label it Mexico City, following the modern usage.

Figure 2: Map of New Spain in the early eighteenth century

While Mexico expanded and became increasingly more independent economically, Spain underwent a political and economic crisis. Driven by the rivalry with European powers, statesmen and pamphleteers called on the crown to reassert control by disciplining the bureaucracy, raising tax revenue, and gaining more influence over the Church. This program caused significant tension with inhabitants of the American colonies that increased over time. Hence, in early-eighteenth-century Mexico conflicts were in place that foreshadowed the independence phase and later periods: the debate about official and contraband commerce, the attempt to build an effective state while reducing the power of Church, especially that of the religious orders such as the Dominicans, as well as the pervading influence of patronage networks.

Embattled during the War of the Succession, the new Bourbon king selected the Duke of Alburquerque as viceroy of New Spain to appease the pro-Habsburg aristocrats at the Spanish court. Therefore, Philip V and his French counsellors did not expect this viceroy to play an active role in regaining control over Mexico. Starting in 1709, however, the French advisors at court lost much influence due to the increasingly diverging viewpoints of France and Spain on the conduct of the war. This process culminated in the dismissal of the powerful Princess des Ursins and her allies in 1714/1715. Madrid began to pursue more exclusively Spanish interests, and the results became apparent in New Spain too.

3

COURT AND CORRUPTION IN COLONIAL MEXICO

In the past forty-five years, historiography has paid increasing attention to the problem of corruption in early modern Europe and America. The current debate involves three main questions: how to explain the endemic non-compliance with the law or other ethical guidelines; how contemporaries viewed corruption; and whether the term *corruption* is applicable to the *ancien régime*. In order to evaluate the extent to which a viceroy's tenure in office can be characterized as corrupt, it is necessary to understand the broader framework of this phenomenon and clarify the terminology concerning it.

Among the first scholars to discuss the subject comprehensively within the Spanish Empire was Dutch historian Jacob van Klaveren.[1] He argued that bureaucrats and municipal aristocrats who controlled the enforcement of trade laws willingly accepted bribes to suspend these regulations to the detriment of merchants, the crown, and the public. Only when merchants evaded paying customary kickbacks did bureaucrats and municipal aristocrats intervene, ostensibly in defence of royal prerogatives. Van Klaveren postulated that the corruption of the executive violated the principles of mercantilism, the idea of a freer flow of merchandise within the realm and the exclusion of foreign goods. Ultimately, he described corruption as a conflict among crown, bureaucracy, nobility, merchants, and others over the access to the country's wealth. Soon after van Klaveren's book was published, Ramón Carande and Richard Konetzke, both prestigious economic historians of Spain and her empire, challenged these conclusions. The scholars attacked the Dutch historian for not having documented his conclusions concerning corruption with primary sources. In their view the series of *juicios de residencia* located in the Archive of the Indies demonstrate that the state successfully reined in this abuse.[2]

In Anglophone historiography, John Leddy Phelan distinguishes between the legal or moral ideal of a loyal bureaucracy and the de facto systematic circumvention of the law.[3] Phelan holds that "[t]he basic cause of the considerable avarice throughout the bureaucracy was the inadequacy of the salary scale."[4] Among the lower ranks, in which individuals had no prospect of adequate remuneration, massive corruption prevailed. Officials receiving a better salary inclined somewhat less towards corruption. Therefore, "the viceroys [were] as a group remarkably honest."[5] Royal officials, however, usually had no hope for promotion, a salary raise, or reliable and significant retirement benefits. Once they had set foot in the New World, royal ministers were there to stay, and, torn from their cultural moorings, were ripe for moral decay.[6] Phelan argues that the pervasiveness of corruption in Spain's empire was partly a structural problem. Nonetheless, he continues to view corruption, to a degree, as an individual moral problem.

Horst Pietschmann maintains that widespread corruption existed in Europe but pervaded the Indies more thoroughly.[7] Pietschmann identifies four forms of corruption in the empire: illegal trade, bribery, favouritism and clientelism, as well as the sale of offices and official services. For him corruption is not a static concept. Its pervasiveness changes over time. He points out that in the mid-sixteenth century, the crown began selling offices. Consequently, the officeholders increasingly diverged from the legal mandates. At the same time venality opened avenues of social advancement for Creoles. From 1710 onward, after the crackdown on Alburquerque and several inspections of the treasury and the *audiencia*, the monarch progressively reined in the administrators, thereby diminishing corruption.

In his analysis of the representation of viceregal power, Alejandro Cañeque cautions against employing the term *corruption*. Cañeque holds that the sale of offices cannot be considered a corrupt practice. Patron-client relationships impregnated the bureaucracy so much that contemporaries did not consider the exchange of favours as illicit but rather as a customary practice.[8] Clearly, Cañeque is right in criticizing a tendency in Latin American scholarship to assume implicitly that the pre-modern state functioned like the modern state. He also correctly underlines the power of patronage in the *ancien régime*. Nevertheless, the sale of offices probably was more controversial than Cañeque holds. As mentioned before, the crown could sell offices without jurisdiction, such as the post of *regidor* (councilman) on town councils, without incurring legal problems. The law, however, did not permit the sale of those offices that carried jurisdiction, such as the posts of *alcaldes mayores* and *audiencia* ministers. That is precisely why the crown reverted to the practice of *beneficio de empleo*. The vehement resistance of the Council of the Indies to the monarch's planned sale of offices with jurisdiction illustrates the controversial nature of this practice. When in 1633 the Count-Duke of Olivares offered to sell two posts in the financial administration in Veracruz, the Council weighed in with a long *consulta* (a political or judiciary recommendation to the king) full of angry objections. Beyond that, a number of jurists even considered the sale of notarial positions distasteful.[9]

Many statesmen therefore anticipated detrimental results from the sale of offices and did not view every infraction of the law with indifference. Although client-patron relationships pervaded the early modern state, and contemporaries did not view clientelism, within limits, as immoral, there are clear indications that officials who exceeded these limits faced consequences. For example, in 1704 the councillors of the Indies, although largely favouring the aristocratic party at court, revoked Alburquerque's measures to imprison members of a powerful merchant family. The Council suggested admonishing the viceroy sternly and fining two of his allied *audiencia* ministers.[10] As another example of this ongoing conflict, the seventeenth-century monarchy had ordered a series of inspections of the treasury of Veracruz to examine excessive deviance.[11]

Early twentieth-century constitutional historians have debated the problem of using modern terminology for historical phenomena. Over sixty years ago Otto Brunner asserted that sources from the Middle Ages never used the term *state*. He warned against applying current concepts of the modern state to previous epochs. Doing so would distort the functioning and ethos of officials of the past.[12] For example, nineteenth-century German historiography consistently applied the term *Reichskanzler* or chancellor of the Reich, to the office of the *cancellarius* in the Holy Roman Empire. Yet medieval sources simply use the phrase *aulae regalis cancellarius* (chief scribe) of the royal (or imperial) court. The *cancellarius* bought his office to supervise the scribes at the court. He did not hold a political office and had little in common with the most powerful appointed politician in the late-nineteenth-century German Reich.[13]

The term *corruption* does not appear in the Spanish sources of the early eighteenth century either. Rather, the authors usually speak of "abuse" or "lack of integrity." In a modern sense, corruption can be defined as the deviation from legal or moral rules out of self-interest. The democratic process in Western states theoretically determines the criteria of office holding. Yet we cannot apply this idea fully to the *ancien régime*. We would impose our conceptions on the past and be inclined to adopt the standard of the European "motherland" as a measure for moral conduct. When the crown defended the restrictions on trade, it hampered the Mexican economy. Labelling contraband merchants corrupt for evading an unsustainable legal and commercial system would be absurd.

Historiography has shown that over the course of the early modern period the European monarchies successfully increased bureaucratic compliance with the law. For a long time in the *ancien régime*, the crown meted out retribution only against those officials who broke the law and did not have powerful enough political connections. Their opponents blamed them of "lack of integrity," yet their censure bore the mark of political vengeance. We can only talk about corruption in the narrower modern sense once the judiciary had reached sufficient independence to prosecute disobedience even of those belonging to the dominant clique. Only when the state had matured into its modern form as a neutral arbiter between contending parties did corruption evolve from a constituent characteristic of the state into an ethical problem for the individual.

Circumscribing this process consistently with terms such as *deviance* or *abuse* would render the text cumbersome. Instead of avoiding the term corruption altogether – or any other concept that has undergone marked change in content or did not exist in historical sources, such as state or gender – one has to be aware of the semantic drift of the term and define the concept properly. One of the aims of this work is to evaluate precisely the viceregal court of Alburquerque by gauging the scale of non-compliance with royal directives. Therefore, I apply the term *corruption* as an analytical tool to grasp a political process of a past time without invoking a moral judgment.

The Viceregal Court of Colonial Mexico

Among historians of Europe, there is no scarcity of literature on the courts, yet there are few precise definitions of this institution. The Spanish Renaissance preacher Antonio de Guevara characterized the court plainly as "a group of men who meet to deceive one another."[14] Apart from the functional definition – deception – the quote is concerned with personnel. For Elias, the personnel of the court were those individuals incorporated into the royal household:

> What we describe as the "court" of the ancien régime is, to begin with, nothing other than the vastly expanded house and household of the French kings and their dependents with all people belonging to them.... The king's rule over the country was nothing other than an extension of and addition to the prince's rule over his household. What Louis XIV ... attempted, was to organize his country as his personal property, as the enlargement of the household.[15]

For Elias, all people whose life revolved around the royal palace such as courtiers, domestics, and others could live either in the royal palace or in their own dwellings in the capital.[16]

Geoffrey Elton echoes Elias's concept when he argues that the sixteenth-century English court "comprised all those who at any given time were within 'his grace's house'; and all those with a right to be there were courtiers."[17] These conceptions explain who belonged to the court, but they do not provide clear delineations of the institution. Ronald Asch argues that the distinction between court and household is insufficient because it draws a blurry line between those who belong to the king's household proper, the court, and those who have access to the ruler and participate in courtly functions while not being in "his grace's house".[18] This is particularly relevant for the court in New Spain. The viceroy did not command a commensurate private household that incorporated the colonial officials and dignitaries, unlike the French nobles Elias had in mind. Any definition based on belonging to "his grace's house" seems flawed because of the limited number of members of the viceregal household proper.

A spatial view of the court adds further clarity. Peter Burke describes the court in Europe "as a place, usually a palace with gatehouse, courtyards, hall, and chapel … but including a chamber where the ruler could withdraw and one or more antechambers where suitors waited for audience."[19] Nevertheless, Burke is quick to add that the court formed part of the "social milieu" of the Renaissance and moved to wherever the ruler journeyed.[20] Solely considering the spatial concept of the palace remains difficult. The viceroy frequently travelled outside the palace, both within the city and occasionally to other urban centres such as Veracruz, to supervise royal defence or construction projects.

The question arises whether any courtiers existed outside of the viceregal entourage. In Europe there were counsellors or politicians who did not permanently reside at the court or in the capital and yet wielded significant influence.[21] In New Spain, many members of the higher social echelons, while not living in the palace, participated in and even determined the operation of the court. The viceroy Count of Revillagigedo closely collaborated with the regent of the tribunal of accounts, who allegedly advised him on promotions in the royal exchequer (financial administration).[22] Private persons such as businessmen built relationships with the viceroy or married into retainers' families and thereby established ties to the viceroy. Participation in viceregal politics could be achieved by virtue of office holding or through contact with the viceroy. Royal ministers and clergy held their positions by royal appointment or promotion within the Church. Therefore, they did not depend on the viceroy to the same extent as the aristocrats and bureaucrats in Spain relied on the king. *Audiencia* ministers quarrelled with the viceroy but did not necessarily face the same consequences as a councillor in Madrid falling out of favour with the king.

In New Spain the household of the viceroy consisted of the entourage of *criados* (clients brought from Spain). Whether viceroys had favourites (*validos*) among his *criados* is a question historiography has barely touched upon.[23] In addition to these courtiers, the whole palace bustled with activity. Virtually all royal ministers and officials reported to the palace for work, while mint officials laboured in the building immediately to the northeast of the palace. In contradistinction to the court in Madrid, however, none of these officials served a household function for the viceroy such as nobles did for the king. With the exception of the palace guard and possibly the *alcalde del crimen* the ministers did not reside in the palace. Rather, they worked in close vicinity to the viceroy. This underscores the importance of personal relationships with the viceroy for individuals with commercial interests or social ambitions.

The viceroy conducted business and ceremonies primarily in the palace, called the royal palace (*palacio real*) or palace of the viceroys (*palacio de los virreyes*, nowadays called the national palace or *palacio nacional*). Located in the heart of the city on the main square (*plaza mayor* or *zócalo*) adjacent to the cathedral, the residence of the archbishop, and the town hall, the palace was situated in close proximity to rivalling powers in the colony. The architecture of the palace – with the current uppermost floor added in the national period – symbolized royal power to the colonial crowd. At the same time, the building was exposed to the populace on the *plaza mayor*. In the turmoil of 1692, rioters destroyed most of the viceroy's residence in the palace and threatened his safety. Nonetheless, the official and his family resumed residence in the palace after its blessing in 1697.[24]

The viceregal palace in Mexico City consisted of four patios: the principal patio was built on the northwest with the viceregal chambers facing the main square (*plaza mayor*); the patio of the *audiencia* towards the southwest; the prison patio (*patio de la cárcel*) on the southeast; and the stable patio (*patio de la caballeriza*) with a passageway to the royal treasury on the northeast corner of the palace. On the lower floor of the palace, staircases provided access to the mezzanine and the upper floor and housed the lower *criados*, horses, and carriages. Thirty soldiers of the viceregal guard also inhabited this floor. The mezzanine or second floor stretched over most of the palace except for the northwest section.

The southern wing contained several offices of the royal treasury such as the *alcabala* and the tribute collection (rooms no. 20–24). The prison patio housed the *alcalde del crimen* and a special chamber for prisoners of more notable social standing (25–27, 28).

The ministers and subordinate employees of the *audiencia* met in several offices on the third floor around the southwest patio. The ministers split up into the *sala de lo civil* for civil cases and the *sala del crimen* for criminal trials (rooms no. 25 and 33). Their secretaries laboured in rooms no. 6 and 28 as well as in 35 and 36, respectively. The *audiencia* shared this patio with the administration of estates (*juzgado general de bienes de difuntos*) located in room no. 37, the tribunal of accounts (the *tribunal de cuentas*) in no. 30 as well as the accountants of the financial administration (31 and 32). A secret chamber next to the *sala civil* connected with the chapel gallery reserved for the vicereines, located between the principal and the southwest patio.

The viceroy was meant to dominate the upper floor of the principal patio. Here, the viceroy and the *audiencia* judges came together in the hall of the *real acuerdo* to discuss matters of political importance (no. 1). The secretaries of government and war (*oficio de la gobernación y guerra*) assisted in rooms no. 7 and 8. The *consulado* of Mexico, comprised of great merchants, also met regularly on the upper floor (no. 11). The plan of the palace drawn up in 1709 intended for the viceroy, his immediate family, and his *criados mayores* to reside in the section north and west of the consulado hall. The section for the viceroy and his family included the rooms for gentlemen (18 and 19), the viceregal secretary (*secretaría de cámara*), the *salón de puntas* hall, and the antechamber (21, 22, 24). Petitioners waited in these rooms to be admitted to the more secluded sphere of the viceroy in the chambers facing the main square. Here, the salon had twelve balconies for public appearances.[25] This arrangement, smaller than the royal court, possibly resembled a magnate's abode in Madrid, such as Alburquerque's town palace on the Encarnación square. As construction had not finished on large portions of this section, the viceroy probably occupied a group of rooms on the mezzanine along the façade towards the *plaza mayor*.[26] For official occasions, Alburquerque ascended the staircase to the second floor, where he received visitors of higher social standing.[27]

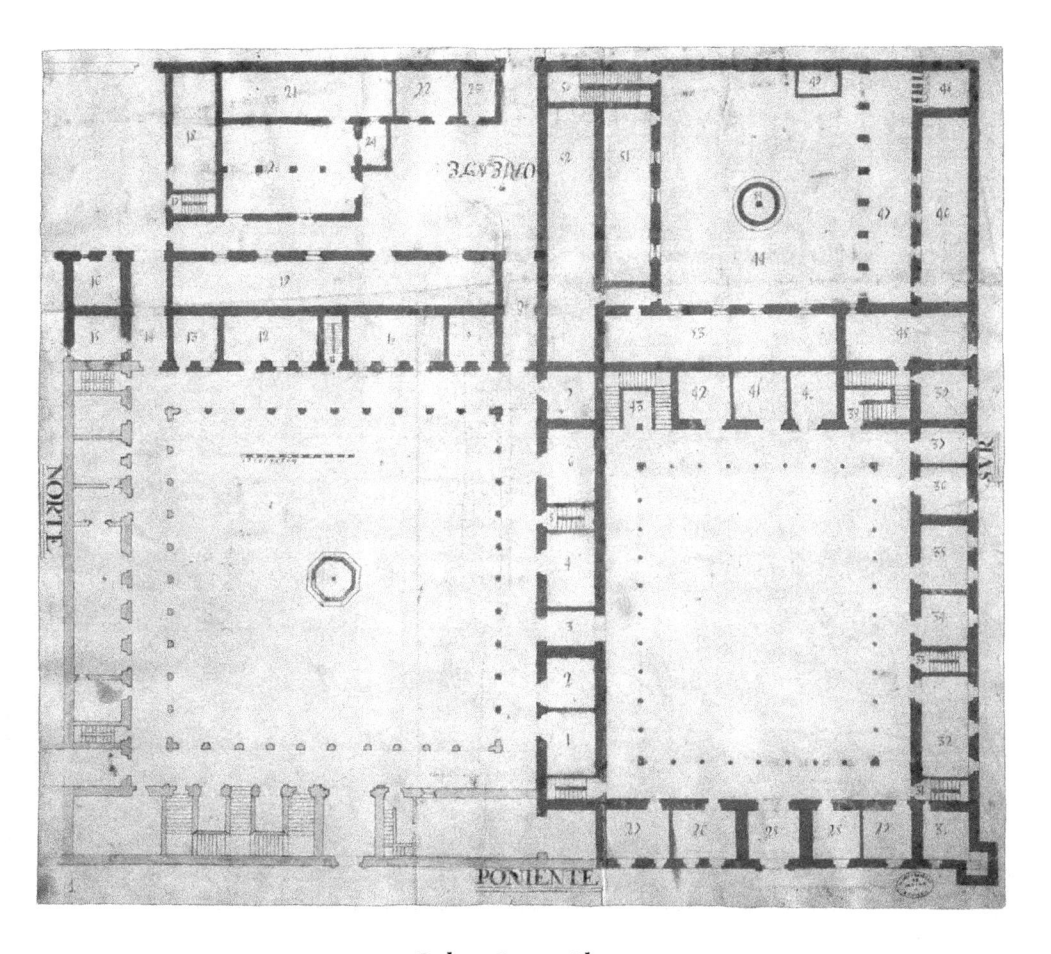

Palace Lower Floor

*Figure 3: 1709 Plan for the reconstruction of the first,
second, and third floor of the viceregal palace*

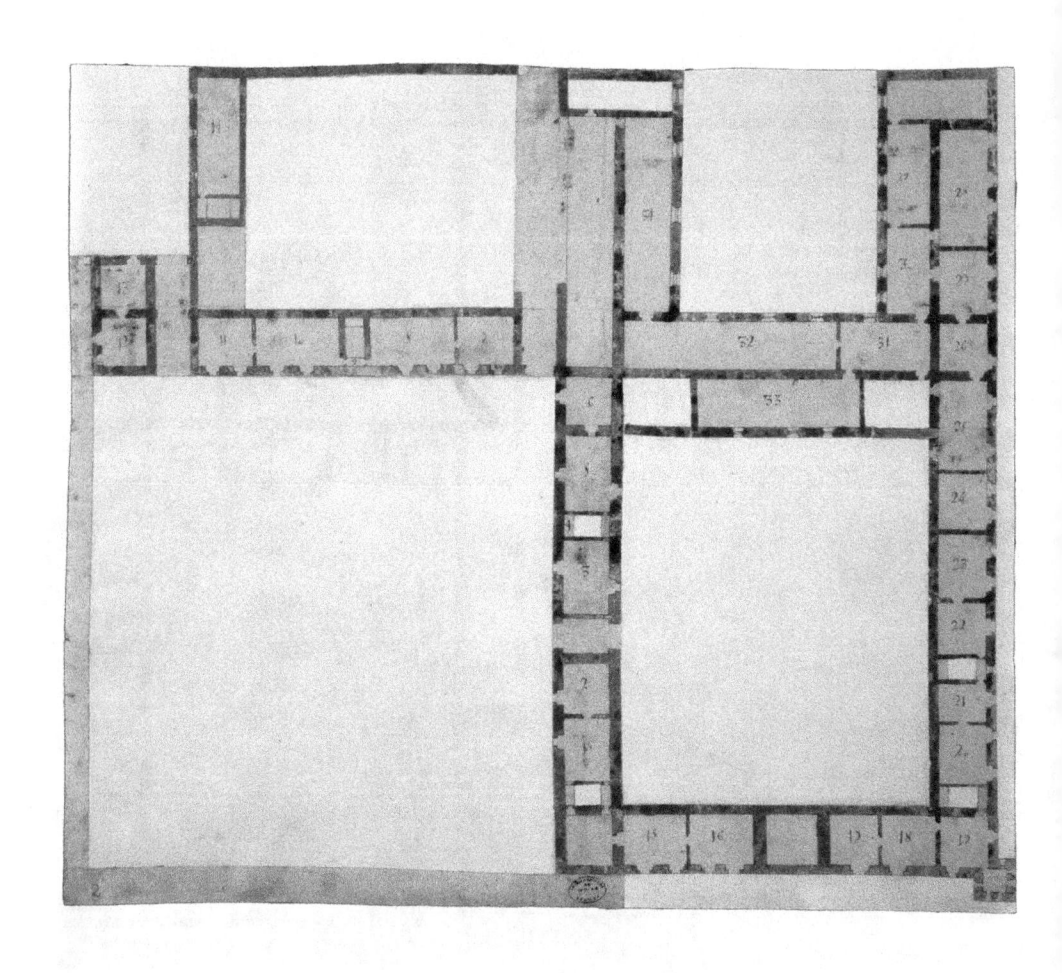

Palace Mezzanine

Continuation of Figure 3

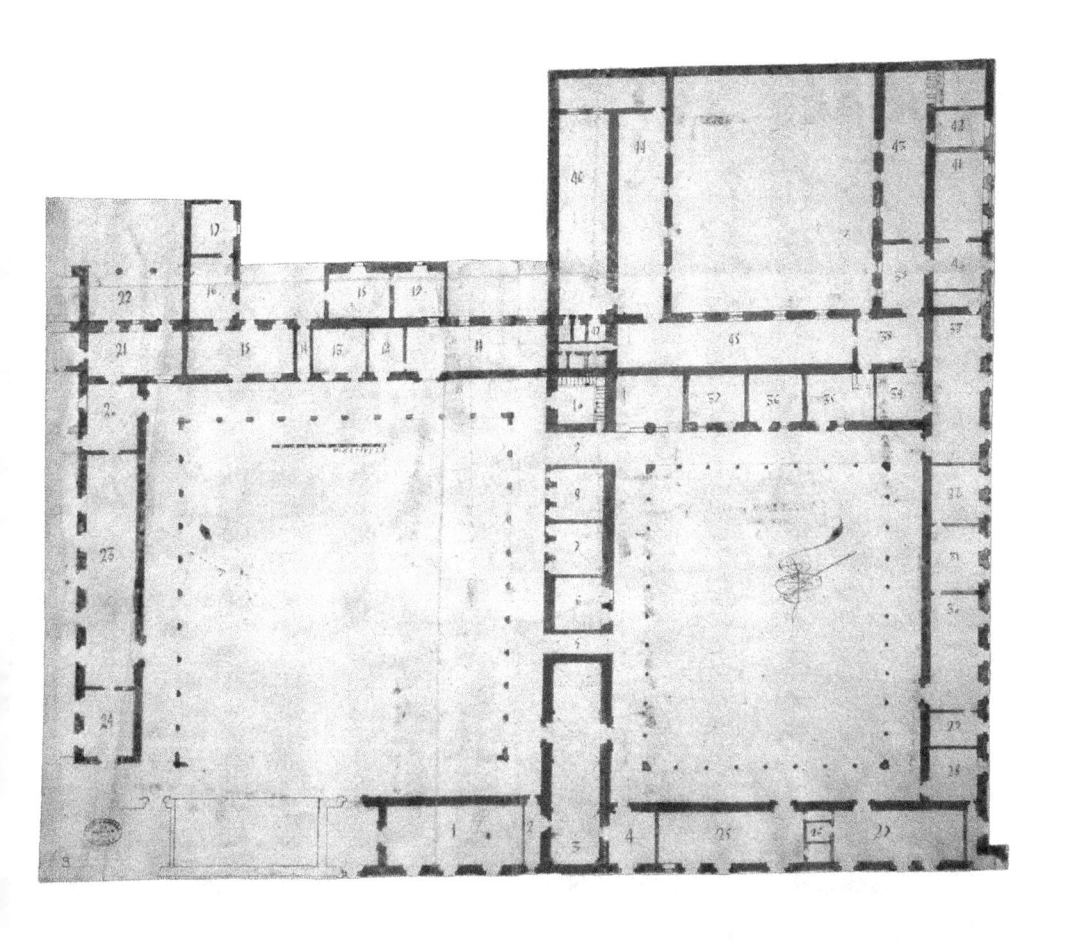

Palace Upper Floor

Continuation of Figure 3

Planta baja=en el Patio principal que da entrada a la vivienda de los S.res Virreyes resta p.r hacer lo que demuestra dha Planta en el Colorido encarnado y sus no.os se entenderan por lo que mira Ala parte deel norte enla man.a sig.te

1. Cochera para dos Coches
2. Otra Cochera para dos Coches
3. Paradiso de Patio a Patio
4. Otra Cochera
5. Encalera [sic!] para Entresuelos
6. Otra Cochera para dos Coches
7. Aposento de lacayos
8. Paradiso al Patio de Caballerizos
9. Aposento de lacayos
10. Aposento de lacayos
12. Otro Almacen
13. Aposento de lacayos
14. Otro Paradiso q.e ba p.a el lado dela Caja
15. Aposento de Lacayos
16. Otro aposento
17. Escalera para Entresuelo
18. Pajar
19. Caballeriza
20. Caballerizas de dos naves
21. Otra Caballeriza
22. Sala para Guarnel
23. Aposento de mosos
24. Tanque en el Patio de Caballerizas
25. Saguan y entrada al Patio dela R.l audienz.a

26. Sala baja p.a Oficio de Provincia
27. Otro Para Otro Oficio de Provincia
28. Otro Para Otro Oficio
29. Aposento de Lacayos
30. Otro Aposento
31. Escalera de entresuelso
32. Almacen para Bullas
33. Otra escalera de entresuelos
34. Aposento de Mosos
35. Almacen p.a papel sellado
36. Aposento de Mososo
37. Aposento p.a el oficio de ss.no de entradas
38. Saguan de la Carcel
39. Aposento del Carcelero
40. Una Cochera
41. Otra Cochera
42. Otra Cochera
43. Casa de escalera Principal de la audienz.a
44. Patio dela Carcel
45. Un quarto para el Alcayde
46. Galera de Presos
47. Portalon
48. Caja de lugares
49. Tanque de Agua
50. Escalera que sube a las Galeras de Pressos
51. Galera
52. Calaboso
53. Galera Calaboso
54. Pila

Lo hecho en esta Primera Planta es lo que denota el Color azul

Segunda Planta que demuestra la vivienda de los entresuelos en esta Manera

1 y 2 Salas sobre las Cocheras n.s 1 y 2
3. Otra Sala
4. Caja de escalera
5. Otra Sala
6. Su aposento
7. Sala
8. Sala
9. Casa de escalera
10. Sala
11. Aposento
12. Aposento que une con las viviendas que estan ya hechas
13. Otro aposento
14. Cebadero sobre el Pajar del n. 18
15 y 16 Salas que toman la entrada para la escalera de el Rincón
17 y 18 y 19 tres salas al otro lado deel saguan para la escalera del otro rincón
20 y 21 dos Piezas para el oficio de Alcabalas que caen por el
22 y 23 dos piezas para Tributos
24. Una pieza para archivo del Trib.l deq.tas q.o baja por su escalera de arriba

25. Sala deel Alcayde de la Carcel
26 y 27 dos piezas para dho Alcayde
28. Sala p.a Caballeros presos sobre el Portalon
29 y 30 dos Piezas para Reos
31. Antesala de la Carcel de Mugeres
32. Sala de Pressas
33. Sala de Deudas
34. Otra Sala separación de sujetos que se entra por la escalera que sube a las Galeras

Tercera Planta que es la que denota las Viviendas Principales y Salas de los Tribunales

1. Sala Para el Real Aquerdo q.e cae sobre el Patio Principal donde esta la armeria y asu lado una Pieza secreta con su escalera que da subida a la Tribuna de la Capilla R.l p.a las S.ras Virreynas q.e es la n. 2
3. Capilla R.l con puertas a ambos Corredores
4. La sachristía
5. Paradiso de Corredor a Corredor
6. Oficio de Camara dela audienz.a
7 y 8 Oficios de Govierno con puertas al corredor deel Patio Principal
9. Paradisso
10. Aposento y asulado escalera para subir ala azotea
11. Sala deel Consulado
12. Su escribania
13. La Chanzillería
14. Paradisso que da entrada a una sotehuela para las viviendas que hade tener y faltan por hacer al encuentro dela obra nueba
15. Una sala
16. Recamara
17. Aposentto
18 y 19 dos quartos p.a Gentilhombres
20. Antesala que da Passo a la
21. que puede ser ss.ria de camara
22. Corredor o Mirador sobre la obra hecha de la R.l Caja y sus oficios corresponde y falta por haserla antesala del n 20 y en lo restante un salon de puntas que es el n 23
24. Antesala para ellado de las viviendas hechas que miran a la plaza mayor
25. Sala para la R.l audienzia
26. Sus secrettos
27. Sala de menor quantia
28. El otro ofiz.o de camara dela audienz.a
29. Aposento del Contt.or dela Messa de Memoria
30. Sala deel Trib.l de quentas
31. Sala de Cott.res ordenadores
32. Sala de Contt.es de Resultas y escotillon citado
33. Sala de el Crimen
34. Casa de escalera y sobre ella el antesala p.a q.u salgan los reos a la visita
35 y 36 los oficios de Camara deel Crimen
37. Jusgado grâl. de Vienes de difuntos
38. Sala de Armas
39. Sala de tormentos
40. Sala donde estenlos S.res Alc.des
41. Capilla de la Carcel
42. Aposento
43. Sala de Reos separados
44. Galera Alta
45. Otra Galera
46. Galera enfermeria
47. Bartolinas

Asimismo se han de hacer en el Patio Principal dos tramos de Corredores alto y bajo y en el lado q. esta hecho dela R.l Caxa el alto q.u le falta y el Patio dela audiencia sus quatro corredores Altos y bajos Como demuestra la Planta

Source: Mapa y explicación de la Planta de lo que falta por hazer en el Real Palacio que es en esta manera," in a *cuaderno* titled "Superior Govierno. Año de 1709. Testimonio de autos hechos en virtud de Real Zedula en que aprueba S.M. a su Excelencia los reparos que se hizieron en el Real Palazio de esta Corte," AGI, Mapas y Planos, México 105 a, b, c.

Some corporations, such as the town hall, the archbishopric, the religious orders, or the craftsmen guilds (*gremios*), never formed part of the palace.[28] Yet, the prelate or the councilmen could become part of the court upon gaining access to the viceroy, his household, or the royal officials working in the palace. Although located within the palace, the prison did not belong to the court. Neither did the archiepiscopate across the street or the town hall, yet undeniably they both exercised influence on it. The archbishop resided in a magnificent palace and controlled a good deal of patronage in the Church. Because of his position he probably held court in his own right. Nonetheless, the court of the king's alter ego remained the most important in the colony.

The protection provided by a personal guard of twenty-five halberdiers endowed the viceroys of Peru and New Spain, as the only crown officials in America, with the aura of royalty. The palace guard's tasks of protecting the entrance and halls of the palace resembled those of the three guard units at the court in Madrid. The viceroy also commanded an infantry company (*compañía*), which guarded the palace and the treasury and policed the city. A privately funded company of cavalry and nine infantry companies (the *tercio de comerciantes*), paid for by the *consulado* and headed by the chief official (prior) of the institution, supported the regular infantry. These units replaced the infantry in the palace when the soldiers were deployed outside of the city. The bakers and bacon traders (*tocineros*) also maintained two companies, and other guilds supported another battalion. In addition, the companies, of *pardos o mulatos*, the units composed of those officially of mixed African and European descent, patrolled the city and paraded at times.[29] They accompanied the viceroy in parades on the *plaza mayor*, underlining royal might, the elevated rank of the viceroy as well as the role of the officers and their soldiers in society. During these occasions, four black slaves brandishing arms marched in front of the viceroy and his personal guard. The other units of the realm followed them. Nonetheless, the loyalty of some of the companies to the viceroy may have been dubious at times. In the early years of the eighteenth century, the *Maestre de campo* (equivalent to a brigadier) Luis Sánchez de Tagle, and his nephew, the prior of the *consulado*, Pedro Sánchez de Tagle, were both sworn enemies of Alburquerque. They commanded the guild and the *consulado* companies.[30]

Besides the limitations that the Mexican society imposed on the viceroy, the monarch intended to restrict the social ties the officials established with colonial society. The laws of the Indies tightly circumscribed the social life of the court. Viceroys and *audiencia* ministers could not visit members of the colonial society, attend burials, weddings, or baptisms, or act as best men or godfathers of inhabitants of New Spain. The viceroy and the magistrates could only attend such functions for themselves, their families, and their *criados*. The law prohibited the viceroys and their wives from participating individually in festivities and barred the vicereines from entering nunneries. Unmarried viceroys could not join in wedlock without a royal licence and certainly not with persons native to the district.[31] As a result the viceroy could eat only in the company of his wife and *criados*, eschewing the presence of the local society. The king also prohibited the viceroy's children from accompanying him to America.[32] The law forbade the viceroys and their wives to own any real estate such as haciendas, houses, or gardens. They were not allowed to run any business, conduct trade and mining, or participate in explorations or conquests of unconquered territory (*entradas*). A viceroy could not accept credits or gifts; Indians could not labour for him nor could more than four slaves serve him.[33] In theory, these laws cut off the viceroy from most of the social life of the colony and reduced him to a detached and loyal servant of the crown – a form of "philosopher-king," as Phelan remarked about the *audiencia* ministers.[34] If these regulations had been obeyed, the palace would have become a sombre place to live in, perhaps mirroring Francisco de Quevedo's observation that "palaces are the sepulchres of a living death."[35]

In practice, the viceroys and local society flouted these rules. The officials relied on contacts with local social networks, and socializing formed part of politics. Because of the clandestine character of viceregal social interactions, however, the sources are opaque about the day-to-day life at court.

The celebration of important religious festivals served the purpose of cementing social relationships. Elites flocked to the main square to celebrate the king's or the queen's birthday, the birthday of the viceroy or his spouse, and great religious holidays such as Christmas or Easter. On 4 February 1708 Alburquerque ordered nine days of observance and jubilation (a *novena*) for the birth of King Philip's heir Luis Felipe, beginning with the procession of the statue of Our Lady of Succour to the cathedral. At night, actors performed comedies in the palace. The inhabitants of the city kept the lights outside of their dwellings lit well into the night, and fireworks exploded over the *plaza mayor*. Bullfights entertained the populace on San Diego square until they ended on Ash Wednesday. After Easter, the festivities resumed with a parade of floats clad with images of the cities of New Spain.[36]

On 5 October the *regidores* and *alcaldes ordinarios* swore homage to the young prince. They attended mass in the cathedral dressed in gala attire and then entered the palace to congratulate the viceroy and the vicereine. In the afternoon the councilmen gathered again with other *beneméritos* in the town hall and proceeded in orderly fashion towards the palace to salute the viceregal couple. Afterwards, the dignitaries ambled through the principal streets until the notary publicly read the homage to the prince. More celebrations followed the event.[37]

During the mid-eighteenth century, for example, the ministers of the *audiencia* and the tribunals (such as the tribunal of accounts) as well as the higher clergy, including the archbishop and canons, assembled in the palace to congratulate the viceroy on his birthday. Town councilmen and *consulado* merchants joined them. Following a grand assembly in the Alameda square, the musicians gathered in the palace and performed for the occasion. The viceroy and vicereine opened the dance and then were joined by the invited dignitaries. The celebration continued until midnight. The next day the invitees attended mass in the form of a Te Deum in the cathedral. The palace infantry paraded on the *plaza mayor*, where artillery and infantry fired three salvos to salute the viceroy.[38]

On other occasions the members of the elite proceeded after mass to the palace for the *besamanos* – to kiss the hands of the viceregal couple.[39] The palace hosted musical performances and comedies attended by the secular and religious dignitaries.[40] Because of the importance of these public spectacles, the palace probably followed a finely tuned choreography according to which the invitees entered the viceregal chamber and participated in pageants. These public spectacles

Source: Museo Naval, Madrid.

Figure 4: Fernando Brambila, Plaza mayor of Mexico City (to the left the viceregal palace)

show that the royal officials ignored the strict stipulations of the law. The celebrations served to demonstrate the legitimacy and power of the colonial order to the public.[41] Bitter quarrels erupted occasionally concerning an individuals' position in a pageant or access to the viceroy. These conflicts reflect a society obsessed with social hierarchy. Similarly, the French Duke of Saint-Simon agonized about preference of birth and prestige bestowed upon members of the court of Versailles.[42] Akin to the conduct of the French nobles described by Norbert Elias, the conflicts about social hierarchy in New Spain revolved also around the possibility of social advancements and patronage. By participating in viceregal festivities, Mexicans demonstrated their acceptance of colonial order and their own place within.[43] This explains why population segments such as Indians and Afro-Mexicans voluntarily participated in the pageants. Finally, as the lavish pageants also entertained the populace, they fulfilled a part of the patron's obligation towards his clients in exchange for their support. As *panis et circenses* (bread and circuses) had kept the Roman populace happy, the Mexican spectacles also diverted attention from the more distressing aspects of colonial life.

During the eighteenth century, enlightened attempts by the crown to enforce the legal conduct of its officials help explain the importance of social gatherings in the palace. In the *juicio de residencia* of Viceroy Count of Fuenclara, in office from 1742 to 1746, friendly witnesses admitted that the count had permitted illegal gambling in the palace, following the long-established customs of his predecessors. The witnesses stressed that Fuenclara had allowed games only with "great reluctance" or "with great moderation."[44] According to them, the nocturnal reunions in the antechamber always ended at ten, when the viceroy retired to his chamber.[45] Not surprisingly, most viceroys socialized with friends and *criados* on a regular basis. These social gatherings served not only to entertain the viceroy but, like the pageants, helped to strengthen the social fabric.

Although Alburquerque resided in the palace on the *plaza mayor* most of the time, he also moved around the city and outside for relaxation or official inspections. The duke travelled to Veracruz twice to examine the state of the port fortifications and to supervise his commercial schemes with foreign merchants. Alburquerque and other viceroys retired frequently to San Angel and to San Augustín de las Cuevas (now Tlalpan), both wealthy towns south of the city. The crown did not own any property on the outskirts of the city, and the viceroy could not legally possess any in his own right. The viceroys relaxed in the gardens of their allies' haciendas, supposedly to seek cures for their failing health. For example, the treasurer of the tribunal of accounts, Francisco de Medina Picazo lavishly hosted Alburquerque on his property in San Augustín. Medina Picazo also sponsored a luxurious boat ride to Ixtacalco for the viceroy and the vicereine.[46] A mid-century successor of Alburquerque, the first Count of Revillagigedo, and his family frequently stayed on the property of their friend Jacinto Martínez de Aguirre in San Angel.⁴⁷ Many ministers, officials, and merchants also socialized in their leisure in the outskirts.

Another important opportunity to forge a link with society was the arrival of a new viceroy in New Spain. This spectacle exposed the incoming official to populace and dignitaries along the road from Veracruz to Mexico City. The choreography varied in detail. After disembarkation the viceroy customarily rested for a few days in Veracruz, where he symbolically received the keys to the city. Then the entourage ascended to Jalapa, escorted by a cavalry company. The councilmen of the towns en route came out to salute the new representative of the king. In Jalapa, two canons of the cathedral chapter and a town hall notary, all from Puebla, joined the procession. The train then wound its way through the adorned street towards Tlaxcala, where a multitude of Indians cheered the new viceroy. Traversing the city, the Indian nobles marched ahead of the dignitary followed by musicians.⁴⁸ The prelates of the religious orders and representatives of the cathedral chapter who had descended from Mexico City extended their welcome to the viceroy. For Alburquerque's convenience, Archbishop Ortega y Montañés sent two gilded carriages and seven mule teams, two of them loaded with silver cases and another two with confectionary.⁴⁹ After a brief sojourn in the predominantly indigenous town, the viceroy elect continued his way towards Puebla, where the corporations of Mexico City greeted him. In Puebla, Alburquerque spent eight days presiding over bullfights and splendid public ceremonies. The voyage then took him to Otumba to meet his predecessor. Before entering Mexico City, the viceroys visited the shrine of Guadalupe and then spent a few more days in the small residence at Chapultepec, a crown property that was a precursor of Emperor Maximilian's palace.⁵⁰ In proper sequence, the ministers of the tribunals, the cathedral chapter, the inquisition, and other clerics passed by to salute the viceregal couple. A multitude convened around the castle to marvel at the richly decorated dwelling containing two silver-plated desks valued at 15,000 pesos. Bullfights in one of the courtyards and a host of public vendors added to the festive mood at Chapultepec. The viceroy entered Mexico City when the town hall had completed its preparations. After praying in the cathedral he approached the viceregal palace under a velvet canopy. On Monday, 27 November 1702, with the reading of the *reales cédulas* (a royal communication requiring some action) in the *sala civil*, Alburquerque formally took possession of the offices of governor, captain general, and president of the *audiencia*.[51] The duke's entry culminated in a parade through the lavishly decorated capital on 8 December, accompanied by representatives of the *audiencia*, the university, and the city as well as by the vicereine and her ladies-in-waiting. The festivities terminated with bullfights and fireworks. During his entry, Alburquerque passed through triumphal arches of the city and the ecclesiastical corporations. Here, he swore to uphold the privileges (*fueros*) of the city and to protect the Church.[52] In allegories to classical legends, these arches usually depicted the viceroys as heroes and the Spanish king as a god.[53] By choosing Achilles as the motif for its arch, the city flatteringly underlined Alburquerque's exalted standing as a grandee.[54] At the same time the *cabildo* (municipal council) alluded to the fate of the classical hero, thus reminding the duke and the populace of the dangers of hubris. The city emphasized the contractual nature of government in New Spain. Under these terms the viceroy observed the rights of the corporation that considered itself the *caput*, the head and foremost representative of the entire realm.

At the end of a viceroy's term, upon receiving notice that his successor was en route from Veracruz towards the capital, the viceroy called upon the archbishop in his palace to bid him farewell. The prelate, joined by the *audiencia* ministers, reciprocated with a visit to the viceregal palace. All paid their respects to the viceregal couple and expressed regret about their departure. The vicereine also made a farewell tour of the convents in the capital that she had visited frequently with her daughters – if she had any in Mexico – *criadas*, and ladies of colonial society.[55] In fact, even before Alburquerque's term, Archbishop Ortega y Montañés complained that viceroys and vicereines visited the nunneries so often as to disturb the convents' peace. The prelate asked the crown to prohibit further visits to the nunneries – apparently to no avail.[56]

In due time, the viceroy left the capital to the sound of the mighty cathedral bells. Riding in carriage, followed by the black guard and dignitaries with their wives, the entourage set out to the shrine of the virgin of Guadalupe. The departure of the first Count of Revillagigedo in 1755 demonstrates the size of the secular procession. Two hundred mules loaded with property allegedly accompanied the outgoing viceroy.[57] At the shrine, members of Mexican society paid their respects and returned to the capital.[58] The viceregal train then proceeded to the compound of royal houses in Otumba on the northeastern fringe of the valley of Mexico, where the viceroy expected to meet his successor.[59] Here, he handed over the baton symbolizing governance over New Spain.

During their voyage the viceroys and their entourage stayed in crown buildings in Otumba as well as in Chapultepec. Lucas Alamán also mentions royal property in Tlaxcala. Nevertheless, viceroys sometimes eschewed staying in these residences, preferring to sojourn with local persons of importance. The first Count of Revillagigedo awaited his successor at his friend's hacienda San Bartolomé de los Tepetates *"alias de los vireyes,"* adjacent to Otumba.[60] This hacienda probably received its denomination "of the viceroys" because other viceroys had frequented it on their journeys to and from Veracruz.[61]

The viceregal court expanded temporarily when Alburquerque travelled outside of the palace. Meanwhile, several viceregal clients and most functionaries continued their labours in the palace. Their activities belonged to the court, because ultimately most decisions of clients depended on the viceroy. The situation became more complex when both the outgoing and incoming viceroy resided in the colony. Hopefuls vied to set up alliances with the incoming viceroy while the outgoing one still wielded influence. Since Alburquerque returned to Spain over two years after the end of his tenure, he must have set up residence somewhere in the capital. His patronage system survived well into the period after tenure, even departure and death. For example, the Osorio merchant family was loyal to Alburquerque in the showdown against the Sánchez de Tagle network. In 1738, five years after Alburquerque's death, Julián de Osorio's heirs appealed to Alburquerque's son to support their aspirations for promotion.[62]

European historiography has considered the question whether institutions of government like the judiciary or the Parliament belonged to the royal courts or formed a separate sphere. In the course of the sixteenth and seventeenth centuries, a marked change occurred in the royal residencies. Various departments of state, such as the administration of justice and finance, began to "move out of court."[63] After this move, most officials did not have regular access to the sovereign, although in the seventeenth century some nobles still held positions in institutions as well as in court offices. These nobles bridged a gap between household and government.[64] The move signalled the separation of professional bureaucracy and the king's court, further carving out the distinction between the state and the person of the monarch.

In the early modern period, we also observe the comparable move of the royal European court "out of the capital." In the sixteenth century Philip II of Spain moved the court to Madrid to rule away from the traditional aristocratic strongholds.[65] In the sixteenth and seventeenth centuries, the construction of princely residences, such as the Escorial and the palaces at Bonn or Versailles, followed a similar logic.

In New Spain, a similar tendency can be observed. In the eighteenth century sections of the government started "leaving" the court. In the appointment of Juan José de Veytia Linage as accountant of mercury residing in Puebla, we can see a precursor of this separation, since the crown intentionally moved the office outside the viceregal palace into a different city. The tribunal of the miners, a corporation founded in 1776 and charged with settling litigation and fostering business, never formed part of the palace.[66] Viceroy Bernardo de Gálvez (1785–1786) periodically relocated the viceregal residence to buildings in Chapultepec Park well outside the city proper.[67] This residence removed the viceroy from a potentially angry crowd on the *plaza mayor* as well as putting some distance between his court and rivalling civil and ecclesiastical powers. At the same time, the dissolution of the traditional unity between administration and the viceregal residence signalled a reduction of the court's function as a space where political negotiations occurred. The separation hampered personal contacts among power elites and bureaucracy. It heralded the rationalization and professionalization of the bureaucracy, which grew increasingly loyal to the crown's demands. It is possible that the viceregal buildings in Chapultepec served primarily as a source for entertainment rather than having a significant political function. Once again this development parallels contemporary European courts.[68] How Bernardo de Gálvez and his successors intended the new residence to function needs to be further researched, as do the implications of this process for the independence of Mexico.

The court in New Spain was the place where the viceroy, his retainers, power elites, and royal officials negotiated politics and their standing in society. Norbert Elias's model, although inspiring, suggests many problems for the Mexican case, because the court did not consist principally of the king's household. Instead, officials, clergymen, and the commercial elite held positions in their own right and did not depend on the viceroy to the same degree as courtiers depended on the king in Versailles. Theoretically, the laws barred the viceroy and the vicereine from socializing with local society. In reality, however, the viceroy and his family participated in colourful pageants and even gambling, developing close-knit ties with society. Nevertheless, in this period we already see precursors of late eighteenth-century Bourbon policies separating the society from the administration to curb overly unlawful behaviour. Corruption engulfed viceroys just as any other royal official of the *ancien régime*. Using the term *corruption* with its modern connotation is problematic because it implies an individual moral failure. I employ the concept here, however, to describe a form of administrative conduct which in the early modern period was endemic and often considered acceptable. The aim is here to understand what constituted excessive infraction of the law at a time when the European states were rolling back corruption in their home countries and their colonies.

4

Clients and Creatures: Alburquerque's Pervasive Patronage

Mexican viceroys bolstered their regime by appointing *criados* (minions who had accompanied the viceroy from Spain) and clients to offices in the colony. An analysis of these appointments therefore provides important insight into viceregal power. Choosing *alcaldes mayores* or *corregidores* (district officials whose functions were by this time almost identical) gave the viceroy two benefits. First, the functionary exercised judiciary tasks and supervised the civil administration in the Spanish and Indian towns, collecting taxes and enforcing the law. In addition, as lieutenants of the captain general, the *alcaldes mayores* performed, at least formally, certain military roles. The viceroy could increase his control over the colony by placing his *criados* or clients in these offices. Patronage remedied the weak viceregal oversight over the outer provinces of the colony. The viceroy had less effective means of coercion over district officials who had bought their offices from the crown. In contrast, the viceroy could better impose his will, even in remote areas, when he took advantage of personal bonds. As *alcaldes mayores* built alliances with the local elites, they extended viceregal patronage into the provinces. The increased exchange of information and resources mattered, especially around major cities and commercial hubs, such as Antequera, or close to strategic places like Veracruz.[1] The viceroy rewarded loyal service and set incentives to collaborate with him by appointing allies to lucrative offices while cutting off opposing groups from patronage.

Tracking all viceregal appointments poses a methodological problem because the available sources are diverse. The viceroy probably also chose many officials clandestinely, especially if doing so was to break the law. A range of sources nevertheless allows insight into nominations. A crucial one is the *memoria de los criados*, which the Duke of Alburquerque provided in his *juicio de residencia* (the inquiry into the conduct of an official at the end of his tenure). The *memoria* lists all the retainers that had accompanied Alburquerque from Spain.[2] The viceregal correspondence and diaries also offer valuable information about patronage and nominations.[3] Additionally, the records of the *media anata* tax reveal serial patronage patterns. The crown established this tax in 1631, stipulating that anyone assuming a crown office needed to pay half of one year's salary in advance and a third of all future fees one could legally levy by virtue of office. The *ramos* (sections) *media anata* and *archivo histórico de la hacienda* (the formerly separate historical archive of the treasury) in the Mexican National Archive (AGN) contain long runs of dated receipts specifying the amount of *media anata* paid by various officials. The papers mention the future officeholder, the witnesses, and often the *fiador* (a bondsman vouching for the official in case of abuse of office, especially if he defaulted on tax collection). The documents also state the estimated duration of the appointment and, occasionally, whether the monarch or the viceroy had appointed the official. Absent such specific designation, one can in many cases distinguish between crown and viceregal appointments by duration of the appointment. The monarch always designated district officials for a five-year period, whereas the viceroy appointed usually for one year, occasionally two.[4]

The crown or the viceroy did not name officials in the territories of the Marquis of the Valley of Oaxaca and of the Duke of Atrisco. These aristocrats picked the *alcaldes mayores* (district officials) in their jurisdiction. The marquisate of the Valley of Oaxaca consisted of the remnants of Conquistador Hernán Cortés's former estate, which by the early eighteenth century had fallen through inheritance to an Italian aristocrat, the Duke of Monteleone. The *alcaldías mayores* Charo, Coyoacán, the Cuatro Villas de Oaxaca, Cuernavaca, Jalapa, Toluca, and Tuxtla made up the marquisate.[5] In December 1707, however, the king sequestered the districts, because Monteleone rallied to the Habsburg cause. Additionally, the Duke of Atrisco appointed *alcaldes mayores* in Atrisco (modern spelling of the town is Atlixco), Tepeaca, Ixtepeji, and Tula. The monarch created the duchy with a royal decree from 1706 to reward the Count of Montezuma's loyalty during the evacuation of Madrid in that year.[6]

Caution is necessary with the sources that reflect appointments. The viceroy and other officials could tamper with the papers when it served their needs. For example, Alburquerque's client Diego Marquina, an assistant notary (*escribano*) of the criminal chamber, received an *alcaldía mayor* under a false name, because the *fiscal del crimen* prosecuted against Marquina in 1710.[7] In addition, the series of the *media anata* tax are probably not entirely complete, and some series contain more specific data than others. The section *archivo de la hacienda* in the AGN, which historians and cataloguers have only recently begun to tackle, still includes further information. Despite these shortcomings, the amount of data available for determining patterns of viceregal patronage is impressive in detail and quantity and sufficient to allow for solid conclusions.[8]

Diaries written between the mid-seventeenth century and the mid-eighteenth century also provide details on patronage and the viceregal court. The writings of Antonio de Robles cover one full year of Alburquerque's administration and are therefore especially valuable. The diaries of Gregorio Martin de Guijo and Joaquín Castro Santa-Anna, covering 1648–1664 and 1752–1756 respectively, reveal the general working of patronage and politics in New Spain.[9] Castro Santa-Anna, an attorney at the *audiencia*, chronicled the viceregal term of the first Count of Revillagigedo in an especially lucid fashion.[10] He wrote, "[T]his morning [13 October 1755] the loads and luggage of His Excellency Señor Viceroy Count of Revillagigedo departed, more than two hundred mules loaded with garments and confectioners, and it is believed to be certain that none of the viceroys who have governed this realm have furthered their interests as this one."[11] Castro Santa-Anna's acrimony against the viceroy could stem from the fact that he had received two *alcaldías mayores* from Revillagigedo's predecessor and that the arrival of the new viceroy blocked future prospects of promotion.[12] Furthermore, Castro Santa-Anna's father worked as an accountant of the *alcabala* tax of Mexico City. Revillagigedo de-privatized the tax administration against the protest of the *consulado* and many Creoles. Castro Santa-Anna resented the reformist approach of Revillagigedo.

Another source reveals sinister aspects of Alburquerque's administration. In May 1710, the Inquisition confiscated several copies of a satirical poem about Alburquerque entitled "Confession, which His Excellency Viceroy Duke of Alburquerque, Don Francisco Fernández de la Cueva, makes in the last days of his government."[13] The document revisits most of the scandals and quarrels surrounding the viceroyship and was well informed about the duke's favourites and enemies. The Inquisition suppressed the verses as irreverent towards the viceroy and the religious orders. For example, some lines attack the clergy close to the viceroy by imagining the duke's search for a confessor in the last hours of his sinful life:

... *En el Cabildo esta Gama*	... *In the chapter Gama*
penitenciario doctor	*Doctor of penitence*
que absuelve, como examina	*Who absolves just like he examines*
con gran pacificacion ...	*With great serenity*
Si murió vro Navarro	*If your Dominican Navarro died*
Dominico, Sucesor	*A successor*
quedó desus caravanas	*Remained from his caravans*
el Seraphico Dañon....[14]	*The Franciscan Dañon....*

These lines depict the conduct of the Mexican Cathedral Canon Antonio de Gama in an unfavourable light. His alleged tendency to absolve indiscriminately contrasts with the prebendary duties of a *penitenciario doctor* to administer penance judiciously to sinners. A colonial résumé (*relación de méritos*) proves that Antonio de Gama did in fact sit on the cathedral chapter.[15] The satire, when read critically, can provide important information on courtly entanglements that the official sources do not regularly reveal. The satire satirically reprises the 1708–1710 antagonism between Alburquerque and the merchant Juan Fernández Cacho over the meat monopoly in Mexico City:

...*Tercera carnicería*	There is a third butchery
después de la una, y las dos	After the first and the second
es, la que ninguno ignora	This everyone knows
digalo el Corregidor	The corregidor may say so
Y cacho que por hazerme	And cacho who raised his bid
con mejora apocision	
como por luna, por carne	For the moon, for meat
iva, y mondado quedo.	Went and I was pruned
Papa cacho, para cacha	Papa Cacho, to the buttocks
nora en tal el porcachon	In bad time the swine
vos contrapeso a mi carne	You counterpoised my meat
vos mi sobregueso, vos[16]	You, my toil, you

Clients and Creatures 57

On the factual level, the *confession* speaks from the perspective of the viceroy and alludes to the implication of the *corregidor* in the quarrel, Fernández Cacho's bid for the monopoly, his ensuing voyage to the Council of the Indies, and the defeat of Alburquerque and the municipal council at the hands of the Council (*hazerme con mejora, iva, mondado quedo*).[17] The author of the *confession* also played with words that sound similar to the monopolist's last name, such as *papa cacho, para cacha, porcachon*. On a metaphorical level, the puns are rather piquant, as the fifth line "hacerme cacho" could also be understood as "he cuckolded me" and *luna* (moon) alludes because of the tipped shape of the crescent to the same idea. *Cacho* in Spanish also means jest or broken-off piece, and the ninth line could also be read as "Papa jest, to the arse." Although very informative, satires or other marginalized sources from the *ramo* Inquisición have so far garnered little attention among political historians.[18]

The *confession* followed the custom of composing satires about affairs at the court in Madrid. The personnel at the viceregal court also reflected in many ways the practices of the royal court. In Madrid three principal courtiers, usually of grandee origin, attended to the king's material necessities. The *mayordomo mayor* or lord high steward held the highest office and supervised the entire palace functions, controlling the king's feeding and housing. The *camarero mayor*, the grand chamberlain, or, as the office fell into disuse, the *sumiller de corps* (groom of the stole), organized the king's personal service. The master of the horse (*caballerizo mayor*) supervised the stables and transportation. Each of these officials had his own extensive staff consisting of *gentileshombres* (gentlemen), who accompanied the king as well as lower officials, such as *ayudas* (aides) and *mozos* (servants), who took care of the menial functions in the palace.[19]

The viceregal retainers served in similar functions in Mexico. When Alburquerque left for America, he brought with him an entourage of about one hundred dependents. While his son remained in Spain, Alburquerque's official retinue consisted of his wife and daughter, a personal secretary, a *camarero*, a majordomo, and a *caballerizo* as well as three chaplains, eighteen *criados mayores* (retainers of higher station) and sixteen pages.[20] These *criados* organized the operation of Alburquerque's court and provided the duke with the necessities of life.

For example, Gentleman José de Escolar transmitted the correspondence between Alburquerque and Archbishop Ortega y Montañés in 1707.[21] Dozens of minions and four black slaves carried out the lower tasks in the household.[22] Alburquerque just as other viceroys brought a physician to attend to his family's medical needs.[23] Cooks and pastry bakers prepared food.[24] The vicereine had several chambermaids at her disposal, although the viceroy did not list them officially among his *criados*. For example, Leonor Fernández de Córdoba had travelled from her hometown in Castile to New Spain, belonging as a damsel (*doncella*) to Alburquerque's family.[25] An Irish chambermaid assisted the Countess of Revillagigedo.[26] This arangement resembled the royal court in small.

Many of the *criados* travelled with their wives and children and other relatives. Other *criados* embarked clandestinely with the duke in La Coruña, exceeding the officially permitted limits. For example, José Munarris, the brother of the duke's treasurer, Miguel Munarris, does not appear in the official records as Alburquerque's *criado*. Yet José Munarris received an *alcaldía mayor* in New Spain. He probably came with the entourage from Spain, and Alburquerque considered him his *criado*.[27]

Although in the course of the eighteenth century the royal regime tightened its control over America, subsequent viceroys brought only slightly smaller retinues. In 1755 the Marquis of Amarillas disembarked in Veracruz with a total of eighty-one minions,[28] while twenty-four male clients plus their families escorted the younger Revillagigedo in 1789. They formed a splendid entourage.[29] His father, the first Count of Revillagigedo, officially brought only four *criados*, although other relatives joined him in Cuba and in New Spain.[30] Such a small entourage was an exception even in the eighteenth century. Revillagigedo was of *hidalgo* origin and obtained the title of nobility only in 1749. As former Captain General of Cuba, he could not claim such a large retinue as other viceroys.[31]

While in New Spain, the viceroy built up a network of new clients through appointments to various offices, especially the *alcaldías mayores* and *corregimientos*. Many of those appointees did not originally belong to Alburquerque's entourage but came to view themselves as *criados*. For example, in November 1704 Alburquerque appointed Martín Ajolesa as *alcalde mayor* of Mestitlan. In 1705 Ajolesa corresponded with the viceroy about the seizure of Portuguese property in his district. Although Ajolesa's name does not appear in Alburquerque's *memoria*,[32] the district official ended the letter with the phrase "I kiss the feet of your Excellency, your most humble *criado*."[33] Testimonies of witnesses in a boundary dispute prove that the *alcalde mayor* of Mestitlan bought land in that jurisdiction before the arrival of the duke and cannot have travelled with Alburquerque from Spain.[34] By receiving the district officialdom, possibly in exchange for a bribe, Alojesa became, at least in his view, a client of Alburquerque. In contrast, the *alcalde mayor* of Nejapa, a crown appointee, reported on the same issue to the viceroy. The official eschewed any embellishments in his correspondence, not even including the popular "May God protect your Excellency."[35] Clearly, a larger social distance separated the viceroy from the crown-appointed *alcalde mayor* than from his own appointee.

The following is an overview of the *criados mayores*, pages, *criados* of lower station, and close clients of the viceroy (Table 1). The information that the duke gave in his *memoria de los criados* has to be taken with a grain of salt, and I have therefore added other clients to the list. Often in the households of Spanish magnates, the *criados mayores* and pages belonged to the lower nobility or families of some social standing. The grandee accepted them into his household and groomed them for court service. Five of Alburquerque's *criados* belonged to a military order, a sign of social distinction. For example, Alburquerque's secretary, Juan de Estacasolo y Otalora joined the order of Santiago, considered by some to be socially more prestigious than those of Alcántara and Calatrava. Two relatives of Estacasolo sat at one time on the Council of the Indies. All other *criados mayores* and pages boasted the honorary title "Don," traditionally reserved for the nobility. In the eighteenth century, however, the designation *Don* or *Doña* no longer carried the same prestige as it had in the previous centuries. Even commoners had begun using the address. In the late eighteenth century, the density of *hidalgos* north of the Duero River in Spain made the distinction between these and commoners somewhat fluid. In the province of Guipúzcoa, all inhabitants claimed inclusion in the *hidalguía*, whereas in Vizcaya one half and in Asturias one sixth of the populace asserted their status of low nobility.[36] The claim to nobility of Alburquerque's retainers was therefore tenuous, but the address *Don* does reflect a social distinction of the *criados mayores* and pages.

Table 1 also lists those retainers who had come from the peninsula while not being mentioned in the *memoria*. It also shows those clients who entered into the viceroy's services in New Spain. I have only incorporated clients into this list if they were appointed more than twice to an *alcaldía mayor*, or if they obtained one of the most profitable districts from the duke (for a full view of all viceregal appointments, see Appendix 5). Even an official who bribed the viceroy to obtain a coveted position could become his client, because the exchange of favours or gifts was a hallmark of patronage. Often, it served the viceroy for political and social purposes to appoint well-established members of society, as in the case of José Nuñez de Villavicencio. Since 1687 Nuñez de Villavicencio had served as *corregidor* of Mexico City. He belonged to an influential family from Jérez, Spain, which had produced an *alcalde ordinario* (a town councillor who sat as judge in cases of first instance) and another *corregidor*. Alburquerque assigned Don José to one of the wealthiest *alcaldías mayores*[37] to foster the alliance. In exchange, Don José's family members vouched for the viceroy in his *juicio de residencia*.[38] The appointments served to establish a patron-client relationship with important individuals in the colony.

In addition to his *criados* and clients at court, Alburquerque collaborated with four legal advisors during his viceroyship. At least four clergymen said Mass in the palace. Officiating in the palace did not necessarily indicate a good relationship with the viceroy, as the case of the bishop of Oaxaca demonstrates. Angel de Maldonado fought with the duke over the sequestration of Dominican parishes in his see. Bishop Maldonado arrived in Mexico City and offered Mass for the duchess to win her over to his political purposes – much to her husband's displeasure.[39]

Alburquerque also used his influence in Spain to recommend promotions in the Church. For example, in 1703 Alburquerque suggested that his faithful ally *Oidor* Baltasar de Tovar should be granted a prebend in the cathedral of Mexico City.[40] In another squabble, the duke picked six clerics for consecration, diverging from the hierarchy of candidates (*terna*) suggested by the archiepiscopate. This provoked considerable ire among the archbishop and clergy. Alburquerque chose his cronies for important positions. They obtained posts at the *sagrario* (the cathedral church), at the Veracruz parish church in Mexico City that served mainly Spaniards as well as at two parishes located just outside of the capital.[41] The duke used his right as vice-patron of the Church moderately. He rewarded loyal clients and extended his influence.

The duke, his wife, and their daughter	
Francisco Fernández de la Cueva	Duke of Alburquerque
Juana de la Cerda y Aragón	Marquise of Cadereita, his wife
Ana-Catalina Fernández de la Cueva y de la Cerda	their daughter

Criados Mayores, addressed as "Don"		
1.	Juan de Estacasolo y Otalora	secretario, o. Santiago
2.	Domingo Valles	camarero, capitán guardia alabarderos
3.	José Alvarez del Valle	mayordomo, capitán infantería palacio, o. Santiago
4.	Francisco Diez de Ulzurrun	caballerizo, capitán infantería palacio, o. Santiago
5.	José Félix de Escolar	gentilhombre, maestresala, o. Santiago
6.	Miguel de Munarris	tesorero
7.	Blasco Ruiz de Herrera	gentilhombre, o. Calatrava
8.	Andrés Alvarez de Maldonado	gentilhombre
9.	Pedro de Alcántara Laris	gentilhombre
10.	Jerónimo Alvarez del Valle	gentilhombre
11.	Bernardo de la Cantera	gentilhombre

Pages (Paje), addressed as "Don"		
12.	Manuel Vellosillo Hienostrosa	capitán de la infantería española
13.	Francisco Saenz Daza	
14.	José Tiburcio Boets y Villalón	
15.	Pedro Manzano	
16.	Juan Manzano	
17.	Diego de Molina	
18.	Francisco Javier de la Mata	
19.	Francisco Maldonado	
20.	Antonio Santos	
21.	Pedro de Arzapalo	
22.	Francisco Sanz Daza	
23.	Doña Leonor Fernández de Córdoba	doncella

Chamber Aides, not addressed as "Don"

24.	Pedro de Ellauri	veedor
25.	Juan Flores Fernández	guardaropa
26.	José de Nieva	ayuda de cámara
27.	José Cazetas	ayuda de cámara
28.	José de Velasco	ayuda de cámara
29.	Alonso de Carmona	ayuda de cámara
30.	Augustin de Buda	portero
31.	Pedro de Franco	repostero
32.	Antonio Alvarez	repostero
33.	Manuel García	cocinero

Other Criados

34.	Fernando de Ortega Patiño	oficial de la secretaría, contador de resultas
35.	Estéban Rodríguez Santa Cruz	oficial de la secretaría, criado
36.	Leandro de Buendía	
37.	Diego Peramato	recomendado to the viceroy
38.	Francisco Peramato	
39.	José Munarris	brother of criado M. Munarris

Clients from New Spain, not listed as Viceregal Criados

1.	José Alarcón, tie to Martin Alarcón	appointment to AM
2.	Martin Alarcón, sargento mayor, o. Santiago	3 appointments to AM
3.	Marcos Ayala	appointment to wealthiest AM (value one)
4.	Castañeda, Francisco	ditto
5.	Ignacio Giniales Lasarte	ditto
6.	Francisco Gorostiza	ditto
7.	Bernardo Izoain	ditto
8.	Pedro Llerena Lazo	ditto
9.	Miguel López Grajal	ditto
10.	Isidro Félix Luna, alférez	two appointments
11.	José Antonio Martínez de Lejarsar	appointment to wealthiest AM (value one)
12.	Pedro Mier Caso Estrada	two appointments to AM
13.	Andrés de la Mora, capitán	three appointments to AM
14.	José Nuñez de Villavicencio	appointment to wealthiest AM (value one)
15.	Nicolás Ordos Laya	ditto, capitán de caballos corazas
16.	Diego Palacios	three appointments to AM
17.	Tomás Ponce de León	appointment to wealthiest AM (value one)
18.	José Ramrírez de Arellano	ditto
19.	Tomás de la Riva	ditto
20.	Coronel Pedro de Rivera	ditto
21.	Andrés de la Serna	3 appointments to AM
22.	Diego Rivas	appointment to wealthiest AM (value one)
23.	Lucas Rosal	ditto

Clients and Creatures

24.	Capitán Mateo Antonio Rueda	ditto
25.	Juan Antonio Sáenz Valiente	ditto
26.	Manuel Bernardo Santerbas Espinosa	ditto
27.	Diego Sotomayor	ditto
28.	José Taboada Ulloa	ditto
29	Capitán Tomás Terán de los Ríos	ditto
30	Juan Torres Camberos	ditto

Legal advisors

1.	Dr. Carlos Bermudes	
2.	Dr. José de León	
3.	Lic. Clemente Buqueiro	
4.	Maestro José Sáenz de Escobar	

The viceregal secretariat

1.	Juan de Estacasolo y Otalora	private secretary of the duke, criado mayor
2.	Estéban Rodríguez Santa Cruz	oficial de la secretaría, criado
3.	Fernando de Ortega Patiño	oficial de la secretaría
4.	José de la Cerda Morán	escribano mayor de gobernación
5.	Francisco de Morales	teniente de escribano de gobernación
6.	Tomás Fernández de Guevara	teniente de escribano de gobernación

Criados and clients in the palace guard

1.	Domingo Valles	capitán guardia alabardero, criado mayor, then capitán guardia del palacio
2.	José Alvarez del Valle	capitán guardia del palacio, criado mayor
3.	Francisco Díez de Ulzurrun	ditto
4.	Manuel Vellosillo H.	capitán, infantería española, criado, paje
5.	Juan de Acosta	alférez, guardia del palacio, client, activities in Habsburg conspiracy

Clergy at court

Antonio Beltrán, a Jesuit	confessor of the viceroy
Bartolomé Navarro, a Dominican	confessor, successor of Beltrán
Francisco Esquivel y Mansilla	viceregal chaplain
Juán Fermín de Armendáriz, Augustinian	trusted clergy, calificador of the Inquisition
Br. Garavato, of the order St. Hippolyte	trusted clergy

Four black slaves

Table 1: The viceregal court of the tenth Duke of Alburquerque

> *Criados are defined as retainers who accompanied the viceroy to New Spain, while clients may have built their relationship in New Spain. The military orders of Santiago and Calatrava are abbreviated as o. Santiago or o. Calatrava. See explanation of the wealthiest AM of value 1 below. Sources: AGI, México 657, cuaderno 2; Memoria de los criados, Francisco Félix Hidalgo to Juan Valdés, Mexico City, 23 November 1710, AGI, México 658, f. 31v–34v. Confession, s. n., AGN, Inquisición 740, 3, f. 56–67; Alburquerque's will, Mexico City, 27 June 1711, AHAGN, Escribano José de Ledesma, No. 340, vol. 224.*

The duke could also built clientage by appointing an individual to administer a district, such as an *alcaldía mayor*, a *corregimiento*, or a governorship. The salaries of these offices did not appeal highly to candidates. Nominally, a district official received an annual salary of between 100 and 600 pesos. The practice of compensating officials, however, dwindled between 1699 and 1717, and hereafter most officials never saw a peso from the fisc. The officials stood to gain much more by siphoning off crown revenues and through the *repartimiento de mercancías*, the illegal but tolerated trade with Indians. An *alcalde mayor* built an alliance with a merchant who advanced credits and merchandise to the Indians. The official sold livestock, lent money, and bought Indian goods. Meanwhile, he could undermine mercantile competition by using his civil and judiciary powers. The official or an agent appointed by the merchant manipulated prices on sales and purchases to the detriment of the Indians. The merchant, often located in Mexico City, also advanced the official's *media anata* obligation and furnished the deposit in case the *alcalde mayor* defaulted in his tax collection. Aspirants who purchased a five-year term of a district official often paid high prices, occasionally surpassing 16,000 pesos. Often they also had to bribe the viceroy. This suggests the profitability of the office and the *repartimiento de mercancías*.[42]

This is not to say that Indians stood by as hapless victims. Their communities circumvented the *alcalde mayor*'s power by reverting to regional markets for more advantageous prices. Often, the *alcalde mayor* depended to a degree on Indian collaboration, since he had little means of coercion at hand. Nevertheless, in a system where clientage ruled the relation between Indian *caciques* (chiefs) and *alcaldes mayores*, there were limits to thwarting the monopoly trade. The formation of prices reflected ultimately a power negotiation among local contenders, following the mechanisms of the *ancien régime*. The crown sold appointments to the district offices and, as we would say today, outsourced the administration. The district officials took their cut from transactions to recoup their investments.

Until the early seventeenth century, the viceroys assigned all *alcaldías mayores* and *corregimientos* for a term of three years. The monarch reserved several districts and appointed officials for five years. Towards the end of the seventeenth century, the crown expanded the practice of selling offices through *beneficio de empleo* (a form of venality where the crown appointed candidates to offices with judicial authority in exchange for donations) to enhance royal income. The advisors of Charles II therefore tried to limit viceregal prerogatives while also discussing a complete overhaul of district administration. Under the law then, the viceroys could appoint *alcaldes mayores* to fill vacancies and to the poorer districts that the crown could not sell. Additionally, the crown limited the viceroys' faculties of designating retainers for *alcaldías mayores*. Not more than twelve *criados* could hold office simultaneously.[43]

A look at the evidence shows that this royal reform was not entirely effective. The crown did sell through *beneficio de empleo* most *alcaldías mayores* in the rich rural districts, those with a dense indigenous population where the *repartimiento* yielded high profits, and most of those in the major urban centres. In the first half of the eighteenth century, the monarch sold all the successive *corregimientos* and *alcaldías mayores* in the cities of Mexico and Antequera. In Puebla, the *alcalde mayor* Juan José de Veytia Linage received his position apparently without paying more than his fee for the combined position on the tribunal of accounts and the Mexico City *alcabala* administration. The monarch did not sell the posts of *corregidor* of Veracruz (also known as castellan of the fortress San Juan Ulúa) or castellan of Acapulco, positions equivalent to an *alcalde mayor* yet with more defence responsibility. Instead, these ports of strategic importance went to officials with military qualification, loyal service to the crown, or political connections.

From Madrid's perspective, officials who bought their posts usually lacked the qualifications to defend the fortresses adequately. The imperial administration hoped to maintain minimum vigilance in Veracruz and Acapulco.[44] This policy, nonetheless, did not prevent Alburquerque from appointing his clients to these offices. This way he could furnish his clients with lucrative posts in the ports that drew bribes from illegal commerce. Alburquerque also further reduced the effectiveness of trade supervision. In 1707 the viceroy named Francisco Manso de Zúñiga as interim *corregidor* of Veracruz. The crown had previously appointed Manso de Zúñiga as *corregidor* of Veracruz (1700–1705). He probably had some military experience as a *maestre de campo*, a rank similar to a brigadier. In 1711 Inspector Félix González de Agüero found Manso de Zúñiga guilty of operating contraband trade with French men-of-war.[45] Alburquerque also named two officers who succeeded Manso de Zúñiga as interim *corregidores*, Colonel José Ramírez de Arellano in 1709 and Colonel Pedro de Rivera in 1710. The crown even approved of the appointment of *Corregidor* Ramírez de Arellano until the return of the crown appointee, Andrés de Pez, who sailed with the fleet at that time. Additionally, the viceroy named a castellan in Acapulco and in 1710 an *alcalde mayor* of Querétaro. These cases demonstrate that Alburquerque was able to appoint his men even in the strategic ports and an important city of New Spain.[46]

To evaluate whether the crown excluded the viceroy from appointing officials in the wealthier districts, we need to assess the profits that an official could draw from his jurisdiction. Two colonial indices provide an approximation. One index, labelled the *Yndize comprehensibo* was drawn up in the 1770s by an anonymous author who assessed the districts according to economic profitability for the officials on a scale from 1 through 8 and an additional category, *ínfima* (minimal). In some cases, the worth of a district lay in between two values, such as 1 and 2. I include these districts in the group of the lower value.

When the Marquis of la Ensenada (prime minister from 1743 to 1754) pondered a reform of the district administration, he had the secretariat of New Spain conceive a second index between 1746 and 1750.[47] This index registers prices paid for *alcaldías mayores* and *corregimientos*, among other offices.[48] These prices reflect the evolution of the expected returns from different districts over a period of fifty years. It is not without problems to infer the value of a district in the early eighteenth century from these indices, since the economic and demographic dynamics of some districts changed considerably. For example, according to Ensenada's index the *beneficio de empleo* of the *alcaldía mayor* of Guanajuato fetched rather low prices between 1708 and 1748. Yet the *Yndize comprehensibo* estimated its value as most profitable, reflecting the region's surge in silver mining.[49] One should also be wary about districts such as Guatulco and Guichiapa, which the *Yndize comprehensibo* lists as most profitable, although Ensenada's register indicates a poor profit. In any case, I will consistently use the *Yndize comprehensibo* as a guideline to judge the districts' value, because Ensenada's data is difficult to compare. Drawing up a new, even more reliable economic assessment of each district's economic performance in the early eighteenth century would be beyond the scope of this book.

Appendix 5 contains the complete listing of viceregal appointments, their values, duration, sources, and in several instances, the bondsmen as well. Judging from this list, the monarch predominantly sold the most profitable rural districts that the *Yndize comprehensibo* classified with a 1. The crown entitled the buyer to take office (*posesión*) either immediately or once the post vacated (*futura*). Because the monarch often sold several *futuras* for the same district, a successful bidder might have to wait years before assuming his office. The viceroy could therefore only occasionally appoint a dependent as an interim *alcalde mayor* in many of these districts.[50] For example, Alburquerque appointed only one official in the *alcaldías mayores* of Tlapa, Celaya y Salvatierra, Miaguatlan and Guajuapa. When he was able to assign interim officials to these districts, Alburquerque chose only minions of higher station. José Alvarez del Valle, majordomo of the viceroy's household and captain of the palace infantry, and Miguel de Munarris, the duke's treasurer, belonged to the upper echelon of viceregal *criados* and received the lush positions of Tlapa and Celaya y Salvatierra, respectively. Out of forty-three viceregal appointments to *alcaldías mayores* of the category 1, eleven went to *criados* of the duke.

The fact that the duke nominated in a row three *alcaldes mayores* of Maravatio y Taximaroa, San Miguel de las Villas y San Felipe, and

Zimatlan y Chichicapa show that he could place his dependents in some of the most prosperous districts on a regular basis. These districts all received the value 1 on the *Yndize comprehensibo* and were sold in Madrid for handsome amounts of money, between 2,400 and 3,000 pesos. As an example, in 1702, 1703, 1706, and 1707, Alburquerque named four *alcaldes mayores* in Teutila, while probably no crown appointee assumed office in this period.[51] In 1703 and in 1706, the viceroy even named his *caballerizo* (master of the horse) to that *alcaldía mayor*. There are several reasons for the duke's success in appointing these officials. Often, purchasers of an office arrived in New Spain only after considerable delay because of the hazardous transatlantic voyage – especially during the War of the Succession. Then, at least according to rumours spread against the duke, Alburquerque charged some crown appointees an additional fee for permitting them to take office (*dar paso*), perhaps equalling the amount paid for the *beneficio de empleo*. This illegal procedure caused further delay. Additionally, viceroys often chose interim officials although crown appointees had arrived and held a title, thus extending their waiting period further. The monarchy issued *reales cédulas* exhorting the viceroys to suppress the practice – apparently without much success.[52] Finally, when the king sequestered the marquisate of the Valley of Oaxaca in December 1707, Alburquerque seized the opportunity. He appointed two pages to the lucrative positions, one in 1708 in the Cuatro Villas de Oaxaca, valued 1, and in 1709 in Cuernavaca, valued 2. The viceroy ensured with this array of manoeuvres that his dependents received a share of the wealthiest posts in the *gobierno* of New Spain.

Officially, the viceroy appointed almost all of these interim officials for a one-year period. The actual duration of the officials' terms, however, differed markedly. Tenure of office ranged from less than one year to three, with most officials remaining in office for about two years. For example, General Carlos Samaniego Pacheco, knight of the order of Calatrava, served the *alcaldía mayor* of Xochimilco for over three years, whereas Lorenzo Ochoa held Justlahuaca for less than ten months.[53] The viceroy named most officials in a one-to-two-year rhythm in many poorer *alcaldías mayores*, which the crown could not sell. His *criados* often obtained longer tenure. In the period from 1703 to 1710, Alburquerque named five officials to the *alcaldía mayor* of Tacuba, who each stayed for one and a half to two years. The duke first appointed his *criado* José de la Cerda Morán, who served the office from 15 February 1703 for two and a half years. The next official stayed from about August 1705 to about mid-1707. In this year two appointees paid the *media anata* tax for the same position, indicating either that one of the officials did not assume his post at all, that he held the position for a brief period, or that he began serving the post at a considerably later time similar to a *futura* issued in Spain. The next official came in 1709. The last *alcalde mayor* appointed by the duke took office in June 1710, just before Alburquerque handed over power. Similar patterns can be observed for several poorer districts, among them Aguatlan and Teopantlan, Chiautla de la Sal, and Coatepec.

In total, the Duke of Alburquerque made approximately 281 appointments in *alcaldías mayores*, *corregimientos*, and *gobiernos*. The viceroy assigned forty-three posts of value 1 districts, and fifty-eight of value 2. The duke named sixty-four officials in districts of the category 3, and twenty-two in those of value 4. For the lower numbers, there were fifteen appointments in districts of value 5, eight in those of value 6, none in value 7, and six in 8. Finally, Alburquerque provided thirteen appointments in those provinces described as *ínfima* (lowest profitability) and fifty-two to officialdoms to which the *Yndize comprehensibo* did not assign a value. Most likely, the crown could not sell these *alcaldías mayores* because of their low profit. Peter Gerhard describes at least two of these jurisdictions, Coatepec and Atlatlauca de Oaxaca, as poor.[54]

The ratio of the top two groups of districts (value 1 and 2) to those of value *ínfima* and those that did not receive a value is 101 to 65. The relation between the top two districts and the bottom two on the index (8 and *ínfima*) is an astounding 101 to 19. The ratio of the upper five values to the lowest five, including those without an assigned value, is almost two and a half to one (200 to 81). These numbers show that, despite crown intentions to the contrary, Alburquerque appointed most of his men in the wealthiest districts.

During Alburquerque's eight years of tenure, both he and the monarch assigned officials to 126 districts and to four northern-frontier *gobiernos*, such as New León (*Nuevo Reino de León*). The incoming viceroy found many provinces filled, so he could effectively begin appointing only after these positions vacated. The number of all possible appointments during this time was 520, assuming that the viceroy chose officials for these posts every two years. The duke appointed 281 officials. Therefore, he filled more than half of all vacant districts. This calculation is admittedly problematic, because the king appointed officials for five-year periods, that is, three years longer than the viceroy did. Additionally, the divergent sources provide information that makes comparison difficult. Regardless, this approach shows a clear tendency and illustrates the considerable appointment powers of the Mexican viceroy.[55]

Thus, the viceroy was able to appoint his clients and *criados* mostly in the wealthier districts. Overall, he provided almost half of all possible appointments in the *gobierno* of New Spain. The officeholder retained vast patronage powers despite earlier royal measures to curb this. By appointing scores of *alcaldes mayores* and *corregidores*, the viceroy secured his hold over the colony. In the first decade of the eighteenth century, the crown made no effort to restrain the power of the viceroy in this regard.

The Duke of Alburquerque furnished at least twenty-six of his *criados* with positions in the colony, predominantly *alcaldías mayores*. Most of his *criados* received two districts, some of them only one, one of them even three (see Table 2). The duke also appointed his *criados* of lower rank, that is, the chamber aides (*ayudas de cámara*) to *alcaldías mayores*. Under the law Alburquerque could have up to twelve *criados* serve as district officials at the same time. According to the sources the duke did not break the rules in this regard.

Wardrobe attendant Juan Flores Fernández was nominated *alcalde mayor* of Amula in July 1703, valued 2, but located at a considerable distance from Mexico City close to the border to New Galicia. A merchant and viceregal ally acted as his *fiador*. In 1704 another chamber aide received the district of Izatlan, which was so poor that the crown could not sell it. Among the *criados mayores*, Bernardo de la Cantera, one of the viceroy's gentlemen-in-waiting received three *alcaldías mayores* from Alburquerque. Cantera became official of the valuable district Teozacualco y Tesocuilco on 13 August 1704, a position he held until 16 December 1706. Less than ten months later, around 6 October 1707, Alburquerque appointed him to the rather unprofitable post of Guajolotitlan, which Cantera kept for about two years. Possibly, the *alcaldía mayor* in a remote district in the Sierra Madre del Sur in present-day eastern Guerrero was only meant as a sinecure. In 1710 finally Cantera received the wealthy *alcaldía mayor* of Miaguatlan.[56] The Steward (*mayordomo*) José Alvarez del Valle served in an even more decorated position, supervising all proceedings at court. In 1702 the knight of the order of Santiago became captain of the palace guard. In November 1706 Alburquerque appointed Alvarez del Valle as interim district official of Tlalpa, although the majordomo probably never assumed that post, because he died soon after. Alburquerque provided *alcaldías mayores* for his *criados* and often allotted the best districts to his *criados mayores* and pages.

Three Appointments to Alcaldías Mayores			
1.	Bernardo de la Cantera		Guajolotitlan
			Miaguatlan
			Teozacualco
Two Appointments to Alcaldías Mayores			
1.	Pedro de Alcántara Laris	Villa de los Valles	Chicantepeque Guayacocotla
2.	Leandro de Buendía	Zempoala, 28 August 1707	San Juan Teotihuacan, 12 March 1709
3.	Francisco Díez de Ulzurrun	Cuautitlan, 7 November 1709	Teutila
4.	Diego Mtz. de Molina	Tula, 19 August 1709	Cuernavaca, 8 August 1709
5.	Miguel de Munarris	Tehuantepec, 28 September 1705–1 November 1707	Celaya with Salvatierra, 18 December 1708
6.	Blasco Ruiz de Herrera	Guajotzingo, 4 September 1709	Macuilsuchil with Mitla y Tlacolula
7.	Antonio Santos Pérez	Papantla, 22 January 1706	Guaxyapa, 23 May 1710
One Appointment to Alcaldías Mayores			
1.	Andrés Alvarez de Maldonado	Tula, 12 June 1705	
2.	José Alvarez del Valle	Tlalpa, 13 November 1706	
3.	Jerónimo Alvarez del Valle	Tabasco, 23 January 1703	
4.	José Cazetas (chamber aide)	Atitalaquia, 5 June 1704	
5.	José Félix de Escolar	Xicayan, 20 December 1702	
6.	Juan Flores Fndz. (chamber aide)	Amula	
7.	Pedro Manzano	Guajalotitlan, 5 September 1709	

8.	Diego Peramato	Tlaxcala, 2 March 1707
9.	Francisco Peramato	Zempoala, 2 January 1710
10.	Francisco Sáenz Daza	Malinalco, 14 May 1707
11.	José Velasco (chamber aide)	Izatlan, July 1704
12.	Manuel Vellosillo Hienostrosa	Cuatro Villas del Marquesado de Oaxaca, 18 December 1708
13.	Francisco Javier de la Mata	San Luis de la Paz, 14 July 1710

APPOINTMENTS FOR CLIENTS WHERE STATUS AS *CRIADO* CANNOT BE PROVEN

1.	Martin Alarcón	3 appointments to AM
2.	José Alarcón	1 AM, tie to Martin Alarcón
3.	Isidro Félix Luna	alférez, loyal role in conspiracy
4.	Pedro Mier Caso Estrada	2 appointments to AM
5.	Andrés de la Mora	3 appointments to AM
6.	José Munarris	brother of M. Munarris
7.	Diego Palacios	3 appointments to AM
8.	Andres de la Serna	3 appointments to AM

Table 2: Appointments of criados *to alcaldías mayores*

The viceroy overwhelmingly nominated officials within the *gobierno* of New Spain. In the early eighteenth century, the crown usually appointed the governors of the northern frontier, such as in the *gobierno* of New León.[57] The viceroys, however, appointed the governors of New Mexico and could on occasion place an interim official in other frontier provinces. Alburquerque named one governor of New Mexico as well as two interim officials in Coahuila and in New León.[58]

Many officials, especially the *alcaldes mayores* and *corregidores*, never actually served their office or dwelt in their districts. Officials put a lieutenant in charge of administrative and commercial duties. The position became a sinecure, profitable for the incumbent but with few official responsibilities. When postmaster Diego de Iglesias carried the announcement of Alburquerque's *residencia* in 1710 from Toluca towards Guadalajara (the northwest districts of the *gobierno* of New Spain), at least every third *alcalde mayor* of the thirty in that region was not present, while his lieutenant confirmed the receipt of the correspondence.[59] On the other hand, along the routes that the four postmasters took to distribute the communication in the viceroyalty, at least nine *criados* of Alburquerque confirmed the receipt. Doubtless, the signature could have been forged, especially since many minions were probably illiterate, but some of the *criados* may in fact have lived in the districts. At least according to the sources, the treasurer of the duke's household, one gentleman-in-waiting, four pages, and several officials resided in their *alcaldías mayores*.[60] These *criados* did not wait on the viceroy in Mexico City, and Alburquerque's entire entourage of higher *criados* never convened in totality at the court. Of all *criados* mayores only the duke's secretary, Juan de Estacasolo y Otalora, and the chamberlain and captain of the halberdiers' guard, Domingo Valles, never received an *alcaldía mayor* and remained in the presence of the viceroy at all times.

Apart from appointments of *alcaldes mayores* and governors, the viceroy also designated officials in the royal exchequer. The crown reserved the right to name employees for lifespan (*en propriedad*) in this important administrative branch. As with *audiencia* posts, Philip V increased the sale of treasury offices in the first decade of the eighteenth century under pressure of war.[61] Nevertheless, Alburquerque designated ten interim financial officials. Five of them laboured as accountants in the tribunal of accounts and one each as treasurer in Guanajuato, Pachuca, and the Yucatan. The viceroy also appointed one royal official in the treasury of Veracruz and one *alcalde* (a police official) in the Mexico City mint.

The viceroy regularly recommended his interim appointees to the crown to confirm them. The king did not approve of the suggestion in many cases, because he had already sold the position. Of Alburquerque's ten interim appointees in the *real hacienda* (royal treasury), only two received the coveted confirmation under the viceroy's watch. These officials acquired tenure and could usually bequeath the post for a fee. The crown turned down three of Alburquerque's designees. Yet these viceregal clients did not necessarily leave the financial administration. In 1705 Alburquerque named his *criado* Estéban Rodríguez de Santa Cruz as accountant (*contador de resultas*) on the tribunal of accounts. The crown denied possession in 1706, but Rodríguez de Santa Cruz stuck around, probably with the help of his brother, the bishop of Puebla. In 1738 Rodríguez de Santa Cruz snared the position of an honorary accountant at the tribunal, and in 1754 he retired from that tribunal as a regular accountant (*contador ordenador*) who had received possession of the office.[62]

Another interim accountant of the tribunal of accounts, Isidro Ruano de Arista, also laboured without royal confirmation, because others had already acquired a title to his position. Soon after, however, Ruano de Arista continued as a lieutenant of the accountant of Indian tribute, waiting for an opportunity to advance in the financial administration.[63]

	Appointee	Position, all interim	Year	Trajectory	Relation to Viceroy	Source
1	José de Chave	Tesorero, Yucatán treasury	1703	Possession denied, 23 May 1709		AGI, México 475.
2	Estéban Rodríguez de Santa Cruz	Contador de resultas, tribunal of accounts	1705	Possession denied 1708; honorary contador 1738; retired as contador ordenador 1754	Criado and testamentary agent (testamentario) of Alburquerque; brother of bishop of Puebla	AGI, México 474, 516; royal title, 18 November 1738, AGS, Hacienda 180-136.
3	Francisco Medrano	Contador, tribunal of accounts	1705	?		AGN, AHH 931.
4	Fernando de Ortega y Patiño	Contador de rentas, tribunal of accounts	1706	Possession on 8 November 1709	Criado and testamentario	AGI, México 480; rel. de méritos, AGI, Indiferente 142, N 10; AGN, AHH 931.
5	Joaquín de Morales	Tesorero, Guanajuato treasury	1706	?		AGI, México 479.
6	Luis Ibáñez de Ocerin	Contador de resultas, tribunal of accounts	1706	?		AGI, México 479.
7	José Tiburcio Boet y Villalón	Tesorero, Pachuca treasury	1706	Possession in 1708, still sitting in 1747	Page of Alburquerque	AGI, México, 479; relación de méritos, AGI, Indiferente 152, N 7.
8	Pedro Carrasco de Aguilar	Royal Oficial, Veracruz	1706	1711 guilty of fraud		AGI, México 377, 479.
9	Lic. Clemente Buqueiro	Alcalde (police official) of the mint	1708		Legal advisor (asesor)	AGN, MA 50; AGI, México 657
10	Isidro Ruano de Arista	Contador ordenador, tribunal of accounts, despite futuras for this post	1709	1709 interim tribute accountant; 1711 lieutenant of the tribute accountant		AGI México 377, 482; AGN, MA 27.

Table 3: Appointments in the real hacienda[64]

Some of the *real hacienda* appointees came from a Creole background and became the viceroy's clients. For example, Joaquín de Morales, appointed to the treasury in Guanajuato in 1706, originated from that city, where a relative worked as a silversmith around 1665.[65] Patronage opened the door to the posts in the *real hacienda* for Creoles for whom purchasing the office in Madrid would have proved more difficult than for peninsular Spaniards.

These offices in the royal exchequer along with the *corregimientos* in the ports offered the best prospects for a viceregal client. They allowed for social advancement by aligning with the local elites in exchange for illicit services. Confidants among the royal officials in Veracruz also helped any viceroy involved in contraband trade.[66] For this reason, the viceroy named three of his *criados* of higher station to the positions in the royal exchequer, as was the case with the treasurer of Pachuca and two accountants on the tribunal of accounts. Historian Michel Bertrand demonstrates that Alburquerque's successor, the Marquis of Valero (1716–1722) skilfully exploited changes in appointment procedures in the *real hacienda* by designating twenty-five interim officials, four of whom were his retainers.[67] Although he had left the helm only six years earlier, Alburquerque could not nearly match Valero's exploits.

Apart from these important positions in the bureaucracy, the viceroy appointed a number of persons to posts such as interim notary of government (*escribano mayor de gobernación y guerra*) and interim *relator* (an official who summarized trial documents for the *audiencia*). Alburquerque also named an overseer of the hospital of the Indians (*administrador mayordomo* of the *hospital de los Indios*) and filled the attractive post as general administrator of the marquisate of the Valley of Oaxaca with his collaborator in contraband commerce, Jerónimo Monterde.

When the duke left Mexico for Spain in 1713, he took back with him the majority of his one hundred *criados* and family members.[68] Alburquerque's *criados* who obtained profitable and enduring positions or built social connections stayed in the realm. Those who did not expected to benefit further from the duke's patronage upon return to the peninsula. The three *criados* named to treasury posts remained in Mexico. Even a number of *criados* who did not obtain long-term posts stayed on. The most striking case is the duke's secretary, Juan de Estacasolo y Otalora. Although tied to the (by then ex-) secretary of the *despacho universal*, this *criado* remained in New Spain. In 1719 he died wealthy in Mexico City, his son having married into a local family.[69] One of the duke's pages replaced Estacasolo as Alburquerque's secretary. This minion helped in channelling funds from Mexico to Spain and paying the huge indemnity to the king.[70]

The duke's treasurer Miguel Munarris settled in Cadereyta, where he engaged with his brother in *repartimiento* commerce. They used their connections with Alburquerque's clients and *criados*, such as one of the duke's ex-gentlemen-in-waiting. Ironically, among Munarris's debtors also appears the duke's political adversary, the bishop of Oaxaca.[71] Out of the thirty-seven *criados*, seven remained in Mexico after the duke's departure and two had died before (see Table 4). The duke described five of the seven retainers remaining in New Spain as his *criados mayores* or pages. The two other *criados* must also have belonged to a higher social station. Estéban Rodriguez Santa Cruz was the brother of the bishop of Puebla, and José Munarris was the brother of Miguel Munarris, *criado mayor* and treasurer of the duke. Therefore, the sources reveal that minions of the upper echelon successfully built ties to local society and obtained occupational positions that made the stay in New Spain promising.

Name	Station	Residence after the duke's departure	Sources
Juan de Estacasolo y Otalora	*criado* mayor, secretary of the duke, order of Santiago	Mexico City	AGI, Escribanía 234 A, f. 33; AGN, Bienes Nacionales 813, exp. 5.
Miguel Munárriz	*criado* mayor, treasurer of Alburquerque	Cadereyta	AGI, Contratación, 5469, N 1, R 36, 1, f. 11-15r
José Munarris	not specified, brother of Miguel Munarris	Cadereyta	ditto
Blasco Ruiz de Herrera	*criado* mayor, gentleman-in-waiting, order of Calatrava	Mexico City	ditto
José Tiburcio Boets y Villalón	page	Pachuca	AGI, Indiferente 152, N 7; AGI, México, 479.
Fernando de Ortega Patiño	criado	Mexico City	AGI, México 480; AGI, Indiferente 142, N 10.
Estéban Rodriguez Santa Cruz	page	Mexico City	AGI, México 474, 516; AGS, Hacienda 180-136.

Table 4: Criados remaining in New Spain

To sum up, when Alburquerque travelled from Spain to Mexico to assume his viceroyship, a retinue of about one hundred *criados* accompanied him officially. Others joined him clandestinely in America. The viceroy's power of patronage was limited compared to early-seventeenth-century predecessors. Regardless, the duke appointed about 281 *alcaldes mayores, corregidores,* and governors. He assigned forty-three officials to districts of value 1, fifty-eight of value 2, sixty-four officials of 3, and twenty-two of 4. The viceroy provided fifteen officialdoms of value 5, eight of value 6, none in 7, six in 8, thirteen in value *ínfima*, and fifty-two to poor jurisdictions without an assigned value. The relation of the two top groups of districts (value 1 and 2) with the lowest categories (value *ínfima* and no value given) is one hundred and one versus sixty-five. The ratio of the districts of the upper five values to the lower five is almost two and a half to one (two hundred against eighty-one). The duke also appointed 281 officials of about 520 vacancies in the *gobierno*, thus filling more than half of all vacant districts posts. Therefore, despite earlier royal attempts to limit viceregal patronage, Alburquerque appointed most officials to the wealthier districts of New Spain. Eleven of the designations to the richest districts (value 1) went to his *criados*. Alburquerque provided almost all of his creatures at some point with an *alcaldía mayor,* although many of his appointees never served in their districts. Instead, many, maybe a third, held their posts as sinecures, while a lieutenant took care of the administrative duties. Officially, the duke named most of these interim functionaries for a one-year period. Yet tenure of office ranged in reality from less than one year to three, with most officials remaining in office for about two.

Additionally, the duke named nine clients and *criados* to posts in the treasury, and fifteen obtained positions in the military. The duke chose six clergymen for consecration to coveted positions diverging from the proposal list submitted by the secular Church. In 1713 at the end of his term, the majority of Alburquerque's *criados* joined him on the voyage back. At least seven *criados* of higher social station stayed on. This data suggests that the viceroy in this period retained vast patronage privileges and used them to secure his hold over the colony. The first Bourbon king made no effort to restrain his power in this regard.

5

THE CLASH OVER CONTRABAND COMMERCE AND THE *CONSULADO*

The crown defended the principle of exclusive Spanish trade with the colonies in the early eighteenth century. The mercantilist vision held that foreign countries should not have commercial access to the colonial markets. New Spain should produce unprocessed materials for sale exclusively to the Iberian Peninsula and buy manufactured goods only from Spain to guarantee wealth for the metropolis. Madrid issued a series of *reales cédulas* (a royal communication demanding some action) stipulating that only the Spanish fleet and, within strict limits, the annual galleon shuttling between Manila and Acapulco (the *nao*), could trade with Mexico.[1] Frequently, the historiographical literature qualifies the trade of the official fleet with America as a monopoly. Although the law prohibited competition outside of the fleet merchants, the traders did compete against each other to a degree. More than a monopoly, this structure resembles an oligopoly. An institution in Seville (Spain) called the *consulado* represented the interests of the oligopolist merchants. This body had pressured the crown successfully to outlaw any naval trade among New Spain and the other Spanish American colonies. Yet over time these rules fell by the wayside. The fleet could not meet the demand of the Mexican market, and locals sought to avoid the elevated prices of the oligopoly. Foreign and colonial merchants stepped in. Britain, France, and the Netherlands, above all, supplied the colonies from their bases in the Caribbean, frequently anchoring clandestinely in the smaller, less supervised Mexican ports.

Other Spanish colonies, such as Peru and the Philippines, also traded with New Spain. The law mandated that the galleon travelling between Manila and Acapulco could not exceed 400 Spanish tons (one *tonelada* equals about 979 kg.) and the value of goods not surpass 250,000 pesos on its way to New Spain.[2] Traders consistently exceeded these limits, especially after commerce in the Pacific began to expand in the 1680s.[3] Manila developed into a hub of commerce between Spain and the Asian countries. Ships from China, Japan, India, and other Asian realms sailed into the Philippine port to sell their goods. The American importers found prices in Asia attractive, because silver had a higher purchasing power than in inflation-ridden Europe. Mexican merchants imported a range of products, usually luxury goods such as porcelains, musk, tapestries, spices, and ivory. Silk from China was especially popular. The trade among the Spanish American colonies also picked up. Some merchants simply re-exported Asian goods from Acapulco to Callao, Peru. Mexican manufacturers produced textiles, clothing, jewellery, leather, and books for the Peruvian market. The South Americans contributed silver, quicksilver, wine, and cacao to the exchange.[4]

In theory, the Spanish fleet sailed from Seville once a year, but over the course of the seventeenth century the intervals became longer, with the convoy arriving in Veracruz only every other year. The beginning of the War of the Succession in 1700 hampered transatlantic travel further, and no important convoy reached Mexico between 1700 and 1706.[5] In the initial years of his reign, Philip V permitted French warships to enter Mexican ports and sell limited amounts of merchandise. Mexicans interpreted these orders loosely and traded wholesale with French merchants.[6]

The crown officials were in no position to curb the vibrant illegal trade. Almost all collaborated and accepted bribes for their acquiescence. By the end of the seventeenth century, the Spanish trade had fallen into such a state of disrepair that only 5 per cent of the fleet cargo was of Spanish origin. Although it had once been heavily supplied by Spanish products, New Spain became economically almost independent from the mother country.[7] These circumstances enabled the merchants based in Mexico to gain leverage over the *flotistas*, the fleet merchants. In the entire seventeenth century no trade fair was held. The fleet merchants had to bring their goods immediately up to Mexico City, where the local traders waited with their purchases until just before the fleet set sail, forcing the oligopoly merchants to lower prices. The Mexico City merchants controlled access to the silver coming in from the great northern mines. The contraband commerce undercut fleet merchants' attempts to obtain higher prices for their goods. The struggle between the two groups intensified in the early eighteenth century, reverberating in the Mexican *consulado*. The representatives of the Seville oligopoly in Mexico clung to their privileges guaranteed by crown policy, although their power was on the wane.[8]

When Alburquerque arrived in New Spain, the commercial community was divided about the role of the official Spanish trade and contraband trade. This conflict also extended to trade with other Spanish colonies such as Peru. At this time, the social network around the wealthy merchant and silver banker Luis Sánchez de Tagle wielded considerable influence in the realm. Sánchez de Tagle, like most businessmen of the early modern period, did not specialize in one occupation. Rather, he engaged in an array of commercial activities. As an *aviador*, he provided credit to the great silver mines in the north and bought their silver. Coining his and the crown's silver in the mint of Mexico City proved to be very lucrative. Sánchez de Tagle also operated one of the leading import businesses in the colony. His success rested on widespread connections. A branch of the family held important positions in Manila – one of the commercial hubs in the Spanish empire. A cousin of Don Luis married the sister of a Mexican aristocrat, and their son became a *regidor* (a town councillor) in the municipal council of the great silver mining centre Zacatecas. The family diversified its fortune by investing much in sizeable haciendas in the north.

The family was able to lend more than 850,000 silver pesos to the crown over the period from 1683 to 1698. Between 1700 and 1703 Luis Sánchez de Tagle loaned another 500,000 pesos *de oro común* (worth about 1.5 silver pesos) to the new dynasty. Philip V granted him the title of Marquis of Altamira in 1704, reflecting Sánchez de Tagle's good standing with the new dynasty.[9]

Furthermore, Luis Sánchez de Tagle represented the *consulado* of Seville together with Miguel de Ubilla y Estrada, Marquis of Santa

Sabina. The Marquis of Santa Sabina held a position as accountant on the tribunal of accounts, and he could also rely on his tie to the secretary of the *despacho universal* (a secretary that belonged to the inner circle of power) at the Spanish Court, Antonio de Ubilla. The great merchant Lucas de Careaga Sanz de Urrutia, Marquis of Santa Fe, joined these two as agents (*apoderados*) of the *consulado*. Together, this triumvirate defended the interests of the Spanish fleet merchants with the authorities in New Spain.[10] For example, in 1703, the *consulado* of Seville asked the three representatives to press for reimbursement of credits that the *consulado* had previously advanced to the crown.[11] Additionally, these representatives, along with other merchants, influenced the Mexican *consulado*. This body had a tradition of defending oligopoly interests, at least officially, while a significant portion of Mexican merchants had by this time become active in contraband commerce. The economic interests of the triumvirate were not in complete accord with those of the oligopoly. Although the group around Sánchez de Tagle participated in the official trade, it also operated clandestine trade with other colonies. In 1712, for example, the *fiscal* of the Mexican *audiencia* confiscated 50,000 pesos belonging to Pedro Sánchez de Tagle, Luis Sánchez de Tagle's nephew and son-in-law. Don Pedro had shipped silver to the Philippines in excess of legal restrictions. Luis Sánchez de Tagle, with the approval of viceroy Duke of Linares, had directed the castellan of Acapulco to permit the embarkation of the illegal funds.[12]

The involvement of the Sánchez de Tagle family in the Philippine trade had a long tradition. In the last decade of the seventeenth century, the network built ties to Fausto Cruzat, who had served as governor of the islands since about 1688. They jointly traded through the Manila galleon. Fausto Cruzat had paid 50,000 *reales* by way of *beneficio de empleo* (a donation to the crown in exchange for an appointment) to obtain his position in Manila.[13] Like most officeholders in similar circumstances, he needed to recoup his investment and plan for the future. Cruzat collaborated in illegal commerce, probably by taking bribes to circumvent the strict rules of the galleon, and even sold an unuseable ship to the crown. Luis Sánchez de Tagle's nephew Domingo Ruiz de Tagle served in the military company commanded by Fausto Cruzat. The partnership with the Sánchez de Tagle family culminated in the betrothal of the governor's daughter, Ignacia Cruzat, to Domingo Ruiz de Tagle.[14]

The competitors of Sánchez de Tagle's network forged an alliance with the newly arrived Viceroy Alburquerque. These merchants also operated contraband and vociferously rejected the oligopoly trade. Alburquerque accepted the predominant conditions of commerce in New Spain like most viceroys before him. The viceroy received bribes for his acquiescence to contraband trade and even mounted his own business scheme to market illegal merchandise. His choice of factions and his activities led to confrontation with the Sánchez de Tagle network. In 1703 the duke accused Domingo Ruiz de Tagle, Luis Sánchez de Tagle's nephew, of breaching the trade restrictions of the Manila galleon. As general of the *nao*, Don Domingo had shuttled funds between Acapulco and the Philippines without registering. On 6 February 1703 Alburquerque imprisoned the Tagle scion for this violation.[15]

The showdown between Alburquerque and the Sánchez de Tagle family continued when the duke and several of his allies tried to derail the marriage of Domingo Ruiz de Tagle to Ignacia Cruzat. Returning from the Philippines on 26 November 1702, Governor Fausto Cruzat died, and his alliance with the Sánchez de Tagle fell apart.[16] Cruzat's sons objected to the planned wedding. They sensed a chance to link up with the socio-economic network tied to the new viceroy. The newly appointed *Oidor* José Joaquín de Uribe proposed marriage to Ignacia Cruzat. Also known as "La China" because of her upbringing in the Asian Philippines, Doña Ignacia was to bring a significant dowry into marriage. Alburquerque backed the judge, one of his favourites on the high court. The viceroy and the judge had met sharing the same ship on their voyage to New Spain.[17]

The sons of Fausto Cruzat settled in San Cosme just outside of Mexico City and kept their sister in seclusion. Domingo Ruiz de Tagle could not visit her, while *Oidor* Uribe continued to woo her. On 13 May 1703 Ruiz de Tagle complained to Juan de Ortega y Montañés, archbishop of Mexico, about this change of fortune. The cleric took up the issue. With an *alcalde del crimen*, the archdiocesan *provisor* (a clerical judge), a notary, and some minions, Ortega y Montañés travelled to San Cosme. The archbishop interviewed Ignacia Cruzat in presence of the functionaries. She expressed her desire to be removed from her brothers' abode in order to contract marriage with Domingo Ruiz de Tagle in liberty. The archbishop escorted Doña Ignacia out of the residence despite the angry protest of her brothers, and placed her in the convent of San Lorenzo.[18]

The intervention of the archbishop did not result exclusively from principles of clemency. The archbishop firmly belonged to Luis Sánchez de Tagle's network of allies.[19] Since the viceroy opted for their enemies and manipulated the *audiencia*, the Tagles appealed to the apex of the ecclesiastical hierarchy. Ortega y Montañés could look back on a stellar career in the New World. The cleric had arrived in New Spain in 1660 as *fiscal* (prosecutor) of the Inquisition and rose through the bishoprics of Guatemala and Valladolid (today Morelia) to the archbishopric in 1700. Twice interim viceroy of Mexico, in 1696 and in 1701–1702,[20] Ortega y Montañés had built connections with the *cabildo civil* (town hall) and the *audiencia*.[21] He bolstered his power by placing members of his episcopal *familia* in the palace guard and in the district administration.[22]

Traditionally, archbishops and viceroys viewed each other with some suspicion and jealously guarded their prerogatives. In 1704 Ortega y Montañés felt snubbed when Alburquerque failed to honour the archbishop with the etiquette owed to a former interim viceroy.[23] A year earlier Alburquerque had told Ortega y Montañés of the crown's decision to deny him the dignity of a former viceroy.[24] Over the course of the Tagle-Cruzat conflict, the archbishop and the duke developed a mutual antipathy that persisted until Ortega y Montañés's death on 16 December 1708.[25]

The Cruzat brothers retorted to the intervention of Ortega y Montañés by challenging the impending marriage in an ecclesiastical court. The Cruzat brothers presented at the trial a letter from a Guadalajaran woman who claimed that Domingo Ruiz de Tagle had seduced her more than fourteen years earlier in that city, fathering two children with her. According to her tale, Ruiz de Tagle had taken her virginity and promised to wed her.[26] Domingo Ruiz de Tagle admitted in court his liaison with the woman whom he supported even after his return from the Philippines with a payment of 2,300 pesos as a token of respect. Yet he denied any promise to marry her. Ruiz de Tagle also acknowledged an affair with another woman with whom he also had a child and whom he furnished with 3,000 pesos.[27]

The allegations of Ruiz de Tagle's affairs did not convince the ecclesiastical court that the bridegroom had vowed to marry anyone but Ignacia Cruzat. The court, composed of Archbishop Ortega y Montañés and his *provisor*, instead blamed the Cruzat brothers for manipulating the Guadalajaran and hiding her from archiepiscopal authority. Since she refused to appear in court, the archbishop asked the *audiencia* for help (*real auxilio*) to enforce her obligation to the Church. The *audiencia*, under the influence of Alburquerque, declared the request invalid for not meeting formal requirements. The high court also turned down the archbishop's angry appeal from 25 May. Five *oidores* signed this decision, indicating that Alburquerque could rely on the majority of the bench in this issue.[28]

The viceroy had issued a decree before the trial ordering Luis and Pedro Sánchez de Tagle, under punishment of 10,000 pesos, not to influence the proceedings of the ecclesiastical court against Ruiz de Tagle. The duke also opined that Ruiz de Tagle had to fulfill his pledge to marry the Guadalajaran lady.[29] The undeterred archbishop concluded from the circumstances that the charges against Ruiz de Tagle were malicious fabrications. Hence, no impediments existed against the marriage to Doña Ignacia.[30]

The Tagle family failed to win over Alburquerque despite putting out peace feelers. Don Domingo passed a note to the viceroy's *mayordomo* (steward) promising Alburquerque 6,000 pesos if he supported him in his bid to marry Ignacia Cruzat. The viceroy refused and publicly displayed great indignation over this attempt to bribe him.[31] Only the daughter of Luis Sánchez de Tagle maintained good relations with Alburquerque's wife.[32] This connection contributed to the duchess's disagreement with Alburquerque's actions during the ensuing conflict.[33]

Ruiz de Tagle continued the preparation for the nuptials on 14 June. The archbishop declared that he was willing to perform the ceremony. Don Domingo called together his family and minions to the convent of San Lorenzo where the bride resided. The Tagles also assembled armed guards of the *consulado* "to embarrass any movement the Cruzats may intend."[34] As prior of the *consulado* of Mexico, Pedro Sánchez de Tagle safeguarded the wedding with a show of force that only the viceregal palace guard could challenge with a notable escalation of violence. The Tagle camp later denied any such preparations. One of their dependents claimed that he and some friends just happened to linger in the vicinity of the San Lorenzo convent, "drinking chocolate," when suddenly and to their great surprise Pedro Sánchez de Tagle and the archbishop appeared in their carriages.[35] According to this client, he and his friends did not carry arms. The Cruzat brothers and their followers appeared at the convent shortly after and attacked them. The Tagle followers fought back, preventing their opponents from disturbing the wedding.[36]

That evening, Alburquerque called in the *real acuerdo*, the joint conference of viceroy and *audiencia*. Weighing the charges, the officials could not agree on how to proceed. Most magistrates were inclined to sidestep the whole issue and call for further investigations of the turmoil. Only a minority supported immediate sanctions against the Tagles. Alburquerque ignored the majority vote of the *real acuerdo* – an advisory vote – and declared the Tagles in breach of his decree not to obstruct the trial against Domingo Ruiz de Tagle in the ecclesiastical court. He ordered the criminal prosecutors to arrest Pedro and Luis Sánchez de Tagle, fine them each 10,000 pesos, confiscate all their property, and exile them from Mexico City. Luis Sánchez de Tagle was deported to the grim prison of the fortress San Juan de Ulua in Veracruz. Don Pedro shared his lot in the fortress of Acapulco. Alburquerque also relieved Don Pedro from his post as prior (chief official of the *consulado*) and cancelled Don Luis' profitable privileges at the silver mint. The viceroy punished Domingo Ruiz de Tagle with a penalty of 20,000 pesos, had him interrogated in the *cabildo civil*, and in October shipped off to Veracruz as well.[37] Apart from the damage to their health and reputations, the prison term also seriously disrupted the Tagles' commercial activities.

The future of the Tagles after the wedding seemed bleak. The bride languished in the convent "out of sorrow to see her husband imprisoned."[38] The following year, she came down with typhus and drafted her last will dated 15 August 1704. Soon after, she died in the convent. Doña Ignacia left most of her estate to her grandmother, and in case of her death to her brothers, yet she still bequeathed her husband 10,000 of her 50,000-peso fortune.[39] Nothing indicates that anyone conspired in her death, although much of the information about her untimely departure came from the Tagle group. Two Tagle clients also perished during incarceration in the harbour fortresses. In August Alburquerque ordered Pedro Sánchez de Tagle moved to the town of San Martín de Tixtla for interrogation.[40] On 22 October 1703 Alburquerque released Luis and Pedro Sánchez de Tagle from jail, and on 5 November Don Luis returned to Mexico City. Alburquerque's allies, the Cruzat brothers, came off lightly. The viceroy merely placed them under house arrest.[41]

News of Alburquerque's clash with one of the first families in New Spain reached Madrid. Archbishop Ortega y Montañés complained bitterly to the king about the viceroy and the *audiencia* in four letters dated 14–16 December 1703.[42] In 1704 a representative of the Tagles defended the family at the Spanish court. Luis Sánchez de Tagle also charged that Alburquerque and his two loyal *oidores* Tovar and Uribe had forged the records of the *real acuerdo* falsely to express unanimous support for the imprisonment of the Tagles.[43]

On 19 June 1704 the Council of the Indies discussed the issue in a *consulta* (a recommendation to the king), culminating in a resounding rebuke of Alburquerque and his party. The Council suggested in harsh language that Alburquerque should immediately release the Tagles and their dependents from prison, return their property including the heavy fines, and restore them to their offices. The Cruzat brothers had to pay 4,000 pesos to the Tagles for damages and another 2,000 to the royal treasury in Spain. The crown did, however, fine Domingo Ruiz de Tagle 1,000 pesos for trying to bribe the viceroy. In a *real cédula* to the *audiencia*, the king lambasted above all the conduct of the *fiscal de lo civil*, José Antonio Espinosa, and Judge Alonso Abellafuentes of the *audiencia* of Mexico, charging them 200 pesos each.[44] The *fiscal* of the Council recommended in his *parecer* (his assessment to the Council) that the viceroy should be excluded from any jurisdiction over the matter. The following *real cédula* stipulated that Alburquerque could only proceed in any matter regarding the Tagles with a majority vote (*voto decisivo*) of the *audiencia*. The viceroy should also immediately reimburse the loan of 110,000 pesos he had exacted from Don Luis.[45] The Tagles furthermore won an initial victory over the Cruzat family regarding the inheritance of Ignacia Cruzat. The king ordered the House of Trade in 1704 to confiscate several crates stored in Cadiz belonging to the Cruzats – an issue the parties were still feuding over in 1710.[46] The Cruzat family, however, pulled some strings at the court too. Their lobbying brought the penalty down to 3,000 pesos total, and in September 1704 the king ordered to discard the penalty entirely and reimburse the Cruzat brothers.[47]

The Purge in the Mexican Consulado

While the conflict about the marriage unfolded, the viceroy moved to knock his opponents out of their institutional strongholds. First, he wrested away the grip of the Sánchez de Tagle alliance on the Mexican *consulado*. Luis Sánchez de Tagle's son-in-law Pedro Sánchez de Tagle held the position of prior of the *consulado*, the head position of the corporation, continuously from 1700 to October 1703, when the viceroy imprisoned him. In 1701 the Sánchez de Tagle network had fended off a political attack, presumably from anti-oligopoly merchants, who intended to elect a new prior.[48] The consuls (senior officials below the prior) and Pedro Sánchez de Tagle asked the king at that time to issue a royal decree suspending further elections and maintaining Don Pedro in office until Madrid ordered otherwise.[49] In 1703, during the showdown with the viceroy, the two consuls, Lucas de Careaga and Captain Juan del Castillo, supported the Sánchez de Tagle network.[50] Shortly after Pedro Sánchez de Tagle's deportation to Acapulco, the consuls protested to the king against the "indecorous violence" perpetrated by the viceroy.[51] The consuls also reported that the viceroy began conspiring with the councilmen of the town hall to decree price ceilings on certain import goods from Spain – iron, paper, olive oil, cinnamon, and saffron. These products arrived typically in Mexico from or through the peninsula on the Spanish fleet. Prices ran high, because the convoy did not reach Mexico between 1700 and 1706 and war disturbed commerce. On 7 May 1703 the town hall asked the king to permit the city to use its jurisdiction freely in implementing price ceilings on these goods.[52] Almost two months later the city again bemoaned the tyranny of arbitrary prices leading to the ruin of the republic. The *cabildo* once more affirmed its jurisdiction over the matter within the city limits and asked the viceroy to curb excesses in the entire realm.⁵³

On the same day the viceroy ordered the *corregidor* of Mexico City to inquire secretly into the merchants who allegedly curbed the free sale of these goods and arbitrarily forced up prices. The *corregidor* obeyed and did not have to look for long. After conducting nineteen interviews among the commercial community, his *informe* (report) closely mirrored the complaints of the town hall. According to the crown official, several merchants sold products from Spain at exorbitant prices. With this finding, the city now asked for a lowering of the prices to about a third or a half of the current market rate.⁵⁴

On 9 July the viceroy followed suit. In a *bando* (a published proclamation) he decreed that prices of iron, paper, saffron, and cinnamon be lowered in Mexico City as well as in other important urban centres such as Puebla and Antequera. For example, merchants could not sell a ream of paper (500 sheets) for more than six pesos compared to the current market price of fourteen. A pound of cinnamon would go at six pesos instead of at twelve.⁵⁵ This proclamation snubbed those traders associated with the oligopoly trade who had remained in the colony after the departure of the fleet. Complaints came from other quarters as well. The small shop owners and peddlers (*tenderos* or *los que menudean en tiendas*) in Mexico City claimed that they had previously acquired products wholesale at the very price they could sell them for under the terms of the viceregal *bando*. These new prices would invariably lead to their ruin.⁵⁶ The viceroy ordered the *cabildo civil* to hold a session on 23 July to discuss the petition of the small shopkeepers. The city pondered the claim and weighed it against the alleged threat of unregulated prices. The corporation then suggested that the retailers should be able to vend with an adequate profit and recommended raising the price for paper and other goods.⁵⁷ Alburquerque again literally executed the demands of the city, decreeing that ceilings for retail prices be raised.⁵⁸

The Mexican *consulado*, in accordance with the view of the Seville *consulado*, opposed the decisions of town hall and viceroy and sharply criticized the price caps. In their letter to the king, the consuls warned that a loss of over 500,000 pesos threatened the merchants. Consuls Lucas de Careaga and Captain Juan del Castillo, both friends of Luis

Sánchez de Tagle, signed the letter.[59] According to later accusations Alburquerque also used the ceilings for his own shady business. The viceroy coerced the oligopoly merchants into selling their goods to his commercial agents at the mandated price. When market forces battled viceregal decrees, the former quickly gained the upper hand and supply dried up. Alburquerque revoked the ceilings again and his agents sold the merchandise at soaring prices.[60]

When Pedro Sánchez de Tagle lost his office as prior of the Mexican *consulado*, his network ceased to play a prominent role in the corporation for the rest of Alburquerque's term. As was customary, Pedro Sánchez de Tagle still acted as *consejero*, that is, counsel to the incumbent prior and consuls. He did not, however, hold a position as consul or prior again. Consequently, the anti-oligopoly group allied with the duke took over the *consulado*, completely reversing previous policies. In 1706 the Spanish fleet pulled into Veracruz after six years of absence. When sales commenced, the prior and consuls of that year complained about the tremendous mark-up the fleet merchants charged on the same merchandise that figured in the quarrel of 1703. The Mexican *consulado* now petitioned the viceroy to implement price ceilings, claiming that the fleet merchants gained a profit of up to 1,200 per cent on their products.[61] This time the viceroy did not follow the recommendation.

The crown took considerable time to respond to this issue. Both the Mexican *consulado* of 1703 and its Sevillian counterpart had sent strong démarches to the Council of the Indies attacking Alburquerque's behaviour. The *fiscal* of the Council pondered the affair on 11 November 1704 but did not pursue the issue further.[62] Almost five years later the Council returned to the subject and on 22 June 1709 drafted a *real cédula* justifying the attempts of the oligopoly merchants to negotiate high profits in the interest of trade and the empire. The king was by then more amenable to the demands of the Sevillian *consulado* and ordered the viceroy to disregard similar pleas for price fixing in future.[63]

In another quarrel in 1706, the viceroy collaborated once again with the prior and consuls against the fleet merchants. He ordered the sale of the fleet's merchandise in Veracruz instead of permitting their free sale in any city of the realm. The duke also mandated – citing military reasons – that the fleet extend its stay in the port. These measures won the acclaim of the *consulado* and its *diputados* for giving the local merchants more bargaining strength with the Spaniards.[64]

The *consulado* of 1706 also collaborated closely with the viceroy in the related squabble about illegal commerce with French warships carrying merchandise. The *consulado* rejected requests by the oligopoly traders for an investigation into the amount of the contraband commerce and the persons involved. In a statement dated 20 March 1706, the prior and consuls suggested that little damage had been done to crown or commerce. In their view, demand for textiles in Mexico had run so high that the influx of contraband goods did not adversely affect the official Spanish traders. Any of the small profits had gone to France, Spain's ally, who protected the sea routes from British and Dutch attacks. The *consulado* concluded that all inquiry into illegal trade would only further disturb the realm.[65] With this recommendation the corporation backed the commercial interests of most local merchants and veiled its and the viceroy's implication in the contraband trade.

The prior and the consuls of the *consulado* in 1706 all had established alliances with the viceroy. The prior, the Count of Miravalle, had gained his wealth through mining in the north of Mexico, investing heavily in haciendas, and participating in contraband operations.[66] Given his economic profile, he opposed the oligopoly's privileges. When he held the office of *alcalde ordinario* of Mexico City in 1703, the count supported the city's petition to the viceroy to decree price caps.[67]

The senior consul in 1706 opposed the Sánchez de Tagle family for other reasons. Nicolás López de Landa competed with Luis Sánchez de Tagle as one of the three silver bankers in the royal mint. The bankers bought silver from the mines and coined it in the mint, sharing access to the two existing furnaces to melt silver. In 1703 López de Landa won a skirmish when the viceroy cancelled Sánchez de Tagle's access to the mint during the merchant's deportation to Veracruz. The *real cédula* from 1704 ordered the viceroy to reinstate Don Luis at the mint, but the *audiencia* still prevented Sánchez de Tagle from minting the silver of the royal exchequer.[68] Alburquerque continued to manoeuvre against Sánchez de Tagle's privileges. The duke suggested repeated inspections of all silver bankers to enforce the minting laws. That gave the viceroy further leeway to harass Sánchez de Tagle in his office. With the viceroy's backing, López de Landa tried to edge out his two rivals in 1706 by suggesting to the crown increased gains of about 28,000 pesos by paying 13 *tomines* more to the exchequer per mark (*marco*) of royal silver struck. His suggestions would have included a strengthening of his standing in the mint.[69]

Nevertheless, Luis Sánchez de Tagle's family returned to full influence. In 1717, after the death of Don Luis, the crown rewarded Pedro Sánchez de Tagle with the exclusive operation of one of the furnaces for two years, leaving his two rivals to share the other. Following this defeat, López de Landa, as the weakest of the three silver minters, faced an uphill battle. In 1727 he quit, transferring his rights to the Fagoaga family.[70] López de Landa also participated in other political schemes of Alburquerque's network that persisted after the duke's departure. López de Landa vouched along with the viceroy's secretary and the legal advisor for an allied *oidor* in his *residencia* in 1715.[71]

In 1707 Alburquerque bestowed a habit of the order of Santiago on the son of Domingo de la Canal, junior consul in 1706. De la Canal maintained a good relationship with the viceroy and had extended a generous credit to the crown in 1706. The consul also vouched for Alburquerque in his *residencia*.[72]

Two long-term partners of the Cruzat family and allies of the viceroy were also chosen *diputados* (deputies) in the *consulado* election of 1706. These *diputados* travelled to Veracruz to negotiate price caps with fleet merchants. Both Juan de Garaicoechea and Julián de Osorio had been involved in illegal Pacific trade along with Governor Fausto Cruzat.[73] Don Fausto gave Garaicoechea, his brother-in-law, the command of the *nao* to oversee the legal and illegal Asian trade.[74] Julián de Osorio, consul from 1707 to 1708, acted in that period also as the viceroy's agent in illegal commercial activities. Alburquerque recommended Osorio to the crown for his generous donations.[75] Both of these merchants had supported the Cruzat sons in the wedding conflict.

Alburquerque's Alliance	The Sánchez de Tagle Network
Immediate Relatives	*Relatives of Luis Sánchez de Tagle*
Juana de la Cerda, Alburquerque's wife	Luisa Sánchez de Tagle, daughter
	Pedro Sánchez de Tagle, nephew
Audiencia of Mexico	and son-in-law
José Joaquín de Uribe Castejón	Domingo Ruiz de Tagle, nephew ∞
Baltasar Tovar and others	Ignacia Cruzat
	Several relatives in Zacatecas
Trade	*Trade*
Cruzat brothers	Several relatives in Manila
Julián de Osorio	Juan del Castillo
Juan de Garaicoechea	
Alonso de Dávalos Bracamonte, Count of Miravalle	
The Mint	Trustees of the Seville Consulado
Nicolás López de Landa	Lucas de Careaga, Marquis of Santa Fe
	Miguel de Ubilla y Estrada, Marquis of Santa Sabina
	Ecclesiastical Hierarchy
	Archbishop Ortega y Montañés

Table 5: The Alliances of Alburquerque and Luis Sánchez de Tagle in 1703

The commercial elite of New Spain in the early eighteenth century formed networks according to their economic and social interests. In this time two major networks around the viceroy and, on the other side, the Sánchez de Tagle family dominated the scene. Nonetheless, members of either network could maintain social ties that reached across this division of oligopoly and contraband trade. For example, the Count of Miravalle forged an alliance with the viceroy, yet he abstained from severing his accord with the Tagle family. According to rumours, the count even godfathered Domingo Ruiz de Tagle's illegitimate child.[76] This strategy proved appropriate, since the viceroy dispensed patronage for a limited time. When he left, the powerful Tagles would still be around to play their hand in politics – in fact, branches of the family exercised influence throughout the eighteenth century and well into independence.[77] A similar pattern can be observed with the Marquis of Santa Sabina, who, as the most active of the trustees of the Seville *consulado*, could be seen as a natural viceregal foe. Yet the marquis managed to avoid conflict with the viceroy, partly, because clientage linked him to Alburquerque. The marquis's father had come to Mexico as a page of Alburquerque's grandfather, former viceroy of the colony. At least until 1705, Santa Sabina very likely also enjoyed the support of the powerful secretary of the *despacho universal*.[78]

Social networks probably maintained much of this ambiguity even into later periods. Research on nineteenth-century Latin American politics, for example, challenges the dichotomous idea of rigid conflict lines between liberals and conservatives. Ties of clientelism and kinship often superseded the ideological orientation, so that alliances frequently breached party lines.[79] The social networks of the early eighteenth century certainly corresponded to this pattern, especially as the ideological framework was less clearly developed.

This ambiguity can also be observed for the allies of the Seville *consulado*. According to rumours Lucas de Careaga originally hit it off with Alburquerque, initially even acting as the duke's agent in contraband trade. Then the relationship deteriorated. A *real cédula* of 17 September 1707 gave the Duke of Alburquerque the opportunity to assault Careaga. The *cédula* ordered the viceroy to inquire into the whereabouts of over one million pesos in Mexico that belonged to the *consulado* of Seville. The duke accused Careaga of embezzlement and seized his property. Careaga asserted that he was responsible for only about 350,000 pesos of the missing funds and was willing to reimburse the *consulado*. Alburquerque nonetheless imprisoned him, sanctioned by a *real cédula* of 1708. Only towards the end of Alburquerque's term, the *real cédula* dated 31 August 1710 ordered Careaga's release from jail and the restitution of his property. Careaga, however, found himself a ruined man, since large parts of his wealth had disappeared during the confiscation.[80] It is possible that Careaga truly mishandled *consulado* funds, yet it is somewhat ironic that the duke could oust one of his local adversaries based on the very complaint of his major foe, the *consulado* of Seville.

In the conflict between the Sánchez de Tagle and the contraband commerce network, Alburquerque suffered a setback at the hands of the crown when he had to restore Sánchez de Tagle to his privileges. Nevertheless, the duke did not face any serious consequences. His strength resulted from his position as a viceroy, on his connections to the aristocratic party in Madrid, and on his alliances with the merchants and *oidores* in Mexico. Luis Sánchez de Tagle bitterly complained about Alburquerque's kinship ties and the use of his viceregal powers to keep the *oidores* in line: "The duke is powerful because of his relatives ... and there is no audiencia that may resist him, for everyone fears their own ruin and not without cause."[81]

The conflict between the two merchant groups reveals a shift in party formation and commercial interests within the *consulado*. According to the historiography, in the mid-seventeenth century the Mexican *consulado* overwhelmingly supported the oligopoly trade from which it drew substantial profits.[82] In the quarrel in the first decade of the eighteenth century, Alburquerque and the anti-oligopoly party succeeded in weakening the influence of the Seville *consulado* over its Mexican pendant. In 1712 a *junta de comercio* (the gathering of *consulado* merchants) pondered the case of a ship anchoring in Veracruz under dubious circumstances. The majority of the junta suggested disembarking its goods, while the minority suggested following the royal guidelines and prohibiting the sale of its goods. The majority carried the day. This case demonstrates that the pro-Sevillian group expressed its opinion in the second decade but lost out to the contraband traders.[83] By the mid-eighteenth century, however, the commercial interests had changed. At this time two parties labelled Basque and Montañés quarrelled over influence.[84] Formally, these groups were composed of people of common regional background in the Iberian Peninsula. The Montañeses came from the mountainous region between Santander and Burgos in northern Spain. The Basques have lived east on the border to France. By this time, the corporation broke apart along "ethnic" lines. Most of the members of the Mexican *consulado*, active in contraband, now opposed the limitations of the oligopoly trade.

A common regional background could play an important role in the constitution of networks, including mercantile alliances. New immigrants from Spain were especially likely to rely on contacts with their transatlantic kin. For example, Lucas de Careaga served as rector of the

Basque *cofradía* (sodality) "Our Lady of Aranzazu," and the Marquis of Santa Sabina succeeded him in this post in 1704. Careaga also preferred clients of predominantly Basque background.[85] Ties of common ancestry also influenced the politics of commerce in Mexico. Archbishop Ortega y Montañés mentioned the quarrels between different regional groups, when in his function as interim viceroy he once ordered Luis Sánchez de Tagle not to leave his house, citing the dispute between the Montañeses and another unnamed group.[86] Alburquerque argued in 1703 that he had to intervene in the Tagle-Cruzat wedding because of the "imminent risks that loom in general because of this unheard-of accident, and in particular mainly with the experiences that we have of lamentable occurrences between Montañeses, Vizcaínos, and Navarrians."[87] Vizcaínos refers to the Basques, and Navarrians to those from the province of Navarre east and southeast of the Basque region.

An analysis of the regional background of the actors involved in the fight indicates, however, that the formation of parties at this time did not depend exclusively on regional descent. For example, the Sánchez de Tagle family considered themselves Montañés. The two other agents of the Seville *consulado*, the Marquis of Santa Sabina and Lucas de Careaga, were of Basque stock.[88] These merchants came from northern central Spain but represented the interests of the Andalusian merchants. Among the opposing alliance around the viceroy, we find individuals from Navarre, Galicia, León, and the Basque region as well as one Creole (a Spaniard born in the Americas).[89] Antonio Fernández de Tubera, who replaced Pedro Sánchez de Tagle as prior of the *consulado* on 28 October 1703, came, just like the Tagle family, from the Montañés region. Therefore, we cannot discern here the formation of opposing camps based on the regional background of the actors. Patterns of economic interest determined the formation of merchant parties within the *consulado* more than regional origin.

In 1736 the Montañeses claimed in a trial before the Council of the Indies that the Basques had distorted the elections of the *consulado* between 1730 and 1733. By the 1730s the Basques and Montañeses had established themselves as groups in the corporation. Both parties, however, still claimed that a leading member of the *consulado*, a member of the Sánchez de Tagle family, appeared as *calificador* (a *consulado* election official) for their respective group in the election.⁹⁰ The *calificador* eventually lined up with the Montañés party. The case again illustrates a fairly flexible adherence to the two parties in the corporation up to the 1730s. This observation then also casts doubt on a generally held opinion about the rigidity of party adherence in the *consulado* in the later eighteenth century.⁹¹

There is also no evidence that Alburquerque favoured one of the ethnic groups in the *consulado* or outside of it. As far as the duke's origins are concerned, his family traced its roots to the town of Alburquerque in Extremadura on the Portuguese border and to Cuéllar, north of Segovia in the region Old Castile. Extremadurans or Castilians did not form an established group in the corporations of New Spain, and Alburquerque did not display a preference for allies of such a background within the corporations. Therefore, regional background mattered for the construction of social ties in New Spain. Yet the alliances in the fight over oligopoly trade and the networks within the *consulado* depended primarily on economic considerations, not on regional background.

This is not a systematic study of the Mexican *consulado*. It would be necessary to trace the regional background of priors and consuls over an extended period and scrutinize the voting patterns of merchants in general. In the present study, we can only focus on some of the involved key actors under Alburquerque's watch.

Name	Post	Regional Origin	Military Order
The Consulado of Mexico, 1703			
Pedro Sánchez de Tagle	prior	Montañés	Calatrava
Lucas de Careaga	senior consul	Basque	–
Juan del Castillo	junior consul	Montañés	Santiago
Antonio Fernández de Tubera	prior since 28 Oct.	Montañés	Santiago
The Sánchez de Tagle Network			
Luis Sánchez de Tagle		Montañés	Alcántara
Domingo Ruiz de Tagle		Montañés	Alcántara
The Consulado of Mexico of 1706, allied with the viceroy			
Alonso de Dávalos Bracamonte, Count of Miravalle	prior	Creole (New Galicia)	Santiago
Nicolás López de Landa	senior consul	Basque	
Domingo de la Canal	junior consul	Leonés	Calatrava
Other great merchants allied with the viceroy			
Julián Osorio	senior consul in '08	Galician	Santiago
Juan de Garaicoechea		Navarrian	Santiago
Fausto Cruzat y Góngora (son of Governor Cruzat)		Navarrian	Santiago
Geronimo and Luis Monterde			Calatrava

Table 6: Regional background and membership in the military orders among the feuding mercantile networks, 1703–1706[92]

These considerations also contradict the traditional thesis of a basic antagonism between Creoles and Spaniards in New Spain, which twentieth-century scholars such as Lesley B. Simpson and Jonathan Israel have upheld.[93] Israel draws attention to the actions of a powerful viceroy and the bureaucracy in the interest of the crown. The Creoles rallied around the archbishop to resist them. Israel argues that although the bishops usually originated from the peninsula, they allied with the Creole party to obstruct royal demands for increased taxation and control. Israel's thesis may very well be sound for the viceregal tenure of the Marquis of

Gelves, whom the Count-Duke of Olivares had entrusted with reining in the most blatant violations of the law. A loyal servant to Olivares' program, Gelves encountered the opposition of Mexican inhabitants to his project of a heightened imperial unity, or Union of Arms.[94] The idea of an underlying and more or less permanent confrontation between Spaniards and Creoles, however, has already been rejected by a variety of historians. Under Alburquerque's tenure, most of the merchants involved in the struggle came from Spain. They nonetheless fought amongst each other with little regard to Creole or Spanish descent.[95]

Nor did the opposing camps align clearly with membership in the military orders. While most merchants had a penchant for the order of Santiago, which was considered by some a socially superior group of knights, we also find merchants represented in the two other orders, Alcántara and Calatrava. Luis Sánchez de Tagle and his nephew Domingo Ruiz de Tagle belonged to the order of Alcántara, but Prior Pedro Sánchez de Tagle had joined Calatrava. Domingo de la Canal, who belonged to the anti-oligopoly camp, had also joined this order. His ally Julian de Osorio had taken the habit of Santiago along with some of his antagonists, such as Juan del Castillo.

In conclusion, in early-eighteenth-century Mexico two major networks fought over influence on trade and the Mexican *consulado*. The network around the Sánchez de Tagle family officially represented the interests of the Spanish fleet merchants, and the archbishop backed them. Meanwhile, Viceroy Alburquerque built an alliance with contraband merchants opposed to the Seville trustees. During the tumultuous 1703 wedding of Merchant Luis Sánchez de Tagle's nephew to the daughter of the ex-governor of the Philippines, the viceroy and his allies ousted the Sánchez de Tagle network from the Mexican *consulado*. The corporation then called for price ceilings on Spanish imports, a measure that previous *consulado* officers had sharply criticized. The viceroy imprisoned Don Luis, who also temporarily lost his hold on the mint. Although the king restored him to his coinage privileges, the *consulado* remained in the hands of the contraband traders. This contention may have paved the way for later conflicts in the corporation between groups labelled Basques and Montañeses, who both objected to commercial restrictions.

The mercantile conflict described in this chapter suggests a quarrel among heterogeneous networks of Spanish immigrants and Creoles over economic and political issues rather than a fight of Creoles versus peninsulars. Merchants of various origins in Spain and one Creole collaborated in fighting a mélange of traders of similar provenance. Membership in the military orders did not define these social networks, nor did Viceroy Alburquerque or Archbishop Ortega y Montañés show any preference for an alliance of Spaniards against Creoles.

6

FIGHTING THE FAUX HABSBURG CONSPIRACY, 1706–1708

The Persecution of Economic Adversaries

After the accession of King Philip V to the throne of Castile, a number of influential Spanish nobles resisted the political changes that came with the new regime and openly bemoaned their loss of privileges and power. Some of them defected to the Habsburg camp, including the Admiral of Castile and a former viceroy of Catalonia, who both switched sides in 1702.[1] When Allied troops took Madrid in 1706, the Count of Oropesa and other aristocrats went over to Archduke Charles, and again when Allied troops occupied the capital in 1710 a number of nobles defected.[2] Bourbon politicians at court not only worried about the situation in Spain but also feared problems in America. Bad news reached Madrid from Venezuela in 1702.

Bartolomé de Capocelato, sent out by the archduke to garner support for the Habsburg cause in Caracas, won over part of the society. According to historian Analola Borges, the captain general of Caracas backed the cause and hoisted the flags of the Empire in honour of the Habsburg pretender. Then the bishop and the *alcaldes ordinarios* (town councilmen who also sat as judges in first instance) of Caracas intervened. After a tumult, the guards arrested Capocelato and several conspirators fled. His movement collapsed as the captaincy general returned to Bourbon loyalty. The crown replaced the captain general but never clarified the affair entirely.[3]

The monarchy was very concerned about losing New Spain to the enemy, especially since the colony continued to provide millions of pesos to support the Bourbon campaigns in the peninsula. Madrid repeatedly sent orders to the American governors to expect British and Dutch attacks and to fortify the ports. The crown also warned Viceroy Alburquerque that a group of friars were travelling to Mexico to hatch a plot against the Bourbon regime.[4] Well informed of events in Spain, Mexicans conversed in the streets about war, trade disruptions, and European politics. Rumours abounded. In 1702 purportedly twenty thousand Spaniards went over to the archduke.[5] This raises a major question. Since most bureaucrats and clergy had obtained their positions under the old dynasty, did sections of Mexican society favour the Habsburg claimant? Moreover, if some inhabitants of the colony supported the archduke, did the colony experience significant tension while adhering to Bourbon rule?

In 1706 confidants of the viceroy reported to Alburquerque that several merchants, shopkeepers, craftsmen, and clerics as well as a hacienda administrator had spoken treacherously against King Philip. The viceroy and trusted *audiencia* ministers pursued these suspects vigorously, accusing them of supporting the Habsburg dynasty. At the same time, the duke faced down two hostile *audiencia* ministers and their allies, accusing them of treason.[6] Spanish historian Luis Navarro García has accepted Alburquerque's allegations as a proof of Mexican support for the archduke. Navarro García argues that the defendants spread Austrophile propaganda and possibly conspired against the Bourbon regime. For the historian, their regional backgrounds in the rebellious principality of Catalonia (Spain) and in Portugal explain partly their disloyal attitudes.[7]

An analysis of the sources taking into account the political and commercial interests of the viceroy and his allied *audiencia* ministers, however, vitiates this thesis. None of the suspects participated in a plot against the Bourbons. There is little indication of a Mexican opposition to the Bourbon dynasty. Instead, the duke and loyal *audiencia* ministers established a series of trials as a scheme to crack down on their enemies, some of whom were tied to the oligopoly trade. The trials of these merchants and shopkeepers nurtured the viceregal client-patron relationship, rewarding clients by punishing their foes. The duke bound to his cause local figures such as the wholesale merchants Alonso de Asinas Duque de Estrada and Juan de Garaicoechea as well as the financial official Antonio Gómez Lobato. The prosecutions also publicly demonstrated to the Bourbon king the duke's character as a loyal supporter. This came in handy at a time when the viceroy's patron, the Duke of Medinaceli, was falling out of favour with the dominant French clique at the royal court. Additionally, Alburquerque's accusations against hostile *audiencia* ministers and secular clergy who were tied to the archbishop served to suppress political opposition to his viceroyship.

The character of the penal justice system determined the course of the trials. Because it was an open system, external considerations heavily influenced its decisions. Outside pressures affected the choice of judges for trials, and magistrates tended to interpret the laws flexibly, often in their own interest. Social and personal ties substantially determined the opinions of ministers and subordinate officials such as *relatores*, who prepared the trials, so that sentences reflected the power of a particular social network rather than an impartial judgment on a case.[8]

Similarly, the viceroy of New Spain could manipulate the proceedings of the court substantially. He could rely on those *audiencia* judges who aligned with him hoping to benefit from his patronage. Others impressed by or timorous of the viceroy's power went along. In the conspiracy trials of 1706, decisions about who was accused as a traitor, imprisoned, and tried reflected the political interests of the viceroy and the *oidores* and the capability of their opponents to exert political pressure in warding off the assault. Rather than comprising a neutral process about treason and loyalty, trials in the *ancien régime* frequently emerged from or evolved into a power struggle.

After Alburquerque received the denunciations of the alleged traitors, he passed the information on to Baltasar Tovar, who was Alburquerque's most trusted *oidor* on the bench. As civil judge (*oidor*), Tovar at that time substituted for the position of a criminal magistrate (*alcalde en turno*).[9] According to the viceroy, Tovar would hear criminal cases, since only two criminal judges (*alcaldes del crimen*) and the crown prosecutor (*fiscal del crimen*) served on the chamber (*sala del crimen*).[10] Staff at the *audiencia* was stretched thin because legally, the criminal chamber should have consisted of four *alcaldes del crimen* and the crown prosecutor. Nonetheless, the foundation for Tovar's action was precarious. *Oidores* could hear a criminal case only in the absence of all criminal judges. If any were serving, the *oidores* were barred.[11] Alburquerque's ally apparently stretched his powers to skew the prosecution of the "Austrophiles."

On 17 November 1706 the accountant of the Mexico City treasury, Antonio Gómez Lobato, accused the wealthy Galician merchant Gregorio Gasco Suárez of disloyalty to the king. In the presence of Judge Tovar, the official claimed that he did not know Gasco personally but had received notice that the merchant "has always been impassionate for the mentioned archduke speaking in his favour and against our king."[12] Seconding the accuser were Gómez Lobato's brother and Antonio Freire y San Martín, both of whom were from Galicia and shopkeepers on the *plaza mayor* in Mexico City. Freire y San Martín declared that he had seen Gasco in "very silent conversations" with his assistant, a blacksmith, a clergyman, and other shopkeepers.[13] Antonio Gómez Lobato, a resident of Mexico even before the duke's arrival, became a client of Alburquerque. The treasury official participated in several mercantile schemes of the viceroy and vouched for the duke in his *juicio de residencia* (the mandatory assessment of an outgoing official's term). Francisco de Pagabe, *visitador* (inspector) of New Spain's financial administration from 1710 to 1715, fined Gómez Lobato for assisting a *junta* (council) in 1709 that, contrary to royal order, withheld the annual proceeds of the mercury sale.[14]

Judge Tovar arrested the merchant Gasco on the same day as the accusations were levelled against him and prosecuted him and most other suspects for *infidencia*, an offence consisting of the violation of fidelity owed to the king. The criminal prosecutor, Gaspar Blas Cepeda y Castro Gil de Gibaja, added that the suspects had uttered blasphemy and formed a conspiracy. He suspected them of *crimen laesae majestatis*.[15] The precise legal definition of those malefactions in the early eighteenth century remains murky. King Alfonso X's medieval law code

Siete Partidas distinguish between treason and *malquerencia*, or speaking badly about the king. Treason or *crimen laesae majestatis* usually involved a violent act against the monarch, such as assassination, ousting the king, or removing his authority over his lawful territory. Treason carried the death penalty, confiscation of all property, and the infamy of the offender's sons.[16] The *Siete Partidas* considered *malquerencia* a grave offence. As it undermined the king's honour and reputation, it could be punished as regicide. The suspect had to be delivered to the king, who could adjudicate more leniently when extenuating circumstance called for it. The punishment for *malquerencia* could then be mercifully reduced to cutting out the culprit's tongue.[17] Blaspheming, although originally exclusively a sacrilege, included by the sixteenth century the offence of speaking derogatorily about the monarch.[18] The nineteenth-century legal dictionary of Joaquín Escriche, written before 1847 and expanded in 1874, defines *infidencia* principally as the political crime of exchanging information with an enemy of the king or the state. The penalty varied according to the circumstances but could be death during wartime.[19] Magistrates Tovar and Cepeda probably knew *infidencia* as a recognized criminal offence. The criminal judges did not overstep their jurisdiction in arresting the suspects, and if evidence pointed towards *malquerencia*, they could have the culprits shipped to Spain to be judged by the king.

During the trial initiated by the court (*de oficio*), Tovar invited several witnesses to back up the allegations against the merchant Gregorio Gasco.[20] The judge called on individuals who buttressed the prosecution case and supported the interests of the viceroy and his clients. The most striking witness was the merchant Juan de Garaicoechea, already known as a close viceregal ally from the fight against the trustees of the Seville *consulado* (the corporation representing Spanish fleet merchants) in the Tagle-Cruzat wedding. Garaicoechea damningly claimed, "Don Gregorio Gasco generally has been taken for and reputed as disposed towards the [Holy Roman] Empire and the English and totally disaffected from the Spaniards and the French."[21] Garaicoechea considered this view as "public and notorious," although he admitted not knowing Gasco. Garaicoechea also volunteered that the accused blacksmith and the shopkeeper were "Sebastianists and they follow the opinion of D[o]n Gregorio and the other ones estranged from our king."[22]

Garaicoechea's charge indicates that something different was at stake in the conspiracy trials. The suspects around Gregorio Gasco formed a network of commercial partners and dependents, mainly shopkeepers, some of them of Galician origin like Gasco himself.[23] As a wealthy and successful wholesale trader (*cargador de flota*), Gasco dealt with the oligopoly commerce of the Spanish fleet.[24] For this reason, the contrabandist Garaicoechea attacked the merchant. This fight reflects a parallel conflict of the viceroy and his allies with the Sánchez de Tagle network, which officially represented the interests of the Spanish fleet merchants. Nevertheless, the trials were not exclusively based on the row between the oligopoly trade and contraband merchants. Personal animosities played an important role as well. Some enemies tried to settle scores with Gasco, who had refused a credit to one of his denouncers.

During the trial against Gasco, the criminal judges did not present any reliable proof that Gasco had uttered irreverent remarks against the Bourbons. In the proceedings against Gasco's servant Joaquín Puyol, Tovar produced two supposedly incriminating letters exchanged between Puyol and Gasco. The first letter pertained to a quarrel between Puyol and a merchant named Coto over business fraud involving the fortresses (*presidios*). This individual could have been the Captain Juan Coto who testified against Gasco.[25] Gasco's client Puyol claimed the second letter had been forged to incriminate Gasco and himself. It is impossible to assess the veracity of this claim since the letter is unavailable in the documentation. In his declaration to Judge Tovar, Gasco discussed at length European politics, the war in Spain, and its impact on maritime trade. Gasco also elaborated on how to reconquer Gibraltar from the English, all views supportive of the Bourbon cause. His statement sheds light on the travel of information across the Atlantic and Mexican knowledge about the fate of the empire. Since Gasco had moved to Mexico seven years before and his fortune was tied to transatlantic commerce, the merchant's intimate knowledge is hardly surprising. Some incriminating data beyond the dubious accusations of two personal enemies seem necessary to explain why a wealthy merchant would get involved in such a risky business as a conspiracy. It is possible that the fleet merchants had reservations about the attempt of the Bourbon dynasty to wrest away trade from the Seville *consulado*. Nevertheless, the sources do not reveal that Gasco felt any fidelity to the House of Habsburg analogous to that of the Spanish grandees who defected to Philip. One would also expect a successful merchant to be cautious enough not to express anything damaging around his commercial rivals who also happened to be well connected to the hostile viceroy.

The entire trial against Gasco illuminates a feud between two social circles about mercantile and personal issues. These groups consisted of import merchants such as Garaicoechea and Gasco and their client shopkeepers on the main square of Mexico City. The trial against one of Gasco's partners confirms the view of a vendetta. This wealthy shopkeeper on the main square – Judge Tovar confiscated almost 17,000 pesos in property – called several witnesses to his defence. These merchants or shopkeepers testified that Gómez Lobato and Gasco's partner had had a falling out long before.[26]

To refute accusations, the suspects sometimes summoned witnesses in their favour, preferably individuals of respectable social standing, especially those connected to the viceroy. The supportive testimony of Luis Ibáñez de Oserin, an accountant (*contador de resultas*) on the tribunal of accounts, significantly helped Gasco's client.[27] Alburquerque had appointed the accountant although no vacancy existed on the tribunal. The defendant had known Ibáñez for twenty-two years and operated his shop in the residence of another accountant on the tribunal, also tied to the viceroy.[28] In addition, this accountant could boast connections to the senior *oidor*, Miguel Calderón de la Barca, a friend of Alburquerque.[29] In another trial, an incarcerated blacksmith linked to Gasco effectively relied for support on a person living in the house of the merchant Julián de Osorio, a close collaborator of the viceroy.[30] Calling in witnesses in trials buttressed the defence in two ways. First, the higher the social standing of the witnesses, the more convincingly they could guarantee the honour of the accused. This issue might gain particular importance if the Council of the Indies reviewed the case. Additionally, the witnesses indicated the strength of the defendant's social network and the political pressure it exerted in the judicial process.

The trial documents for Gasco's clients went back and forth between Alburquerque and the criminal chamber with considerable delay. Prosecutor Cepeda routinely asked for a guilty verdict.[31] In the case of

Fighting the Faux Habsburg Conspiracy, 1706–1708

Gasco's client Antonio de Villar, Cepeda admitted that the evidence was ambiguous but demanded capital punishment anyway to set an example.[32] Frequently, colonial prosecutors (*fiscales*) demanded harsh sentences as a way of expressing crown interests – in Mexico as in other parts of the empire.[33] Cepeda's quarrel with the viceroy also explains the prosecutor's call for stern justice. Alburquerque wrote to the Council of the Indies that Cepeda favoured the defendants.[34] This accusation caused Cepeda to ask for harsh sentences to erase any doubts about his loyalty to the embattled Spanish monarch.

After some suspects had spent up to nineteenth months in jail, the *audiencia* decided most cases between October and November 1707. One case dragged on until the chamber revised the sentence on 3 October 1708. The criminal judges found five suspects innocent. Gasco's aide Joaquín Puyol was to be set free but had to shoulder the costs of the trial.[35] The ministers decided to ship Gasco to the dungeons of Spain without reaching a guilty verdict.[36] Gasco, however, died in jail before departing from New Spain, as did Puyol and another client. The Council of the Indies, reviewing the case of Gasco's aide Puyol on 4 June 1712, threw out the *audiencia*'s verdict and declared him innocent.[37]

Puyol was unable to mount an effective defence in Mexico. With his patron Gasco jailed, Puyol lacked the requisite finances, good social connections, and competent legal representation. Instead, the viceroy appointed a *procurador de pobres* (an attorney representing the poor), who defended him badly. The *audiencia* did not permit Puyol to call any supporting witnesses to the bar. All this led to his initial conviction. When the *audiencia* finally revised his sentence and declared him free in October 1708, Puyol had already died. His patron, Gregorio Gasco, tied to the enemies of the viceroy, bore the brunt of the attack. Nonetheless, the court never executed any punishments that could have drawn reprimand from Madrid. It sufficed wholly to keep Gasco and Puyol confined and threaten the death penalty to ruin their business and health. Under these strains they finally died. Since Gasco belonged to the fleet merchants, one would also suspect the influence of the Sevillian *consulado* on a final verdict of the Council of the Indies.

In the course of the proceedings, Judge Tovar also planned to interrogate two clerics, one of them Gregorio Gasco's confessor. On 2

November 1706 Tovar asked Alburquerque to obtain permission from the archbishop to interrogate the priests. The request met with a cool response. The relation between the archbishop and the viceroy had suffered markedly since the Tagle-Cruzat wedding. Archbishop Ortega y Montañés probably grasped that the whole process against the "austrophile party" served a self-interested political end rather than the suppression of a dangerous conspiracy. Consequently, he rejected Alburquerque's plea, arguing that in matters of such gravity prelates could not allow their subordinates to appear before the secular courts.[38]

The archbishop then forestalled possible manoeuvres of the viceroy to portray him as a Habsburg loyalist. He ordered the *promotor fiscal* (the chief advisor on canon law and lawsuits at the archbishop's court)[39] to interrogate one of the accused clerics.[40] The *promotor* arrested Lorenzo González de Figueroa on 30 November 1706 and found two incriminating letters among the cleric's belongings. In the first letter, the cleric criticized the archbishop for levying the tenth of Church income for the king while the funds in fact ended up with the English. In the second document, González satirized the Bourbon dynasty, calling the new king *duque de ajos*, that is, garlic duke, instead of *duque de Anjou* or Duke of Anjou. The cleric labelled Philip's brother *duque de berros*, that is, watercress duke, instead of *duque de Berri* or Duke of Berri.[41] González admitted to have copied the letter for entertainment.[42] If this is a true statement, it represents the only written proof of a critical attitude towards the Bourbon rulers in the entire series of trials. The phrase, however, does not necessarily indicate a preference for the Habsburg dynasty. Satirical writings against the authorities were not unusual in the *ancien régime* and do not constitute a conspiracy or a pro-Habsburg attitude.[43] In any case, on 19 April 1707, the ecclesiastical court sentenced González for these irreverent letters to two years of exile outside of Mexico City and withdrew his licence to hear confessions.[44] With this verdict, given the nature of the evidence, the cleric came off lightly and evaded the harsher secular prosecution that his friends suffered.

Fighting the Faux Habsburg Conspiracy, 1706–1708

Name of Defendant	Origin	Occupation	Relationship	Verdict	Trajectory	Attorney
Gregorio Gasco Suárez	Galicia	Fleet merchant (*cargador de flota*)		To be deported to Spain	Died in prison	Carlos de Navia
Antonio Caballero	Montañés	Shopkeeper	Client	Absolved	Died in prison	Félix Hidalgo
Juan López Camaño	Galicia	Blacksmith	Client	Absolved		Miguel Leonardo de Sevilla
Pedro Collazo de Soto		Wealthy shopkeeper	Unclear	Absolved, case reviewed by Council		Carlos de Navia
Lorenzo González de Figueroa	Galicia	Cleric	Gasco's confessor	Guilty of irreverence by ecclesiastical court	Exile from Mexico City, lost license to hear confession	
Joaquín Puyol	Catalan	Gasco's aide	Client	To be set free, liable for costs of trial	Died in prison	Attorney for the poor
Antonio del Villar Bahamonde	Galicia	Shopkeeper	Client	Absolved		Carlos de Navia
José Pardo	Galicia	Shopkeeper	Client	Absolved		José de Ledesma
Juan Antonio Pardo	Galicia	Shopkeeper	Client, nephew of José Pardo	Absolved		José de Ledesma

Antonio Gómez Lobato, an accountant of the Mexico City treasury, his brothers Pedro and Bernardo Gómez Lobato as well as Antonio Freire y San Martín, accused Gregorio Gasco and his clients of treason. All of the accusers came from Galicia and, save Antonio, worked as shopkeepers on the *plaza mayor*. Contraband merchant Juan de Garaicoechea backed their cause against Gasco. The quarrel revolved around the oligopoly issue, personal animosities, and a credit that Gasco had denied his enemies.

Name	Relationship	Occupation	Verdict	Attorney
Benito Cartagena	Marquis of Buenavista, Count of Galve	Merchant	Absolved	Carlos de Navia

Merchant Alonso de Asinas Duque de Estrada and Tomás Fernández de Guevara, assistant notary of government, accused Cartagena of infidelity. At the core of the denunciation lay a conflict over the playing card monopoly.

Name	Occupation	Verdict	Trajectory	Attorney
Manuel de Sousa y Prado	Operated skinner workshop	To be deported to Spain	Died in prison	Carlos de Navia

Sousa y Prado was denounced by Diego de Vera. Sousa's creditor Pedro Urtazu backed the accusation.

Name	Occupation	Verdict	Trajectory	Attorney
Salvador Mañer	Hacienda administrator	Guilty	Deported to Spain, in 1714 sentenced to six years of forced military duty	Attorney for the poor

Juan de Acosta, *alférez* and head of the palace guard, accused Salvador Mañer.

Table 7: Defendants in the conspiracy trials, 1706–1708[45]

The trial against Benito Cartagena, a merchant and erstwhile district official, confirms even more clearly the character of a personal vendetta. Captain Alonso de Asinas Duque de Estrada and Tomás Fernández de Guevara denounced Cartagena as a traitor. They claimed to have talked with Cartagena at Fernández de Guevara's house. There Cartagena reported that a friend, holding a napkin in the German style (*servilleta alemanisca*) in his hand, declared "he cannot be content until he saw these raised in Mexico."[46] Soon after, Asinas went to the palace, threw himself "on his knees," and told the viceroy about the incident.[47] The denunciations carried weight, as both accusers stood in favour with the viceroy. The duke twice recommended Asinas, a wealthy merchant and monopoly contractor for gunpowder, to the crown. The assistant government notary (*teniente de escribano de gobernación*), Tomás Fernández de Guevara, worked closely with the viceroy.[48]

Cartagena, who was arrested on 1 November 1706, vehemently denied these charges, claiming he merely visited the assistant notary to inquire about the upcoming auction of the playing card monopoly. Cartagena and Fernández de Guevara had originally planned to bid jointly in the auction. Asinas then convinced the notary to join him in acquiring the monopoly and used the opportunity to incriminate his competitor with the viceroy. In his defence Cartagena could call on important witnesses, such as the Marquis of Buenavista, with whom he had shared the same patron, the former viceroy Count of Galve. With the backing of the witnesses, Cartagena got off the hook.[49] The *sala del crimen* declared Cartagena innocent on 16 March 1707.[50]

To gather more information about the supposed conspiracy, Alburquerque also ordered the questioning of cooks who assisted at the reunion where Cartagena allegedly uttered his disloyal phrase. In November 1706 Tovar interrogated two chefs who usually cooked in the house of their patron Lucas de Careaga – the very enemy of Alburquerque. Another cook worked in the residence of Archbishop Ortega y Montañés, also known to be hostile to the duke.[51] Alburquerque steered the inquiries towards the activities of his opponents with whom he had already clashed in the wedding scandal. This attempt did not deliver any tangible results, but the documents hint at a tie between Benito Cartagena, his friend accountant José de Careaga, and the wholesaler Lucas de Careaga.[52]

Doubts remain also about the trial of Manuel de Sousa y Prado, who operated a skinner workshop in Mexico City. Early in January 1707 *Oidor* Tovar arrested Sousa y Prado. According to hostile witnesses, the defendant had said, "Spain had sworn allegiance to the archduke and that Philip V … had usurped the crown from the archduke to whom it belonged exclusively."[53] Additionally, Don Pedro Urtazu, an individual of some social standing who was in contact with the *alcalde del crimen*, Manuel Suárez Muñoz, claimed that Sousa had suggested a bet on the war in Spain. Sousa had wagered that Badajoz had fallen to the Portuguese and that Philip V had not been able to reconquer Barcelona.[54]

Manuel de Sousa y Prado rejected most of the accusations. Born in Portugal, he claimed to resent people speaking badly about the king of that realm. He did admit, however, to the bet with Pedro Urtazu. Sousa maintained that he accepted the wager because he owed Urtazu money. According to Sousa, he did not bet "because he was against the king but because the bad news about the events in Spain are generally known."[55] Several other witnesses supported Sousa's claim of innocence. According to witness Marcos de Sola, some time before, Urtazu and some of his fellows had caused a nighttime commotion in front of Sousa's residence, drawing their swords and throwing stones at the house.[56] Regardless, on 21 June the executioner dragged Sousa into the torture chamber and demonstrated to him the instruments. Shortly after, the criminal chamber declared Sousa guilty of pronouncing "irreverent and scandalous words."[57] Sousa, liable for all trial costs, was to be shipped out to Spain. In December 1708, while waiting in prison for the fleet, Sousa died.[58]

The case against Salvador Mañer, an administrator of a hacienda in Toluca, took a different course because the *audiencia* ultimately deported him to Spain and his trial continued until 1714. According to an *alférez* (standard-bearer) of the palace guard, Mañer had stated, "he would bet two hundred pesos that all of Spain would be for the archduke."[59] Mañer came under further suspicion because of his stay in Venezuela and his continuing contacts with his uncle in Caracas, where the governor had briefly gone over to the Habsburg cause.[60] *Oidor* Tovar confiscated Mañer's property, a procedure following the law, since the defendant could be fined or forfeit his property if convicted.[61] By seizing Mañer's goods, however, the judge also conveniently prevented Mañer from hiring an effective lawyer. On 23 June 1708, the *audiencia* convicted Mañer for being "disloyal to and disaffected from His Catholic Majesty."[62] Nothing substantial in the records supports this conviction or any loyalty towards the archduke. After his transfer to the prison of the House of Trade in Seville, Mañer escaped on 8 June 1711. Soon after, the local *corregidor* captured him in Córdoba. At that time, according to the *fiscal* of the Council of the Indies, Mañer was carrying papers that discussed the legitimacy of the Bourbon succession. Mañer stated he had simply agreed to copy these documents for others. Twice again Mañer fled and was caught. Finally, on 22 August 1714 the Council of the Indies sentenced him to six years of forced military service in a port fortress (*presidio*).[63] Once released from his gruelling term, historian

Luis Navarro García claims, Mañer gained access to the court in Madrid and established himself as a successful political writer under the protection of Secretary José de Patiño.[64]

Doubts remain about the truthfulness of the accusations against Mañer. According to the *fiscal*, in one letter from 1711 Mañer discussed the succession, yet the writing cannot be found in the archive. One can only speculate whether Mañer truly harboured subversive ideas at all, or if he developed them during four and a half years in jail. Either way, his later career in Madrid seems inconceivable. In any case, none of the *fiscal's* charges against Mañer amounted to a conspiracy in New Spain.

One additional element helped decide the fate of the defendants: access to a good attorney. Four lawyers represented the alleged conspirators: José de Ledesma, Félix Hidalgo, Leonardo de Sevilla, and Carlos de Navia. Three of them had built ties to the viceroy. In 1708 the duke appointed Leonardo de Sevilla as attorney (*procurador*) of the *audiencia*,[65] while Ledesma and Hidalgo both acted later as Alburquerque's legal counsel in the *juicio de residencia*. Ledesma also represented other *oidores* tied to the viceroy in their *juicios de residencia*.[66] Attorney Félix Hidalgo testified for Judge Miguel de Calderón in the *residencia* and intervened as an attorney in a high-level dispute over the alum monopoly.[67] These bonds contributed to the verdicts of innocence for all clients of Ledesma, Hidalgo, and Sevilla, although Hidalgo's defendant had died by then. The judges freed three of Carlos de Navia's defendants, but they also convicted two. In 1711 Navia reluctantly represented a viceregal enemy in the fight about the meat monopoly. The attorney lacked similar access to powerful networks.[68] He could not prevent guilty verdicts against all his clients.

Opposition to Alburquerque in the Audiencia and the Secular Clergy

Ministers of the *audiencias* in the Spanish Empire usually sought to establish a good relationship with the viceroy – and the laws of the Indies exhorted them to do so. The *oidores* could inform the king without royal order about occurrences in the colony as long as their report did not directly criticize the viceroy.[69] The viceroys as presidents of the *audiencia* could receive information about the misconduct of a minister and secretly pass it on to the Council of the Indies. The laws required the viceroy to advise the crown on the conduct and qualities of all persons in his jurisdiction, including men trained in law and members of the Church. The crown considered these recommendations as a basis for promotions to the *audiencia* and to canonries or prelacies.[70] For example, Alburquerque recommended his confidant *Oidor* Baltasar Tovar for a canonry in the cathedral chapter of Mexico City as a way to secure a more comfortable retirement for the elderly judge.[71] A smooth relationship between *audiencia* ministers and the viceroy was usually profitable in several ways. A disgruntled viceroy could undermine a minister's standing with the crown and damage (arguably vague) prospects of promotion. Since several ministers in the early eighteenth century owned landed property in the colony or pursued some clandestine business in violation of the law, the vigorous opposition of the viceroy could pose dangerous risks. Yet, if a viceroy fell into disgrace, Madrid could interpret a magistrate's distance to the viceroy as sign of service to the crown.

Earlier, Alburquerque had favoured Judge José Joaquín de Uribe in the quarrel with the Sánchez de Tagle family. Their relations later deteriorated. Both sides increasingly reverted to mudslinging. Uribe reported to Spain that the viceroy coerced the *audiencia* ministers into supporting him in his illegitimate activities.[72] Uribe also charged that *Oidor* Miguel de Calderón, a viceregal collaborator, abused his powers and provided credits to the Rayas mine in Guanajuato – prohibited by the laws of the Indies.[73] Some of these allegations may have been true, yet they do not entirely explain the falling out between Uribe and Alburquerque, since Uribe pursued illicit interests in a very similar fashion.[74]

When the new *fiscal del crimen* Gaspar Cepeda arrived in New Spain, he strengthened bonds with Uribe, whom he had met as a fellow student at the archiepiscopal *colegio mayor* (a residence hall or confraternity) at the University of Salamanca.[75] Cepeda later substituted for Uribe's chair at the Spanish university in 1701.[76] Cepeda fell into disgrace with the duke, because the *fiscal* insisted on his participation in some meetings of the *real acuerdo*. Alburquerque did not permit his presence there.[77] The prosecutor also clashed with the *corregidor* of Mexico, a viceregal crony, about jurisdiction in a murder trial.[78] Subsequently, relations worsened when Cepeda attacked the assistant notary of the *sala del crimen*, a viceregal client. Cepeda jailed the notary during the proceedings against the merchant Gasco, charging him with stealing 80,000 pesos of Gasco's property. The prosecutor also challenged the viceroy's exclusive authority as captain general in trials against military personnel, and he wrangled with the duke about how to prosecute the alleged Habsburg conspirators.[79] Cepeda finally maintained that the viceroy had artificially delayed the taking of office (*dar paso*) of a district official appointed by the king and recently cleared of charges of infidelity. In the meantime, Cepeda stated, Alburquerque had already named an interim official to the wealthy district of Tepeaca and Tecali, charging him 14,000 pesos.[80]

In return, the viceroy complained bitterly to Madrid about Uribe's and Cepeda's conduct.[81] Alburquerque suggested that Uribe had taken offence because he did not entrust him with the *auditoría de guerra* – the viceroy's legal counsel on military affairs. The duke also humiliated Cepeda in the *real acuerdo*, claiming among other things that Cepeda had committed adultery with a married woman.[82] The quarrel reflected a social difference. The Duke of Alburquerque belonged to one of Spain's premier families. In 1520, Emperor Charles V had included the family among the twenty lineages of grandees (*grandeza*), the uppermost echelon of Castile's aristocracy.[83] Under Charles II in the later seventeenth century, the high aristocracy also came to consider state affairs as their prerogative. As a viceroy Alburquerque was not, unlike several predecessors, the second-born son of the uppermost aristocracy, or offspring of a lower or more recent branch of titled nobility. Accustomed to enjoying deferential treatment in his ducal residence and at the royal court, he resented officials of, in his eyes, humble origins who consistently challenged his authority. This partly explains Alburquerque's haughty attitude towards the *audiencia* ministers. In particular, the aristocrat vented his wrath towards both Uribe and Cepeda in his letters to the king when he labelled the magistrates as *mozos* and *muchachos*, in other words, 'young fellows.' The duke's derision against the vexatious ministers culminated in accusing them of disloyalty towards the monarch.[84]

Little evidence points to this claim. Unlike most contemporary judges on the Mexican bench in that era, both owed their appointments to the new dynasty. The causes of the dispute between Alburquerque and the ministers revolve around power, etiquette, and vanity. The conflict shows the usual symptoms of a clash between two rival networks. The viceroy attacked his enemies in the *audiencia* and those linked to the archbishop of Mexico.

Ministers José Uribe and Gaspar Cepeda did not, as they claimed, strictly defend crown interests against the powerful duke. As did most officials in the early eighteenth century, both ministers came to Mexico planning to profit socially and economically. After Alburquerque's departure, Cepeda aligned with other *audiencia* ministers and the Puebla oligarchy in their schemes against Superintendent Juan José de Veytia Linage, who considerably raised the yield of the sales tax (*alcabala*) in that city. Cepeda eventually retired into the Church – as a canon in Puebla, where other *oidores* joined him later.[85] After his wedding plans with Ignacia Cruzat fell through, Uribe married a wealthy heiress to landed estates in the Puebla region. He then bought further haciendas in that region, owning property worth more than 44,000 pesos.[86] One can only speculate on the origins of his wealth. Uribe thus strengthened his bonds to the Puebla oligarchy. Following this rather customary conduct of royal officials, Uribe and Cepeda were not the disinterested wardens of crown prerogatives. Criticizing Alburquerque's abuses helped fend off the viceroy's attack. In hindsight, however, both judges acted with political astuteness, distancing themselves from the viceroy when Alburquerque's fortune in Madrid waned.

The manoeuvres in Mexico received attention in Madrid. On 16 April 1708, after a series of letters from the duke and Uribe lambasting each other, the king ordered Uribe and Cepeda to travel to Spain immediately.[87] They were to be joined by their friend Canon Andrés Costela, who had arrived in New Spain in 1702 sailing in the same French squadron as Uribe and Alburquerque.[88] With this decision the Council of the Indies intended to end the dispute in the *audiencia* and investigate charges of treason. Yet on 10 August 1708, the Council discussed the memorandum drawn up by Cepeda's brother, who defended the prosecutor's integrity. The corporation then reversed its decision and suggested Cepeda not be required to return to Spain. The Council also recommended naming a junta of the four oldest *audiencia* ministers to assess the prosecutor's conduct. The councillors proposed excluding the viceroy from any jurisdiction in the inquest. Cepeda in the meantime should leave Mexico City.[89] Through a *real cédula* (a communication from the monarch) to Alburquerque dated 7 January 1709, the crown also suspended Uribe's return to Spain. The matter then dragged on without resolution beyond Alburquerque's departure. His successor investigated the issue, and finding no guilt, he restored Costela and Cepeda to their offices in 1710 and 1711, while the crown reinstated Uribe.[90]

Sala Civil	Relation to Alburquerque
Oidores	
Calderón de la Barca, Miguel	ally, leaves *audiencia* in November 1703
Escalante Mendoza, Juan	cooperative
Luna, José	ally
Uribe Castejón M., José Joaquín	ally
Tovar, Baltasar	ally, adviser (*asesor*) of the viceroy
Valenzuela Venegas, Francisco	ally, adviser of the viceroy
Fiscal de lo civil	
Espinosa Ocampo C., Dr. José A.	cooperative
Sala del Crimen	
Alcaldes del crimen	
Abellafuentes, Alonso	ally
Ozaeta Oro, Juan	cooperative
Sarace Arce, Francisco	unknown
Suarez Muñiz, Manuel	cooperative

Source: See the prosopography of audiencia ministers in Appendix 3.

Table 8: The Mexican audiencia *during Alburquerque's clash with the trustees of the Sevillian* consulado, *1702–1703*

Sala Civil	Relation to Alburquerque	
Oidores		
Abellafuentes, Alonso	ally	*oidor* since 1705
Luna, José de la	ally	
Tovar, Baltasar	ally, adviser	died before September 1707
Valenzuela Venegas, Francisco	ally, adviser, *auditor de guerra*	
Escalante y Mendoza, Juan	conflictive	died 3 September 1706
Uribe Castejón M., José J.	hostile	
Soria Velásquez, Jerónimo	ally	possession in December 1704
Diez de Bracamonte, Juan	ally	supernumerary, possession in 1705
Pérez de Villareal, Dr. Cristóbal	ally, advisor	supernumerary, purchased in 1707
González de Agüero, Félix	cooperative	supernumerary, purchased in 1707
Valdés, Juan de	cooperative	supernumerary, bought in 1707
Fiscal de lo civil		
Espinosa Ocampo C., Dr. José	cooperative	
Sala del Crimen	**Relation to Alburquerque**	
Alcaldes del crimen		
Eguaras Fernández de Hijar, Pedro	cooperative	appointed 1705
Ozaeta y Oro, Juan	cooperative	
Suárez Muñoz, Manuel	cooperative	
Casa Alvarado, Francisco de	ally	supernumerary, purchased in 1706
Peña y Flores, Juan Francisco de la	unknown	supernumerary, purchased in 1707
Robles y Lorenzana, Augustín	unknown	supernumerary, purchased in 1707
Peña y Flores, Juan Francisco de la	unknown	supernumerary, purchased in 1707
Fiscal del crimen		
Cepeda, Gaspar	hostile	possession in 1705

Source: Razon de los Oydores, y Alcaldes del Crimen del numero, y supernumerarios, que ay en la Audiencia de Mexico, s. n., drawn up around 1712, AGI, México 377; see also Appendix 3.

Table 9: The Mexican audiencia *during the conspiracy trials, 1706–1708*

Tables 8 and 9 offer an overview of the relationship between *audiencia* ministers and the viceroy. The absence of the *audiencia* proceedings for this period encumbers tracing the relationships of all the members with the viceroy. For the purposes of this analysis, I define a minister as an *ally* when the viceroy employed him as his legal advisor or if there are signs of a continuous collaboration. If the record does not allow for conclusions on a close relationship and nothing indicates a conflict, the minister is labelled *cooperative*. In Uribe and Cepeda's case, the relationship turned *hostile*. In 1706 and 1707, during the critical phase of the war, the crown flooded the *audiencia* with supernumerary ministers. The crown may have used the appointments to pack the high court with people more loyal than the previous Habsburg appointees. Most of these new magistrates, however, had paid several thousand pesos into the royal coffers for their position. The recent arrivals were therefore inclined to cooperate with the viceroy in order to recoup their investments. Consequently, in 1719 Inspector Francisco Garzarón removed most of these corrupt ministers. The overview of the *audiencia* shows that the viceroy collaborated during the Tagle-Cruzat conflict with all *audiencia* ministers. This does not mean that they simply executed orders from the duke. Ministers sometimes disagreed with the viceroy on issues. When Juan de Escalante y Mendoza and the duke clashed about the farming out of the alum monopoly and the subsequent fire in the building, each supported his own client.[91]

Before their fight with the viceroy, Magistrate José Uribe, Canon Andrés Costela, and their friend, Inquisitor José de Cienfuegos, built links to other Mexican clergy. Costela could rely on some of his colleagues in the cathedral chapter. This ecclesiastical chapter (*cabildo eclesiástico*) composed of clergymen appointed by the king governed a Cathedral church. The clerics drew an income and organized the cult of the church. At the top of the chapter hierarchy sat the dignities (*dignidades*), that is, the dean (*deán*), archdeacon (*arcediano*), precentor (*chantre*), school master (*maestrescuela*), and the treasurer (*tesorero*). The next in rank were the canons (*canónigos*) followed by prebends called *racioneros* and, below them, the *medio racioneros*.[92]

Facing deportation, Canon Costela rallied clerics for support. These clergymen vouched for Costela's loyal character. Two supportive canons had participated as Archbishop Ortega y Montañés's confidants in the Tagle-Cruzat wedding. Since they consistently supported the archbishop, both of these canons can be considered as the archiepiscopal party in the cathedral chapter. Another canon joined them, criticizing Alburquerque for embezzling royal funds.[93] The support of Ortega y Montañés's confidants for Costela also demonstrates that the archbishop himself backed Alburquerque's opponent. The duke complained several times to the crown that the archbishop supported the Uribe alliance.[94] For the archbishop, opposition to the viceroy had become an established policy. Uribe and Inquisitor Cienfuegos, however, had changed their alliance remarkably. Opponents of the Sánchez de Tagle group in the wedding conflict, the minister, and the cleric aligned with the archbishop after their falling out with the viceroy. With the support of the prelate and his allies, Costela and Inquisitor Cienfuegos could avoid loss of their offices. The crown and Alburquerque's successor reinstated the two clergymen.[95]

Paradoxically, in 1710 Alburquerque recommended Costela among other cathedral canons to the crown as a "person of my confidence,"[96] while the canon still awaited the final decision on his deportation to Spain. The reason for this apparent contradiction can be found in Alburquerque's conflict with the cathedral chapters of the vacant sees of Mexico and Valladolid. Acting on a *real cédula* dated 2 December 1706, the viceroy insisted on the prerogative of the church vice-patron to send an observer to the process (*oposición*) that examined and selected clergymen for future positions in parishes. The chapters objected. In this traditional patronage conflict, Mexico's chapter even circulated a printed rebuttal.

ECCLESIASTICAL CHAPTER	POSITION
Malpartida Centeno, Diego	dean
Suazo y Coscojales, Diego	archdeacon
Gómez de la Madrid, José	treasurer
Ibañez de la Madrid, José	school master
Avalos, Pedro	canon
Barrera, Ignacio Diez de la	doctoral canon
Flores, Rodrigo	lectoral canon
Franco, Diego	canon
Parcero, Francisco	canon
Villaseñor y Monroy, Antonio de	canon
Millán, Juan	racionero
Narváez, Juan	racionero
Cabañas, ?	medio racionero
González, Miguel	medio racionero
Mendoza, Lorenzo	medio racionero
Vallejo, ?	medio racionero
VICEREGAL PARTY	
Bayón Vandujo, Domingo	canon
Gama, Antonio de	canon
González de Valdeosera, Miguel	canon
Panyagua, Francisco Jiménez	racionero
Castorena, Juan de	medio racionero
Menéndez, Alonso	medio racionero
ARCHIEPISCOPAL PARTY	
Aunisbay y Aznaya, Antonio	precentor
Torres y Vergara, José de	*medio racionero* since 1706, doctoral canon in 1709
Costela, Andrés Pérez de	canon
Parcero Ulloa, Francisco	canon

Sources: ACCM, Actas del Cabildo Eclesiástico, vols. 25, 26; Robles, *Diario*, 3: 288, 308-309; AGI, México 657, cuaderno 2, f. 118v-35; AGI, Indiferente 132, N 98, ff. 1-2v.

Table 10: The Cathedral Chapter of Mexico City in 1706.

Alburquerque retorted by publishing a defence of royal patronage, written by none other than Canon Costela, with support from several colleagues. When the viceroy increased pressure, the ecclesiastical *cabildos* finally backed down. By writing the defence, Costela ingratiated himself with the crown but faced the rejection of the majority of the Mexican chapter, including Canon José de Torres, who had just vouched for him and led the charge against the viceroy.[97]

At least four of the five cathedral capitulars who supported Costela's defence were the viceroy's cronies. These four testified in support of Alburquerque's conduct in his *residencia*.[98] In this case, Costela aligned with the four capitulars. That does clearly not mean that Costela backed the viceregal party in all instances. His position could reflect a regalist attitude or his need to curry favour with the crown or the viceroy. Costela also sought support of those prebendaries close to the duke when he faced deportation to Spain.

Apart from these political and economic conflicts between the viceroy's alliance and his local enemies, little evidence in the sources supports the thesis of a Habsburg conspiracy in Mexico. In a curious draft to the Duke of Florence written after Philip V's death, the Jesuit Cayetano Francisco Javier de Ayala disputed the legitimacy of the Bourbon succession and claimed the throne for himself. Ayala claimed to be the great-grandson of María Ana of Austria and either Philip Baltasar, son of Philip IV of Spain, or the prime minister, Fernando Velanzuela Marquis of Villa Sierra, called *El Duende* (the Phantom). According to Ayala, Doña María Ana's son married the daughter of the Duke of Medinaceli.[99] This is the only documentary evidence, however peculiar, of a local challenging the succession. The author did not in any case flirt with pro-Habsburg arguments. He simply laid claim to the throne for himself.

The true sentiments of colonials for the dynasties are hard to fathom. Having acceded to the throne, Philip asked the merchants and bureaucrats in New Spain to contribute to the cause with a voluntary contribution (*donativo gracioso*). Alburquerque soon complained about the difficulty of raising money. Although he offered his daughter as hostage to the *consulado*, the merchants contributed only meagre amounts.[100] Some smaller cities paid only a few hundred pesos.[101] In 1706 Alburquerque again asked for a loan of one million pesos to the crown and reached this figure only after pressuring the merchants. In 1705 Alburquerque had already forced his enemy Luis Sánchez de Tagle to lend 110,000 pesos to the crown.[102]

Previously, the last Spanish Habsburg king, Charles II, had acquired the approval of Pope Innocent XII to levy a tenth (*décima*) on all Church income in America. The crown argued the funds would be used to expel Scottish Protestant settlers from the Yucatan. Philip seized on this opportunity and reiterated the order on 11 April 1700. In November of that year, Archbishop Elect Ortega y Montañés presented fifteen doubts about the legitimacy of the tax. According to him, the Protestants had already been driven out, and the Mexican clergy resented the fact that the funds would not strengthen the defences of New Spain. Rather, they would be drained off to Spain.[103] When Alburquerque tried to collect the tenth, he met the resistance of the Church. Despite the efforts of the duke and his successors, only a scant 58,350 pesos reached the royal coffers by 1719. The crown had originally envisioned raising half a million pesos from the entire archdiocese, Central America, the Caribbean, and the Philippines.[104]

These episodes do not indicate a principled opposition to the House of Bourbon. The Habsburg kings had tried squeezing the colonies through extraordinary contributions and calls for donations before and had met a similar lacklustre response. The Mexican Church simply resisted any new form of taxation.

In New Spain, many colonials stood by and waited to see who would prevail in the struggle between the Bourbon and Habsburg aspirants. Accustomed to centuries of Habsburg rule, many Mexicans may have supported the Bourbon cause somewhat hesitantly, especially those in the bureaucracy and clergy appointed by the outgoing dynasty. Unlike the Spanish nobles, however, most inhabitants did not immediately stand to lose power or prestige by the ascendancy of the French counsellors at court. Those tied to the Spanish fleet trade could have differed. One cannot entirely exclude the fact that merchant Gregorio Gasco had a critical opinion about the onslaught on the Sevillian *consulado* and the opening of trade to French merchantmen. Defendant Manuel Sousa y Prado, born and raised in Portugal, even admitted to having an affinity for the king of his native country.[105] Nonetheless, the majority of the power elites in New Spain perceived no need to support the Habsburg camp as long as they could co-opt the viceroy into foiling nascent Bourbon reform initiatives. Alburquerque used his powers widely to attack his enemies and those of his clients. Some of these opponents were tied to the Spanish fleet merchants, others sat on the *audiencia*. None of these opponents, however, hatched a pro-Habsburg plot in Mexico. Alburquerque's collusion with certain local interests kept the colony loyal to the new dynasty and, simultaneously, successfully restrained rising royal control.

7

ALBURQUERQUE RESISTS
ROYAL REFORMS

In 1707 the bishop of Oaxaca, Angel de Maldonado, attacked the Dominican friars in his diocese, charging that "the intention of the friars was to destroy the royal patronage of Your Majesty in their parishes."[1] Maldonado suggested a way to defend royal authority in ecclesiastical affairs. In 1704 the prelate recommended turning over ten wealthy parishes administered by the friars to the secular Church, a process called secularization. The monarch, for whom secularization resulted in more influence over the Church, issued a *real cédula* (royal communication) in 1705 that gave the seculars the right to take over the next ten Dominican parishes to vacate. Although the bishop, a regalist or defender of royal authority over the Church, did not obtain the coveted affluent parishes, he made significant inroads into Dominican territory. Viceroy Alburquerque, in contrast, backed the friars in fending off the secular Church. He delayed the execution of the communication until 1706. The duke also opposed the bishop's recommendation to carve new parishes out of existing Dominican ones and have secular clergy administer them. Furthermore, Alburquerque objected to the introduction of a new fee guideline (*arancel*) drafted by the bishop on the grounds that it presented a "strange and impractical novelty."[2] The viceroy supported the corporation in defending its traditional autonomy and rejected changes in the structure of the *ancien régime.*

The role of the bishop of Oaxaca parallels the position of Juan José de Veytia Linage, since 1695 superintendent of the Puebla *alcabala* (a sales tax). With Veytia Linage's appointment, the crown intended to raise tax proceeds from New Spain's second most populous city. By cutting corruption, the superintendent delivered. Soon after the crown also named him accountant of the mercury distribution in the entire realm and judge over illegally arriving ships in Acapulco. Alburquerque again opposed these changes and forged an alliance with those social groups that had benefited from the lax enforcement of treasury laws. The Puebla oligarchy, composed of merchants and clergymen as well as treasury officials and miners, resisted Veytia Linage's work. The superintendent held out with the support of the Council of the Indies. Yet after his death the monarch rescinded most of Veytia Linage's special powers. This phase illustrates that the crown gave temporary commissions to provincial administrators to improve tax collection. This step preceded the 1786 introduction of the intendancy system, a radical reorganization of royal power in the Americas. Alburquerque acted again in a very different manner from the energetic viceroys under the Count-Duke of Olivares or the Marquis of Ensenada who enforced royal interests in the colony. Alburquerque's attitude as a representative of the high aristocracy surely mattered in this conflict. Policies designed to heighten monarchic authority affected his estate's privileges too. The duke followed the argumentation of those defending their privileges by emphasizing the legitimacy of tradition.

Both of these agents of disciplining tendencies, the superintendent and the bishop, held an important and independent position in the colony and took on the interests of social groups or corporations that resisted the rise of crown power. None of them, however, laboured wholly disinterested because Maldonado and Veytia Linage stood to gain from these changes as well.

The Antagonism over the Puebla Alcabala Tax

When the new Bourbon King Philip arrived in Spain in 1701 with his entourage, the political situation appeared calm. Soon, the king and his advisors attempted to reduce some of the inefficiency in the overseas treasury. The monarch ordered the elimination of all supernumerary positions in New Spain and prohibited further *beneficio* of offices, that is, awarding positions in exchange for donations to the crown.³ A *real cédula* dated 6 March 1701 mandated the reduction of the number of officials on the tribunal of accounts to that stipulated in the founding instructions (*ordenanza*).⁴ The crown also suppressed the office of the treasurer of the half real (*medio real*) collected from the Indians to pay for their legal defence and ordered the accountant of tributes to administer the tax.⁵

During his term in office, Alburquerque permitted some changes in the royal treasury. In 1703 Alburquerque decreed a reform in procedure drawing upon recommendations from his precursors and pleas from the tribunal of accounts. The viceroy authorized the junior accountants (*contadores ordenadores*) of the tribunal to summarize the receipts and to relinquish the time-consuming work of copying all receipts and putting them into order. This reduced the large backlog of the receipts that arrived at the tribunal of accounts from the regional treasuries.⁶ The change also suited the accountants on the tribunal, because it reduced their workload substantially.

In 1704 the viceroy also executed a *real cédula* from 21 February 1690 ordering the tighter regulation of the Indian community treasuries. The crown had charged the *audiencia* of La Plata (Buenos Aires, now Argentina) with a review of the *bienes de comunidad* (the Indian community treasuries) that were no longer able to pay their debts (*censos*) or the salaries of the Indian officials.⁷ The *fiscal de lo civil* in Mexico took up the issue and commented that in New Spain few if any indigenous communities possessed a treasury. He proposed a tighter financial oversight over Indian communities by suggesting that in future the district officials (*alcaldes mayores*) approve of any community expenditure. The viceroy should sign off on any transaction surpassing 20 pesos.⁸

Alburquerque and the *fiscal* achieved meagre results with the inquest. The *alcaldes mayores* and some Indian governors usually claimed in their replies to the central authorities that tribute payable to the monarch did not enter into the community treasury. According to the local officials, the towns owned only a little property such as a strip of land or a small herd. The Indians declared they used the community income in the range between 15 to 30 pesos for their town fiestas, for maintaining the local church, and for supporting visiting clergy.⁹ The viceroy dropped the issue, and Spain could not gain additional revenue through these means.

The clash between the duke and the superintendent of the *alcabala* in the city of Puebla de los Angeles demonstrates Alburquerque's resistance to the expansion of royal control and revenues. During the government of the Count-Duke of Olivares, Puebla had already resented rising fiscal demands under the project labelled *Union of Arms*. Olivares attempted with this program to coerce the realms and provinces of the empire into contributing more to the war against the Netherlands, thus releasing Castile from some of her crushing obligations. In 1628 Viceroy Marquis of Cerralvo (in office 1624–1635) coaxed Puebla and Mexico City to accept a raise of the *alcabala* from 2 to 4 per cent.[10]

At the end of the seventeenth century, the crown introduced several superintendencies in the American fiscal administration. These superintendents held commissions, usually limited in duration, for specific tasks dealing with the treasury. They focused on improving yields from a crown monopoly or a specific tax, such as the *alcabala*. During most of the seventeenth century, the *consulado* of Mexico City levied the sales tax of the capital while paying an annual fee to the monarch. Farming out the tax had proved an acceptable solution for the crown, because it could rely on predictable revenue at a fixed date. Yet as the end of the term for the *alcabala* administration in 1677 drew near, the crown quarrelled with the *consulado* about the value and the conditions of the new instalment (*encabezamiento*) of nine years. Anticipating a significant raise in revenue, the crown refused renewing the contract. As the administration reverted to the monarch, the results rose impressively under the watchful eyes of the acting superintendent of the *alcabala* accountancy.

In 1685 the crown confirmed Juan José de Veytia Linage as administrator (*juez administrador*) of the Mexico City *alcabala*. Veytia Linage had purchased this position for at least 14,000 pesos. The monarch formally extended to him the title of a superintendent. Veytia Linage had already previously advanced to a supernumerary superior accountant at the tribunal of accounts in Mexico.[11] Veytia Linage continued to raise revenues effectively in Mexico City. Then in 1696, after twenty years of royal administration, the *consulado* improved its offer for the

Mexico City *alcabala*. The administration reverted to the corporation. Just about at the same time, an imbroglio between the town hall and several merchants of Puebla about the *alcabala* in that city called for a resolution. The crown received only meagre proceeds in New Spain's second-largest city. The monarch applied the same remedy as in Mexico City by seizing the administration in 1695 and appointing Veytia Linage as its superintendent.[12]

Seasoned from his travails in Mexico City, Veytia Linage soon discharged the existing staff and hired new personnel. To levy the *alcabala* on products brought into Puebla effectively, he constructed inspection posts on the incoming roads. Efficacious collection began in 1698, and soon merchants and clerics involved in trade clamoured for an end to the new system. The town hall, the bishop of Puebla, and the cathedral chapter openly challenged Veytia Linage. The *alcalde mayor* colluded with the oligarchy. Bishop Manuel Fernández de Santa Cruz was said to dominate the local political scene to such a degree that he effectively controlled municipal council appointments. Alburquerque and Bishop Fernández forged an alliance through the bishop's brother, who in 1702 accompanied the duke as a page to New Spain.[13] Consequently, the viceroy supported the bishop and his clients in their conflicts with Veytia Linage. Originally, the prospects of building confidence between Veytia Linage and Alburquerque had looked promising. Veytia Linage's uncle thrived under the patronage of the eighth Duke of Medinaceli, prime minister under Charles II and father-in-law of Alburquerque. Yet, because of Veytia Linage's course in the *alcabala* collection, their relationship failed.[14] Veytia Linage expressed his dissatisfaction about *audiencia* ministers who heard legal recourses in violation of his exclusive jurisdiction.[15] Later, Veytia Linage excoriated the conduct of several magistrates who, in conjunction with Alburquerque and his successors, collaborated with the Puebla clique to derail the superintendent's work.[16] While levying the impost, Veytia Linage also received death threats. In 1706 opponents assaulted him while he was travelling on the outskirts of the city. Veytia Linage continued with the *alcabala* collection despite the resistance. He raised the annual tax proceeds in Puebla from 27,000 pesos to 100,000 pesos.[17]

In April 1703 Alburquerque recommended Veytia Linage for the presidency of the *audiencia* of Guadalajara, and in December 1704 for the presidency of Guatemala.[18] Sending Veytia Linage off to Guadalajara or Guatemala would terminate his successful endeavours in Puebla and remove him from the *gobierno* of New Spain. This would have served the oligarchy in Puebla as well as Alburquerque. Yet the Council of the Indies ignored the duke's recommendation and appointed other officials to the presidencies. In 1703 the viceroy called on Veytia Linage to deal with the problem of illegal trade in Acapulco. Veytia temporarily moved to Acapulco and confiscated some ships, among them the *Nuestra Señora de Guadalupe*. This merchantman had arrived from Peru in violation of the ban on intercolonial commerce. Veytia Linage recommended selling both the ship and its cargo, and he received the support of *Fiscal* José Espinosa. Instead, the viceroy, in consultation with his legal advisor, decided simply to charge the captain twice the amount of the regular sales tax. The duke argued that he could not disprove the captain's claim that he had anchored in Acapulco because of the bad weather. When the Council of the Indies got wind of the affair, it rebuked Alburquerque harshly for this decision. On 30 December 1705 the Council appointed Juan José de Veytia Linage as judge of all illegally arriving ships (*juez de arribadas*).[19] Veytia Linage received thus a second commissarial function with exclusive jurisdiction. The Council specified that neither viceroy nor *audiencia* could challenge his decisions. A case could only be appealed to the Council of the Indies in Spain. In the following year Veytia Linage began complaining to the crown about the viceroy's machinations against his work in Acapulco. In Veytia Linage's eyes, Alburquerque attempted to "frustrate any operations that could be favourable to the royal service."[20] In 1709 the superintendent apparently had enough. He asked for a release from the task in Acapulco, maintaining that he needed to relocate to Puebla to supervise the effective collection of the sales tax. The Council of the Indies, however, rejected Veytia Linage's plea.[21]

The most serious conflict between Veytia Linage and the viceroy arose over the sale of mercury. In 1709 the crown split the responsibility for mercury sales from the tribute collection. Traditionally, these functions had been united in the accountancy of mercury and Indian tributes (*contaduría de azogues y tributos*).[22] The accountancy was part of the

Mexico City treasury staffed by royal officials. The viceroy as superintendent of the royal exchequer also oversaw the accountancy. The crown now endowed the mercury administration with exclusive (*privativa*) jurisdiction along the lines of the superintendency of the *alcabala* and terminated the viceroy's authority to monitor this branch. The mercury administration was not restricted to a certain region as in the case of the *alcabala*. Rather, it held jurisdiction over the entire viceroyalty with the aim of improving the distribution of mercury and the collection of remittances. This task then became the third independent commissarial office for Veytia Linage. He also received an annual allowance of 1,000 pesos for this task (*ayuda de costa*).[23]

With his customary zeal Veytia Linage put the mercury distribution on a new footing by excluding the traditional circles from its administration. He negotiated a lower price for the mercury transportation from the fleet anchoring in Veracruz to Puebla, saving the fisc 8,000 pesos. In Puebla he rented a suitable storage site and hired several trustworthy officials to manage distribution. These measures cut costs at the expense of those treasury officials who had traditionally profited from the distribution. In 1709 Veytia Linage reported to the Council of the Indies that the viceroy, the tribunal of accounts, and various treasury officials threatened to sabotage the success of the new quicksilver administration. The crown called the duke to order. When the Spanish fleet left Veracruz in 1709, however, Alburquerque expressed his discontent. The duke began circulating a rumour among miners that Veytia Linage only accepted cash for mercury while raising the price. In fact, Veytia Linage demanded 900 pesos more for a *quintal* (one hundred Castilian pounds or forty-six kilograms) of quicksilver than customary. As the conflict escalated, the duke exiled Veytia Linage's accountant from Puebla.[24]

On 11 November 1709 the duke assembled a junta of ministers drawn from the *audiencia* and the treasury to discuss the issue. The members of this general junta consisted only of handpicked *oidores*, such as José de Luna, and loyal treasury officials, such as Antonio Gómez Lobato. The junta lamented the sad state of the Spanish fortresses (*presidios*) in New Spain and the Caribbean. The junta suggested spending all proceeds from the mercury sale to support the military posts in the urgency of the war. The ministers decided with this recommendation to ignore royal orders explicitly giving Veytia Linage jurisdiction over mercury.[25] Veytia Linage responded to this affront by sending the viceroy a copy of his secret instructions that outlined his prerogatives. The viceroy disregarded the correspondence and ordered the treasuries of the colony to send all their reserves, including those from the mercury sale, to Veracruz. In the summer of 1710 the windward armada shipped the funds off to the fortresses in the Caribbean.[26] The viceroy's alliance with the traditional bureaucracy and the miners had dealt a serious blow to Veytia Linage's project. Financial crisis loomed for him. While the viceroy had stripped Veytia Linage of his proceeds, the superintendent still had to pay the fixed costs for the mercury administration, especially salaries. Veytia Linage managed by transferring funds from the Puebla *alcabala,* and much depended on Madrid's response to the crisis.

Veytia Linage had ingratiated himself with the administration in Madrid and, in particular, with the Council of the Indies, even after the purge of councillors in 1706. Consequently, when news of Alburquerque's scheme reached Madrid, the *fiscal* of the Council of the Indies in attendance at a special junta on this issue reacted sternly. He censured the viceroy and the Mexican ministers who had decided to deliver the funds to the Caribbean fortresses. The *fiscal* deemed all the justifications, including the alleged necessity of the fortresses, as manoeuvres to discredit the new mercury administration. The crown prosecutor recommended approving all the measures taken by Veytia Linage and suggested upholding the superintendent's honorary seat on the Council of the Indies. The *fiscal* sought a further strengthening of Veytia by conferring on him civil and criminal jurisdiction over his employees that could only be challenged in the Council of the Indies. This jurisdiction would then bypass the regular course of justice through the *alcaldes ordinarios* (municipal councillors) of Puebla and the *audiencia* of Mexico City. They had amply demonstrated their hostility to Veytia Linage.[27]

The strong position of Juan José de Veytia Linage signified a legal check on viceregal power. The viceroy had lost supervision over three important parts of the royal treasury: The *alcabala* in Puebla, the mercury distribution throughout New Spain, and the control of illegal trade in Acapulco. The crown also appointed Veytia *alcalde mayor* of Puebla, so that he controlled the local judiciary and tax collection and influenced the municipal council.[28] The local oligarchy had dominated these offices for decades and considered them their birthright. As a result Veytia's opponents assaulted him politically with a stream of complaints to the Council of the Indies. Veytia received the support of the Council of the Indies and held out.

The special mercury junta convened in Madrid in 1711 affirmed that the duke had disobeyed royal communications in order to undermine the new treasury arrangement. The viceroy intended to protect his allies who siphoned off funds from the treasury, and he favoured the miners by charging them less than mandated. The junta recommended castigating all ministers who had participated in the scheme with a fine of 300 pesos and suggested a penalty of 100,000 pesos for the duke.[29]

This episode shows that Madrid tried to clean up the royal exchequer in New Spain, but there was no consistent effort. After Veytia Linage's death, the crown revoked most of the special attributes of his office. The path towards social disciplining meandered. Granting special powers to Veytia Linage reflects a general tendency in early modern European states to tackle problems with temporary commissions. In 1786 the monarch converted these administrators into a permanent institution known as intendancy with a wider range of assignments. The superintendence of *alcabalas* thus constituted one of the precursors of the intendancy system, insofar as a powerful, well-remunerated, and independent officer, increasingly loyal to crown interests, appeared in the province of New Spain and took on the local elites, the viceroy, and the central bureaucracy. The process was decentralizing in character vis-à-vis Mexico City, since the viceroy and the *audiencia* had to relinquish jurisdiction to the provincial official. In particular, the mercury administration (*contaduría de azogues*) relocated from the capital to Puebla. Nonetheless, by joining the *alcabala* and mercury office with the *alcaldía mayor*, jurisdiction was also centralized on a district level. The metropolis gained influence over a provincial city where, so far, locals had conducted politics without considerable outside interference.

The Secularization of Indian Parishes in Oaxaca

Secularization in Oaxaca resembles the Puebla conflict in that a proponent of royal authority clashed with the viceroy allied to local groups who opposed the rise of crown power. In Oaxaca, the bishop took on the Dominican monks. In early sixteenth-century New Spain, the mendicant orders had formed the spearhead of the mission. These friars or regulars lived in principle by strict rules (*regula*) in monasteries. Dominican, Franciscan, and Augustinian monks, however, did not withdraw into seclusion. Rather, they continued to administer the sacraments to Indians in their parishes after the establishment of Spanish order. In comparison, the priests of the secular church lived in the world or in the age (*saeculum*). The parish priest resided close to the parochial church within the community and his bishop supervised the ministry.[30]

In the eyes of the crown, the task of friars was to missionize. The monarch permitted them to serve their parishes as a privilege until enough secular (also called diocesan) clergymen were available to replace the regulars. By the late sixteenth century, the monarch began to turn over several parishes from the friars to the secular clergy, a process known as secularization.

Secularization continued in the later seventeenth century. The state sought to gain more control over the Church, which at times could be a formidable power contender. The reform program of the Count of Oropesa, president of the Council of Castile since 1684 and prime minister from 1685 until 1691, included an attack on Church privileges. Oropesa called for a halt to new religious foundations and a temporary suspension of ordinations to reduce excessive recruitment of priests. The prime minister also assaulted the powers of the Inquisition, especially its jurisdiction in civil and criminal cases. Although most of these measures faltered, the state again had exerted pressure on the Church.[31]

The renewed secularization in New Spain in the late seventeenth century has to be seen within the context of Oropesa's onslaught on the Church. By wresting parishes from the regulars, the crown gained influence over the Church, because the monarch could not invest the regular prelates or the friars administering the parishes. These decisions were made in Rome or within the order itself. In contrast, the monarch appointed the secular bishops and could influence the nomination of parish priests by choosing one of three candidates suggested by the clergy. Secularization also suited the interests of the diocesan clergy, who enviously eyed the wealth of the regulars and rejected their independence. In 1573 the crown had already rescinded the privileges of the regulars in matters involving marriage and the *Ordenanza de Patronazgo* (the patronage ordinance) of 1574 rolled back their independence further.[32]

During the late seventeenth century the monarch backed the seculars in their conflict with the friars in the diocese of Guadalajara. In 1678 the bishop sequestered two regular parishes. In 1708 the prelate recommended to the Council of the Indies the secularization of the entire diocese, arguing that a large number of clergy were unemployed while the Franciscans administered forty-one of seventy-six parishes in the diocese. Gradually, the secular Church took control of the parishes until at the end of the eighteenth century the Franciscans only retained two.[33]

Philip V appointed Angel Maldonado as bishop of Oaxaca shortly after acceding to the throne. Maldonado had received a doctorate in theology from the University of Alcalá and then joined the Cistercian order. The king designated him as his personal secretary and confessor, both titles probably honorific. Maldonado left the court in Madrid and took possession of his see on 2 July 1702.[34]

After his arrival in Oaxaca, Maldonado rushed straight into battle by inspecting the parishes in the densely populated Villa Alta region, located in the mountainous north of the diocese. The Council of Trent had mandated these visitations, annually if possible, to ensure that the prelates thoroughly familiarized themselves with their diocese and flock and to reduce absenteeism among the bishops.[35] As was customary, Maldonado also ventured into the Dominican parishes. When the bishop ended his inspection after several years, he had visited one hundred out of the one hundred and sixteen parishes in the diocese. Maldonado proudly pointed out that his was the first thorough *visita* of the bishopric.[36]

The energetic bishop, in tandem with the secular clergy, searched for ways of making inroads into the coveted Dominican territory. On 28 September 1704 Maldonado wrote to the king that the secular Church in Oaxaca administered sixty parishes and the Dominican order forty-five.

Maldonado argued that many secular clerics could not find a ministry or hope to obtain a better one as long as the friars officiated in forty-five *doctrinas*, especially the wealthy ones.[37] In principle, a *doctrina* was a parish administered by the regulars for Indians just beyond the initial stage of conversion, whereas a *curato* referred to an ordinary parish. By the eighteenth century, however, the sources often speak interchangeably of *doctrinas o curatos* for the Indian parishes. The terms evidently had become interchangeable.[38]

In Bishop Maldonado's view, the friars oppressed the Indians and imposed more economic demands on the Indians than the secular clergy did. The Indians not only had to support the priest but also the vicar, other friars, the provincial, and the monastery. According to the bishop, the secular Church controlled its priests more closely than the Dominicans did.[39]

In September 1704 the *promotor fiscal* (the chief advisor on canon law) of the bishopric appealed to the crown in the name of all secular clergy to secularize ten wealthy Dominican parishes located in the fertile valleys of Oaxaca. The *promotor* pointed out that many descendants of the original conquistadors lived in this region. These should benefit from the wealth rather than the Dominicans, who were composed of individuals from many nations.[40]

Thus, the bishop based his demand for secularization on two traditional leitmotifs of regalist conviction: The royal duty to protect the Indians and to increase supervision over the Church, especially over the regulars. The particular argument of the *promotor fiscal* to foster the conquistadors and their offspring strayed somewhat from this regalist line. Favouring the conquistadors had long been publicly avowed policy of the crown, but by the eighteenth century, this idea increasingly collided with the monarchic aim of increasing control over America.

In a *real cédula* to Alburquerque dated 24 November 1705, the king approved of the demands and gave permission to secularize ten parishes in Oaxaca. At the behest of the *fiscal* of the Council of the Indies, who opposed the move, the communication stipulated that the seculars could not simply sequester the wealthiest *doctrinas*. Instead, the Dominicans had to relinquish the first ten parishes to be vacated, usually through the death of the incumbent friar.[41]

The *procurador general* (the representative) of the Dominican province rejected the demands of the bishop by pointing to the insufficient qualification of the secular clergy in Oaxaca. The *procurador* asked the crown to reconsider any change (*novedad*) in the distribution of parishes.[42] The prior of the Santo Domingo monastery in Antequera, fray Jacinto de Coria, also asked the viceroy on 7 July 1706 not to execute the order until Madrid had reconsidered the issue, a suggestion that Angel Maldonado quickly rebutted.[43]

Alburquerque hesitated to execute the *real cédula* immediately, assembling the *real acuerdo* (the joint meeting of viceroy and high court *oidores*) to consider the issue. The ministers recommended suspending the *cédula* and asking the *alcaldes mayores* and prelates of Oaxaca for their views on secularization, especially whether the secular clergy were adequately qualified to replace the regulars.[44] In their answers, the prelates of the Franciscans and the Jesuits cautiously backed the Dominicans, knowing secularization could affect them next. Even the *alcaldes mayores* in Oaxaca supported the friars revealing their attachment to the powerful Dominican order and to the central authorities in Mexico.[45] While the correspondence went back and forth, the viceroy gained time. Alburquerque could also count on support in the Council of the Indies in his opposition to secularization.[46] On 19 November 1706, however, the *fiscal* of the Mexican *audiencia*, José Antonio Espinosa Ocampo, requested the execution of the *real cédula* without further delay. The viceroy finally yielded.[47] On 23 December Maldonado and the secular clergy began sequestrating ten parishes from the Dominicans. Although some Indians resisted, the bishop completed the secularization before 13 April 1707.[48]

As secularization proceeded, Maldonado also aimed at carving new parishes out of existing Dominican ones and introducing a uniform schedule of fees (*arancel*) in the diocese that the secular and regular clerics should charge for ecclesiastical services. On 20 March 1703 he presented his case to the viceroy. The bishop lamented that a great number of Indians in the Villa Alta lived in settlements removed from their corresponding Dominican priests who dwelt in the head towns of the parish (*cabecera*). The Indians could not attend mass or receive the sacraments. As a consequence, idolatry flourished. The bishop suggested a temporary solution until the king reviewed the issue. Maldonado called for dividing twelve of the Dominican *doctrinas* into thirty-two, that is, creating new parishes out of the twelve that were too large to execute their spiritual duties adequately. If the Dominicans could not staff the new parishes, Maldonado offered to appoint secular priests to these ministries.[49] Subsequently, Maldonado asked the viceroy repeatedly to turn over some of the new parishes to the secular Church.[50] Again, the Dominican provincial rejected Maldonado's demands. In order to take out the wind of Maldonado's sails, the provincial agreed to nominate Dominican friars in the remote settlements to improve access to mass and sacraments.[51] Alburquerque and the *real acuerdo* approved of the provincial's measure.[52]

Theological arguments alone did usually not determine politics in colonial Mexico. While appealing to the viceroy, the friars drummed up support in Oaxaca as well as at the viceregal court. Several *alcaldes mayores* from the Oaxaca region eulogized the missionary efforts of the regulars. The *alcalde mayor* of Antequera also provided testimonies from some Indians in Sanatepec and Tecomatlan denying they had ever written to the bishop about the friars' abuses – as Maldonado had claimed.[53] The notaries (*escribano*) in Antequera even asserted that the appointees to the ten recently secularized parishes had bribed the bishop with up to 1,100 pesos to obtain their ministries.[54] Most important, the Dominicans could rely on *Oidor* Baltasar Tovar to represent them in Mexico. Maldonado complained about Tovar's support for the order and reiterated what had been apparent since the Tagle-Cruzat conflict that Tovar stood "in extraordinary favour with the viceroy."[55]

On 1 September 1707 Alburquerque and the *real acuerdo* discussed the question whether the case should be heard at all. Maldonado disavowed the institution's jurisdiction over this case, since under the law he only owed responsibility to his conscience. With Alburquerque and several ministers leaning towards the order, the Dominicans carried the day. The majority of the *acuerdo* upheld the monarch's prerogative to settle the issue. In the meantime the *doctrinas* would remain untouched.[56] After this stinging defeat, the bishop left his see and travelled to Mexico to continue his fight in the capital. When he arrived in Mexico City, he attempted to win over the duke and the duchess. Acting as the viceroy's chaplain, the bishop frequently said mass at the viceregal court. Apart from Maldonado's edifying labour – which he hoped would impress the pious duchess – he also conferred with several *audiencia* ministers. On 19 January 1708 the *real acuerdo* again pondered the issue. Maldonado reported that the majority now supported his suggestions, while the viceroy only registered some "opposing votes."[57] In this situation, Alburquerque called together a junta consisting of three theologians and three attorneys to counsel him.[58] Following *ancien régime* consuetude, at least three of the six handpicked members had benefited from viceregal patronage or were known as confidants. Their consultation would produce the desired results and justify Alburquerque's proceeding in the case. The first member of the junta, the rector of the university, testified for Alburquerque in the viceroy's *juicio de residencia*.[59] The duke had previously appointed the second junta member as a priest in the cathedral, although he was placed second on the proposal list, much to the archbishop's chagrin. In exchange, the archbishop had labelled this junta member as "somewhat confused and stuttering."[60] The third member of the junta, Dr. José de León, was a professor of canon law at the university. He had acted as Alburquerque's legal advisor in several delicate affairs such as interrogating Pedro Sánchez de Tagle after his detention. Alburquerque's favourite, Judge Tovar, who had already recommended León for promotion to the *audiencia* in 1695, established this link.[61]

According to Maldonado, the viceroy opened the junta with the sentence "I have been pleased to call together Your Honours because the Señor Bishop of Oaxaca is wrong."[62] The predictable recommendations of the junta suited Alburquerque, shrewdly repudiating the viceroy's authority to divide the parishes. Instead, the bishop of Oaxaca needed to confer further with the Dominicans. Ultimately, the junta counselled again that the decision rested with the monarch, to whom the Mexican authorities should send all documents. Consequently, the bishop and the friars expressed their variant opinions to the Council of the Indies. Maldonado charged that the viceroy had delayed a solution to the quarrel by interfering with ecclesiastical jurisdiction. In Maldonado's view, Alburquerque displayed an attitude "highly passionate for the Dominicans."[63] The viceroy manipulated the junta and the *real acuerdo* to vote along his lines and openly criticized the bishop's conduct.[64] Alburquerque retorted to these accusations in the same tone.[65]

The issue lingered on until after Alburquerque's departure. On 11 April 1712, the provincial of the Dominicans, the bishop, and several important clergymen in Oaxaca finally discussed the issue to settle their differences. The friars yielded twenty *doctrinas* to the secular Church, which in exchange handed over five to the regulars. The contract also arranged for the division of several parishes, calling for the creation of new ones in some and the installation of friars in others. On 14 June 1713, however, the Council of the Indies threw out the entire agreement, branding it as another scheme by the bishop to secularize further parishes beyond the ten he had already gained in 1705. The Council argued, much like the *real acuerdo* under Alburquerque, that the redistribution of the *doctrinas* fell alone under jurisdiction of the king.[66] In 1707 and 1709 during the hot phase of the peninsular war, the *fiscal* of the Council had already recommended revoking the secularization from 1705.[67]

It is noteworthy that on 25 November 1705 the crown had issued the *real cédula* to secularize the parishes. The monarch risked confrontation with the religious order even as the military situation deteriorated after the Allied invasion in Catalonia. Bishop Maldonado aggressively pursued secularization and the introduction of the fee schedule in the conflict with the Dominican order. Meanwhile Alburquerque sought to delay changes in the traditional arrangement. This conflict had a long history and smouldered on beyond Alburquerque's return to Spain. The issue culminated in the years 1749 to 1756 when the crown mandated the sequestration of a string of parishes. By the end of the colonial period, the secular church administered almost all parishes in New Spain.

8

Reform and Revenge: The Fall of Alburquerque, 1711–1715

Shortly after his accession to the throne, Philip V permitted French warships to enter Mexican ports for repairs. In 1701, in a stunning reversal of traditional Spanish trade policy, the monarch also permitted Gallic men-of-war to trade small quantities in exchange for fresh food.[1] According to several *reales cédulas* (communications from the monarch) of similar content, French frigates defending the sea routes to America were allowed to engage in trade not exceeding 1,000 to 2,000 *livres* in order to pay for provisions and refurbishing.[2] Since the Spanish fleet did not travel to Veracruz between 1700 and 1706, the prices for import goods soared. The Mexicans willingly bought merchandise from the French ships anchoring legally in Veracruz. Very soon, the *consulado* of Seville (the corporation guarding the interests of the Spanish fleet merchants) assailed the French for not observing the stipulations and for trading freely with the locals.

Alburquerque rebutted the contention of the *consulado* on several occasions during his viceroyship, arguing in favour of fewer restrictions on trade among the colonies.[3] He acknowledged that Spanish goods had become scarce. At the same time the duke held that they did not compete with textiles and other merchandise arriving from the Philippines, because the Asian products were cheaper and served mainly the poor. Even if the merchants of the Manila galleon exceeded the legal restrictions and arrived in Mexico with plenty of cargo, the Spanish fleet merchants would not have to fear any competition, because any occasional abundance of Asian goods was siphoned off to Peru.[4] Rather than enforcing the strict trade laws, Alburquerque argued that lifting the ban on free trade (*comercio libre*) within the empire would strengthen the crown. Since the ban had become effective, the royal treasury had lost 200,000 silver ducats in sales taxes from intercolonial trade. The duke also claimed that in Mexico alone 13,000 textile looms producing for Peru had gone out of business as a result of the restrictions. The families who had worked them lived in miserable poverty.[5] Alburquerque believed that it was impossible to curb contraband commerce in the Pacific, and all efforts of the viceroys had failed. Confiscating illegal cargo only sent prices soaring and resulted in higher profits for the traders. The true problem, according to the duke, lay with the great merchants of the Spanish fleet. They bought up merchandise to heighten scarcity and thus artificially forced up prices. Foreign traders damaged imperial interests by buying into the Spanish fleet and running contraband commerce.

Although Alburquerque's observations were from a modern perspective surprisingly accurate in some regard, they also served his own interests. The viceroy knew well that the Manila galleon shipped mostly luxury goods such as silk, porcelain, and so forth, and did not supply the indigent. His concerns demonstrated the economic distortions of the impractical commercial rules and defended the mercantile interests of his constituency. Several of the merchants linked to the viceroy prospered through contraband trade and stood to profit from a relaxation of the rules on intercolonial trade. Alburquerque's position also justified his clement clampdown on contraband commerce, for which he was soon to draw fire from Madrid. Because the duke could not directly attack the Spanish trade houses for political reasons, he lambasted foreigners who dominated the official overseas trade. Thus, he could criticize the oligopoly trade as damaging to Spain's imperial interests without criticizing the official policy.

Alburquerque's view coincided with the 1705–1709 attempt of the crown to confine the power of the *consulado* of Seville. This anticipated later policies in favour of less restricted trade. In 1765 the Marquis of Esquilache opened the Caribbean Islands to free trade with important ports in Spain, and José de Gálvez extended this idea with the decree of 1778 (*reglamento de comercio libre*) to the colonies except Mexico and Venezuela. These regulations were designed to stimulate the local economy, improve royal taxation, and reduce foreign competition. The crown expected these changes to translate into a stronger defence of its American dependencies. In part, the new policies were due to the recognition that the old system was untenable and that previous attempts to enforce it had shipwrecked on economic reality. Gálvez, however, did not envision an unrestricted trade of the colonies with other states. The laws of the late eighteenth century still sought to maintain the protectionist framework.[6]

Despite the permits for the French men-of-war in the early years of Philip's reign, neither the crown nor the *consulado* of Seville agreed with the views of the viceroy on inter-American commerce. The crown repeatedly censured Alburquerque for absolving those merchants who arrived illegally from Peru. Under the law royal officials should confiscate these ships and their merchandise and punish the captains. The duke, however, only charged elevated sales taxes. In 1705 Madrid fined Alburquerque's legal advisors 2,000 pesos for counselling not to enforce the laws.[7]

On 23 August 1708 General Andrés de Pez, who commanded the Spanish fleet anchored in Veracruz, raised serious allegations against the duke. Pez wrote to Gaspar de Pinedo, secretary of the Council of the Indies, that Alburquerque tolerated and profiteered from illegal trade. According to the general, Alburquerque had permitted eighty ships from France and the Canary islands to anchor in Veracruz to sell foreign goods. (Although subjects of the Castilian crown, Canarian tradesmen frequently did not purchase their goods at the Sevillian exchange. Rather, they shipped merchandise from third countries to America.) Pez complained that French merchants systematically exceeded the limits stipulated by the *real cédula* from 1703. They bribed the royal officials to circumvent the sales tax (*alcabala*) in the value of about three million pesos. By abundantly supplying the market, prices fell and, according to Pez, the Spanish merchants of his fleet lost three fourths of their profits. In Pez's view, the viceroy deliberately turned a blind eye on the contraventions.[8] The general's vitriol against Alburquerque reflects a mercantilist vision of Spanish trade, which the Sevillian *consulado* also espoused.[9]

In 1710 another author anonymously alleged the duke's malfeasance in a similar fashion. According to this letter, Alburquerque charged every foreign ship entering Veracruz between 30,000 and 60,000 pesos. Additionally, the duke's agents in the port bought illegal merchandise and sold it in Mexico City at a 100 to 130 per cent mark up. While price caps for Spanish import goods mandated by the duke kept prices down, Alburquerque forced some oligopoly merchants to sell their goods to his agents Julián de Osorio and Augustín de Palma. These merchants then waited until the revocation of the price ceilings and, when market prices soared again, they sold the merchandise. Furthermore, the viceroy traded through the Manila galleon. The author finally claimed that the royal officials in Veracruz colluded with the viceroy, accepting bribes from the French merchants. The custom officials set aside a fifth of the extortions as a slush fund to finance possible indemnities in case of a royal investigation. They labelled this procedure *engordar el cochino*, to fatten the pig – a custom already well established in the seventeenth century.[10] When Alburquerque travelled to Veracruz in 1709 to supervise work on the fortifications, he purportedly confiscated half of the *cochino*, arguing that the remainder would be enough to buy a crown pardon if necessary. The anonymous author also insinuated that the duke had extorted friars seeking prelacies. Furthermore, Alburquerque had withheld a percentage from remittances (*libranzas*) from Spain.[11] This second letter reiterates Andrés de Pez's accusation in more detailed fashion. Several other oligopoly merchants as well as the notary of Diego Fernández Santillán's 1706 fleet also made accusations of contraband trade and abuses in Mexico.[12]

In a very different circumstance, a witness who supported the clerics assailed by Alburquerque in the conspiracy trials confirmed the truthfulness of the contraband claims. According to this purveyor of the Inquisition, the merchants of Mexico City and the viceroy collaborated in transporting contraband goods from Veracruz to the capital. Two *regidores* (members of the town council) in Veracruz, the castellan of the port, and Alburquerque's pages bought textiles from French merchantmen. They stored some of the merchandise in the Jesuit college in Veracruz before carrying it to Mexico City. The Count of Miravalle (senior consul of 1705) and a viceregal friend both received the merchandise outside of the capital.[13] Judge (*oidor*) Miguel Calderón, who was tied to a powerful merchant family, turned a blind eye on the unlawful import. The textiles were smuggled into the capital hidden in sugar packages and sold.[14]

So far, Alburquerque had remained in fairly good standing with the crown. He had suffered harsh criticism in the Tagle-Cruzat wedding and on trade issues. Yet Alburquerque did not face serious consequences. In 1707 the Council of the Indies even extolled the duke's decision to dispatch the fleet from Veracruz despite the menacing British squadron anchored in Jamaica. The fleet delivered one million silver pesos to Spain, where the Bourbons urgently needed the funds for the war. The Council of the Indies consequently recommended the duke for the order of *cordon bleu* or the *toison de oro*. The king chose the lesser *toison de oro*.[15] To date, the crown did not overly frown on its viceroy in New Spain.

In summer 1708, things began to look darker for the viceroy. On 17 August the king ordered him to investigate contraband trade in New Spain more thoroughly and appointed the supernumerary *Oidor* Félix González de Agüero as inspector (*visitador* or *juez de comisión*) of illegal commerce.[16] The Bourbon king at this time still struggled against the allied forces. The commission for González de Agüero also has to be seen as a means of confiscating funds and channelling them into the peninsula military machine. In the consulta from 10 December 1708, the Council of the Indies furthermore recommended providing the *fiscal* of the Council of the Indies with a copy of Pez's incriminations for the *juicio de residencia* of the duke.[17]

During González de Agüero's investigation, customs officials in Veracruz confessed to accepting kickbacks from merchants and French captains. One trader admitted bribing the *corregidor* and the officials of Veracruz with 89,400 pesos to let French ships enter the port and sell their merchandise. The officials each received 610 pesos and the *corregidores* 12,400 pesos. In 1709 the viceroy intervened when royal officials confiscated the French frigate *Daubenton*. Alburquerque ordered the ship and all its merchandise returned to its captain without penalty.[18]

When González de Agüero concluded his inquiry, he imprisoned several officials but disregarded calls in the Council of the Indies for harsh prison sentences, transfer to Spain, or the death penalty as stipulated by law.[19] The *oidor* charged some merchants several thousand pesos as an indemnity (*indulto*), while the royal officials faced stiffer fines. Two officials together contributed 50,000 pesos to seek a pardon from the monarch. In November 1711, the Council of the Indies applauded González de Agüero for raising 185,673 pesos in indemnities, calculating the *oidor* would be able to collect a total of 300,000 pesos.[20] González de Agüero's success should, however, not be interpreted as great zeal for the royal cause. The *oidor* had bought his office and had to collaborate with colonial society to recoup his investment. Subsequently, González pursued his own interests so successfully that Inspector Francisco Garzarón dismissed him from the bench in 1719.

Possibly because of González de Agüero's collusion, most of the culprits escaped with comparatively light sentences. None of the accused lost their posts in the financial administration or faced any physical punishment. Even the indemnities seem rather low in relation to the profits drawn from the illegal trade. With the support from their contingency fund, the convicted officials did not succumb to bankruptcy. Rather, they returned to business as usual at the end of the inspection. Since the crown was in no position to replace contraband trade with the ineffective Spanish oligopoly on commerce, the penalties levied from the royal officials had evolved into a form of import tariff. Foreign traders bribed the royal officials. These pocketed most of the funds and occasionally spent the remainder to buy a royal pardon after an inspection.

Beyond González de Agüero's inquiry and the concurrent irritations in the Council of the Indies, nothing unusual presaged Alburquerque's end of tenure in 1710. The king appointed *Oidor* Juan de Valdés as judge of Alburquerque's *juicio de residencia* (the comprehensive assessment of the conduct of any outgoing royal official) as stipulated by the law.[21] Drawing upon Andrés de Pez's complaints, the *fiscal* of the Council instructed Valdés to elucidate Alburquerque's role in the illegal entry of French ships and the obstruction of the sales fair in Veracruz in 1708. The *fiscal* also ordered Valdés to verify if Alburquerque had demanded bribes from crown-appointed *alcaldes mayores* (district officials) and provincials of the religious orders before allowing them to assume their offices.[22]

The *juicio de residencia* consisted of two parts, the public and the secret inquiry. Inhabitants of the colony, including Indians, could complain to the judge in the public section about the conduct of the outgoing official. Two merchants accused the duke of undermining the monopoly to sell meat in Mexico City (*abasto de carne*). The merchant who had acquired the 1702 monopoly contended that Alburquerque's majordomo José Alvarez del Valle illegally sold licences to market meat for 1,500 pesos a year, chipping away at the profits of the monopolist and the crown.[23]

It seems impossible that Alburquerque did not tacitly approve of Alvarez del Valle's conduct. The viceroy may even have profited from it. Probably, Alburquerque and his majordomo had not even invented the scheme. They solely continued a time-tested practice from their predecessors. Most likely, the monopolist had received wind of Alburquerque's falling out of grace and sought to enhance his profit by charging the duke's majordomo in the *juicio de residencia*.[24] By fostering competition, the viceroy and his majordomo may have contributed inadvertently to lowering meat prices. In any case, *Oidor* Valdés struck down the complaint of the meat monopolist.

The merchant Juan Fernández Cacho had obtained the exclusive right to supply the city with meat in 1708. This plaintiff alleged that he had already invested heavily in livestock when Alburquerque revoked his rights and entrusted the town hall with the meat monopoly. According to Fernández Cacho, his livestock perished and he suffered substantial loss.[25] He travelled to the court in Spain to seek redress for his damages, while his wife pursued the claim in Mexico. After reviewing the case, Valdés argued that he could not resolve the issue, because the suit was pending in Spain.[26] Although the claims against the viceroy may have been reasonable, the *oidor* turned the public inquest into an ineffectual tool.

On 15 August 1710 the Council of the Indies settled the claims of Fernández Cacho. The institution ordered the *cabildo civil* (town council) of Mexico City to compensate the merchant by handing over the city's herds to him. The viceroy was to reimburse all penalties that he had imposed on the merchant for challenging his orders. Although the Council of the Indies severely castigated the town hall, Alburquerque yet again escaped with a stern admonishment.[27]

In the private inquest of Alburquerque's *juicio de residencia*, a group of witnesses responded to a written questionnaire about the official's conduct. Few criticized the duke, and none substantiated the crown allegations of contraband trade. As the judge carefully orchestrated the choice of witnesses, most of them are familiar as staunch allies of the duke. Among them the *corregidor* of Mexico, the treasurer Antonio Gómez Lobato, and merchant Juan de Garaicoechea lauded Alburquerque's conduct. Ironically, even González de Agüero, who was still investigating contraband commerce, testified in favour of the duke.[28]

To rebut the accusations of tolerating contraband commerce, Alburquerque's attorneys claimed that since 1705 the duke had repeatedly published orders prohibiting illegal trade and exhorting the royal officials to exercise vigilance. The duke also referred to a 1706 *parecer* (a recommendation on political issues) by the Mexican *consulado* applauding the duke's actions against contraband. The body rejected the necessity of an investigation and jettisoned the reproaches of the fleet merchants about damages caused by French importers. Furthermore, the *real acuerdo*, the joint meeting of the viceroy and the *audiencia* judges, had seconded the Mexican *consulado* in 1706 with a similar advisory statement (*parecer consultativo*). Yielding to all these arguments, the lawyers contended, the duke had not ordered an inquest into the matter.[29]

Alburquerque knew that at this time González Agüero investigated the viceroy's implication in contraband schemes. The duke returned to Cadiz in 1713, over two years after handing over power. Possibly Alburquerque intended to influence the inspection and his own *juicio de residencia* by extending his stay in the colony. Additionally, the judge of the *residencia*, Juan de Valdés, favoured collaboration with the duke, since he had acquired his *audiencia* position for 6,000 pesos.[30] Consequently, when Valdés concluded the *juicio de residencia*, he declared Alburquerque innocent of all applicable charges.[31]

In light of these findings, it is somewhat surprising that José María Mariluz Urquijo considered the *juicios de residencia* an efficient tool for controlling royal officials.[32] This researcher concedes that during some phases of the Spanish empire the rigour of the process relaxed and illicit agreements between judge and defendant resulted in inappropriate sentences. Nonetheless, the mere threat of the *juicio de residencia* reined in abuse of office. Complaints by the viceroy of Peru, the Count of Chinchón, corroborate the effectiveness of the *juicio de residencia*. The official remarked that he enjoyed the honour of entering the viceregal palace under a canopy, yet faced the humiliation of justifying his activities at the end of his tenure.[33]

Mariluz Urquijo's defence of the *juicios de residencia* challenges the judgment of two prestigious scholars of the old guard, Clarence H. Haring and Ernst Schäfer, who emphasize the frequently unreliable character of the process. In their view, strong ties of a high crown official to the court in Madrid could save the official from accusations and prosecution. Witnesses followed their personal interests, and enemies tried to avenge old grudges.[34] Haring argues that despite all problems the *juicio de residencia* remained a useful tool especially for controlling the lower levels of administration: "In case of less important officials the *residencia* was probably more effective than for the viceroys. For most of them throughout three centuries of colonial rule, the residencia, ... served as a formidable institution of royal control."[35] Historian Horst Pietschmann, on the other hand, holds the diametrically opposed opinion that the *residencias* of *alcaldes mayores* had become almost ineffective by the eighteenth century. The outgoing district officials customarily bribed their judges with sums between 800 and 1,000 pesos. This scholar, however, emphasizes the effectiveness of the *residencia* in reining in higher officials.[36]

Four types of inspections developed over time. First, the *visita de comisión* comprised a targeted inspection of one treasury, such as the one in Veracruz, or of a group of royal officials, with the principal aim of restoring the orderly functioning of that particular body or group. Second, the *visita general* constituted an occasional but sweeping inquest, such as José de Gálvez's *visita* of the royal financial administration or an inspection of the entire administration of the viceroyalty. Thirdly, the crown usually employed *pesquisas* as a secret punitive measure of criminal character against one official or a particular treasury (*caja*) to redress a specific and limited wrong. Finally, the *juicio de residencia* routinely assessed the conduct of all outgoing royal officials.

French historian Michel Bertrand demonstrates that between 1660 and 1730 royal delegates conducted a *visita* or *pesquisa* every five or six years in New Spain.[37] Some of them failed, such as Francisco Pagabe's *visita general*, whereas others unveiled substantial infractions, such as the Veracruz treasury inquiry of *Alcalde del crimen* Jerónimo de Osilia y Rayo in the 1720s. Backed by energetic Viceroy Marquis of Casafuerte, Osilia y Rayo suspended three royal officials.[38] Bertrand contends that not all royal control mechanisms in Mexico foundered automatically. Instead, their success depended on the political alliances of inspectors and defendants.[39]

The *visita* and *pesquisa* can be distinguished from the *juicio de residencia* by the habitual character of the latter. This is not the place to analyze exhaustively the efficacy of this instrument in the early eighteenth century. A cursory review of nine available *residencias* of high crown officials between 1700 and 1755 reveals, however, that the *residencia's* secret inquest regularly turned into hagiology of the assessed.[40] Therefore, this process offered very limited utility for the crown. The public inquiry could be more effective, because opponents used them to avenge perceived wrongs. Nevertheless, the judges found few officials guilty. Only one judge suggested fining Archbishop Juan de Ortega y Montañés, interim viceroy in the period from 1700 to 1702, 5,480 pesos for having appointed *alcaldes mayores* who had not yet passed the *residencias* of their previous offices. Petitioned by the archbishop's attorney, the Council of the Indies eventually waived the penalty.[41] Although some *oidores*, such as Miguel Calderón de la Barca, struggled with serious allegations of abuse, the trial usually was guaranteed to declare the innocence of the official. Arguably, the process's favourable conclusion depended more on the relation between the judge and the outgoing official than on a true finding of facts.

By this time the crown knew of the secret inquiry's limited effectiveness. The 1715 special junta in Madrid that adjudicated Alburquerque pondered the statements of witnesses with considerable suspicion. The unanimous testimony in favour of Alburquerque caused the junta to state that "favour disguises, power obscures, and timidity dissimulates" the facts surrounding the viceroy's conduct.[42] Witnesses did not speak out against higher officials. Previously, crown officials had criticized the utility of the process. As a result Madrid began dispensing with this procedure in 1757.[43]

Political changes at the Spanish court also had their impact on Alburquerque's fate. With the recall of the French ambassador, Amelot, and the apparent military victory over the allies, the king's counsellors increasingly guarded Spanish interests. In March 1711 a special junta (labelled the *junta de azogues* or mercury junta) discussed Alburquerque's manoeuvres to derail Juan José de Veytia Linage's quicksilver distribution.[44] The presenting *fiscal* of the Council of the Indies summed up the allegations against Alburquerque and described the former viceroy's conduct acerbically as "disobedience, feigned resistance and ... persistent excess" and suggested a penalty of 100,000 pesos.[45] The majority of the junta voted along with the *fiscal*. The Councillor Alonso de Araciel, however, disagreed on the duke's punishment and instead recommended appointing a minister to investigate the treasury in New Spain. Such an investigation could easily have rendered similar results as Alburquerque's *residencia*, absolving him.

All members of the junta, none of them a titled noble, sat on the Council of the Indies. Judging from their background, most of the members were allies of the French party around the Princess de Ursins. Two councillors had survived politically from the Habsburg period, among them the dissenting magistrate. This possibly explains his reluctance to condemn the duke.[46] At this time, the junta did not take any further action against Alburquerque.

On 22 June 1711 Philip entrusted the *visitador* Francisco de Pagabe with the bookkeeping review of the Mexican mercury supply for the silver mines.[47] The king also excluded the Council of the Indies from further jurisdiction in this particular case. In November 1711 a special commission (*junta de indultos*) charged with the sentencing of royal officials implicated in illegal commerce agreed with *Oidor* González de Agüero that royal officials in Mexico could not have tolerated this traffic without Alburquerque's consent. Even if the king decided not to sentence the duke, the junta urged an indemnity corresponding to the "grave guilt."[48] In comparison to the mercury junta, this junta owed its unanimous vote on this issue to the absence of Councillor Alonso de

Araciel, who had previously voted in favour of delaying a sentencing of the duke.[49]

Alburquerque's ties to some councillors also explain why the crown did not try the case in the Council of the Indies.[50] Juan de Otalora Bravo de Laguna, a patron and kinsman of Alburquerque's secretary Juan de Estacasolo y Otalora, sat on the Council since 1708. Along with one of the "old guard" councillors, Otalora voted in 1712 against granting a seat on the Council to the Mexican *Oidor* José Joaquín Uribe, an enemy of the duke.[51]

When Alburquerque finally arrived in Cadiz in 1713, more than two years after the end of his term, the king seized his entire luggage, including a respectable sum of 150,000 pesos.[52] The duke travelled towards Madrid to enter the court and present himself to the king, but Philip ordered him to remain in Villaverde just outside of Madrid.[53] The French Counsellor Jean Orry, as *veedor general de la real hacienda* responsible for supervising the royal exchequer,[54] began negotiations with the duke. On a convenient occasion, the Count of Moriana, in charge of administering the war treasury,[55] indicated to Alonso de Herrera, Alburquerque's secretary, that a substantial donation to the monarch would help the duke in the light of the serious charges against him. Soon enough, an unnamed individual approached Orry's aide Moriana and offered a donation of 162,000 pesos in the name of the duke. Orry made it clear that he considered this offer wholly insufficient. Moriana recalled, "I reported to him [Orry] and he said if this ever occurred to me I should strive much harder."[56] In Orry's opinion, Alburquerque needed to provide at least 1.5 million pesos. "This notice," wrote Moriana, "made the heart of Don Alonso sink, and equally that of the duke and the duchesses."[57] Moriana referred here to the duke's mother, wife, and Alburquerque's secretary. Alonso Herrera continued to call on Orry's aide and raised the offer from 200,000 to 300,000 and finally to 500,000 pesos. Orry, however, had given orders not to receive Herrera until the duke was willing to pay at least one million. The monarch also ordered the duke to retire to Segovia – further away from the machinations at court. When, during the negotiations, the duke had exhausted all potential funds, his mother spectacularly offered to add her private jewellery, elevating the proffered donation to 700,000 pesos. Orry's representative remarked that the king appreciated Alburquerque's repeated pecuniary remittances to Spain in moments of great urgency for the monarchy. If the duke and duchess could add just another 50,000 pesos to the sum, the duke would likely be absolved of all charges. Alburquerque would be allowed to leave his exile in Segovia and return to his home in Madrid to reunite with his family.[58]

After Orry's ouster in the first week of February 1715 and the changes in the government of Spain, a special junta composed of an entirely different set of people conjoined on this matter in June 1715. Unlike the mercury and the indemnity junta of 1711, this special junta drew no personnel from the Council of the Indies. The closest relationship was that of one member's brother who sat on the Council. All ministers of the 1715 junta were drawn from the Council of Castile, by then the most influential conciliar body of the state. Of these six junta members, Charles II had named three. With the fall of Orry and the powerful Princess des Ursins and the ascent of the so-called Italian clique, some councillors of the Habsburg period rose again in esteem provided they had not conspired with the archduke. Three councillors owed their advance to Philip V. At least four had taught law as chairs (*catedráticos*) at one of the great Spanish universities, Alcalá, Salamanca, or Valladolid. Two individuals had recently received titles of nobility.[59]

In the consulta from 24 June 1715, the junta weighed the charges against the duke. The ministers found that Alburquerque had tolerated and profited from illegal commerce with French frigates, thus damaging Spanish commerce and depriving the king of taxes. Additionally, the viceroy had not properly supervised the royal officials who levied taxes on French men-of-war. The junta jettisoned all other charges, arguing that there was no clear further offence they could penalize. Numerous witnesses stood against the accusations that the general of the fleet, Andrés de Pez, and the anonymous author levelled. Nonetheless, the junta found the uniformity of the testimonies exculpating the viceroy curious in light of the massive contraband trade in New Spain. The junta considered Alburquerque at least negligently ignorant of these activities. Given the legal problems, the junta believed that the duke could be formally sentenced to a penalty of 100,000 pesos. Yet the most convenient way of resolving the issue would be to accept the 700,000 pesos that the duke and his mother had offered as a sign of their zeal for the monarchy. The king should absolve the duke with this extrajudicial indemnity from the charges in the *juicio de residencia*, the inquiry into trade in Veracruz, and the investigation of the mercury distribution.[60]

Whereas Jean Orry had bothered little about the legal problematic, the junta ministers, trained jurists, had some trouble adjudicating the case. Considering the irksome problems of reaching a formal conviction of Alburquerque, they suggested that accepting the "donation" was preferable to a penalty of 100,000 pesos. This way, the monarch received the indemnity and the duke avoided the embarrassment of a formal trial.

After 6 July 1715 the king discussed the matter with his confessor Guillaume Daubenton. Although the French Jesuit had replaced the former confessor Jean Robinet, a close collaborator of Orry's, this change did not signify relief for Alburquerque. Daubenton closely followed the recommendations of the junta and drew up a note in French – for the king had considerable trouble mastering Spanish. The confessor argued "that the king may receive without scruples the seven hundred thousand pesos in question from the Duke of Alburquerque."[61] Daubenton held that the junta had found Alburquerque guilty on the count of illegal trade. The duke himself had offered the indemnity voluntarily, and finally, the duke had thus admitted his transgressions in order to evade a formal trial. For these three reasons, the confessor recommended accepting the indemnity.

The king apparently showed some concern as to whether the junta had dealt adequately with the duke. Since the process involved a member of Spain's premier stirpes, the king became involved in the matter. The somewhat twisted arguments of the confessor sufficed, and the king agreed to the indemnity.[62] By this time, the duke had been successful in lowering the indemnity from 750,000 pesos to 700,000 pesos. Alburquerque accepted the arrangement and paid most of the sum by September 1715.[63] The king absolved him of all charges, expressed his gratitude for the duke's service, and ordered perpetual silence on this affair.[64]

The crown had not systematically tracked the transgressions of the viceroy over a long period. No dossier of past malfeasance is available, and, for example, the Cruzat-Tagle scandal does not appear in the files, although the crown had severely reprimanded the duke. Alburquerque had ingratiated himself to the monarch by remitting one million pesos to the treasury each of the three times that the fleet crossed the Atlantic. Some tacit understanding governed Alburquerque's tenure suggesting that a person of his rank was entitled to compensation beyond the mere 20,000 pesos annual salary. While the crown warded off the Allies, the affairs of a Mexican viceroy seemed acceptable as long as the colony stayed loyal to the throne.

Several reasons came into play in Alburquerque's fall. The general political weakening of the high aristocracy and especially the trial and death of Alburquerque's brother-in-law Medinaceli eroded much of the viceroy's backing at court. The French party around Orry and Ursins sought to take revenge on a partisan of their formerly feared foe and the entire pro-Habsburg clique. When the various juntas sat in judgement from 1711 through 1715, punishing even the grandees of Spain had lost some of its spectacular character after many of Spain's nobility had fallen into disgrace.

The juntas before Orry's ouster charged Alburquerque on several counts, among others, ironically, for permitting trade with French vessels. Orry himself did not specify the charges against Alburquerque. Willing to serve the Spanish state, he did not stand in the way of prosecuting the duke even on the count of illegal trade.[65] With the fall of *Veedor* Orry, the new party at court (sometimes labelled the Italian) attempted to strengthen Spanish control over trade. The councillors on the 1715 junta judged trade infractions to be the only viable charge against the duke. This change in emphasis reflects the shifts in Spanish commercial policy. In the first years of the Bourbon regime, the French party tacitly approved of the illegal trade between French warships and colonial Americans. King Louis XIV of France considered it among his premier tasks to open the Indies for French commerce and had instructed Philip's entourage correspondingly. In 1705, as a part of this policy, Philip's French advisors launched an investigation into the massive tax evasion at the Sevillian exchange. Merchants regularly paid an indemnity upon arrival of the fleet from the Indies to evade the confiscation of unregistered silver. Substantial bribes – sources mention three million pesos paid on top of the official indemnity – disappeared into the pockets of the royal officials and the Seville *consulado*. The crown imprisoned the priors and consuls of the years 1689 to 1705 and confiscated their property. Yet at this time the Seville *consulado* thwarted attempts to loosen its grip on the profitable system. When Ambassador Amelot left the court in 1709, the crown returned to protecting the mercantilist interests of Spain and increasingly heeded the demands of the *consulado* of Seville. In 1717 the crown released the incarcerated *consulado* officials. In the following year, when the monarch concluded the inspection, he declared the Sevillian priors and consuls "true and good administrators."[66] Well entrenched and with jurisdiction over the international trading community in Seville and Cadiz, the *consulado* staged a comeback in power.[67] The 1711 complaints of the oligopoly traders against Alburquerque apparently brought results.[68]

Philip's counsellors also called for tighter supervision of the bureaucracy, and one has to see the trial of the duke as a part of a general cleanup. The penalty was specifically aimed so "that it may serve other viceroys as an example."[69] In 1705 the crown had confiscated one million pesos from the estate of the deceased Peruvian viceroy, the Count of Monclova. As in Alburquerque's case, the judge of the *juicio de residencia* in Peru absolved the Habsburg favourite. Madrid, however, censured him posthumously for fraud on a large scale.[70] Alburquerque's trial and substantial indemnity followed this punitive measure. The stiff penalties for the two viceroys presaged a change in direction. By contrast, in the entire seventeenth century the king never seriously castigated a Mexican viceroy. Only in a few cases did the overseas *juicios de residencia* end with penalties. The Count of Baños, viceroy of New Spain (1660–1664), was sentenced to pay 2,000 ducats for rerouting a Corpus Christi procession, a rather trivial infraction. In the early seventeenth century, a judge handed down a 200,000-peso penalty against Viceroy Count of Monterrey (1595–1603), who had tolerated financial abuse in the Indian parishes. Nonetheless, the Council of the Indies discarded the sentence and cleared the count of the accusations.[71]

Whether Alburquerque was more corrupt than his predecessors remains somewhat open to question in the absence of detailed studies on the second half of the seventeenth century. Spanish historian Cayetana Alvarez de Toledo argues that the Count of Salvatierra, viceroy from 1642 to 1647, appointed relatives of *audiencia* ministers to district officialdoms to wrest away influence over the body from Bishop Juan de Palafox, visitor-general of New Spain (1639–1647). The viceroy also illicitly collected 650,000 pesos for naming *alcaldes mayores*. According to Palafox, Salvatierra derailed the inspection of illegal Veracruz commerce in which several *audiencia* magistrates, the viceroy, and his clients participated. Additionally, the viceroy colluded with a corrupt merchant in the farming out of the stamp tax.[72] Alvarez de Toledo holds that Bishop Palafox represented an idea of consensual government that relied on Creole participation, whereas the viceroys "promoted a more authoritarian approach to government, designed to intensify royal control and raise more revenue."[73]

I hypothesize that the scions of Spain's premier families in late seventeenth Mexico conducted politics and patronage in a fashion similar to that of Alburquerque. Yet, they maintained a firmer support at the Spanish court than the duke. Viceroys had acquiesced and participated in circumventing the inoperative trade oligopoly. Alburquerque's fall and subsequent trial simply offers a lucent panorama of ongoing viceregal corruption because of the political transformation in Spain. While Alburquerque utilized his powers of patronage extensively, his interests and manifold ties to the local society curbed his role as a royal agent, so that he acted rather as a brake on royal initiatives – an observation that could hold true for Habsburg officials as well.

With the harsh penalties for Alburquerque and Monclova, the new Bourbon regime pushed for tighter control of viceroys. The battle at Villaviciosa on 10 December 1710 cleared the way for the Bourbon victory and Philip's political survival. The archduke left Barcelona on 27 September 1711, and peace negotiations with the British started shortly afterwards. Since the king had defended his claim, his advisors could now move the agenda of imperial reform forward. In 1710 Francisco de Pagabe started the *visita general* of the exchequer in Mexico.[74] The new counsellors in the metropolis sidestepped the traditional councils, such as the Council of the Indies, in the effort to punish viceregal abuses effectively.

This imperial policy of disciplining the administration slowly affected the governance of Alburquerque's successors. The Duke of Linares, viceroy from 1710 to 1716, may have been a more trustworthy and pious administrator[75] – although he also helped circumvent the stipulations of the Manila galleon.[76] Some historians consider the Marquis of Casafuerte (1722–1734) to be the first loyal and efficient bureaucrat of the eighteenth-century Mexican viceroys. The crown had not promoted him to this post because he was an offspring of a Spanish grandee, but as a reward for his loyal and effective military services.[77] Casafuerte reduced graft in the treasury and the tribunal of accounts and streamlined the military by cutting costs as well as boosting morale.[78] A Spanish historian describes the Count of Fuenclara (1742–1746) as an "active administrator, vigorous, and intelligent, ethical."[79] Furthermore, the first Count of Revillagigedo (1746–1755) has recently received a glowing treatment as a man of probity.[80] These analyses of viceroys are, perhaps, a bit favourable towards their subjects, tending not to discuss the officials within the panorama of corruption. The research, however, indicates a trend among the "king's living images" in New Spain. The Bourbon secretaries of the Indies increasingly chose loyal and effective viceroys who executed more closely the metropolitan agenda.

After paying the indemnity to the monarch, Alburquerque returned to Madrid, where he did not hold further political office. On 23 October 1733 he died in his palace on Encarnación Square (the *plazuela de la Encarnación*).[81] The duke's fall did not hinder his family's return to favour with the House of Bourbon. Alburquerque's son served close to the monarch as Philip's *gentilhombre* (gentleman-in-waiting) and as *caballerizo mayor* (master of the horse) of Prince Ferdinand, and continued to do so after Ferdinand's accession to the throne in 1746.[82] Alburquerque's son married the daughter of the Duke of Infantado, a successful match from a dynastic viewpoint.[83] The unfortunate dénouement of Alburquerque's viceregal career did not hamper his son's standing in the Spanish court society.

In conclusion, officials and merchants associated with the Spanish fleet denounced Alburquerque for permitting French merchantmen to exceed the limits of what they could sell in America. The duke also allowed the illegal entry of ships from other Spanish colonies. The 1708 inspection of Judge Félix González de Agüero corroborated the charges against the viceroy and royal officials. In 1711 and 1715, three juntas in Madrid called for penalizing the duke sternly. When Alburquerque returned to Spain in 1713, the king seized his property and forced the duke to agree to an extrajudicial indemnity of 700,000 pesos. This unusually harsh punishment of a viceroy came about because Alburquerque lost his political backing in Spain with the wane of the aristocratic party and the demise of his brother-in-law, the Duke of Medinaceli. The French counsellors at court, who were largely responsible for the fate of the aristocrats, had originally favoured French commercial expansion in America. When French influence in Madrid diminished after 1709, the *consulado* of Seville rose again in power. Together with Spanish advisors, the *consulado* pressed for the enforcement of trade laws and the punishment of Alburquerque. In this sense, the fall of the duke precedes the later "Bourbon Reforms," because the adjudication sent a message to viceroys and bureaucracy alike not to ignore the laws too ruthlessly.

9

Conclusion

Historians of colonial Mexico have almost completely ignored the early eighteenth century. This study addresses this oversight by focusing on the political culture of court society from 1702 to 1710. The Bourbon dynasty had just replaced the House of Habsburg, and Spain entered a transitional phase. Philip V defended the throne against the Alliance of European powers comprised of Great Britain, the Netherlands, and the Holy Roman Empire. In 1702 a beleaguered Philip appointed the Duke of Alburquerque as viceroy of Spain's most valuable colony. By designating this grandee, Philip and his circle of advisors did not intend to recruit a loyal and efficient administrator. Rather, the move was an attempt to appease the aristocratic party at home that opposed the new dynasty and its French counsellors.

When the monarch tried to tighten his grip over the colonial treasury, trade, and the Church, Alburquerque resisted most of these measures. Alburquerque favoured defending the interests of the traditional bureaucracy and the religious orders against the monarch. Cooperating with some groups of locals in Mexico and accepting their rewards for permitting contraband commerce suited Alburquerque's material interest and reduced the possibility of opposition to his governance. Most important, his politics helped to keep the colony loyal to the Bourbons.

In doing so, Alburquerque widely used his patronage powers. The duke appointed 281 district officials (*alcaldes mayores* and *corregidores*) and governors. Forty-three times the viceroy appointed officials in the wealthiest districts of Mexico, eleven of which went to his *criados* (clients that had accompanied the viceroy from Spain). The ratio of his appointments in the five wealthiest districts to those in the lowest five was nearly two and a half to one (two hundred versus eighty-one officials). The duke filled more than half of all vacant district officialdoms. Furthermore, Alburquerque assigned ten clients and *criados* to posts in the financial administration. Fourteen of his dependents obtained positions in the military or the militias. The duke chose six clergymen for consecration to coveted positions diverging from the order of the proposal list (*terna*) submitted by the secular Church. Therefore, although the monarchy during King Charles II's reign (1665–1700) had made efforts to limit viceregal patronage, Alburquerque retained and used his significant privileges to secure his hold over the colony and to profit from the appointments. Philip V made no effort to restrain the power of the viceroy in this regard.

At the viceregal court, Alburquerque communicated on a daily basis with bureaucrats, lawyers, merchants, clergy, and his entourage. Key colonial institutions such as the *audiencia* (high court), the treasury, or the *consulado* (merchant guild and court) were located in the palace in proximity to the viceroy's residence. The court buzzed with activity and performed a central function in political manoeuvring. Because Alburquerque usually acted as a brake on royal reforms, his court did not function typically as an institution that subjected Mexican power elites to the will of the metropolis. To a large extent, local society co-opted the viceroy, and together they resisted the disciplining currents originating from Madrid.

In his collaboration, Viceroy Alburquerque aided contraband merchants in circumventing the impractical limits of the official oligopoly trade that produced soaring prices and inadequate supply. As a result, Alburquerque's network clashed from 1702 to 1704 with the merchants tied to the powerful wholesaler Luis Sánchez de Tagle. This merchant represented the *consulado* of Seville, the body guarding the interests of the Spanish fleet merchants. Alburquerque and his allies even attempted to derail the wedding of Sánchez de Tagle's nephew to Ignacia Cruzat, the daughter of the former governor of the Philippines. The Sánchez de Tagle family temporarily lost their mint privileges in the course of the power struggle. The viceroy's alliance also succeeded in loosening the influence of the oligopoly representatives over the Mexican *consulado*. When in

1703 Alburquerque deported Sánchez de Tagle's son-in-law, who was at that time prior of the *consulado*, the family relinquished its sway over the body. The anti-oligopoly merchants took over, applauding the viceroy's measures to permit commerce formally considered contraband trade. This shift in the *consulado* possibly led to the later quarrels between Basques and Montañeses, who both rejected the fleet merchants' privileges. Some historians, most recently Jonathan Israel in his observations on the Viceroy Marquis of Gelves (1621–1624), have noted a pattern of collaboration between the viceroy and the Spaniards against the archbishop and the Creoles.[1] Yet Alburquerque aligned with both Creoles and Spaniards of various regional extractions. The duke and his network fought their opponents for commercial, political, and personal reasons, but the alliances did not run along clearly demarcated lines of regional background. The archbishop followed suit, backing the representatives of the Seville *consulado*, also of variegated origins.

Between 1706 and 1708 the duke with high court judges ostensibly persecuted a circle of traders and salesmen around fleet merchant Gregorio Gasco. The criminal court charged Gasco and his clients with treason against the House of Bourbon. Yet, in contrast to the theory of Spanish historian Luis Navarro, little evidence points to a conspiracy or even a significant inclination to support the Habsburg cause among elites and popular classes in colonial Mexico. The fight bore the marks of a struggle between social networks for personal and commercial reasons in which oligopoly trade also played a role. The same holds true for the altercation between the viceroy on the one side and *audiencia* ministers and clergymen on the other.

Alburquerque also rebuffed the accountant of mercury sales and superintendent of the Puebla sales tax (*alcabala*) collection, Juan José de Veytia Linage. This royal minister successfully raised proceeds for the crown. Alburquerque sided with the bishop of Puebla and the local oligarchy in opposing an efficient *alcabala* levy. In 1709/1710 the duke also confiscated the proceeds of the quicksilver sale, thus imperilling Veytia Linage's work. After Alburquerque's departure, the coalition hostile to Veytia Linage adjusted to the circumstances when two *audiencia* ministers, enemies of the duke, joined the Puebla oligarchy in thwarting the superintendent's efforts. With the support of the Council of the Indies, however, Veytia Linage held out. His successful superintendency marked a step towards the introduction of provincial military governors in Puebla in 1754 and, ultimately, towards the intendancy system in 1786. These well-paid officials with a record of loyal service to the crown increasingly resisted the demands of the local oligarchy and the Mexican central bureaucracy.

Among the steps that he to took to win support, Alburquerque manoeuvred against the secularization of Dominican parishes in Oaxaca. Allied with the religious order, Indian caciques, and district officials, the viceroy delayed the execution of a *real cédula* (a royal communication) mandating the sequestration of regular parishes. His opponent, the bishop of Oaxaca, Angel de Maldonado, furthermore demanded the creation of new parishes out of existing ones. In the bishop's view, secular clergy would then be appointed to these parishes. The duke helped in thwarting this proposal.

Marked by excessive corruption, Alburquerque's regime did not contribute to greater royal power overseas. By allying with local society and widely using his patronage powers, the duke continued a tradition of late seventeenth-century viceroys that emphasized governance in accord with large parts of the Mexican elites. Ultimately, however, as the influence of the pro-Habsburg party and the high nobility at the Spanish court declined, the viceroy's support in Madrid crumbled too. The fall of Alburquerque's brother-in-law, the Duke of Medinaceli, further eroded the viceroy's backing. Although Philip V and his counsellors successively emancipated themselves from French influence after 1709, a mélange of reformists at court and the resurgent *consulado* of Seville sought to take revenge on Alburquerque. Several juntas blasted Alburquerque for tolerating contraband trade. In 1715 the duke had to pay an extrajudicial indemnity of 700,000 pesos to the monarch for malfeasance during his viceroyship. In doing so, the crown sent a warning to Alburquerque's successors and the bureaucracy not to flout the laws too ruthlessly.

Alburquerque's governance differed therefore from that of the viceroys under the Count-Duke of Olivares (1621–1643) who, although no strangers to clientelism and corruption, served as agents of royal prerogatives. These viceroys also intended to collect higher tax revenues for the crown. The cautious reforms that the first Bourbon king put in place during Alburquerque's tenure such as the appointment of the Puebla *alcabala* superintendent continued changes instigated by seventeenth-century statesmen such as Olivares and the Count of Oropesa (1685–1691). Only in his laissez-faire approach to commerce did Alburquerque's actions foreshadow to a degree José de Gálvez's later free trade decree, although the motivation of the two men was entirely different. Gálvez sought to relax rules for commerce within the empire to strengthen tax revenue, while Alburquerque allowed contraband trade with foreigners, probably even enemy states. The novel trial of and significant penalty against Alburquerque (and Peruvian Viceroy Count of Monclova), partially reflected the resurgent power of the Seville *consulado*. At the same time, the punishment marked a step towards the "Bourbon Reforms."

Historians have discussed the question whether these reforms failed or succeeded. The term "Bourbon Reforms" is only loosely defined. Usually, historians refer to those political changes that occurred under the energetic king Charles III (1759–1788). His prime minister, the Marquis of Esquilache (1759–1766), attempted in vain to break the power of the Andalusian *consulado* (that had by this time moved to Cadiz), parts of the aristocracy, the upper clergy, and the graduates of the select colleges of the Spanish universities. José de Gálvez, secretary of the Indies in the period from 1776 to 1787, shifted the attention overseas by introducing a new style of regional governance. Viceroy Alburquerque, in contrast, opposed those incipient political reforms that preceded later more radical changes.

Towards the end of the eighteenth century, bureaucratization and rationalization of the administration increasingly may have replaced the negotiating function of the viceregal court typical of Alburquerque's tenure. Further research needs to determine whether a gradual reduction of courtly influence contributed to the independence of Mexico. When Madrid denied the colonial elites their share in the exchange of resources at court, their interests in upholding imperial unity withered away. Additional scholarship will pave the way for a better understanding of the role of the viceregal court at the crossroads of clientelism, corruption, and the state in the history of Mexico. Even today, the interaction of patronage and state power is a critical determinate of the development of Modern Mexico.

APPENDICES

1. *Glossary*

abasto de carne. The monopoly on the local meat supply.

alcabala. A sales tax.

alcalde de crímen. A criminal judge of the *audiencia*.

alcalde mayor. A district official akin to a *corregidor*.

alcalde ordinario. A town councillor who also sat as a first-instance judge.

alférez. A standard-bearer of a political unit; an ensign.

alguacil. A constable; an official with police functions.

apoderado. An agent, usually with power of attorney.

arbitrista. An author of a treatise urging change in Spain.

asesor letrado. Legal advisor of the viceroy.

audiencia. The high court that reviewed civil and criminal cases and wielded some political authority in its district.

auditor de guerra. A viceregal advisor in military jurisdiction, often an *audiencia* minister.

aviador. Someone who advances loans to a business.

ayuntamiento. A municipal council.

ayuda de cámara. A chamber aide.

bando. A public proclamation.

beneficio de empleo. A form of venality where the crown appointed candidates to offices with judicial authority in exchange for donations.

benemérito. A merited member of society.

caballerizo. A master of the horse, an important *criado*.

cabildo. The *cabildo civil* was a municipal council, whereas the *cabildo eclesiástico* (or in the archdiocese, the *cabildo metropolitano*) equals the cathedral chapter.

caja real. A treasury.

cámara de Indias. A chamber, that is, a committee of the Council of the Indies that dispensed patronage.

camarera mayor. The head of the queen's household.

cargador de flota. A merchant dealing with the Spanish fleet and its oligopoly traders.

casa de contratación. The house of trade, an institution in Seville that supervised and taxed the traffic with America.

castellano. A warden of a fortress.

cofradía. A sodality, a lay society for social purposes.

colegio mayor. An exclusive residence hall or confraternity associated with one of the three foremost universities of Spain, Salamanca, Valladolid, and Alcalá.

colegial mayor. A university graduate who had belonged to a *colegio mayor.*

compadrazgo. Coparenthood, that is, the bond between parents and godparents.

consul. One of the two officials below the prior, who acted as judges and administrators of the *consulado.*

consulado. The merchant guild and its court, located in Mexico City, Lima, and Seville.

consulta. A written recommendation.

contador. An accountant.

contador de penas de cámara. Accountant of the fines imposed by the *audiencia.*

contaduría de azogues y tributos. The accountancy of mercury and Indian tributes.

Council of the Indies. A council in Madrid that advised the king or decided on American affairs. The Bourbon dynasty reduced the body's role to that of an appellate court.

corregidor. A district official akin to an *alcalde mayor.*

créature. A client or a minion.

criado. A client who accompanied the viceroy from Spain.

criado mayor. A *criado* of higher social standing, sometimes a kinsman of the patron, such as the *secretario,* the *caballerizo,* or the *gentileshombres.*

curato. A parish.

decretales mayores. Papal decrees.

de oficio. A trial that is initiated by the court and not by a private individual.

diputado. A *consulado* representative.

despacho universal, secretario del. A secretary who relayed messages among the various councils of the Spanish court and the king.

doctrina. In principle, a parish for recent converts administered by friars.

en propriedad. See *propriedad.*

escribano. A notary.

escribano de gobernación y guerra. A notary dealing with government and war.

fiador. A bondsman; a guarantor.

fiscal. A prosecutor. *Fiscales de lo civil* sat on the *audiencia* or the Council of the Indies and were in charge of civil matters. The *fiscal del crimen* presented criminal causes in the *sala del crimen* of the *audiencia*. The prosecutor of the Inquisition was also known as *fiscal*.

fiscalía. The office of a *fiscal*.

flotista. Merchants associated with the Spanish fleet.

fuero. A law, a legal privilege.

futura. The title to serve an office once it vacated.

gentilhombre. Gentleman-in-waiting.

gobierno. A province administered by a governor.

gobierno superior. Here, the viceroy in his civil function; in general, the colonial civil authority superior to other governors.

grandeza. Grandeeship, that is, the uppermost echelon of Spanish nobility.

hidalgo. A member of the lower nobility of Spain's empire.

hidalguía. The lower nobility of Spain.

house of trade. See *casa de contratación.*

intendente. An intendant or regional royal governor, an office introduced to New Spain in 1786.

infidencia. Violation of fidelity.

informe. A report.

juez de arribadas. Judge of ships that arrive illegally in an American port.

juicio de residencia. The inquiry into the conduct of an official at the end of his tenure.

junta. A council.

maestre de campo. A military position equivalent to a brigadier.

malquerencia. Speaking offensively about the king.

mayordomo. A steward.

media anata. A tax of half of an annual salary and a third of all future fees that anyone assuming a crown office needed to pay.

medio racionero. A prebend below a *racionero*.

memoria (de los criados). The list of retainers who accompanied the viceroy from Spain.

montañés. Refers to the natives and their descendants from the mountainous region between Santander and Burgos in northern Spain.

New Spain. Colonial Mexico.

nao. The galleon shuttling annually between Manila and Acapulco.

novohispano. Adjective of New Spain.

oidor. A judge on the *audiencia*.

oligopoly. Refers here to the oligopolistic trade of the Spanish fleet between Seville and America.

ordenanza. Founding instructions.

parecer. A recommendation or expertise, usually provided for a council or the king.

pesquisa. Usually a criminal investigation.

plaza mayor. The main square in Mexico City, also known as the *zócalo*.

presidio. A fort or fortress.

prior. The elected head of the *consulado*.

procurador. An attorney or representative.

procurador de pobres. An attorney representing the poor.

procurador general. A representative of a corporation or an institution.

promotor fiscal. Chief diocesan advisor on canon law and lawsuits.

propriedad. Possession. In this period, appointment *en propriedad* usually meant for a lifespan with the option to bequeath the office for a fee payable to the crown.

provisor. An ecclesiastical judge appointed by a bishop.

provincial. Head of a province of a regular order.

racionero. A prebend.

ramo. An archival section.

real acuerdo. Joint conference of viceroy and *audiencia oidores*.

real cédula. A royal communication requiring some action or bestowing a favour.

real hacienda. The financial administration, the royal exchequer.

regidor. A councilman.

relator. An *audiencia* official who summarized trial documents.

repartimiento de mercancías. The illegal but tolerated trade of a district official with Indians.

residencia. See *juicio de residencia*.

royal exchequer. The royal financial administration.

ruego y encargo. "I request and require," a request of the king or the viceroy for the church to execute something.

sala civil. The *audiencia* chamber dealing with civil and political cases.

sala del crimen. The criminal chamber of the *audiencia*.

sargento mayor. A major or third-in-command of a regiment.

secretario del despacho universal. See *despacho universal*.

superintendente. A superintendent of an administrative unit.

terna. The proposal list with three candidates that bishops submitted to a governor for appointments of secular clergy positions.

tribunal de cuentas. The tribunal of accounts that audited the colonial treasuries.

valido. A favourite.

veedor general de la real hacienda. The chief administrator of the royal finances.

visita. An inspection, usually of the bureaucracy or the church.

visitador. An inspector, someone who conducts a *visita*.

voto decisivo. A majority vote.

2. Biographical Information

Asinas Duque de Estrada, Alonso de. The merchant and viceregal ally denounced his commercial rival Benito Cartagena in the conspiracy trials.

Careaga Sanz de Urrutia, Lucás de. The trustee of the Seville *consulado* was also consul of the Mexican *consulado* in 1703 and 1704. In 1704 the crown titled him Marquis of Santa Fe. The viceroy imprisoned Careaga in 1708 for embezzling funds of the Seville *consulado*.

Cartagena, Benito. *Oidor* Tovar arrested Cartagena in 1706 after the merchant Alonso de Asinas Duque de Estrada and an assistant government notary had denounced Cartagena as a traitor. The accusers bid against Cartagena for the playing card monopoly. In 1707 the *sala del crimen* declared Cartagena innocent.

Costela, Andrés Pérez de. Originally a page of Pope Innocent XI, the former dean of the chapter of Ciudad Rodrigo, near Salamanca, Spain, was promoted to a canonry of the Mexico City cathedral. Costela arrived in New Spain with the same squadron as Alburquerque and *Oidor* José Uribe, and the canon supported the viceroy in the dispute over the Tagle-Cruzat wedding. When Uribe and Costela fell out with the duke, Costela secured the support of Archbishop Ortega y Montañés and his allies to prevent their deportation to Spain.

Cruzat y Góngora, Fausto. The governor of the Philippines (ca. 1688–1700) arranged the betrothal of his daughter Ignacia to Domingo Ruiz de Tagle, nephew of Luis Sánchez de Tagle. After Don Fausto had died on the Manila galleon in 1703, his sons Juan, Fausto, and Martín objected to the wedding.

Cruzat y Góngora, Ignacia, also known as *La china*. The daughter of Governor Fausto Cruzat married Domingo Ruiz de Tagle in 1703 and died the following year.

Estacasolo y Otalora, Juan de. Estacasolo, a knight of the order of Santiago, travelled to Mexico as Alburquerque's secretary. Two relatives of Estacasolo sat on the Council of the Indies, and Don Juan was also related to the secretary of the *despacho universal*, Antonio de Ubilla y Medina. Estacasolo remained in Mexico after Alburquerque's departure and died wealthy in 1719. His son married into a local family.

Frigiliana, Count of. In 1706 Frigiliana joined the Spanish nobles in their deliberations against the Bourbon regime. In 1709 he gained the governorship of the Council of the Indies, and in 1715 he became secretary of state of the navy and the Indies.

Gálvez y Gallardo, José de. Gálvez undertook an important *visita* of New Spain (1765–1773) and then became secretary of state of the Indies (1776–1787). He implemented structural changes often labelled "Bourbon Reforms" by introducing the intendancy system in 1786, among other measures.

Garaicoechea, Juan de. The great merchant and contrabandist cooperated with Fausto Cruzat's sons and the viceroy in the Cruzat-Tagle wedding dispute. Garaicoechea also supported Alburquerque's clients in the conspiracy trials.

Garzarón, Francisco. In 1716 Garzarón began a *visita general* ("general inspection") of all tribunals of New Spain, such as the *audiencia*, the tribunal of accounts, and the *consulado*. He removed several *audiencia* ministers, and he passed away in 1726.

Gasco, Gregorio. Alburquerque's allies Antonio Gómez Lobato and Juan de Garaicoechea denounced the merchant Gasco as a traitor. Alburquerque had Gasco jailed, and the merchant associated with the Spanish fleet died before the *audiencia* could ship him to Spain.

Gómez Lobato, Antonio. The accountant of the Mexico City treasury accused fleet merchant Gregorio Gasco and his allies of disloyalty to the king. Gómez Lobato also participated in Alburquerque's 1709 junta that decided against royal orders to ship proceeds from mercury sale to the fortresses in the Caribbean.

Maldonado, Angel. Maldonado became bishop of Oaxaca in 1702 and called for secularizing Dominican parishes in his see.

Mañer, Salvador. The criminal judges of Mexico found the Toluca hacienda administrator guilty of conspiracy and shipped him to Spain. Mañer escaped from the House of Trade dungeons. In 1711 the *corregidor* of Cordoba caught Mañer and found papers on him that discussed the legitimacy of the Bourbon succession. Sentenced to forced military service in a port fortress, Mañer was finally released and allegedly served later as a writer at the court in Madrid.

Medinaceli, Duke of. From 1680 down to 1685, the eighth Duke of Medinaceli served as prime minister under the last Habsburg king, Charles II. His daughter, Juana de la Cerda, married Alburquerque. Her brother, Don Luis, ninth Duke of Medinaceli, came under suspicion of collaborating with Archduke Charles. King Philip had Medinaceli arrested in 1710, and in 1711 he died in Pamplona.

Miravalle, Alonso de Dávalos Bracamonte, Count of. The count rejected the oligopoly privileges as *alcalde ordinario* in 1703 and as prior of the Mexican *consulado* in 1706. Although he was involved in contraband, he remained in good standing with the Sánchez de Tagle family.

Oropesa, Count of. King Charles II appointed Oropesa as president of the Council of Castile in 1684. By 1685 Oropesa had eased out the Duke of Medinaceli as prime minister. Oropesa envisioned a reform program that included a restriction of church privileges, a reorganization of the royal treasury, as well as a cutback in pensions and bureaucracy. He was dismissed in 1691.

Orry, Jean. The *veedor general de la real hacienda* was periodically in charge of the Spanish treasury. The Frenchman was expelled from Madrid in August 1704, returned in the following year, and left again in 1706. He rejoined the court in April 1713, and the king finally discharged him in February 1715.

Ortega y Montañés, Juan de. He became archbishop of Mexico in 1700 and did not favour Viceroy Alburquerque.

Pagabe, Francisco de. From 1710 to 1715 he conducted a *visita* of Mexico's financial administration. The viceroy opposed the inspector, and the *visita* remained largely unsuccessful.

Pez, Andrés de. The former warden of the San Juan Ulúa fortress and general of the 1708 Spanish fleet accused Alburquerque of malfeasance. Pez became governor of the Council of the Indies in 1717.

Ruiz de Tagle, Domingo. Luis Sánchez de Tagle's nephew and husband of Ignacia Cruzat.

Sánchez de Tagle, Luis. The great merchant and trustee of the Seville *consulado* received the title of Marquis of Altamira in 1704. Don Luis's daughter Luisa married Sánchez de Tagle's nephew, Pedro Sánchez de Tagle. They fought the viceroy over an array of issues such as the marriage of Luis Sánchez de Tagle's other nephew Domingo Ruiz de Tagle, the control of the Mexican *consulado*, the royal mint, and contraband trade.

Sánchez de Tagle, Pedro. The nephew of Luis Sánchez de Tagle served as prior of the *consulado* of Mexico from 1700 through October 1703.

Ubilla y Estrada, Miguel de. The accountant on the tribunal of accounts and premier trustee of the Seville *consulado* was made Marquis of Santa Sabina in 1704.

Ubilla y Medina, Antonio de. As secretary of the *despacho universal*, he supported Philip's accession and was created Marquis of Ribas in 1701. The king demoted Ubilla to a councillor of the Indies in 1705 and dismissed him in 1706 under suspicion of collaborating with the archduke. Philip re-established Ubilla as councillor in 1715, and in 1721 the monarch admitted him to the *cámara de Indias*, the body that dispensed patronage.

Ursins, Princess des. The influential head of Queen Marie Louise's household (*camarera mayor*) was a confidante of French King Louis XIV and partially responsible for streamlining the Spanish government. After Marie Louise's death (1714), the new Queen Elizabeth Farnese dismissed Ursins and several French counsellors tied to the princess.

Veytia Linage, Juan José de. He collected the *alcabala* (sales tax) in Puebla following his appointment as superintendent in 1695. In 1705 he became judge of all illegally arriving ships (*juez de arribadas*) in Acapulco. From 1709 he also administered the mercury accountancy (*contaduría de azogues*) and clashed with the viceroy and the local oligarchy over these issues.

3. Prosopography of Mexican Audiencia Ministers in Relation to the Viceroy

Abellafuentes, Alonso (also Villafuerte or Fuertes y Abella). Probably of Asturian origin, Abellafuentes left in 1687 for the Philippines to become *oidor*. Future Mexican *alcalde* Juan Ozaeta y Oro joined him on the bench in Manila. As dean of that *audiencia*, Abellafuentes held the interim governorship until Fausto Cruzat took office in ca. 1688. In 1699 Abellafuentes advanced to the post of *alcalde del crimen* of the *audiencia* of Mexico and then to *oidor* in 1705. He joined the military order of Calatrava and later of Alcántara. He seems to have been a loyal supporter of Alburquerque, who gave him two commissions. The crown fined him 200 pesos for improper conduct during the Tagle-Cruzat wedding. He fined Juan de Ortega y Montañes, interim viceroy and archbishop, a 5,480-peso penalty in the *residencia* for appointing *alcaldes mayores* who had not yet passed their previous *residencias*. Abellafuentes became well connected to Mexican society and possibly married the widowed Countess of Santiago de Calimaya.

Sources: AGI, Contratación 5448, N 101, Indiferente 135, N 132, México 400, 401, 642.

Calderón de la Barca, Miguel. In 1653 he was born in Spain. Calderón paid 12,000 pesos for a position as supernumerary *oidor* in Mexico, taking possession on 27 November 1692. Appointed senior *oidor* by 1703, he testified favourably in Archbishop Ortega y Montañés's *residencia*. Luis Sánchez de Tagle travelled officially as Calderón's *criado* to Mexico in 1692, and Lucas de Careaga and Miguel de Ubilla supported the *oidor* in his *residencia*. In the eyes of *Oidor* Uribe, Calderón conspired with the viceroy against him. Although certainly a friend of Archbishop Ortega y Montañés during the prelate's interim viceroyalty, Calderón voted with all other *audiencia* ministers to turn down Ortega y Montañés's request for support in 1703. He also gave a supportive statement (*parecer*) on Alburquerque's efforts to curb illegal trade in 1706. In exchange,

Alburquerque's secretary Estacasolo and other viceregal allies testified for Calderón in the *residencia*. Calderón cannot easily be attributed to one camp. There were allegations that he owned landed property in Mexico, advanced loans to the Raya mine in Guanajuato (an occupation called *aviador*), and pursued other commercial contacts with merchants such as Jerónimo de Monterde. The *oidor* may have used the proceeds to acquire a position in the Council of the Indies on 8 June 1707.

Sources: Burkholder and Chandler, *Biographical Dictionary of Audiencia Ministers* (hereinafter abbreviated as BC) 62; AGI, Contratación 5540 B, L 5, ff. 14v; Escribanía 233 A, 236 A; Indiferente, 134, N 4 ff. 1–3r; México 403.

Casa Alvarado, Francisco. Born around 1670, Casa Alvarado received a baccalaureate in canon law from the University of Seville and later a licentiate from Salamanca. He served under the new Bourbon dynasty as district official of Ujijar and then Granada. Casa Alvarado purchased the post of *alcalde del crimen* of Mexico for 1,000 doubloons on 8 October 1706. In 1709 Alburquerque commissioned him to pursue suspected traitors in Guadalcázar. The *alcalde* also sat on the junta that the duke convened to adjudicate quarrels over the governor of New Mexico, the Marquis of la Peñuela.

Sources: BC, 74–75, AGI, México 377; 658, f. 330v; BNM, FR, Archivo Franciscano, Caja 25/486, f. 81v.

Cepeda y Castro Gil de Gibaja, Gaspar Blas de. Cepeda was born in Spain. He studied at the archiepiscopal *colegio mayor* (residence hall) at Salamanca University together with future *oidor* José Uribe, whom he substituted as chair in *decretales* (papal decrees). Appointed *fiscal del crimen* on 20 September 1704, he took possession in 1705 and closely collaborated with Uribe and the archbishop. The two ministers clashed with the viceroy over jurisdiction, and the crown ordered their return to Spain. After their allies intervened, especially Cepeda's brother, the crown revoked the order, and a council declared Cepeda innocent in 1709. When Alburquerque left, Cepeda linked up with the bishop of Puebla. Just before Garzarón's inspection, Cepeda retired as a canon into that chapter.

Sources: BC 370, Bertrand, *Grandeur et misères* (hereinafter cited as Bertrand), 342; AGI, México 376, 377, 403.

Díez de Bracamonte, Juan. Born in Mexico in 1662, he became a priest and a lawyer at the *audiencia*. Diez owned the Rayas mine in Guanajuato and purchased the hacienda Jalpa de Cánovas in Jalisco. In 1708 bankruptcy forced him to sell the hacienda to the merchant Jerónimo Monterde. In 1705 Díez took possession of the position of supernumerary *oidor* for which he paid the *media annata* tax on 14 January 1706. He sat on Alburquerque's mercury junta and joined ranks with the bishop of Puebla. Inspector Garzarón removed Díez de Bracamonte from the *audiencia*, and Diez retired into the Puebla chapter as a cantor and later archdeacon.

Sources: BC 101, Bertrand 342, AGI, México 377, 477.

Escalante Mendoza, Juan de. Probably born in Mexico, he travelled in 1672 to Spain to attend the University of Salamanca. In 1682 he left Spain to become *oidor* of Guadalajara and then advanced to the position of *oidor* of Mexico. In 1703 Escalante voted several times in the *real acuerdo* to turn down requests of the archbishop regarding the Cruzat family. In October 1704 Escalante lost a conflict with Alburquerque when their respective protégés blamed each other for the fire damage to the royal gunpowder factory. In Escalante's view, Alburquerque illicitly reimbursed the monopoly contractor. The *oidor* was possibly a relative of Captain Pedro de Escalante y Mendoza, who held the gunpowder monopoly in the 1690s. Notwithstanding, Judge Escalante praised the viceroy's trade policies in 1706. The crown appointed him president of the Guadalajara *audiencia* in 1705, although he probably never assumed that position, because he died before 1708.

Sources: AGI, Indiferente 123, N 101, 12, ff. 1–1v; México 522, 477, 660; Contratación 5540 A, L 3, f. 4v.

Espinosa Ocampo y Cornejo, José Antonio. In 1665 he was born in Salamanca and went on to receive his doctorate from that university. In 1699 the crown appointed him *alcalde del crimen*, and in 1703 Espinosa advanced to the *fiscalía de lo civil*. In the same year the Council of the Indies recommended the admission of Espinosa in a military order, except that of Santiago; subsequently, he was accepted into that order in the following year. Alburquerque was satisfied with Espinosa's conduct in the Tagle-Cruzat wedding and recommended him to the king on 2 December 1703. The crown, in contrast, fined the *fiscal* 200 pesos. Espinosa disagreed occasionally with the viceroy on the enforcement of trade laws. The *fiscal* testified favourably in Archbishop Ortega y Montañés's *residencia*. Burkholder and Chandler's assertion that Espinosa was considered a "just and humane minister" is in contradiction with Juan Veytia Linage's charge that the *fiscal* lined up with the Puebla oligarchy against crown interests.

Sources: Bertrand, 342; BC, 112; AGI, Escribanía 233 A, México, 475, 604, 660.

González de Agüero, Félix. Born in Fuenmayor, Spain, he purchased an appointment as supernumerary *oidor* on 11 April 1707 for 1,000 doubloons. Gónzalez vouched for Alburquerque in his *residencia*. During his inspection of the Veracruz treasury, however, Gónzalez held the duke responsible for permitting the entry of foreign ships into Mexican harbours. Gónzalez married a Mexican and linked up with the bishop of Puebla. Finally, Inspector Garzarón fired him for abuses in 1719.

Sources: BC, 141–142, Bertrand 342, AGI, México 377, 657, 1. cuaderno.

Luna Arias, José de. His father held a position as *oidor* of Guadalajara, and then became treasurer and dean of the Puebla cathedral, bequeathing 200,000 pesos to his heir in 1700. José Luna, born in Guadalajara in 1683, studied in Puebla and at the University of Mexico and transferred to Salamanca, Spain, where he received a licentiate. Before his return to Mexico, Luna purchased the appointment to *oidor* for 16,000 pesos. He was in good standing with the viceroy, siding with Alburquerque on 12 December 1703 against the archbishop's request for help. Luna also praised the duke's faux crackdown on contraband trade. The viceroy appointed him judge of Indian affairs (*juez de indios*). In 1711 Inspector Pagabe fined him as a member of Alburquerque's mercury junta. The *oidores* Valenzuela and Díez de Bracamonte absolved him in his *residencia* in 1712. Several of Alburquerque's *criados* and friends also testified for the *oidor*, such as Secretary Estacasolo as well as the merchants Nicolás López de Landa and Domingo de la Canal. Luna obtained a canonry in the Puebla cathedral – much like Díez de Bracamonte and other *audiencia* ministers. Luna's brother, Francisco Mateo, became accountant at the tribunal of accounts.

Sources: BC, 191; AGI, Escribanía 234 A, México, 377, 642, 657, 660, Contratación, 5456, N 3, R 27.

Ozaeta y Oro, Juan. He became *alcalde del crimen* in 1695 and there is no indication of a conflict with Alburquerque. In 1703 Ozaeta arrested Pedro de Sánchez Tagle, and in 1706 he voiced his support for the duke's trade policies. Pagabe fined Ozaeta for participating in the mercury fraud.

Sources: AGI, México 377, 660.

Peña y Flores, Juan Francisco de la. Born in Mexico, he practised law at the *audiencia* and on 13 June 1707 acquired the post of a supernumerary *alcalde del crimen* for 3,000 doubloons. Inspector Garzarón removed him from the bench in 1720.

Sources: Hamnett, *Mexican Bureaucracy* (hereinafter cited as Hamnett), 17; AGI, México 402.

Pérez de Villareal y Florencia, Dr. Cristóbal. Born in Florida and educated in Mexico, he earned a doctorate in civil law. Pérez de Villareal held a benefice and practised law in Mexico. On 16 September 1707 he purchased the post of supernumerary *oidor* for 8,000 pesos. Previously, he had already served as Alburquerque's legal advisor. In 1703 Pérez de Villareal recommended to permit a sea captain to sell his illegally traded cacao while paying double taxes on it. The *fiscal* meanwhile demanded confiscation. The crown fined Pérez de Villareal 600 pesos for this advice. The *oidor* also supported Alburquerque in the viceroy's *residencia* against charges of permitting illegal trade.

Sources: BC 360, AGI, México 401, 547.

Robles y Lorenzana, Agustín de. Born in Spain in 1678, he considered himself a resident of the Canary Islands and received his education in Lima. Robles bought the post of *alcalde del crimen* for 9,000 pesos *escudos* in 1707 and probably married a Mexican. He testified for Alburquerque in the duke's *residencia*, rejecting allegations of fraud. Garzarón ousted him in 1719.

Sources: BC 291, AGI México, 657, 1. cuaderno.

Salvatierra, Pedro Eguaras Fernández de Hijar, Marquis of. He studied at Salamanca and served as *oidor* in Guatemala. On 13 March 1705 he advanced to the *alcaldía de crimen* in Mexico. Alburquerque claimed to suspend him from office for illegally marrying. Nonetheless, Eguaras testified favourably in the viceroy's *residencia*. On 20 April 1711 the king awarded Eguaras the honours of a councillor of the Indies, retirement from the *audiencia* with full pay, and the dispensation of the illegal marriage in return for a payment of 7,000 pesos.

Sources: BC, 107–108, AGI, México 377, 657.

Saraza y Arce, Francisco. He graduated in 1662 with a baccalaureate of law from Salamanca and received the position of *oidor* of Guatemala in 1678. Taking possession of the *alcaldía del crimen* of Mexico on 19 July 1688, he advanced to the position of *oidor* on 9 October 1703. He also held the commission to supervise the playing card monopoly. Little is known about Saraza's relationship with the duke. At the end of 1703 the *oidor* left to pacify the Sierra Gorda Indians. He died during the campaign in 1704, thus avoiding the Tagle-Cruzat conflict.

Sources: Robles, 3:307; AGI, Indiferente, 133, N 91, México 400, 475, 476.

Soria Velásquez, Jerónimo de. Born around 1660 in Pátzcuaro, Michoacán, he graduated from the University of Mexico with a degree in philosophy as well as canon and civil law. In 1692 Soria obtained a doctorate in civil law. After residing at the Council of the Indies in Spain since 1702, he took possession of his post as *oidor* of the Mexican *audiencia* in December 1704. Soria sat on Alburquerque's mercury junta and seemed to have built an alliance with the viceroy. In 1711 Soria obtained the title of Marquis of Villahermosa y Alfaro. Inspector Garzarón commended him as one of the few judges of the bench.

Sources: BC, 323–324, AGI, México 377.

Suárez Muñoz, Manuel. He was born in 1660 and gained a licentiate in law. Then he advanced to the post of an attorney at the royal councils. On 30 September 1687 the king appointed him to the post of supernumerary *alcalde del crimen* of Mexico for his "knowledge and good conduct." There is no indication of *beneficio de empleo*. Shortly afterwards Suárez Muñoz advanced to the position of an ordinary *alcalde del crimen*. He testified for *Oidor* Calderón and for interim Viceroy Ortega y Montañés in their *residencias*. The archbishop called on him to escort

Ignacia Cruzat out of the Cruzat residence. On the other hand, Suárez Muñoz praised Alburquerque's trade policies. The viceroy supported his bid for retirement, which the crown approved in 1708. In 1710 the crown ordered him to conduct Alburquerque's *residencia* if *Oidor* Juan de Valdés were absent.

Sources: AGI, Escribanía 233 A, 236 A; Indiferente 132, N 74, 1, 1; México, 377, 642, 658, 660.

Tovar, Baltasar. Born in Spain to a family from Badajoz, he received a doctorate in canon law and was appointed *alcalde del crimen* of the Mexican *audiencia* in 1693. In 1699 he advanced to the position of *oidor*. Alburquerque specially recommended Tovar to the crown in 1703 and suggested granting him a prebend in the Mexico City cathedral. Tovar consistently backed the viceroy, who in return employed him in issues such as in the Habsburg conspiracy trials. On 16 September 1707 Tovar died in the midst of this process. Luis Sánchez de Tagle labelled him the "hidden advisor" of Alburquerque.

Sources: BC, 330; AGI, México 404, 474, 642.

Uribe Castejón Medrano, José Joaquín de. Born in Jeréz de la Frontera around 1666, Uribe received a licentiate from the University of Salamanca, where he was a member of the archbishop's *colegio mayor*. Future *fiscal* Cepeda joined him there. When the crown appointed him *oidor* in 1702, Uribe travelled to New Spain with Alburquerque. The viceroy supported his futile bid to marry Ignacia Cruzat. From 1707 Uribe and Cepeda as well as the clerics José de Cienfuegos and Andrés Costela clashed with Alburquerque over various issues. The viceroy almost obtained their deportation to Spain. In 1706 Uribe married Michaela María de Sandóval, heiress to landed property in Huejotzingo. The spouses then bought additional haciendas in San Juan Molino, Iztacuixtla, and Tlaxcala, valued at around 44,000 pesos. Uribe's property interest in the Puebla region enhanced his connections to the regional oligarchy. The *oidor* subsequently opposed the efforts of the Puebla *alcabala* superintendent, Juan José de Veytia Linage. Uribe died a wealthy man in 1734, and his children married into affluent *oidor* families.

Sources: Bertrand, 342–343, Hamnett, 333–334, AGI, México 646.

Valdés, Juan de. He was born in Mexico in about 1651 and then became an attorney, counselling Viceroy Count of Montezuma and the bishop of Puebla. On 16 September 1707 Valdés bought the position of supernumerary *oidor* for 6,000 pesos. The crown appointed him to take the *residencias* of *Oidor* Miguel Calderón de la Barca and Viceroy Alburquerque. Heavy charges were levelled against the officials, but Valdés absolved them both.

Sources: BC, 340, AGI, México, 403, 657; Indiferente 135, N 80.

Valenzuela Venegas, Francisco. Born in Spain, he embarked in 1687 to assume the position of *oidor* of Guatemala. Before 1697 he advanced to *oidor* of Mexico and then joined the military order of Santiago. The *fiscal* of the Council of the Indies in Madrid called him Alburquerque's assessor, and there is a record of consistent support for the viceroy. Valenzuela participated in the mercury junta, backed Alburquerque in jurisdictional squabbles with the *sala del crimen*, and testified for the duke in the *residencia*. Inspector Pagabe fined him 300 pesos, and Garzarón suspended Valenzuela's tenure due to misconduct.

Sources: Gómez Gómez, *Las visitas*, 146; AGI, Contratación 5449, N 66; México, 89, R 1, N 7; 377, 479, 660.

4. The Mexican Consulado and the Alcaldes Ordinarios of Mexico's Cabildo Civil

The Consulado

This overview lists the prior (head of the *consulado*), the senior consul (*consul mayor* or *antiguo*), and the junior consul (*consul moderno*), in that sequence.

1695 Damarze de Zaldívar, died in office, Felipe Vélez de Escalante, Pedro Sánchez de Tagle.

1696 Antonio Fernández de Tubera, Pedro Sánchez de Tagle, Felipe González de Arnaes.

1697 Antonio Fernández de Tubera, Felipe González Arnaes, Juan Luis de Baeza.

1698 Antonio Fernández de Tubera, Juan Luis de Baeza, Pedro de la Puente Ascarai (died in office).

1699 Antonio Fernández de Tubera, Joaquín de Zabaleta, Domingo Palacio Jaez.

1700 Pedro Sánchez de Tagle, Domingo de Palacio Jaez, Matias Tarto.

1701 Pedro Sánchez de Tagle, Matias Tarto, Antonio Carrasco de Retortillo.

1702 Pedro Sánchez de Tagle, Antonio Carrasco de Retortillo, Juan del Castillo.

1703 Pedro Sánchez de Tagle, on 28 October replaced by Antonio Fernández de Tubera, who died in office; Juan del Castillo, Lucas de Careaga.

1704 Alonso de Ávalos Bracamonte Count of Miravalle, Lucas de Careaga, Juan Hernando de Gracia (died in office).

1705 Count of Miravalle, Jerónimo Monterde, Nicolas López de Landa.

1706 Count of Miravalle, Nicolas López de Landa, Domingo de la Canal.

1707 Alonso Morales, Domingo de la Canal, Julián Osorio.

1708 Alonso Morales, Julián Osorio, Juan Bautista López.

1709 Alonso Morales (died in office), Juan Bautista López, Juan Miguel de Vertiz.

1710 Joaquín de Zabaleta, Juan Miguel de Vertiz, Diego Ceballos Villegas.

1711 Joaquín de Zabaleta, Diego Ceballos Villegas, Count of el Fresno de la Fuente.

1712 Felipe Gónzalez de Arnaes, Count of el Fresno de la Fuente, Luis de Monterde.

1713 Felipe Gónzalez de Arnaes, Luis de Monterde, Juan Ignacio de la Vega y Sotomayor.

1714 Juan Luis de Baesa, Juan Ignacio de la Vega y Sotomayor, Pedro Ruiz de Castañeda.

1715 Juan Luis de Baesa, Pedro Ruiz de Castañeda, Juan Bautista de Arozqueta.

1716 Domingo de la Canal, Juan Bautista de Arozqueta, Francisco de Ugarte.

1717 Domingo de la Canal, Francisco de Ugarte, Nicolas de Eguiara.

1718 Domingo de la Canal, Francisco de Ugarte, Nicolas de Eguiara.

Sources: Borrador del Inventario de Libros, Quentas, y Papeles de R.s Alcavalas, desde el año de 1694 hasta el de 1753, Mexico City (?), 1 January 1753, AGN, AHH 129, exp. 15; AHH 1016, exp. 1, f. 98.

Alcaldes Ordinarios of the Mexico City Cabildo Civil

1700 Andrés de Berrio, José de la Fuente.

1701 Bernadino de Meneses Monroy y Mendoza Count of Peñalba, Diego Velázquez de la Cadena.

1702 José Tomás Tioserán de los Rios, Felipe de Estrada Tuno de Castro.

1703 Pedro Alonso Dávalos y Bracamonte, Carlos de Samaniego Gaitán.

1704 Nicolás Altamirano de Velasco Count of Santiago de Calimaya, Alonso de Navia Bolaños, after his death replaced by Pedro Jiménez de los Cobos.

1705 Juan de Padilla y Estrada Marquis of Santa Fe de Guardiola, José Escalante y Mendoza, Count of Casa de Loja.

1706 Pedro de Castro y Cabrera, Juan Leonel Gómez de Cervantes.

1707 Antonio Terán, José Ventura Artiaga y Elejalde.

1708 Fernando de Mier y Albear, Antonio de Urrutia de Vergara y Flores.

1709 Jose Núñez de Villavicencio y Orozco, Luis Moreno Monroy Guerrero y Villaseca.

1710 Miguel González del Pinal, Marcos de Tapia.

1711 Miguel Pérez de Andabolla y Santa Cruz, Marquis of Buenavista, Pedro Luna y Gorraez.

Source: Archivo Histórico del Distrito Federal. Guía General, ed. Lina Odena Güemes H. (Mexico City: Gobierno del Distrito Federal, 2000), 88–89.

5. Index of Alburquerque's Appointments of Alcaldes Mayores (AM), Corregidores (CO), and Governors (GO)

This index lists Alburquerque's appointments to the positions of *alcalde mayor, corregidor, gobernador* (governor), and in the military. The first column registers the name of the appointee; the second, labelled *Approx. date,* indicates the approximate date of the assumption of office. On occasion, the precise date could not be located because the date of paying the *media anata* tax, that is, the fee of half an annual salary, was not identical with the assumption of office. The third column, *Fiadores and testigos,* shows witnesses and those bondsmen who deposited funds with the crown in case the official defaulted on his duties. The fourth column names the appointee, while the fifth renders the office such as *alcalde mayor* (abbreviated as AM), *corregidor* (CO), or governor (GO). By this time the offices of *alcaldes mayores* and *corregidores* were almost identical. For this reason I usually label these two offices in the following index as AM, except for Veracruz nueva, where the *corregidor* held additional military duties. The sixth column shows the *Value* of the position according to the *Yndize* as explained in the text. The seventh column, *Prices usually paid,* shows various sums paid for this particular *alcaldía mayor* in Madrid as given by the records assembled under the Marquis of la Ensenada. I have only entered data here when the prices diverge considerably from the value suggested by the *Yndize*. The next column lists the time an official held the position. Several documents from the Historical Archive of the Hacienda state the exact tenure of office. Some information can be inferred from the date when the successor took possession. In many cases identifying the exact duration of office is difficult, and I had to rely on the official declaration of the *media anata* document, which was normally one year. The duration of office is given in years. In some cases the appointment only lasted months. The final column mentions the source. Abbreviations used for these columns are as follows:

m.	months
ps.	pesos
ps. e.	pesos *escudos*
ps. f.	pesos *fuertes*
rls.	*reales*
ínf.	small, *ínfima* in the *Yndize*
agr.	*agregación*, that is, an *alcaldía mayor* added to another to increase value
RyM	*real y minas*, a mining camp supervised by royal officials
alfz	*alférez*, a standard bearer

The second chart lists appointments exclusively in the military, as opposed to governors or *alcaldes mayores*, who wielded both civil and military authority. Further abbreviations used in this row are:

capitán Atrisco	Captain of the Atrisco militia
capitan comp. ciudad	Captain of the Mexico City battalion, unsalaried

Index of Alburquerque's Appointments of Alcaldes Mayores (AM), Corregidores (CO), and Governors (GO)

NO.	APPROX. DATE	FIADORES AND TESTIGOS	NAME OF APPOINTEE
1	26–Jan–02	Benítez, José, cirujano	Peramato, Diego
2	03–Jan–02	González, Francisco	Aldana y Espinosa, Francisco
3	01–Feb–02	Abarca, Nicolás	Villaroel, Diego
4	01–Feb–02	Asinas Duque de E., Alonso	Ruiz de Herrera, Blasco
5	01–Feb–02	Bustamante, Domingo, almacenista de ropa	Ruiz de Cevallos, Antonio
6	06–Feb–02	Aretio Onda, Manuel	Torre, Mateo de la
7	08–Feb–02	Manrique Alemán, Francisco	Maldonado, Andrés
8	09–Feb–02	Gómez Sánchez, Francisco	Estensoro, José
9	09–Feb–02	Sarmiento de Valladares, Miguel, maestro confitero en la calle de San Francisco	Sáenz Valiente, Juan Antonio
10	10–Feb–02	Valderrabano, Juan Antonio	Varela Moreno, Isidro
11	02–Mar–02	Díaz de la Concha, Juan, alfz. C. Dorado, cacahuateros	Cueba, Juan de la
12	09–Mar–02	Roce Velasco, Jerónimo	Ita, capitán Francisco
13	19–Jul–02		Ochoa Arin Ezeiza, Lorenzo
14	16–Oct–02	Díaz del Campo, Melchor	Izoain, Bernardo
15	14–Nov–02		Mora, capitán Andrés de la
16	20–Dec–02	Urrua, Francisco, Conde del	Escolar, José Félix, orden de Santiago
17	01–Jan–03		Rivaguda Enciso, Alvaro de
18	01–Feb–03	Reinoso Altamirano, Diego	Lejama Altamirano, Fernando
19	07–Feb–03	Aramendia, Martín	Alvarez del Valle, Jerónimo
20	14–Feb–03	Albórnoz, Francisco	Aguirre, Martín
21	15–Feb–03		Cerda Moran, José de la
22	03–Mar–03	Hoya, Juan, cacahuatero	Rojo del Río Fuente, Manuel

OFFICE	VALUE	PRICES USUALLY PAID FOR THIS AM	DURA-TION	SOURCE
AM Tlazazalca	4	1000 ps.–1400 ps. f.	1	AHH 1463
AM Autlan Puerto de la N.	2	2000 ps.	1	AHH 1463
AM Aguatlan Teopantlan			1	AHH 1463
AM Mitla y Teutitlan		2500 ps. escudos	1	AHH 1463
AM Mizantlan, Antigua Veracruz	5		1	AHH 1463
AM Panuco y Tampico	2	1000 ps.–1500 ps.	1	AHH 1463
AM Tula	2		1	AHH 1463
AM Lerma y Tarasquillo	5		1	AHH 1463
AM Villa de los Valles (Santiago de los Valles, close to San Luis Potosí)	1		1	AHH 1463
AM Guajolotitlan	4		1	AHH 1463
AM Atengo y Misquiaguala	3	without Atengo 800 ps.–150 dobloons	1	AHH 1463
AM Tetela del Volcan	8		1	AHH 1463
AM Justlahuaca	3	2400 ps. f.	10 m.	MA 65
AM Teutila	1	2400–2500 ps.	1	MA 34
AM Guichiapa	1	1200 ps.–2300 ps. f.	2	MA 34
AM Xicayan	1		1	AHH 1463
GO Campeche				AGI, Méx. 476
AM Octupan			3	MA 65
AM Tabasco		2000 ps.–2400 ps. f.	1	AHH 1648
GO Coahuila		1000 ps.–7000 ps. f.	1	AHH 1361
AM Tacuba	3		2.5	MA 34
AM Sochicoatlan			1	AHH 1463

Appendices

NO.	APPROX. DATE	FIADORES AND TESTIGOS	NAME OF APPOINTEE
23	03–Mar–03	García del Castillo, Juan	Serna, Andrés de la
24	03–Mar–03	García Cano, Francisco	Barrera, Francisco
25	04–Mar–03	Garcia de Rivas, Pedro	Villa y Cañas, Alonso
26	05–Mar–03	Vega, Isidro Romero	Vargas Lujan, Francisco
27	16–Mar–03	Mendieta Rebollo, Gabriel	Jimeno de Salinas, cap. José
28	04–Apr–03	Angulo, Carlos, vecino	Álvarez Serrano, Pascual
29	05–Apr–03	Luyando Bermeo, Juan cap., o. Alcántara	Alcántara Laris Munabe, Pedro
30	11–Apr–03	Goytia, Juan Victoria, almacenero	Fernández de Oláez, Francisco
31	17–Apr–03	Vildasola, Blas, con tienda de cacahuatería	González de Gamarra, Juan
32	05–May–03	Aguirre Espinosa, Juan, regidor perpetuo de México	Guevara, Juan
33	09–May–03	Ventura de Espinosa, Francisco, mercader	Buendía, Leandro
34	05–Jun–03	Escalante Mendoza, Pedro	González de la Sarte, Ignacio
35	08–Jun–03	Ozuela, Francisco	Gil Joven, cap. Torribio
36	16–Jun–03	Campo, Melchor Díaz	Pérez de la Calle, José
37	10–Jul–03		Morales, Miguel
38	12–Jul–03	Montero, Bartolomé, capitán	Vera, Diego
39	13–Jul–03	Gabiño, Miguel Blas, vecino	Diez de Ulzurrun, Francisco
40	18–Jul–03	Villa y Hano, Antonio	Flores Fernández, Juan
41	18–Jul–03	Dávila Galindo, Juan, general, o. Santiago	Cazate y Vargas, Lorenzo Manuel
42	20–Jul–03	Núñez Vizeo, Diego	Díaz Herrera
43	27–Jul–03		Núñez de Villavicencio, José
44	14–Aug–03	Gabiño, Miguel Blas	Vases, Lorenzo del
45	14–Aug–03	Martínez de Cárdenas, José, dueño, hacienda, Metepeque	Fernández de Angulo, Simón
46	23–Aug–03	Morales, Francisco, teniente de oficios de gobierno	Palacios, Diego

OFFICE	VALUE	PRICES USUALLY PAID FOR THIS AM	DURATION	SOURCE
AM Teusitlan y Atempa	2	1000 ps.	1	AHH 1463
AM Tixtla			1	AHH 1463
AM Ixquintepeque Peñoles			1	AHH 1463
AM Guagacualco			1	AHH 1463
AM Tenango del Valle	2	500 ps.–750 ps.	1	AHH 1463
AM Justlahuaca	3	2400 ps. f.	1	AHH 1463
AM Guayacocotla Chicontepec	3		2	MA 34, AHH 1463
AM Chilapa	1–2		2	MA 34, AHH 463
AM Teotalco, Minas de Atlazingo			1	AHH 1463
AM Coatepec	ínf.		1	AHH 1467
AM Zempoala	3	800 ps. a 20 reales–1400 ps.	1	AHH 1463
AM Tepeji de la Seda	2	1200 ps. escudos	1	AHH 1463
AM Guadalcazar	5/6		1	AHH 1463
AM Iguala	5		1	AHH 1463
AM Tepoztlan, Guaytitlan			1	AHH 1361
AM Guaymeo y Sirándaro	3	15,000 ps. escudos	1	AHH 1463
AM Teutila	1	2400–2500 ps.	1	AHH 1463
AM Amula	2		1	AHH 1463
AM Cadereita, Minas de Escanela	6		1	AHH 1463
AM San Luis de la Paz	2	1000 ps. a 10 rls.	1	AHH 1463
AM Zimatlan y Chichicapa	1		2	MA 34
AM Chinantla	4		1	AHH 1463
AM Metepec e Istlahuaca	2		1	AHH 1463
AM Yagualica	3	500 ps. fuertes	2	MA 65

NO.	APPROX. DATE	FIADORES AND TESTIGOS	NAME OF APPOINTEE
47	25–Aug–03	Martinez de Lejarzar, José A.	Mier Caso Estrada, Pedro
48	13–Sep–03	Fernández, Diego and Augustin Pérez, alférez	Morales Valdes, Miguel Jerónimo
49	17–Sep–03	Jaso Osorio, Pedro, dueño de hacienda de labor en Tula	Jaso Ponce de León, Matías
50	18–Sep–03	Cervantes Casaus, Juan; Cuebas Dávalos, Miguel, regidor; Borja Altamirano Reynoso, Diego, Regidor	Luazes, Lorenzo
51	24–Sep–03	Dunz Laguera, Francisco, dueño hacienda en Chiautla	Hortuño de Aguirre, capitán Tomás
52	28–Sep–03	Lopéz de la Peña, Juan	Covarrubias Cervantes, Juan
53	05–Oct–03	Fuente, Pedro de la	Granada, Pedro
54	11–Oct–03		Aguirre Espinosa, Juan, cap.
55	22–Oct–03	Morales, Joaquín	Tellers Siciliano, Nicolás
56	22–Oct–03	Galain, Juan, o. Santiago	Ibarrola, Juan
57	22–Nov–03	Salazar, Felipe, mercader	Chávez Osorio, Juan
58	22–Nov–03	Monroy, Pedro	Santos Pérez Terán, Antonio
59	24–Nov–03		Vargas Lujan, Francisco
60	26–Nov–03	López de Landa, Nicolás comprador de plata	Chávez Osorio, Pedro
61	06–Jan–04		Luna, alférez Isidro Félix de
62	05–Feb–04	Vivanco, capitán Miguel	Vivanco, Pedro
63	08–Feb–04	Fernández Cacho, mercader	Palacios, Domingo
64	13–Feb–04	Munarris, Miguel, tesorero del virrey Alburquerque	Munarris, José
65	08–Mar–04	Villanueva Sousa de Castro, Alonso	Villanueva Sousa de Castro, Juan José, capitán
66	17–Apr–04	Torre, Diego de la, capitán, mercader	Vargas Lujan, Pedro
67	24–May–04	Osorio, Lorenzo, o. Santiago	Andrada, Alonso
68	04–Jun–04	Gutiérrez, Antonio, mercader	Estrada Galindo, Francisco
69	05–Jun–04	Fernández de Guevara, Tomás	Navarro Cazetas, Juan

OFFICE	VALUE	PRICES USUALLY PAID FOR THIS AM	DURATION	SOURCE
AM Zumpango de Laguna	5		1	AHH 1463
AM Guautitlan	3/2		1	AHH 1463
AM Chilchotla	3		1	AHH 1463
AM Cholula	2		1	AHH 1463
AM Chiautla de la Sal	3		1	AHH 1463
AM Atlatlauca de Oaxaca	ínf.		1	AHH 1463
AM Tlalpujagua	2	3500 ps.	1	AHH 1463
AM Cholula	2		2	MA 34
AM Coatepec	ínf.		1	AHH 1463
AM Zimapan	3		1	AHH 1463
AM Guejutla	1	300–400 ps.	1	AHH 1463
AM Papantla	3		1	AHH 1463
AM Guazacualco	2		2.3	MA 34
AM Guatulco agr. Guamelula	1 ?	800 ps. de a 10 rls	1	AHH 1463
AM Otumba	3	1250 ps. – 2400 ps. de 10 rls.	2	MA 34
AM Temascaltepec	2	500 ps.–690 ps. f.	2	MA 65
AM Tetela del Rio	3		1	AHH 1648
AM Tuzpa Acpotlan y Colima	2/3		1	AHH 1648
AM Apa y Tepeapulco	4		1	AHH 1648
AM Zacatlan de las Manzanas (Gueytlapa)	2		1	AHH 1648, 1361
AM Tabasco		2000 ps.–2400 ps. f.	1	AHH 1648
AM Chinantla y Cosamaluapan	3		1	AHH 1648
AM Atitalaquia	4	with Misquiagual 800 ps. –150 doblones	1	AHH 1361

Appendices

NO.	APPROX. DATE	FIADORES AND TESTIGOS	NAME OF APPOINTEE
70	06–Jun–04	Chofre Morales, Mateo, o. Santiago	Zamora, Félix, capitán
71	14–Jun–04	García de la Vega, Lázaro; Lazo de la Vega, Antonio	Cuervo Valdés, Francisco, o. Santiago
72	20–Jun–04	Vaca, Diego, vecino	Cruz Durango, lic. Alonso de
73	25–Jun–04	Munarris, Miguel, tesorero de Alburquerque	Munarris, José
74	30–Jun–04	Vildasila, Blas, mercader	Bueno Bazori, Bartolomé
75	03–Jul–04	Galayn Berrio, Juan, o. Santiago.	Burrutayn, Berrio, o. San Juan
76	07–Jul–04	Javier, Br. Pedro; José de Castro	Samaniego Pacheco, Carlos, general, o. Calatrava
77	11–Aug–04	López de Landa, Nicolás, capitán, comprador de plata	Velasco Duque de Estrada, Fernando
78	11–Aug–04	Albizba, Juan, cajero de Nicolás López de Landa	Ecelate Luzuriaga, Juan
79	11–Aug–04	Ozerin Jáuregui, Pedro	Maldonado, Francisco Benito maestro de campo
80	13–Aug–04	Rubin de Celis, Juan	Cantera, Bernardo de la
81	20–Aug–04	Bustos, Juan de, oficial de libros del tribunal de cuentas	Alarcón, Martín, sargento mayor, o. Santiago
82	21–Aug–04	Montoya Ochoa, Juan, contador, media anata	Velasco, José Francisco
83	21–Aug–04	Ortiz Mazo, Antonio	Pérez Maldonado, Manuel
84	25–Aug–04	Vellosillo, Manuel, familia de Alburquerque	Sanz Daza, Francisco
85	27–Aug–04	Alvarado, Simón Nieto, receptor de audiencia	Luna, alférez Isidro Félix
86	29–Aug–04	Garabito, Francisco	Ortiz Hora, Cristóbal
87	01–Sep–04	Montesdoca, José, mercader	Alvarez del Valle, José
88	04–Sep–04	Pozo, Francisco, capitán, dueño trapiche, Cuernavaca	Castro, José
89	07–Sep–04	Morales, Miguel, alférez; José Sarmiento	Santerbas Espinosa, Manuel Bernardo
90	08–Oct–04	Mier, Fernando, o. Santiago	Mier, Francisco
91	22–Nov–04	Ruano Arista, Isidro	Ochoa Arin, Lorenzo

OFFICE	VALUE	PRICES USUALLY PAID FOR THIS AM	DURATION	SOURCE
AM Cuautla de las Amilpas	3		1	AHH 1648
GO Nuevo México		4000 ps.–16,000 ps. fuertes		AHH 1648
AM Temascaltepec	2	500 ps.–690 ps f.	1	
AM Guajuapa	1		1	AHH 1648
AM Ismiquilpan	3	1100–1380 ps. e.	1	AHH 1648
AM Tuzpa Acpotlan			1	AHH 1648
AM Xochimilco	4	1000 ps. – 2070 ps. fuertes	3	MA 34
AM Guanajuato, RyM	1?	1200–1900 ps	1	AHH 1648
AM Tanzitaro y Pinsándaro	3	800–1200 ps	1	AHH 1648
AM Zimatlan y Chichicapa	1		1	AHH 1648
AM Teozacualco con agr. Tesocuilco	2	800 ps. e.–2500 ps. fuertes	1.3	MA 34
AM Villa del Nombre de Dios		200 doblones–1200 doblones de a 2 escudos de oro	8 ms.	MA 34, AHH 1463
AM Izatlan y la Magdalena			1	AHH 1648
AM Tulanzingo	2	1000–1500 ps. e.	1	AHH 1648
AM Malincalco			2.5	MA 34, AHH1648
AM Mexicaltzingo	8		1	AHH 1648
AM Tinguindin	2	400 ps.	1	AHH 1648
AM Tlapa	1	4000 ps. de a 10 rls.	2	MA 34
AM Zacatula	4/2	1000 ps. escudos– 2500 ps. fuertes	1	AHH 1648
AM Maravatio y Taximaroa	1	3500 ps. de a 10 rls.	1.25	MA 34, AHH 1648
AM Igualapa			1	AHH 1648
AM Atlatlahuca	4		1	AHH 1648

Appendices

NO.	APPROX. DATE	FIADORES AND TESTIGOS	NAME OF APPOINTEE
92	27–Nov–04	Val de Espino, Juan, oficial de libros del tribunal de cuentas	Riascos, Antonio Lorenzo
93	28–Nov–04		Ajolesa, Martín
94	11–Dec–04	Cos Morante, Juan	Cosio, Bartolomé
95	20–Dec–04	Pérez Terán, Juan, mercader; Díaz Hidalgo, Francisco	Rueda, capitán Mateo Antonio
96	21–Dec–04		Colomo, Carlos
97	22–Dec–04		Valladolid, José de
98	01–Jan–05		Peramato, Diego
99	10–Jan–05	Peña, Antonio de, mercader	Pacheco, Antonio
100	16–Jan–05	Manrique Alemán, Francisco, mayordomo, posito, ciudad	Cuevas Dávalos Luna, Miguel
101	21–Jan–05		Fernández de Córdova, García, coronelo. Calatrava
102	26–Jan–05	Deza, Bernardo	Sota Yrazagorria, Pedro
103	29–Jan–05	Villegas Tagle, Pedro, o. Alcántara, vecino	Hoyuela Velarde, Pedro
104	30–Jan–05	Peña, Francisco de la	Alvarado, Felipe
105	10–Feb–05	Peña, Francisco de la, labrador	Alvarado, Felipe
106	11–Feb–05	Gómez Tagle, Francisco, dueño de almacén de pescado	Argüelles, Alejandro
107	12–Feb–05	Goroy Victoria, Juan	Berrosteguieta, Pedro
108	17–Feb–05	Mendes, Andrés	Gómez Vallesteros, Gregorio
109	19–Feb–05		Loayza Dios, Gabriel
110	28–Feb–05	Sánchez, Francisco, alférez, compañía real palacio	Salinas Barona, Gregorio, capitán, caballos corazas
111	03–Mar–05	Morales, José	Fernández de la Flor, Luis
112	10–Mar–05		Ramos Izquierda, Lorenzo A.
113	12–Mar–05		Villanueva, Juan José
114	13–Mar–05		Alarcón, José

OFFICE	VALUE	PRICES USUALLY PAID FOR THIS AM	DURATION	SOURCE
AM Cordoba	2	2000 ps. escudos–2760 ps. fuertes	1	AHH 1648
AM Mestitlan	2	1600–2800 pesos	1	AHH 1648
AM Motines	4		1	AHH 1648
AM San Miguel de las Villas y San Felipe	1	2,500 ps.– 4,025 ps. fuertes	2	MA 34, AHH 1648
AM Huauchinango	3		1	AHH 931
AM Guipustla y Tetepango			1	AHH 931
AM Tlaxcala			?	AGI, Méx. 658
AM Sinagua y la Huacana	3		1	AHH 931
AM Guichiapa	1	1200 ps–2300 ps. f.	1	AHH 931
AM San Juan de los Llanos	2	1200 ps. escudos	2	MA 65
AM Huejotzingo			1	AHH1648
AM Lerma	5		1	AHH 931
AM Chiconautla			1	AHH 1361
AM Ecatepec, San Cristóbal	6		1	AHH 931, 1648
AM Pánuco y Tampico	2		1	AHH 931
AM Chilapa	1		1	AHH 931
AM Suletepec, RyM			1	AHH 931
AM Cuiseo de la Laguna	3		1	AHH 931
GO Nuevo Reino de León		3000 ps. e. –4200 ps. fuertes		AHH 931
AM Jalapa y Jalatzingo	2		1	AHH 931
AM Mestitlan	2		1	AHH 931
AM Apa y Tepeapulco extensión del oficio	4		1	AHH 931
AM Villa del Nombre de Dios		200 doblones –1200 dobl. a 2 e. de oro	1	AHH 931

Appendices

NO.	APPROX. DATE	FIADORES AND TESTIGOS	NAME OF APPOINTEE
115	30–Mar–05	Flores Loayza, José	Campuzano, Miguel
116	30–Mar–05	Sánchez García, Bernardo	Mora, Andrés de la, capitán
117	31–Mar–05		Arias, Manuel
118	05–Apr–05	Bueno Basora, José, capitán, mercader	Cuellar, José
119	15–Apr–05	Sapa, Francisco Pablo	Martínez Molina, Diego de
120	21–Apr–05		Carrillo Viezma, José
121	21–Apr–05	Quiros, Bartolomé del	Vicuña, Pedro José
122	01–May–05		Terán de los Ríos, capitán Tomás, o. Santiago
123	03–May–05	Carvallido, Diego	Taboada Ulloa, José
124	05–May–05	Pérez Cortes, Pedro Alonso	Cortés, capitán Diego
125	13–May–05	González de Selis, Juan	Iriarte, Juan
126	20–May–05	Cardenas Bermeo, José	Vera, José
127	20–May–05	Nuñez de Villavicencio, Juan	Llerena Lazo, Pedro
128	22–May–05		Laureano Aguilar, Ignacio
129	06–Jun–05		Alarcón, Martín, sargento mayor, o. Santiago
130	12–Jun–05		Villareal y Cevallos, Pedro
131	18–Jun–05	Marreategui, Bernardo	Alcántara Laris Munabe, Pedro
132	27–Jun–05	Riva, Manuel	Ascona, José
133	03–Jul–05	Ledesma, Manuel	Ramos Izquierda, Lorenzo Antonio
134	07–Jul–05		Peñafiel, Nicolás
135	09–Jul–05	Fernández, Diego	Castillo, José del
136	13–Jul–05	Díaz Leal, Gaspar, mercader	Maldonado, Nicolás
137	13–Jul–05	Albizba, Juan, cajero del cap. Nicolás López de Landa	Fellitu, Manuel
138	17–Jul–05		Serna, Andrés de la

OFFICE	VALUE	PRICES USUALLY PAID FOR THIS AM	DURATION	SOURCE
AM Guayacocotla and Chicontepec	3		1	AHH 931
AM Pachuca, RyM	2	2000 pesos	1	AHH 931
AM Guajolotitlan	4		1	AHH 931
AM Izucar y Chietla	2	1000–2000 ps. e.	1	MA 34, AHH 1648
AM Tula	2		1	AHH 931
AM Tenango del Valle	2	500 ps.–750 ps.	1	AHH 931
AM Teusitlan y Atempa	2	1000 ps.	1	AHH 931
AM Tepeaca	1		2.5	MA 34
AM Cuicatlan con agr. Teutitlan y Papalotipac	1		1	AHH 931
AM Justlahuaca	3	2400 ps. fuertes	2	MA 34
AM Tetela y Jonotla	3	800 ps.–2000 ps.	1	AHH 931
AM Nochitlan Tilantengo			1	AHH 931
AM Zimatlan y Chichicapa	1	3,000 ps. e.–4,300 ps. de a 10 rls.		AHH 931
AM Guadalcazar	5/6		1	AHH 931
GO Coahuila		1000 ps. –7000 ps. f.	1.25	MA 65
AM Colima	2/3	1400 ps. escudos	1	AHH 931
AM Villa de los Valles (Santiago de los Valles)	1		1	AHH 931
AM Tepeji de la Seda	2	1200 ps. escudos	1	AHH 931
AM Cadereita, Minas de Escanela	6		1	AHH 931
AM Jonotlan				AHH 931
AM Guautitlan	3/2		1	AHH 931
AM Guaymeo y Sirandaro	3		1	AHH 931
AM Tanzitaro y Pinsandaro	3	800–1200 ps.	por S. E.	AHH 931
AM Zacualpan	2	2000 ps.–2300 ps. f.	1	AHH 931

NO.	APPROX. DATE	FIADORES AND TESTIGOS	NAME OF APPOINTEE
139	18–Jul–05	Jáuregui, José	Cañete, Francisco Antonio
140	20–Jul–05		Figueroa, José
141	20–Jul–05	Cornejo, Francisco Antonio	Trujillo, Diego Francisco
142	24–Jul–05	Vidal, José, tratante de ropa	Rivas Cerecedo, Antonio
143	18–Aug–05	Calderón, Miguel, dueño de hacienda	Vélez, Julián
144	20–Aug–05		Padilla, Gaspar
145	31–Aug–05	Barba de Figueroa, Pedro	Macasaga, Gabriel
146	28–Sep–05	Vertis, Juan José	Munárriz, Miguel de
147	01–Oct–05		Gorraez, Francisco
148	01–Oct–05		Flores de Medina, Juan
149	01–Oct–05		Ortiz, Francisco
150	03–Oct–05	Baltrana, José de	Burgos Osio, Miguel
151	29–Oct–05		Mora, Andrés de la, capitán
152	12–Nov–05		Contreras, José
153	16–Jan–06	Villaroel, Francisco	Sotomayor, Diego
154	22–Jan–06	Salgado, Dr. Marcos, médico	Vázquez Mellado, José
155	22–Jan–06	Díaz de la Concha, Juan	Delgado Milán, cap. Nicolás
156	22–Jan–06	Miranda, Melchor de, oficial real, caja de Pachuca	Argüelles, Juan Manuel
157	26–Jan–06	Peña, Felipe Antonio de la, capitán, mercader	Díaz Leal, Juan
158	20–Feb–06	Ruiloba, Antonio de, dueño de tienda de cacahuatería	Riva, Tomás de la
159	27–Feb–06	Osorio, Lorenzo de, o. Santiago	Ayala, Marcos
160	02–Mar–06	Nadal, Jacinto, dorador	Bolaños, Juan
161	02–Mar–06	Arrieta, Francisco de	Álvarez de Aponte, Jacobo
162	12–Mar–06	Arrieta, Juan de	Ponce de León, Diego
163	10–May–06	Salazar, Juan de, relator de la audiencia	Pérez Maldonado, Cristóbal

OFFICE	VALUE	PRICES USUALLY PAID FOR THIS AM	DURATION	SOURCE
AM Jiquilpa	3		1	AHH 931
AM Jaso y Teremendo	ínf.			AHH 931
AM Tacuba	3		1	AHH 931
AM Peñoles			1	AHH 931
AM San Luis de la Paz	2	1000 ps. a 10 rls.	1	AHH 931
AM Teotihuacan, San Juan	4	600 ps. e.	1	AHH 1361
AM Metepec e Istlahuaca	2		1	AHH 931
AM Tehuantepec	2	3500 ps.	2	MA 65
AM Chinantla Usila	5		1	AHH 931
AM Cholula	2		1	AHH 931
AM Zumpango			1	AHH 931
AM Chiautla de la Sal	3			AHH 931
AM Xilotepeque				MA 34
AM Tlalpujagua	2	3500 pesos	1	AHH 931
AM Guejutla	1	300–400 pesos	1	AHH 1361
AM Aguatlan y Teopantlan			1	MA 42
AM Atengo Misquiaguala	3		1	MA 42
AM Octupan			1	MA 42
AM Tetela del Rio	2–3		1	MA 42
AM Guatulco agr. Guamelula	1 ?	800 ps. de a 10 rls.	1	MA 42
AM Guatulco agr. Guamelula	1	800 ps. de a 10 rls.	1	MA 42
AM Atlatlauca de Oaxaca	ínf.		1	MA 42
AM Coatepec	ínf.		1	MA 42
AM Sochicoatlan			1	MA 42
AM Yagualica	3	500 ps. fuertes	1	MA 42

Appendices

NO.	APPROX. DATE	FIADORES AND TESTIGOS	NAME OF APPOINTEE
164	10–May–06	Patiño, José, oficial de pluma, contaduría de real hacienda	Deza Ulloa, Miguel, capitán
165	20–Jul–06	Espinosa, Francisco de	Galdo, capitán Juan
166	25–Sep–06	Ugarte, alférez Francisco de, mercader	Rasquito, Francisco
167	12–Oct–06	Fernández Cacho, Juan	Fernández Cacho, Pedro
168	06–Nov–06	Aldama, Agustín de, mercader	Torres Camberos, Juan
169	11–Nov–06	Erenchum, Francisco de, oficial de pluma	Fez de Acuña, Manuel, capitán de caballos corazas
170	11–Nov–06	Salazar y Velasco, Felipe de, mercader	Pérez de Bulnas, Antonio
171	11–Nov–06	Abiles, Alonso de, mro. platero	Torres, Juan Francisco Antonio
172	23–Nov–06	Manrique Alemán, Francisco alcalde, albóndiga, México	Aguirre Espinosa, Juan Manuel, capitán
173	27–Nov–06	Domingo de Bildosola, Blas	Iñigo Horcasitas, Tomás
174	27–Nov–06	Velasco, Juan de, alférez, maestro de carrocero	Ordos Laya, Nicolás, capitán caballos corazas
175	04–Dec–06	Noboa, Alejandro de, dueño de hacienda en Teotihuacan	Insa, Martin
176	13–Dec–06	González, alfz. José, mercader	Ponce de León, Tomás
177	23–Dec–06	Morales, Pedro de	Mier Caso Estrada, Pedro
178	23–Dec–06	Alvarez de U., José, mercader	Bueno de Viveros, Fernando
179	04–Feb–07	Prieto, Juan Teodoro, vecino	Prieto Cárdenas, Juan
180	10–Feb–07	Fernández Guevara, Tomás	Monteagudo, Martín
181	02–Mar–07	Sánchez, Delgado, Antonio	Delgado, Manuel
182	06–May–07	Cabrera, Fernando	Polo, Pedro Alejo
183	06–May–07		Trujillo, Estéban José
184	09–May–07	Arce, Matías Francisco	Ruiz de Herrera, Blasco
185	18–May–07	Hidalgo, Francisco Félix, procurador de audiencia	Oveda, Mateo Antonio
186	25–May–07	Garcés, Manuel Francisco	Diez de Ulzurrun, Francisco, o. Santiago

OFFICE	VALUE	PRICES USUALLY PAID FOR THIS AM	DURA-TION	SOURCE
AM Zacatlan de las Manzanas (Gueytlapa)	2		1	MA 42
AM Tanzitaro y Pinsándaro	3	800–1200 ps.	1	MA 42
AM Acatlan y Piastla	2		1	MA 42
AM Mexicaltzingo	8			MA 42
AM San Miguel de las Villas y San Felipe	1	2500 ps. a 8 rls.– 4025 ps. fuertes	1	MA 42
AM Guadalcazar	5/6		1	MA 42
AM Guanajuato, RyM	1?	1200–1900 ps.	1	MA 42
AM Izucar y Chietla	2	1000–2000 pesos escudos	1	MA 42
AM Texcoco	2	800–1300 ps	1	MA 42
AM Mitla y Tlacolula			1	MA 42
AM Taxco, RyM	1	2000 ps. e.	1	MA 42
AM Iguala	5		1	MA 42
AM Teutila	1	2400–2500 ps.		MA 42
AM Atitalaquia	4		1	MA 42
AM Motines	4		1	MA 42
AM Tetepango			1	AHH 1648
AM Cuiseo de la Laguna	3		1	AHH 1648
AM Chiconautla			1	AHH 1361
AM Apa y Tepeapulco	4		1	AHH 1648
AM Atlatlauca de Oaxaca	ínf.		2	MA 34
AM Huejotzingo			1	AHH 1648
AM San Luis de la Paz	2	1000 ps. de a 10 reales	1	AHH 1648
AM Teutila	1	2400–2500 ps.	2	MA 34

NO.	APPROX. DATE	FIADORES AND TESTIGOS	NAME OF APPOINTEE
187	27–May–07	Sánchez Riscos, José	Pintos Caldemoros, Juan
188	28–May–07	Peña, Felipe Antonio, capitán, mercader	Urízar, Tomás
189	10–Jun–07		Manso de Zúñiga, Francisco
190	17–Jun–07	Fernández Salazar, Manuel en casa de Felipe Salazar	Guevara Oteiza, José
191	28–Jun–07	Ponce de León Somoza, Ángel	Chávez, Cecilio
192	12–Jul–07		Trujillo, Diego Francisco
193	01–Aug–07	Cagueñas, José, capitán	Diez de la Mora, Miguel, o. Calatrava
194	03–Aug–07	Mascarua, Manuel, cajero de Lucas de Careaga	Diez de Ulzurrun, Francisco, o. Santiago
195	07–Aug–07	Valdés, Agustín	Garzón, Francisco
196	07–Aug–07	Pérez Romo, José	Pardo Mora, Mateo
197	07–Aug–07	Gálvez, Fernando, procurador de audiencia	Fonseca Enríquez Zúñiga Toledo, Tomás
198	08–Aug–07	Osorio, capitán Lorenzo, o. Santiago	Castañeda, Francisco
199	09–Aug–07	Garzes, Felipe, mro. herrero	Alvarado, Pedro Antonio
200	09–Aug–07	Sánchez Hidalgo, Alonso, mercader	Delgado, Manuel
201	09–Aug–07	Riscos, José	Fdz. Marmolejo, Salvador
202	09–Aug–07	Carballido Surita, Diego M.	Ramírez Valdés, Juan
203	17–Aug–07	Pastrana Mendizábal, Roque	Pastrana Mendizábal, Manuel
204	23–Aug–07	Álvarez, Juan, mercader	Álvarez, Marcos, capitán
205	15–Sep–07	Palacios, Diego, dueño de sombrería	Echevarria, José
206	19–Sep–07	Ganbino, Juan Antonio	Ochoa Lazarte, Marcos
207	06–Oct–07	Rubin de Celis, Juan	Cantera, Bernardo de la
208	04–Nov–07	Vivanco, Miguel	López Grajal, Miguel
209	08–Nov–07	Albornoz, Francis., mercader	Peramato, Francisco
210	11–Nov–07	Lanterin, José J., contador resultas, tribunal de cuentas	Guerrero Dávila, Gabriel Antonio

OFFICE	VALUE	PRICES USUALLY PAID FOR THIS AM	DURATION	SOURCE
AM Pachuca, RyM	2		1	AHH 1648
AM Sinagua y la Huacana	3		1	AHH 1648
CO Veracruz nueva	1			AGI, Méx. 377
AM Cuiseo de la Laguna	3		1	AHH 1648
AM Autlan Puerto de la Navidad	2	2000 ps.	1	AHH 1648
AM Tacuba	3		1	AHH 1361
AM Xochimilco	4		1	AHH 1648
AM Guautitlan	2/3		1	AHH 1648
AM Suletepec, RyM			1	AHH 1648
AM Tetela del Volcan	8		1	AHH 1648
AM Tetepeaca con agr. Santiago Tecali			1	AHH 1648
AM Guatulco con agr. Guamelula	1?	800 ps. de a 10 rls.	1	AHH 1648
AM Chilchotla	3		1	AHH 1648
AM Ecatepec, San Cristóbal	6		1	AHH 1648
AM Pachuca, RyM	2		1	AHH 1648
AM Tacuba	3		1	AHH 1648
AM Chiautla de la Sal	3		1	AHH 1648
AM Teotalco, Minas de Atlazingo			1	AHH 1648
AM Jiquilpa agr. Tinguindin	3		1	AHH 1648
AM Tetela y Jonotla	3		1	AHH 1648
AM Guajolotitlan	4		1	AHH 1648
AM Maravatio y Taximaroa	1	3500 ps. de a 10 rls.	1	AHH 1648
AM Zempoala	3		1	AHH 1648
AM Zumpango de la Laguna	5		1	AHH 1648

Appendices

NO.	APPROX. DATE	FIADORES AND TESTIGOS	NAME OF APPOINTEE
211	22–Nov–07	Samaniego, Juan, teniente de corte	Téllez Girón, Nicolás
212	24–Nov–07	Prado Concha, Lorenzo, mercader	Concha Cueva, Francisco
213	10–Dec–07	López de Santa Ana, Salvad.	Cano Cortes, Lorenzo
214	01–Jan–08		Velosillo Hinestrosa, Manuel, capitán
215	23–Mar–08	San Martín, Juan A., Abajo, M., Mugaguren, D., cajeros del capitán Lucas de Careaga	Gorostiza, Francisco
216	17–Apr–08	Salinas, Pedro, cacahuatero	Cuellar, Pedro Pablo
217	18–Apr–08	Carballido y Surita, Diego	Rubio de Valdés, Manuel
218	28–Apr–08	Cuevas Lunas Arellano, Miguel, regidor	Lezama Altamirano, Fernando
219	02–May–08	Díaz Leal, capitán Gaspar	Suárez Ravelo, Juan
220	06–May–08	Cerda Moran, José	Zorzona, Antonio
221	08–May–08	Menéndez, Bartolomé	Miranda, Sebastián
222	23–May–08	Arnesaga, Antonio	Murga, Antonio
223	18–Jun–08	Gonzáles de Figueroa, Antonio, mercader	Levia y Valdés, Manuel
224	22–Jun–08	Tagle Villegas, Pedro capitán, o. Alcántara	Garcia de Pruneda, Luis
225	06–Jul–08	Torres y Cano, lic. Miguel abogado de audiencia	Mesa, Augustín
226	27–Jul–08	Rubio, Pedro, platero	Ríos, José de los
227	08–Aug–08	Morales, Francisco, teniente, oficios de gobierno	Palacios, Diego
228	27–Oct–08	Barrera, Domingo, mercader	Rivas, Diego
229	05–Nov–08	Vivanco, Miguel Antonio	Vivanco, Pedro
230	08–Nov–08	García Suárez, Juan	Escudero, Cristóbal
231	09–Nov–08	Rieros, Miguel, ministro del juzgado de Indios	Salinas Arce y Vivero, Lorenzo
232	17–Nov–08	Arce, Matías Francisco	Contreras, Lucas José
233	20–Nov–08	Campa, Bernardo de la	Mediavilla y Ascona, Melchor
234	21–Nov–08	Castañeda, Benito Antonio, dueño, hacienda	Herrera, Francisco Isidro

OFFICE	VALUE	PRICES USUALLY PAID FOR THIS AM	DURA-TION	SOURCE
AM Jaso y Teremendo	ínf.		1	AHH 1648
AM Córdoba, S. Guatusco	2	2000 ps. escudos –2760 ps. fuertes	1	AHH 1648
AM Jacona Villa de Zamora			1	AHH 1648
AM Cuatro Villas de Oaxaca	1			AGI, Méx. 658
AM Tepeaca y Tecali	1	Tecali alone is of value 3 at 3500 ps. escudos	1	MA 50
AM Tochimilco	3		1	MA 50
AM Coatepec	ínf.		1	MA 50
AM Atengo y Misquiaguala	3		1	AHH 1466
AM Tetela del Río	2/3		1	MA 50
AM Atlatlauca de Oaxaca	ínf.		1	AHH 1361
AM Tenango del Valle	2	500 ps.–750 ps.	1	MA 50
AM Tanzitaro y Pinsandaro	3	800–1200 ps.	1	MA 50
AM Aguatlan Teopantlan			1	MA 50
GO Nuevo Reino de León			2	MA 50
AM Amula	2		1	MA 50
AM Papantla	3		1	MA 50
AM Yagualica	3	500 ps. fuertes	1	MA 50
AM Guanajuato, RyM	1	1200–1900 ps.	1	MA 50
AM Temascaltepec	2	500 ps.–690 ps. f.	1	MA 50
AM Iguala	5		1	MA 50
AM Atitalaquia	4		1	MA 50
AM Acatlan y Piastla	2		1	MA 50
AM Guaymeo y Sirandaro	3		1	MA 50
AM Mexicaltzingo	8		1	AHH 1648

Appendices

NO.	APPROX. DATE	FIADORES AND TESTIGOS	NAME OF APPOINTEE
235	28–Nov–08	Pérez Navas, Francisco, o. Santiago	Alarcón, Martín, sargento mayor, o. Santiago
236	07–Dec–08	Cornejo, Francisco Antonio	Trujillo, Estéban José de
237	20–Dec–08	Fez, Alonso, mercader	Arroyo y Herrera, Francisco
238	29–Jan–09	Domínguez, Santiago	Montenegro, José García
239	20–Feb–09	Paredes, Francisco de, oficial de gobernación	Lazarte, Ignacio Giniales
240	26–Feb–09	Juan Guerrero de Bocanegra, defensor del juzgado general	Vega, Pedro Carrillo de la
241	12–Mar–09	Salvador de Alaba y Mendiola García, mercader	Buendía Dávila, Leandro de
242	09–Apr–09	Rodríguez de Ledesma, Man.	Munarris, Miguel de
243	04–May–09	Gálvez Sotomayor, Nicolás	García Marino, Pedro
244	08–May–09	Barrera, Nicolás de, dueño hac.da Mexicaltzingo	Barrera Coronado, Diego de la
245	24–May–09	Prado y Zúñiga, Gregorio de	Terrero, Bartolomé
246	28–May–09	Ybarzaval, Juan Bautista de	Goenaga, capitán Martín
247	03–Jun–09	Pacheco, Pedro	Vallejo y Quiniense, Manuel
248	08–Aug–09		Martínez Molina, Diego de
249	19–Aug–09	Alvarado, Sebastián de	Contreras, José
250	05–Sep–09	Asinas Duque de Estrada, Alonso	Manzano, Pedro
251	12–Sep–09	Quintana Calero, José de, mercader	Rosal, Lucas
252	12–Sep–09	Gómez, Francisco	Lemos, José
253	14–Sep–09	Villegas, Francisco de	González de Anzo, José
254	16–Sep–09	Cosio, Alejandro de, mercader	Rebollar, Domingo
255	21–Oct–09	Valdés, Salvador de	Rivera, Tomas Antonio
256	23–Oct–09	Peramato, Diego	Morellón, Juan José
257	29–Oct–09	Roldán, Juan	Roldan, Juan Leonardo
258	29–Oct–09	Mendoza, Juan de	Valverde, Antonio
259	10–Nov–09		Ramírez de Arellano, José
260	05–Dec–09	Sampayo, capitán Francisco	Palacian y Gatica, Ignacio

OFFICE	VALUE	PRICES USUALLY PAID FOR THIS AM	DURA-TION	SOURCE
AM San Miguel de las Villas y San Felipe	1	2500 ps. a 8 rls.–4,025 ps. fuertes.	1	MA 50
AM Lerma y Tarasquillo	5		1	MA 50
AM Sochicoatlan			1	MA 50
AM Tacuba	3			MA 27
AM Maravatio y Taximaroa	1	3500 ps. a 10 rls.	1	MA 27
AM Cadereita, Minas de Escanela	6		1	MA 27
AM Teotihuacan, San Juan de	4	600 pesos escudos	1	MA 27
AM Celaya y Salvatierra	1	3000–6000 ps.	1	MA 27
AM Tinagua y la Guacana			1	MA 27
AM Ecatepec, San Cristobal	6		1	MA 27
AM Zumpango			1	MA 27
AM Pachuca, RyM	2		1	MA 27
AM Tlanatzalca			1	MA 27
AM Cuernavaca	2			
AM Zayula	2	1000 pesos escudos	1	MA 27
AM Guajolotitlan	4		1	MA 27
AM Guejutla	1	300–400 ps.	1	MA 27
AM Veracruz antigua	5		1	MA 27
AM Cuiseo de la Laguna	3		1	MA 27
AM Xiquilpa, with agr. Tinguindin				MA 27
AM Izatlan y la Magdalena				MA 27
AM Chilchotla	3		1	MA 27
AM Atlatlauca de Oaxaca	ínf.		1	MA 27
AM Chiautla de la Sal	3		1	MA 27
CO Veracruz nueva	1			AGI, Méx. 474
AM Tetela del Volcan	8		1	MA 27

Appendices   215

NO.	APPROX. DATE	FIADORES AND TESTIGOS	NAME OF APPOINTEE
261	16–Dec–09	Barreda, Pedro de la	Islaba, Juan Francisco
262	01–Jan–10		Cantera, Bernardo de la
263	27–Jan–10	Gómez, Francisco, mercader	Rivera, coronel Pedro de
264	08–Apr–10	Aguirre, Juan Manuel	Guevara, Juan
265	06–Jun–10	Meléndez, López Manuel	Peramato, Francisco
266	07–Jun–10	Díaz Leal, Gaspar	Aguirre Puentes, Francisco
267	18–Jun–10	Peña y Flores, José de la	Buendía, Pedro José de
268	20–Jun–10	Rocha, Diego de la, dueño de cajón en la plaza mayor	Dávalos Bracamonte, Francisco
269	23–Jun–10	Hugues Lorrilla, Baltasar	Montero de Espinosa, capitán Fernando
270	23–Jun–10	Sánchez de Chavarría, capitán Diego	Cervantes, Andrés Cristóbal de
271	12–Jul–10	Diego de la Rocha	Martínez de Lejarsar, José Antonio, o. Santiago
272	08–Aug–10	Roque Dávila y Quesada, Estéban	Javier de la Mata, Francisco
273	14–Aug–10	Fez de Arellano, Cristóbal, cacahuatero	Castilla, Estéban de
274	21–Aug–10	Ríos, Antonio de los, oficial de platero	Serna, Andrés de la
275	21–Aug–10	Ramírez, Miguel, maestro arcabucero	Ramírez Cortés, capitán Juan
276	21–Aug–10	Ibáñez de Ocerin, Luis, contdor resultas tribunal cuentas	Soto Carrillo, Roque de
277	04–Sep–10	Gorrindo y Navarro, Diego	Delgado, Manuel
278	10–Sep–10	Soto, Pedro Francisco de, con tienda de mercader	García del Rivero, Juan
279	23–Oct–10	Estensoro, José de, dueño de hacienda, Lerma	Hoyuela Velarde, Tomás de la
280	31–Oct–10	Vásquez, Sebastián, procurador del número, audiencia	Adel y Peñarojo, Vicente, o. Santiago
281	13–Aug–14	Romero de la Vega, Carlos	Paredes, Juan

OFFICE	VALUE	PRICES USUALLY PAID FOR THIS AM	DURA-TION	SOURCE
AM Otumba	3		1	MA 27
AM Miaguatlan	1	w. Mitla 3000–5710 ps. fuertes		AGI, Méx. 658
CO Veracruz nueva	1			MA 24
AM Coatepec	ínf.		1	AHH 1361
AM Tanzitaro y Pinsandaro	3	800–1200 ps.	1	MA 24
AM Tetela del Rio	2/3		1	MA 24
AM Tenango del Valle	2	500 ps.–750 ps.	1	MA 24
AM Tacuba	3	2400 ps.–2900 ps. fuertes	1	MA 24
AM Aguatlan Teopantlan			1	MA 24
AM Apa y Tepeapulco	4		1	MA 24
AM Queretaro	1		1	MA 24
AM San Luis de la Paz	2	1000 ps. a 10 rls.	1	MA 24
AM Tetela y Jonotla	3		1	MA 24
AM Suletepec, RyM			1	MA 24
AM Teotalco, Minas de Atlazingo			1	MA 24
AM Veracruz antigua	5		1	MA 24
AM Jaso y Teremendo	ínf.			MA 24
AM Motines	4		1	MA 24
AM Tehuantepec	2	3500 ps.	1	MA 24
AM Papantla	3		1	MA 24
AM Izucar y Cítela	2	1000–2000 pesos escudos	1	AHH 1361

6. Alburquerque's Appointments in the Military

No.	Approx. Date	Name of Appointee	Office	Source
1	01–Jan–02	Alvarez del Valle, José	Capitán, guardia del palacio	AGI, México 658
2	23–Nov–02	Valles, Domingo	Capitán, alabarderos del palacio	AGI, México 659, 4. cuaderno
3	15–Sep–03	Ibarra, Antonio de	Capitán, compañía de Mar y Guerra de la Armada de Barlovento	AGI, México 474
4	15–Sep–03	Simón Pérez, Romero	Capitanía de la almiranta de la armada	AGI, México 474
5	07–Jan–05	Arellano, José	Alférez, compañía de Acazingo	AHH 931
6	28–Jan–05	Morales Bela, Fernando	Capitán de la infantería española de Oaxaca	AHH 931
7	28–Feb–05	Cuervo Valdés, Francisco	Capitán, Atrisco	AHH 931
8	29–Oct–05	Álvarez Nava, Capitán	Alférez, compañía caballos corazas, Nueva Veracruz	AHH 931

No.	Approx. Date	Name of Appointee	Office	Source
9	29–Oct–05	Olazerigui, Francisco	Sargento, compañía de Izucar	AHH 931
10	29–Oct–08	Manzano, Juan	Capitán, compañía caballos corazas Veracruz	AGI, México 659, 4. cuaderno
11	02–Mar–09	Galearo, José Estebes	Guarda mayor, Santa Hermandad, Cerro Gordo Provincial, Santa Hermandad	MA 27
12	25–Apr–09	Diez de Ulzurrun, Francisco, o. Santiago	Capitán compañía caballos corazas Veracruz	AGI, México 659, 4. cuaderno
13	18–May–09	Salinas Barona, Gregorio, capitán	Interim sargento mayor, compañía de Puebla Tlaxcala	MA 27
14	10–May–10	Calderón Salgado y Castilla, Miguel	Capitán, compañía de la ciudad de México	AHH 1188–1

Notes

CHAPTER 1 - INTRODUCTION

1. Roderic Ai Camp, *Mexico's Mandarins: Crafting a Power Elite for the Twenty-First Century* (Berkeley: University of California Press, 2002).

2. Barry Ames, "Approaches to the Study of Institutions in Latin America," *Latin American Research Review* (hereinafter LARR) 34:1 (1999): 221-36.

3. The *Partido Revolucionario Institucional* (PRI) and its predecessor parties continuously held the presidency and the majority of the federal congress in Mexico since 1929; Camp, *Mexico's Mandarins*, 5-6.

4. Historians describe the office of the viceroy as an institution, for example, Sigfrido Augusto Radaelli, *La institución virreinal en las Indias; antecedentes históricas* (Buenos Aires: Perrot, 1957). The viceregal court may be classified as an informal institution.

5. See, for example, José María Ots Capdequí, *El estado español en las Indias* (Mexico City: Fondo de Cultura Económica, 1946).

6. John Leddy Phelan, *The Kingdom of Quito in the Seventeenth Century. Bureaucratic Politics in the Spanish Empire* (Madison: University of Wisconsin Press, 1967); Inge Wolff-Buisson, *Regierung und Verwaltung der kolonialspanische Städte in Hochperu, 1538-1650* (Cologne: Böhlau, 1970).

7. Jonathan Israel, *Race, Class and Politics in Colonial Mexico, 1610-1670* (London: Oxford University Press, 1975), 43.

8. David Brading, *Miners and Merchants in Bourbon Mexico, 1763-1810* (Cambridge: Cambridge University Press, 1971), 33-96.

9. Ibid., 33.

10. Ibid., 33-96.

11. Colin M. MacLachlan, *Spain's Empire in the New World. The Role of Ideas in Institutional and Social Change* (Berkeley: University of California Press, 1988); Mark A. Burkholder and Dewitt Samuel Chandler also back Brading's argument in *From Impotence to Authority: the Spanish Crown and the American Audiencias, 1687-1808* (Columbia: University of Missouri Press, 1977).

12. John Mark Tutino, "Creole Mexico: Spanish Elites, Haciendas, and Indian Towns, 1750-1810" (Ph.D. diss., University of Texas at Austin, 1976), v-vii. Jacques Barbier has also denied the novel character and structural change of the reforms under Charles III, although he sees a number of successful innovations, mostly in the fiscal and military realm; see his *Reform and Politics in Bourbon Chile, 1755-1796* (Ottawa: University of Ottawa Press, 1980), 5, 7-9.

13 Horst Pietschmann, *Die Einführung des Intendantensystems in Neu-Spanien im Rahmen der allgemeinen Verwaltungsreform der spanischen Monarchie im 18. Jahrhundert* (Cologne: Böhlau, 1972).

14 Ibid., 308.

15 Horst Pietschmann, *Staat und staatliche Entwicklung am Beginn der spanischen Kolonisation* (Münster, Germany: Aschendorff, 1980), 17–25; Spanish translation *El estado y su evolución al principio de la colonización española de América* (Mexico City: Fondo de Cultura Económica, 1989).

16 John Lynch, *Spain under the Habsburgs*, vol. 2, *Spain and America 1598–1700*, 2nd ed. (New York: New York University Press, 1984), 271–73, 1st ed. published in 1969. Richard Kontetzke advances the idea of the longstanding quarrel between crown and conquistadors, "Grundherrschaftliche Gerichtsbarkeit im spanischen America während des 18. Jahrhunderts," in *Homenaje a Jaime Vicens* Vives, ed. Juan Maluquer de Motes y Nicolau (Barcelona: University of Barcelona, 1967), 2:281–82.

17 One of the few contributions is Israel, *Race, Class and Politics*; for a recent analysis of Peruvian politics, see Adrian John Pierce, "Early Bourbon Government in the Viceroyalty of Peru, 1700–1759" (Ph.D. diss., University of Liverpool, 1998).

18 Luis Navarro García, "La política Indiana," in *América en el siglo XVIII. Los primeros Borbones*, ed. Luis Navarro García, vol. 11–1 of *Historia General de España y América*, ed. Luis Suárez Fernández et al. (Madrid: Ediciones Rialp, 1989), 3–64; Antonia Herrera Heredia, "México," in ibid., 461–517. The German language *Handbuch* also offers an interpretive outline of political and social transformation in Spanish America; Anthony McFarlane, "Hispanoamerika," in *Mittel-, Südamerika und die Karibik bis 1760*, ed. Horst Pietschmann, vol. 1 of *Handbuch der Geschichte Lateinamerikas*, ed. Walther L. Bernecker et al. (Stuttgart: Klett-Cotta, 1994), 751–88. *Colonial Latin America*, vol. 2 of *The Cambridge History of Latin America*, ed. Leslie Bethell (Cambridge: Cambridge University Press, 1984).

19 Max Weber, *Politcs as a Vocation*, trans. and ed. H. H. Gerth and C. Wright Mills (Philadelphia: Fortress Press, 1965), 4–7, 18–19; Max Weber, *The Protestant Ethic and the Spirit of Capitalism*, ed. Anthony Giddens, trans. Talcott Parsons (New York: Charles Scribner's Sons, 1958), 181.

20 Ibid., 835.

21 Gerhard Oestreich, "The Structure of the Absolute State," in *Neostoicism and the Early Modern State*, ed. Brigitta Oestreich and H. G. Koenigsberger, trans. David McLintock (Cambridge: Cambridge University Press, 1982), 258–73. First published in 1969.

22 Ibid., 271.

23 Ibid., 258–73.

24 Wolfgang Reinhard, "Introduction. Power Elites, State Servants, Ruling Classes and the Growth of State Power," in *Power Elites and State Building*, ed. Wolfgang Reinhard (Oxford: Clarendon Press, 1996), 1–18. See also Peter Waldmann, "Zur Transformation des europäischen Staatsmodells in Lateinamerika," in *Verstaatlichung der Welt? Europäische Staatsmodelle und außereuropäische Machtprozesse*, ed. Wolfgang Reinhard, Schriften des Historischen Kollegs, vol. 47 (Munich: Oldenbourg, 1999), 53–66.

25 Peer Schmidt, "Neoestoicismo y disciplinamiento social en Iberoamérica colonial (siglo XVII)," in *Pensamiento europeo y cultura colonial*, ed. Karl Kohut and Sonia Rose (Frankfurt am Main: Vervuert, 1997), 181–204; John H. Elliot emphasizes the neo-stoic thinking of the Count-Duke of Olivares and of Cardinal Richelieu in *Richelieu and Olivares* (Cambridge: Cambridge University Press, 1984), 26–31.

26 For example, see Steffen Schmidt, *Friends, Followers, and Factions: A Reader in Political Clientelism* (Berkeley: University of California Press, 1977). For a recent overview, see Stanley Wasserman, *Social Network Analysis: Methods and Applications* (Cambridge: Cambridge University Press, 1994).

27 For a suggestive discussion of lineage in France, see Roland Mousnier, *Les institutions de la France sous la monarchie absolue 1598-1789, societé et état* (Paris: Presses universitaires de France, 1974), 1:47–84.

28 I refer here to the excellent study on "spiritual kinship" by Joseph H. Lynch who, despite the narrower title, thoroughly synthesizes the literature on Europe and Latin America, *Godparents and Kinship in Early Medieval Europe* (Princeton: Princeton University Press, 1986). Lynch points to the changing medieval and early modern usage of the coparenthood complex (Latin terms *compatres/comatres* and *patrini/matrinae*).

29 Alex Weingrod, "Patrons, Patronage and Political Parties," *Comparative Studies in Society and History* 10:4 (1968): 379.

30 For a good albeit somewhat dated survey of anthropological and sociological literature on social networks, see Wolfgang Reinhard, *Freunde und Kreaturen. "Verflechtung" als Konzept zur Erforschung historischer Führungsgruppen. Römische Oligarchie um 1600* (Munich: Ernst Vögel, 1979).

31 Sharon Kettering, *Patrons, Brokers, and Clients in Seventeenth-Century France* (Oxford: Oxford University Press, 1986), 3–11. For an early revision on absolutism, see Fritz Hartung and Roland Mousnier, "Quelques problèmes concernant la monarchie absolue," in *Relazioni del X Congresso Internazionale di Scienze Storiche*, Rome 1955 (Florence: G.C. Sansoni, 1955), 4:1–55.

32 Phelan, *The Kingdom of Quito*. For an enlightening quantitative study, Stephanie Blank, "Patrons, Clients, and Kin in Seventeenth-Century Caracas: A Methodological Essay in Colonial Spanish American Social History," *Hispanic American Historical Review* (hereinafter HAHR) 54:2 (1974): 260–83.

33 Tamar Herzog, *La administración como un fenómeno social: La justicia penal de la ciudad de Quito (1650-1750)* (Madrid: Centro de Estudios Constitucionales, 1995).

34 A massive prosopography of a social group between 1680 and 1748 delivers André Zysberg, *Les galériens. Vies et destins de 60 000 forçats sur les galères de France, 1640-1748* (Paris: Editions du Seuil, 1987); for general methodological problems of prosopography, see Françoise Autrand, ed., *Prosopographie et genèse de l'état moderne. Actes de table ronde* (Paris: École normale superieure de jeunes filles, 1986).

35 Michel Bertrand, *Grandeur et misères de l'office. Les officiers de finances de Nouvelle-Espagne XVIIe-XVIIIe siècles* (Paris: Publications de la Sorbonne, 1999).

36 See Antonio del Valle Menéndez, *Juan Francisco de Güemes y Horcasitas. Primer Conde de Revillagigedo. Virrey de México. La Historia de un Soldado (1681-1766)*, in collaboration with Pilar Latasa Vasallo (Santander, Spain: Librería Estudios, 1998); José Antonio Calderón Quijano, ed., *Los virreyes de Nueva España en el reinado de Carlos III* (Seville: Escuela de Estudios Hispano-Americanos, 1967); Bernard E. Bobb, *The Viceregency of Antonio María Bucareli in New Spain, 1771-1779* (Austin: University of Texas Press, 1962). A recent work on viceroys is Asmaa Bouhrass, "La administración virreinal y el comercio en Nueva España (1740-1765)" (Ph.D. diss., University of Seville, 1999). Lewis Hanke also stresses research lacuna on viceroys in *Spanish Viceroys in America*, the

Smith History Lecture 1972 (Houston: University of St. Thomas, 1972).

37 Horst Pietschmann "La corte virreinal de México en el siglo XVII en sus dimensiones jurídico-institucionales, sociales y culturales: Aproximación al estado de la investigación," in *La creatividad femenina en el mundo barroco hispánico. María de Zayas-Isabel Rebeca Correa-Sor Juana Inés de la Cruz*, ed. Monika Bosse, Barbara Potthast, and André Stoll (Kassel, Germany: Reichenberger, 1999), 2:481–97; Pilar Latasa Vasallo, "La Casa del Obispo-Virrey Palafox: Familia y Patronazgo. Un análisis comparativo con la corte virreinal hispanoamericano," in *Palafox. Iglesia, Cultura y Estado en el Siglo XVII. Congreso Internacional IV Centenario del Nacimiento de Don Juan de Palafox y Mendoza, Universidad de Navarra, Pamplona, 13–15 Abril 2001* (Pamplona, Spain: Universidad de Navarra, 2001), 201–28. See also the description of ceremonies and some of viceroy Fuenclara's clients in Eugenio Sarrablo Aguareles, *El Conde de Fuenclara. Embajador y Virrey 1687–1752* (Seville: G.E.H.A., 1955), 183–214.

38 Norbert Elias, *The Court Society*, [1969] trans. Edmund Jephcott (Oxford: Basil Blackwell, 1983), 41–42.

39 Ronald G. Asch, Introduction to *Princes, Patronage and the Nobility. The Court at the Beginning of the Modern Age, c. 1450–1650*, ed. Ronald Asch and Adolf M. Birke (Oxford: Oxford University Press, 1991), 38.

40 Geoffrey Elton, "Tudor Government: The Points of Contact: III The Court," *Transactions of the Royal Historical Society*, 5th ser., 26 (1976): 211–28. See also Antonio Sáez-Arance, "La corte de los Habsburgos en Madrid (siglos XVI y XVII): Estado de la cuestión y nuevos planteamientos historiográficos," in Bosse, Potthast, and Stoll, *Creatividad femenina*, 1:1–16.

41 Robert Forster, *The House of Saulx-Tavanes. Versailles and Burgundy 1700–1830* (Baltimore: Johns Hopkins University Press, 1971), 10–11. Emmanuel Le Roy Ladurie also rejects Norbert Elias' notion that the courtly discipline of Versailles lay at the roots of the bourgeois moderation and conviviality of the post-revolutionary epoch. Regardless, the origins of modern manners and measure are not the focus of this investigation; *Saint-Simon, and the Court of Louis XIV*, in collaboration with Jean-François Fitou, transl. Arthur Goldhammer (Chicago: University of Chicago Press, 2001), especially 349–52.

42 Elias, *The Court Society*, 41–42.

43 Memoria de los criados y allegados y assesores que ha tenido el Excelentisimo Señor Duque de Alburquerque (hereinafter abbreviated as Memoria de los criados), Francisco Félix Hidalgo to Juan Valdés, Mexico City, 23 November 1710, Archivo General de las Indias, Seville, Spain, section audiencia de México, legajo (folder) 658 (hereinafter AGI, México 658), ff. 31v–34v. See also the licencia de embarcación of the Viceroy Marquis of Valero, Cádiz, 3 March 1716, AGI, Contratación 5469, N 2, R 10.

44 Stephanie Blank quantifies status and wealth in a colonial society. Although applying a novel and interesting methodology, the scarcity und unreliability of data poses problems. Applying her method to the viceregal court is impossible because of the lack of comparable sources. Blank, "Patrons, Clients, and Kin."

45 This was evidently the contemporary understanding of the term as well. Alburquerque's legal advisor once defined a client by explaining that he was not a *criado* but accompanied his father, Alburquerque's physician, to Mexico, and then served the viceroy. Another client arrived later as well and attended Alburquerque "no como *criado*; sino como Recomendado" ("not as a *criado* but as a recommended person"); Francisco Félix Hidalgo to Juan de Valdés, Mexico City, 20 January 1711, AGI, México 658, ff. 317–18.

46 For this point see also Burkholder, "Titled Nobles, Elites, and Independence: Some Comments," *LARR* 13:2 (1978): 290–95. Jochen Meissne, in his discussion of the Mexico City *cabildo civil,* delivers a defintion of a functional elite, *Eine Elite im Umbruch: Der Stadtrat von Mexiko zwischen kolonialer Ordnung und unabhängigem Staat (1761–1821)* (Stuttgart: Franz Steiner, 1993). For a recent discussion of elites in Latin America see Bernd Schröter, Christian Büschges, eds. *Beneméritos, aristócratas y empresarios. Identidades y estructuras sociales de las capas altas urbanas en América hispánica* (Frankfurt am Main: Vervuert, 1999).

47 For an early investigation into the etiquette and courtly ceremonies under Philip II, see also Ludwig Pfandl, *Philip II. Gemälde eines Lebens und einer Zeit* (Munich: Georg D. W. Callwey, 1938).

48 This working hypothesis draws from Ronald Asch's interpretation of the European courts in "Introduction," in *Princes, Patronage and the Nobility,* 38.

49 Alburquerque to the Duke of Medina Sidonia, Puerto Rico, 15 August 1702 and Mexico City, 6 January 1703, Latin American Library, Tulane University, Viceregal and Ecclesiastical Collection (hereinafter VEMC) 1, leg. 75, exp. 29. Duke of Linares to king, Mexico City, 6 January 1711, AGI, México 483. The surname of the tenth duke is Férnandez de la Cueva Enríquez, his forename being Francisco; customarily he intituated as follows: "Duque de Alburquerque, Marques de Cuellar, Conde de Ledesma y de Guelma, Señor de las Islas de Mombeltran, La Codozera, Lanzaita, Mijares, Pedro Bernardo, Aldea de Avila, S. Estevan, Uitlarejo, y las Cuevas, Comendador de Guadalcanal en la horden de Santiago, y de Bemsayanen en la de Alcantara, Gentilhombre de la Camara de su Magestad, su Virrey, lugartheniente, Governador, y Capitan General de esta Nueva-España, y Presidente de su Real Audiencia, y Chanzilleria en el reside & c": see, for example, Alburquerque to *alcalde mayor* of Tetela del Volcán, Archivo General de la Nación, Mexico City, *ramo* (section) Indios, *volumen* (volume) 97, *expediente* (folder) 1, *foja* (folio) 13 (hereinafter AGN, Indios 97, exp. 1, f. 13).

50 The eighth Duke of Alburquerque governed New Spain from 1653 to 1660. His daughter, Ana Rosalía Fernández de la Cueva, married her uncle, who later inherited the title. The tenth Duke of Alburquerque was therefore simultaneously grandson and nephew of the former viceroy. The traditional dynastic interpretation has preferred labelling the tenth duke as "nephew" of the eighth; José Ignacio Rubio Mañé, *Introducción al estudio de los virreyes de Nueva España, 1535–1746* (Mexico City: UNAM, 1959), 1:248–51, 294. The governor of New Mexico and client of Alburquerque, Francisco Cuervo y Valdés, founded the "villa de Alburqueq. e" [sic] (town of Alburquerque) in 1706, certificación of Francisco Cuervo y Valdés to the king, Santa Fe, New Mexico, 23 April 1706, Biblioteca Nacional de México, Fondo Reservado (hereinafter BNM, FR), Archivo Franciscano 24/479, ff. 34–34v. The city in New Mexico, named after the duke, shed the first "r" in the course of the region's Anglicization. The toponymy of the town Alburquerque in the province Badajoz, Extremadura, Spain, on the border to Portugal developed from the Arabic *abu l-qurq,* literally father of the cork, that is, place of the cork trees. In Spanish Arabic the term *qurq* is derived from Latin *cortex* (cork); see Emilio Nieto Ballester, *Breve diccionario de topónimos españoles,* in collaboration with Araceli Striano Corrochano (Madrid: Alianza Editorial, 1997), 34.

51 Manuel Rivera, *Los Gobernantes de México. Galería de biografías y retratos de los Vireyes, Emperadores, Presidentes y otros gobernantes que ha tenido México, desde Don Hernando Cortes hasta el C. Benito Juarez* (Mexico City: Imprenta de J. M. Aguilar Ortiz, 1872), 1:308.

52 Francisco Fernández de Bethencourt, *Historia genealógica y heráldica de los grandes de España*, (Madrid: Estab. Tip. de Enríque Teodoro, 1920), 10:297–300. Another laudatory view is José Montoro, *Virreyes españoles en América. Relación de virreinatos y biografías de los virreyes* (Barcelona: Editorial Mitre, 1991), 143–46.

53 Luis Navarro García, "La secreta condena del virrey Alburquerque," in *Homenaje al Dr. Muro Orejón*, ed. Facultad de Filosofía y Letras (Sevilla: Facultad de Filosofía y Letras, 1979), 1:201–14; idem, *Conspiración en México durante el gobierno del Virrey Alburquerque* (Valladolid: Casa-Museo de Colón, 1982); idem, "El segundo virrey Alburquerque y su memoria de gobierno (México 1710)," in *Reformismo y sociedad en la América borbónica. In memorian Ronald Escobedo*, ed. Pilar Latasa Vasallo (Barañáin, Spain: Ediciones Universidad de Navarra, 2003), 195–226.

54 A note on titles, spelling, and terminology: Persons are usually introduced with their full title, such as *Alférez* Juan Vázquez when relevant for the argument. I occasionally use *Don* or *Doña*, the addresses indicating nobility, in order not to repeat the full names excessively. These titles reflect merit according to the colonial order, and I will not repeat them every time a person's name appears. Additionally, names of persons and locations appear in myriad variations in the colonial documents. I have cautiously modernized their spelling and chosen to employ one version consistently. For example, at least three different written versions of the *alcaldía mayor* of Celaya (Zelaya, Celaia) can be found. I shall use Celaya throughout the text. Moreover, some English language works on viceroys, such as Bobb, *The Viceregency of Antonio María Bucareli*, translate the Spanish term *virreinato* as *viceregency* when referring to the tenure instead of the territory. Viceregents, however, have acted as the deputy of the regent, who in turn has been "invested with royal authority by, or on behalf of, another; *esp.* one appointed to administer a kingdom during the minority, absence, or incapacity of the sovereign," the Oxford English Dictionary, 2nd ed. (Oxford: Clarendon Press, 1989), 8:506. The American viceroys did not claim to act as a deputy to the regent. Rather, they represented royal authority under the auspices of the king in the other realms or provinces. The expressions *viceroyalty* or *viceroyship* fit better when referring to the tenure of the viceroy.

CHAPTER 2 - THE POLITICAL AND ECONOMIC CULTURE OF SPAIN'S EARLY-EIGHTEENTH CENTURY EMPIRE

1 Henry Kamen, *Spain in the Later Seventeenth Century, 1665–1700* (London: Longman, 1980), 67–105.

2 Pierre and Huguette Chaunu, *Séville et l'Atlantique, 1504–1650* (Paris: A. Colin, 1955–59), 8:1523–1560; Woodrow Borah, *New Spain's Century of Depression* (Berkeley: University of California Press, 1951).

3 Renate Pieper, "Die demographische Entwicklung," in *Mittel-, Südamerika und die Karibik bis 1760*, 313–28; historians still debate the impact of the conquest on population level: see Bernard H. Slicher van Bath, *Indianen en Spanjaarden. Een ontmoeting tussen twee werelden, Latijns Amerika 1500–1800* (Amsterdam: B. Bakker, 1989), 97–106. Jonathan Israel defends Borah's theory in as far as he argued for a political crisis: see his "Mexico and the 'General Crisis' of the Seventeenth Century," *Past and Present* 63 (1974): 33–57.

4 Louisa Schell Hoberman, *Mexico's Merchant Elite, 1590–1660. Silver, State, and Society* (Durham: Duke University Press, 1991), 13–17, 270–74.

5 Lynch, *Spain under the Habsburgs*, 212–13. See also Ruggiero Romano,

Conjonctures opposées. La "crise" du XVIIe siècle: en Europe et en Amérique ibérique (Geneva: Librairie Droz, 1992), 224.

6. Along with the Count of Monterrey and the Admiral of Castile, see Janine Fayard, *Les membres du Conseil de Castille a l'époque moderne (1621–1746)* (Geneva: Librairie Droz, 1979), 156. Ubilla y Medina was created Marquis of Ribas in 1701, reaping the rewards of the Bourbon accession; Kamen, *The War of Succession in Spain 1700–1715* (Bloomington: Indiana University Press, 1969), 113.

7. *Histoire publique et secrette de la cour de Madrid. Dès l'avènement du Roy Philippe V. a la couronne, avec des considerations sur l'état present de la monarchie espagnole* (Cologne: Pierre le Sincère, 1719), 29; Vicente Bacallar y Sanna, Marqués de San Felipe, *Comentarios de la guerra de España e historia de su rey Felipe V, el animoso,* ed. Carlos Seco Serrano, Biblioteca de Autores Españoles desde la formación del lenguaje hasta nuestros días, vol. 99 (Madrid: Ediciones Atlas, 1957), 5–19.

8. Kamen, *The War of Succession*, 45, 83–86, 113.

9. Alfred Baudrillart, *Philippe V et la cour de France d'après des document inédits tirés des archives espagnoles de Simancas et d'Alcala de Hénares, et des archives du ministère des affaires étrangéres a Paris* (Paris: Librairie du Firmin-Didiot et Cie, 1890), 1:150. Under the Habsburgs, the Council of the Indies in Madrid advised the king or decided de facto on a whole range of American affairs. The Bourbon dynasty reduced the role of the body to that of an appellate court.

10. Alburquerque's sister-in-law, Ana Caterina de la Cerda y Aragón, Duchess of Medina de Río Seco, had married Juan Tomás Enriquez de Cabrera, Admiral of Castile; power of attorney by the Duchess of Alburquerque, Mexico City, 6 May 1710, Acervo Histórico del Archivo General de Notarías (hereinafter abbreviated as AHAGN) Escribano José de Ledesma, número de notaría 340, volume 2247. On the defection of the admiral, see Kamen, *Philip V of Spain. The King Who Reigned Twice* (New Haven: Yale University Press, 2001), 25.

11. Kamen, *The War of Succession*, 90–92, 113.

12. Ibid., 99.

13. Gildas Bernard, *Le secrétariat d'état et le conseil espagnol des Indes (1700–1808)* (Geneva: Librairie Droz, 1972), 3–6, 83, footnotes 43, 44. The king suspended or exiled the following councillors in 1706: José Bolero y Muñoz, Juan de Castro y Gallego, José de Cossio Barreda, Sancho de Castro y Losada, José de Escals, José María Francisco de la Cerda Manrique de Lara Marquis of la Laguna, Pedro de Gamarra y Arriaga, Manuel de Gamboa, Manuel García de Bustamante, Mateo Ibañez de Mendoza, Diego Jiménez de Encina Marquis of Casal, Antonio de Ubilla y Medina Marquis of Ribas, Ramón de Portocarrera, Pascual de Villacampo: Bernard, *Le sécretariat d'état,* ibid., 212–14.

14. Kamen, *The War of Succession*, 52, 185–86.

15. Ibid., 1–24. For an account of mainly military activities, David Francis, *The First Peninsular War 1702–1713* (New York: St. Martin's Press, 1975).

16. Kamen, *The War of Succession*, 233.

17. Ibid., 113–14; idem, *Philip V,* 95–97.

18. Kamen, *The War of Succession*, 88, fn. 15; Frigiliana acted as governor during the absence of president Duke of Uceda from 17 January 1710 to 13 September 1717. The career of Antonio de Ubilla y Medina, Marquis of Ribas, also recovered after the departure of Jean Orry. The king reestablished Ubilla as councillor of the Indies in 1715 and admitted him to the *cámara de Indias* (select members of the Council who

dispensed patronage) in 1721; Bernard, *Le secrétariat d´état*, 211, 214.

19 Consulta of the Council of the Indies, Madrid, 25 February 1702, AGI, México 610.

20 José I. Conde and Javier Sanchiz, *Títulos y dignidades nobiliarias en Nueva España* (Mexico City: UNAM, forthcoming), based on a journalistic article by Fernando Muñoz Altea on the Duke of Alburquerque in the Mexican newspaper *Excelsior*.

21 Alburquerque belonged to the Spanish grandees of the first class and held the office of gentleman with access to the king's chamber (*gentilhombre con ejercicio de la cámara del rey*). The duke married Juana de la Cerda y Aragón, sister of Luis de la Cerda, ninth Duke of Medinceli, both offspring of Juan F.T.L. de la Cerda y Enríquez de la Ribera, eighth Duke of Medinaceli, and Catalina A. de Aragón y Folch de Cardona; Rubio Mañé, *Introducción*, 1:248–51; Lynch, *Spain under the Habsburgs*, 143.

22 On 9 October 1702, Medinaceli formally ended his term but continued in his functions, see Bernard, *Le secrétariat d´état*, 213–34.

23 Alburquerque's will, Mexico City, 27 June 1711, AHAGN, Escribano José de Ledesma, No. 340, vol. 2247.

24 Real cédula, Madrid, 13 April 1702, AGI, México 610.

25 Alburquerque to the Duke of Medina Sidonia, Puerto Rico, 15 August 1702, VEMC 1, leg. 75, exp. 29; Alburquerque to Medina Sidonia, Mexico City, 6 January 1703, ibid. According to the audiencia, the Duke took possession of the viceroyalty on 25 November 1702; audiencia of Mexico to king, Mexico City, 9 April 1703, AGI, México 610. For the departure from La Coruña, see Rubio Mañé, *Introducción*, 1:160.

26 Duke of Linares to king, 6 January 1711, AGI, México 483.

27 Mexico City, 26 November 1712, AHAGN, Escribano José de Ledesma, No. 340, vol. 2247.

28 Pablo Emilio Pérez-Mallaina Bueno, *Política naval española en el Atlántico, 1700–1715* (Seville: Escuela de Estudios Hispano-Americanos, 1982), 14.

29 Pietschmann, *Die Einführung des Intendantensystems*, 14–29.

30 Ibid.

31 MacLachlan, *Spain's Empire*, 67–88. In 1729 Uztariz became secretary for New Spain on the Council of the Indies, Bernard, *Le secrétariat d´état*, 231.

32 Horst Pietschmann, *Die staatliche Organisation des kolonialen Iberoamerika*, Teilveröffentlichung zum Handbuch der Geschichte Lateinamerikas (Stuttgart: Klett-Cotta, 1980), 84–85.

33 Elliott, *The Count-Duke of Olivares. The Statesman in an Age of Decline* (New Haven: Yale University Press, 1986), 653. The observation about the *privados* is also true for the prime ministers of eighteenth-century Spain until Charles III as well as for the government of Cardinal Richelieu in France; Elliott, *Richelieu and Olivares*; Antonio Feros, *Kingship and Favoritism in the Spain of Philip III, 1598–1621* (Cambridge: Cambridge University Press, 2000); James M. Boyden, *The Courtier and the King. Ruy Gómez de Silva, Philip II, and the Court of Spain* (Berkeley: University of California Press, 1995).

34 Israel, "Mexico and the 'General Crisis,'" 38–54.

35 Lynch, *Spain under the Habsburgs*, 271–73.

36 Parry, *Sale of Public Office*, 48–68.

37 John Lynch, *Bourbon Spain, 1700–1808* (Oxford: Basil Blackwell, 1989), 142, 152–54.

38 Michel Bertrand, *Grandeur et misères*, 286–90, 325–33, 405–7.

39 Meissner shows that in the 1761–1821 period, fifty-three merchants joined the *ayuntamiento* through the new offices

whereas only one *regidor perpetuo* (a member of the municipal council who purchased his office) was a merchant. He also points to the four nobles among the *regidores perpetuos* as compared to twenty-four among the annually rotating new members of the municipal council; *Eine Elite im Umbruch*, 81–83, 325–26, 340–46.

40 Stanley J. and Barbara H. Stein see the tenure of Esquilache as the pivotal phase of eighteenth-century "defensive modernization." Segments of the upper clergy, the *colegiales mayores* (the graduates of the universities of Salamanca, Valladolid, and Alcalá who had belonged to the six exclusive confraternities associated with these schools), the *consulado* of Cadiz, and the nobility engineered the riot of 1766 to ward off Esquilache's impending changes: *Apogee of Empire. Spain and New Spain in the Age of Charles III, 1759-1789* (Baltimore: Johns Hopkins University Press, 2003), 28–30, 81–115.

41 Pietschmann, "Consideraciones en torno al protoliberalismo, reformas borbónicas y revolución. La Nueva España en el último tercio del siglo XVIII," *Historia Mexicana* 41:2 (1991): 167-205.

42 Rubio Mañé, *Introducción*, 1:242, 251-64.

43 Ibid., 1:267-70.

44 *Recopilación de leyes de los reynos de las Indias mandada imprimir y publicar por la Magestad Católica del Rey Don Carlos II. Nuestro Señor ...* (1741: Madrid: Consejo de la Hispanidad, 1953) (hereinafter *RLRI*), libro iii, título iii, ley ii.

45 For the guard, see *real cédula* to Viceroy Juan Francisco de Güemes y Horcasitas (viceroy from 1746–1755, Count of Revillagigedo since 1749), Madrid, 28 July 1746, AGI, México 1506, No. 12 and 12b.

46 Informe of the tribunal of accounts, Mexico City, 15 November 1780, BNM, Fondo Reservado, Manuscritos 439, ff.

333–39. See also Rubio Mañé, *Introducción*, 1:211–12. The tribunal of accounts or *tribunal de cuentas* revised the transactions and receipts of all treasuries and accountancies in the realm. One silver peso corresponded to eight *reales*; one *real* equalled twelve *granos*.

47 *RLRI*, lib. iii, tít. iii, ley i.

48 Burkholder and Chandler, *From Impotence to Authority*, 1–3.

49 See for example the case discussed in Pedro del Castillo y Vergara to king, 8 April 1707; Consulta of the Council of the Indies, 2 December 1707, AGI, México 817.

50 *RLRI*, lib. iii, tít. iii, leyes iii, iv; king to Archbishop Ortega, Madrid, 9 August 1709, AGI, México 403.

51 Ernst Schäfer, *El consejo real y supremo de Indias. Su historia, organización y labor administrativo hasta la terminación de la casa de Austria* (Seville: M. Carmona, 1935–47), 1:248.

52 See the relación de Don Francisco de Güemes y Horcasitas [Count of Revillagigedo] a Agustín de Ahumada y Villalón, 8 October 1755, in *Instrucciones y memorias de los virreyes novohispanos*, ed. Ernesto de la Torre Villar (Mexico City: Editorial Porrúa, 1991), 2:826.

53 "Tambien tiene alguna subordinacion â este Gov.no y Capitania Gral. (como que deeste Reyno procede su manutencion) las Yslas Philipinas, y Marianas, la de Cuba, S.to Dom.o, Puerto Rico, Cumana, la Florida, y Yucatan, pero nunca se trata â sus Gov.res como a subditos porque ellos dan quenta â S.M. immediatamente de lo que se les ofrece, y reciven las ordenes delo que han de executar de su R.l mano," Alburquerque's *relación del estado*, Mexico City, 27 November 1710, AGI, México 485, f. 26.

54 According to viceroy Güemes y Horcasitas, the borders of New Spain were defined by the "Reino de Guatemala que rige su Presidente, y Audiencia, sin subordinacion, y Nueva Galicia gover-

Notes   229

nado ... por su Presidente, y Audiencia, en puntos de Justicia, con jurisdiccion absoluta, y sin recursos, y sugeto su Territorio en los del Hazienda, y Guerra a la Capitania, y Superintendencia grâl. anexidades de este Virreinato", Instrucción of Revillagigedo to the Marquis of Amarillas, Mexico City, 28 November 1754, AGI, México 1506, No. 167 a.

CHAPTER 3 - COURT AND CORRUPTION IN COLONIAL MEXICO

1   Jacob van Klaveren, *Europäische Wirtschaftsgeschichte Spaniens im 16. und 17. Jahrhundert* (Stuttgart: Gustav Fischer, 1960).

2   Ramón Carande, "Zum Problem einer Wirtschaftsgeschichte Spaniens," *Historische Zeitschrift* 193:1 (1961): 359–65; Richard Konetzke, "La literatura económica. Así se escribe la historia," *Moneda y Crédito* (Madrid) 81 (1962): 67–77.

3   Phelan, *The Kingdom of Quito*. Compare also Phelan's article "Authority and Flexibility in the Spanish Imperial Bureaucracy," *Administrative Science Quarterly* 5:1 (1960): 47–65.

4   Phelan, *The Kingdom of Quito*, 147.

5   Ibid., 148.

6   Ibid., 147–76.

7   Horst Pietschmann, "Burocracia y corrupción en Hispanoamérica colonial. Una aproximación tentativa," *Nova Americana* 5 (1983): 11–37. For a similar interpretation, see also Eduardo R. Saguier, "La corrupción administrativa como mecanismo de acumulación y engendrador de una burguesía local," *Anuario de Estudios Americanos* (hereinafter AEA) 56 (1989): 269–303.

8   Alejandro Cañeque, *The King's Living Image. The Culture and Politics of Viceregal Power in Colonial Mexico* (New York: Routledge, 2004), 175–83. Solange Alberro warns against generalizing findings exclusively from penal proceedings, yet she argues that clerics frequently overstepped their normative boundaries: "Control de la Iglesia y transgresiones eclesiásticas durante el periodo colonial," in *Vicios públicos, virtudes privadas: la corrupción en México*, ed. Claudio Lomnitz (Mexico City: CIESAS, 2000), 33–47.

9   J. H. Parry, *The Sale of Public Office in the Spanish Indies Under the Habsburgs* (Berkeley: University of California Press, 1953), 51–54, 60–63. Parry holds that the Jurist Juan de Solórzano Pereira did not "question the lawfulness of the practice in general, but he mentions it with evident distaste, and is emphatic on the illegality and immorality of selling judicial offices," ibid., 60.

10 The following ministers attended the Council's meeting: Manuel García de Bustamante, Juan de Castro y Gallego, Martín de Solis y Miranda, Mateo Ibáñez de Mendoza, Pedro de Gamarra y Arriaga, Diego de Hermoso Romero y Aragón, Juan de Aguilera, José Bolero y Muñoz, and Ramón de Portocarrera. In 1706, after the Allied occupation of Madrid, Philip removed all of these except for Solis, Hermoso, and Aguilera; Bernard, *Le secrétariat d´état*, 212–14. The *real cédula* of 1 July 1704 addressed to Alburquerque closely followed the Council's recommendations, AGI, México 1079, ff. 22–27v.

11 The older scholarship such as Parry's views the Council of Indies as the bastion of lawful administration and considers the king's seventeenth-century favourites as corrupted. Parry labels the Count-Duke of Olivares as "the most grasping of favorites," Parry, *The Sale of Public Office*, 22. More recent historians such as Bertrand in his work *Grandeur et misères* tend to perceive the Council as an example of internecine squabbles encumbering vigorous reforms.

12 Otto Brunner, *Land and Lordship. Structures of Governance in Medieval Austria*. [1939] Transl. from the 4th ed. and introduced by Howard Kaminsky and James van Horn Melton (Philadel-

phia: University of Pennsylvania Press, 1984), 95–102.

13 Peter Moraw, "Personenforschung und deutsches Königtum. Über König und Reich," [1975] In *Aufsätze zur deutschen Verfassungsgeschichte des späten Mittelalters, Festschrift Peter Moraw*, ed. Rainer Christoph Schwinges (Sigmaringen, Germany: Jan Thorbecke, 1995), 1–10.

14 Quoted in Peter Burke, "The Courtier," In *Renaissance Characters*, ed. Eugenio Garin (Chicago: University of Chicago Press, 1991), 119.

15 Elias, *The Court Society*, 68–69.

16 Ibid., 71–73.

17 Geoffrey Elton, "Tudor Government," 217.

18 Asch, "Introduction," in *Princes, Patronage and the Nobility*, 8.

19 Burke, "The Courtier," 98.

20 Ibid., 98–101.

21 See the example of Matthäus Enzlin, favourite of Duke Friedrich of Württemberg (1593–1608). Enzlin did not belong to any governing body and usually dwelt in his private residence in Tübingen instead of at the court in Stuttgart; see Ronald G. Asch, "Corruption and Punishment? The Rise and Fall of Matthäus Enzlin (1556–1613), Lawyer and Favourite," in *The World of the Favourite*, ed. J. H. Elliott and L.W.B. Brockliss (New Haven: Yale University Press, 1999), 101.

22 Testimony of Regent Juan Chrisóstomo de Barroeta in the pesquisa secreta, Mexico City, 17 January 1757, AGI, Escribanía 246 B, f. 27 v.

23 Pilar Latasa Vasallo views the administration of the Marquis of Montesclaros's secretary as an example of a viceregal *privanza* (the term of a *privado*); Pilar Latasa Vassallo, *Administración virreinal en el Perú: gobierno del marqués de Montesclaros, 1607–1615* (Madrid: Editorial Centro de Estudios Ramón Areces, 1997).

24 Martha Fernández, *Arquitectura y gobierno virreinal. Los maestros mayores de la ciudad de México siglo XVII* (Mexico City: UNAM, 1985), 248.

25 For the balconies, see ibid., 87.

26 According to Martha Fernández, the viceroy normally resided in the mezzanine: *Arquitectura*, 246.

27 Ibid., 247; testimonios de la pesquisa secreta, juicio de residencia de … Conde de Fuenclara, AGI, Escribanía 246 B.

28 Diego Angulo Iñiguez, *Planos de monumentos arquitectónicos de América y Filipinas existentes en el Archivo de Indias* (Seville: University of Seville, Laboratorio de Arte, 1939), 4:296–305; Enrique Marco Dorta, "El palacio de los virreyes a fines del siglo XVIII," *Archivo Español de Arte y Arqueología* (Madrid) 31 (1935): 103–30.

29 *Relación* of Alburquerque to the Duke of Linares, Mexico City, 27 November 1710, AGI, México 485, ff. 48–50; the *relación* is also published by Navarro García, "El segundo virrey Alburquerque y su memoria de gobierno." See also Revillagigedo's *relación*, in *Instrucciones*, ed. Torre Villar, 827–28.

30 In 1708, the king promoted the *Maestre de campo* Luis Sánchez de Tagle to the post of general (*general de batalla*) and Don Pedro to that of *maestre de campo*: real orden, Madrid, 2 January 1708, AGI, México 377.

31 *RLRI*, lib. ii, tít. xvi, leyes xlviii– l; liv–lviv; lxxv, lxxxii–lxxxvii, xci.

32 Ibid., lib. iii, tít. iii, ley xii.

33 Ibid., lib. iii, tít. iii, ley xii.

34 Phelan, *Kingdom of Quito*, 153.

35 Cited in Burke, "The Courtier," 23.

36 Mexico City, 4 February 1708, AHDF, Actas del Cabildo 36 A, f. 101.

37 Viceregal decree, Mexico City, 27 September 1708, ibid., ff. 54v–55.

38 José Manuel de Castro Santa-Anna, *Diario de Sucesos Notables, 1752 a 1754*,

Documentos para la historia de Méjico (Mexico City: Imprenta de Juan R. Navarro, 1854), 5:7–8.

39   Ibid., 4:51, 250.

40   Antonio de Robles, *Diario de Sucesos Notables (1665–1703)*, ed. Antonio Castro Leal, 2nd ed. (Mexico City: Editorial Porrúa, 1972), 3:259.

41   In her recent publication, Linda Curcio emphasizes that the processions served to impress a subjugated populace with the hegemonic power of the colonial order, Linda Curcio-Nagy, *The Great Festivals of Colonial Mexico City. Performing Power and Identity* (Albuquerque: University of New Mexico Press, 2004), 3–9.

42   Le Roy Ladurie, *Saint-Simon*, particularly 23–61.

43   The costs and efforts of participating in a pageant or perhaps political calculations deterred some. For example, in 1710 the viceroy penalized the *corregidor* and *alcaldes ordinarios* for not tending to their public functions: real acuerdo, Mexico City, 5 December 1710, *Compendio de los Libros Capitulares de la Muy Noble Insigne, y Muy Leal Ciudad de Mexico. Comprehende desde el año de 1702 hasta el de 1742. Hizolo El Licenciado D. Francisco del Barrio Lorenzot Abogado de la Real Audiencia, y Contador de dicha N.C.*, Mexico City, s.d., AHDF, 437 A, vol. 4, ff. 56–56v.

44   AGI, Escribanía 245 A, cuaderno 7, ff. 14–65.

45   Ibid.

46   Robles, *Diario*, 3:264, 270.

47   Castro Santa-Anna, *Diario*, 5:9–39.

48   Rubio Mañé, *Introducción*, 1:117–19.

49   Robles, *Diario*, 3:232–33.

50   Rubio Mañé, *Introducción*, 1:117–19.

51   Robles, *Diario*, 3:239–40.

52   Session of the ayuntamiento, Mexico City, 17 November 1702, *Compendio de los Libros Capitulares*, Mexico City, s.d., AHDF, 437 A, vol. 4, ff. 8–8v.

53   Curcio, *Great Festivals*, 22.

54   Rubio Mañé, *Introducción*, 1:117–19.

55   This section here refers to the departure of Revillagigedo, Castro Santa-Anna, *Diario*, 5:171–72.

56   Consulta of the Council of the Indies, Madrid, 4 July 1703, AGI, México 399. For the Marquise of Cadereyta, Alburquerque's grandmother, visiting the convents in New Spain formed an important part of courtly life; see Artemio de Valle-Arizpe, *Virreyes y virreinas de la Nueva España. Leyendas, tradiciones y sucedios del México virreinal* (Madrid: Biblioteca Nueva, 1938), 179. Robles describes a 1703 visit of Alburquerque and his wife to a convent, *Diario*, 3:252.

57   Castro Santa-Anna on Revillagigedo's departure, *Diario*, 5:173.

58   Robles, *Diario*, 3:217.

59   The treasury paid the chief architects (*maestro mayor*) for the upkeep of the royal buildings in Otumba and Chapultepec, Fernández, *Arquitectura*, 104. Otumba is located due east of Teotihuacán. According to Sarrablo Aguareles, the Count of Fuenclara rested in the monastery of San Francisco in Otumba: *El Conde de Fuenclara*, 2:51–52.

60   Castro Santa-Anna, *Diario*, 5:173.

61   Ibid. On the purchase of the hacienda San Bartolomé around 1749, declaration of Captain Jacinto Martínez, Mexico City, 15 January 1749, AGN, Tierras vol. 3353, exp. 43.

62   Manuel Julián Osorio to the eleventh Duke of Alburquerque, Vich, Catalonia, 21 January 1738, Archivo Histórico de la Casa Ducal de Alburquerque, Cuéllar, Spain, legajo 379, No. 6 (hereinafter abbreviated as AHCDA, 379, No. 6). A *relación de méritos* proves that Manuel Julián and his brother are Julián de Osorio's sons, AGI, Indiferente 144, N 16.

63 Burke, "The Courtier," 103.

64 Asch, "Introduction" in *Princes, Patronage and the Nobility*, 16–18.

65 David R. Ringrose, *Madrid and the Spanish Economy, 1560–1850* (Berkeley: University of California Press, 1983), 1–15.

66 On the mining tribunal, see Brading, *Miners and Merchants*, 163–68.

67 Pietschmann, "La corte virreinal," 488.

68 For the European courts, see Asch, "Introduction" in *Princes, Patronage and the Nobility*, 38.

CHAPTER 4 - CLIENTS AND CREATURES: ALBURQUERQUE'S PERVASIVE PATRONAGE

1 Antequera was the colonial name of Oaxaca de Juárez.

2 Memoria de los criados, Mexico City, 23 November 1710, AGI, México 658, ff. 31v–34, 316–18; Fernández de Bethencourt: *Historia Genealógica*, 10:297–98.

3 See, for example, Robles's and Castro Santa-Anna's diaries. Much of Alburquerque's viceregal correspondence is contained in AGI, México 474–83, 485.

4 See, for example, the *media anata* receipt of Francisco Gorostia for the *alcaldía mayor* Tepeaca y Tecali, dated 23 March 1708. The document mentions that the viceroy appointed Gorostia to this position for "the period at will of said most excellent Señor Alburquerque" ("por tiempo de la voluntad de dicho S.or Ex.mo Alburquerque"), AGN, Media Anata (hereinafter MA) 50. Most of the information used in the analysis of *media anata* records is drawn from AGN, MA 24, 27, 34, 42, 50, and 65 as well as AGN, Archivo Histórico de Hacienda (hereinafter AHH) 213, 223, 931, 1361, 1463, 1466, and 1648.

5 See Bernardo García Martínez, *El Marquesado del Valle. Tres siglos de régimen señorial en Nueva España* (Mexico City: El Colegio de México, 1969), 82–83.

6 Real decreto, Madrid, 23 February 1706, AGI, México 377; *Diccionario Porrúa*, 1:268.

7 AGI, Escribanía 263 A, pieza (abbreviated as pza.) 36.

8 For example, the *media anata* documents in the bundle labelled *octubre 30–* in AGN, AHH 931, mention that the viceroy designated the officials. These papers, however, do not list the bondsmen. Records in section MA 65 meanwhile note the exact dates of tenure while being silent on the appointer; see, for example, entry on Diego Palacios, alcalde mayor of Yagualica from 23 August 1703 to 11 September 1705, f. 185.

9 Robles, *Diario*; Castro Santa-Anna, *Diario*; Gregorio Martín de Guijo, *Diario, 1648–64*, ed. Manuel Romero de Terreros (Mexico City: Editorial Porrúa, 1952).

10 Witness Juan Antonio Casas Novas, mayordomo of the cathedral, Mexico City, 12 July 1748, AGI, Indiferente 152, N 2.

11 Castro Santa-Anna, *Diario*, 5:170.

12 The Count of Fuenclara appointed José Manuel de Castro Santa-Anna to the *alcaldía mayor* of the *real y minas* (mining camp) de Zimapán in 1744 and then to the *alcaldía mayor* of Chalco and Tlalmanalco including the *agregado* (annex) of Tlayacapa. Castro delivered his oath in the *real acuerdo* on 21 August 1746. The official then acquired the *alcaldía mayor* of Tacuba from the king in 1748, possibly with the help of his patron; AGI, Escribanía 245 A and 246 A, cuaderno 1, f. 153v; AGI, Indiferente 171, and Archivo General de Simancas, Spain (hereinafter AGS), Hacienda 182–365. Castro moderated his acrimony towards the end of Revillagigedo's term. Copies of the diary's edition from 1854 are rare; the *Fondo Reservado* of Mexico's National Library and the library of the *Escuela de Estudios Hispano-Americanos* in Seville, Spain, each hold one.

Notes

13 "Confession, que haze, en los ultimos dias de Su govierno; el Ex.mo S.r Duque de Alburquerque D.n Fran. Fernandez dela Cueva Virrey," s.n., AGN, Inquisición 740, exp. 3., ff. 57–60.

14 Ibid., f. 56v. The phrase *Vro Navarro* probably alludes to two personages: On the one hand, it referred to the Dominican Friar Bartomolé Navarro de San Antonio, whom Alburquerque appointed to the chair of Saint Thomas at the University of Mexico in 1703 or 1704; king to Alburquerque, Madrid, 2 September 1704, AGI, México 400; Robles, *Diario*, 3:273. On the other hand, the phrase also adverts to Martín de Azpilcueta, called *el doctor Navarro*, who wrote an important sixteenth-century confessor's manual. I owe the reference to Azpilcueta to Professor James Boyden, Tulane University.

15 Relación de méritos, Madrid, s.d., 1690, AGI, Indiferente 132, N 98, ff. 1–2v.

16 AGN, Inquisición 740, exp. 3, f. 60.

17 Demanda puesta por D.a Sebastiana Fernandes Nolasco muger lex.ma de D.n Juan Francisco Fernandez Cacho contra el Ex.mo S.or Virrey Duque de Alburquerque, Mexico City, 4 December 1710, AGI, México 659, cuaderno 7, exp.1, ff. 11–16v.

18 A useful tool for accessing this material is the *Catálogo de textos marginados novohispános: Inquisición, siglo XVIII y XIX: Archivo General de la Nación*, ed. María Agueda Méndez (Mexico City: AGN, El Colegio de México, 1992).

19 Elliott, *The Court*, 7; Christina Hofmann, *Das spanische Hofzeremoniell von 1500–1700* (Frankfurt am Main: Peter Lang, 1985), 84–87.

20 In 1660 Philip IV prohibited the viceroys from bringing their sons and daughters as well as their respective spouses to America, to maintain the social distance between the official and local society. Nevertheless, the Count of Baños negotiated an exception to that rule before taking office in 1660, and the crown never enforced the law: Rubio Mañé, *Introducción*, 1:116, 152; *RLRI*, lib. iii, tit. iii, ley xii.

21 Ortega to Alburquerque, Mexico City, 29 May 1707, AGN, Bienes Nacionales 477, exp. 10, f. 5.

22 Real cédula to Captain General Ducas, Madrid, 8 May 1702, AGI, México 610. Memoria de los criados, Mexico City, 24 November 1710, AGI, México 658, ff. 33–34v.

23 Alburquerque's physician Buendía died en route to New Spain: Francisco Hidalgo to Juan de Valdés, Mexico City, 20 January 1711, AGI, México, 658, ff. 317–18.

24 Castro Santa-Anna, *Diario*, 4:138, 165.

25 Her father, Andrés Fernández y Cuebas, must have been Alburquerque's relative: Mexico City, 22 December 1704, AHAGN, Escribano Diego Antonio Marquina, No. 393, vol. 2614, leg. 5, ff. 15v–16.

26 "El 11 [January 1754] en el real palacio casó D. Roberto Quilvan con doña María Doile, dama de la Exma. Sra. vireina, ambos naturales de Irlanda," Castro Santa-Anna, *Diario*, 4:203.

27 For the relationship between Miguel and José Munarris, see AGI, Contratación 5469, N 1, R 36, 1, ff. 11–15r.

28 Castro Santa-Anna, *Diario*, 5:167.

29 The second Count of Revillagigedo to the president of the *casa de la contratación* (the clearing house in Cadiz that supervised and taxed the traffic with America); Cadiz, 27 May 1789, AGI, Contratación 5533, N 3, R 8.

30 See Rosenmüller, "Friends, Followers, Countrymen: Viceregal Networking in Mid-Eighteenth Century New Spain," *Estudios de Historia Novohispana* (Mexico City) 34 (2006): 62–64.

31 For the distinction among *hidalgos*, *caballeros*, *títulos*, and *grandeza*, see Antonio Domínguez Ortiz, *La sociedad española en el siglo XVII* (Madrid: Consejo Superior de Investigaciones Científicas, 1963), 189–93.

32 Media Annata payment of Martín Ajolesa, 28 November 1704, AGN, AHH 1648.

33 Martín Ajolesa to Alburquerque, Mestitlan, 12 September 1705, AGN, Civil 455, f. 61; other district officials not mentioned in Alburquerque's *memoria* use similar phrases: see Alfonso de Vargas y Luján to Alburquerque, San Pedro Tlaolan, 1 September 1705, ibid., f. 16.

34 Testimonies of Juan Otidalgo and Jerónimo de Grijalba, Mestitlan, 7 October 1711, AGN, Tributos 22, exp. 4.

35 Felipe de Merezilla Sota to Alburquerque, Nejapa, 3 August 1705, AGN, Civil 455, f. 45.

36 Antonio Domínguez Ortiz, *La sociedad española en el siglo XVIII* (Madrid: Consejo Superior de Investigaciones Científicas, 1955), 77–78.

37 Nuñez de Villavicencio became *alcalde mayor* of Zimatlan and Chichicapa on 27 July 1703: AGN, MA 34; AHH 1463, f. 230.

38 Real cédula, Madrid, 20 March 1686, AGI, Contratación 5447, N 2, R 8. Juan Nuñez and Nuño Nuñez appeared in the *residencia*, AGI, México 657, ff. 423v, 225v.

39 Maldonado to king, Antequera, 17 April 1708, AGI, México 879.

40 Tovar's services in the showdown with the Tagle family surely played a role: Alburquerque to king, Mexico City, 26 March 1703, AGI, México 474.

41 The parishes outside of Mexico City were Zacualpan and Xocotitlan; Archbishop Ortega to king, Mexico City, 31 August 1707; parecer of the fiscal of the Council of the Indies, Madrid, 23 June 1709, AGI, México 480.

42 Horst Pietschmann, "Alcaldes Mayores, Corregidores und Subdelegados. Zum Problem der Distriktsbeamtenschaft im Vizekönigreich Neuspanien," *Jahrbuch für Geschichte von Staat, Wirtschaft und Gesellschaft Lateinamerikas* (now *Jahrbuch für Geschichte Lateinamerikas*, hereinafter JbLA) 81 (1972): 195, 201–2. For a recent publication on the *repartimiento de mercancías*, see Jeremy Baskes, *Indians, Merchants, and Markets. A Reinterpretation of the repartimiento and Spanish-Indian Economic Relations in Colonial Oaxaca, 1750–1821* (Stanford: Stanford University Press, 2000); see also Arij Ouweneel, *Shadows over Anáhuac. An Ecological Interpretation of Crisis and Development in Central Mexico, 1730–1880* (Albuquerque: University of New Mexico Press, 1996), 159–209, originally published in Dutch in 1989.

43 Pietschmann, "Alcaldes Mayores," 186–90.

44 Ibid., 191–92.

45 AGI, Pasajeros, L 14, E 1711; junta de indultos and parecer of the fiscal, Madrid, 14 November 1711, AGI, México 377.

46 For Veracruz, see Alburquerque to king, Mexico City, 21 May 1710; Council of the Indies, Madrid, 16 January 1711, AGI, México 482; king to Alburquerque, Madrid, 29 June 1710, AGI, México 474; Mexico City, 27 January 1710, AGN, MA 24. For Acapulco, Mexico City, s.n, AGN, AHH 1361, f. 22v. Paradoxically, Alburquerque jailed the merchant Juan Martínez de Lejarzar in 1703 for disturbing the Philippine trade, but in 1710 the Duke appointed José Antonio Martínez de Lejarzar, probably a relative of Juan Martínez, to the profitable *alcaldía mayor* of Querétaro; Mexico City, 12 July 1710, AGN, MA 24; Alburquerque to king, Mexico City, 29 November 1703, AGI, México 642. According to Gerhard, in the early eighteenth century the chief magistrate of Veracruz nueva (not to be confused with Veracruz antigua located to the northwest) was referred to as governor. My sources, however, do not always employ this term. The *alcalde mayor* of Acapulco carried the titles of *castellan* and *capitán a guerra*, that is, a magistrate with military duties, and obtained

the title of governor after 1710; Peter Gerhard, *A Guide to the Historical Geography of New Spain*, Cambridge Latin American Studies, vol. 14 (Cambridge, Cambridge University Press, 1972), 40, 360–67.

47 The *secretaría de Nueva España* of the Council of the Indies responsible for this territory.

48 The index named "Yndize comprehensibo de todos los Goviernos, Corregimientos, y Alcaldías Mayores" and the register drawn up for Ensenada are both synthesized in Pietschmann, *Alcaldes mayores*, 239–57.

49 For a discussion of the economic and social development of Guanajuato, see Brading, *Miners and Merchants*, 223–339.

50 In the following *alcaldías mayores* the viceroy could never appoint an official: Chalco y Tlamanalco, Michoacan-Valladolid, Nejapa, Tehuacan de las Granadas, Villa Alta (Oaxaca), all value 1; Orizaba, Nochistlan y Peñoles, both of value 2; Guajocingo, described as between 3 and 2.

51 According to Ensenada's list, the crown sold the first *futura* for Teutila in 1706.

52 The crown still admonished the mid-century Viceroy Revillagigedo to adhere to these rules, indicating lack of abidance: real cédula to Revillagigedo, Aranjuez, 21 April 1752, AGN, Reales Cédulas Originales (hereinafter RCO) 72, exp. 36, f. 74–76v.

53 Samaniego exercised his office from 7 July 1704 to 11 August 1707, Xochimilco, 11 August 1707, AGN, MA 34, f. 259; Ochoa held his position from 19 July 1702 to 22 May 1703, Mexico City, 7 October 1704, AGN, MA 65, f. 196.

54 Gerhard, *Historical Geography*, 54–55, 76–78.

55 This calculation of the number of districts is probably rather liberal. Gerhard, who focuses on the earlier colonial period, counts 129 provinces, ibid. Viceroy Revillagigedo claimed that nominally 137 *alcaldías mayores* and *corregimientos* existed in the *gobierno* of New Spain, but several of these officialdoms had merged into others: Instrucción to the Marquis of Amarillas, Mexico City, 28 November 1754, AGI, México 1506, No. 167 a.

56 Mexico City, 13 August 1704, AGN, AHH 1648, f. 182; Mexico City, 25 May 1707, AGN, MA 34, f. 255; Testimony of Oidor Valdes, Mexico City, 10 November 1711, AGI, México 658, ff. 311–14.

57 Peter Gerhard, *The North Frontier of New Spain*, rev. ed. (Norman: University of Oklahoma Press, 1993), 316–17, 349.

58 For the viceroy's right to appoint the governor of New Mexico, RLRI lib. iii, tít. ii, ley clvi. In the mid-eighteenth century, the crown named these governors too: see José Ignacio de Goyeneche, secretary for New Spain on the Council of the Indies, to Tomás Vélez Cachupin, Buen Retiro, 5 March 1761, AGN, RCO 81, exp. 7.

59 Derrotero de … Diego de Yglesias, 28 November 1710–11 January 1711, AGI, México 659, cuaderno 6, ff. 40–87.

60 For the route towards the south, at least the following four *criados* signed the receipt: Pedro de Manzano, AM of Guajalotitlan and page of the viceroy; page Manuel de Vellosillo Hinestrosa, AM of villa del marquesado del valle; gentleman-in-waiting Bernardo de la Cantera, AM of San Andrés de Miaguatlan; page Francisco Benites Maldonado, AM of Teposcolula; see derrotero de Francisco de la Peña … por la Cordillera dela Villaalta, 27 November 1710–8 January 1711, ibid., ff. 11v–33. See also derrotero … of Diego de Yglesias, correo de S. M.; derrotero … of Miguel de Menchaca; Juachin Cortes and of Juan de Nava, ibid., ff. 40v–237.

61 Luis Navarro García, "Los oficios vendibles en Nueva España durante la Guerra de Sucesión," *AEA* 32 (1975): 133–54.

62 Alburquerque to king, 6 June 1706, AGI, México 474, f. 31v; royal title, 18 November 1738, AGS, Hacienda 180-136; Revillagigedo to Marquis of la Ensenada, Mexico City, 29 June 1754, AGI, México 516.

63 Isidro Ruano de Arista did not leave further traces, but a Fernando Ruano de Arista held the office of *contador* at the Puebla treasury in the 1730s, indicating a tradition in Ruano's family of working in the royal exchequer: Alburquerque to king, Mexico City, 6 April 1709, AGI, México 482; AGI, Contaduría 793. Interim Viceroy Ortega y Montañés must have appointed Francisco Vela de la Torre for the position of interim treasurer of Guanajuato. Vela de la Torre took office on 2 December 1702. The king confirmed the designation on 11 January 1703, too early for Alburquerque's correspondence to reach Madrid: AGI, México 1045.

64 The appointment of *Licenciado* Clemente Buqueiro (no. 9) to *alcalde* of the mint did not match the other ones in importance. Yet in the late seventeenth century, the crown sold even minor offices in the mint such as a guard or a notary for between 18,000 and 25,000 pesos. The post was, therefore, an significant sinecure: Bertrand, *Grandeur et Misères*, 345-46.

65 Treasury register of Guanajuato, AGI, México 1044. I owe this information to Spanish historian José Luis Caño Ortigos.

66 For Alburquerque's six appointments to military posts in Veracruz, see Appendix 6.

67 Bertrand, *Grandeur et misères*, 211, especially fn. 83.

68 Bertrand, *Grandeur et misères*, 210-11.

69 Whether the fall from grace of Antonio de Ubilla y Medina, Estacasolo's relative in the *despacho universal*, influenced the secretary's decision to stay needs further evaluation. Around 1685 Estacasolo y Otalora started to assist his relative Antonio Ortiz de Otalora, secretary of the Council of the Indies for New Spain from 1684-1691: consulta of the Council of the Indies to secretary Pinedo, 28 July 1707; see also Schäfer, *El consejo real y supremo*, 1:371. In 1708 another relative of the duke's secretary, Juan Otalora Bravo de Laguna, obtained an appointment as councillor of the Indies: Bernard, *Le secrétariat d'état*, 215, No. 46.

70 See the document "Quenta de cargo que yo Francisco Sanz Daza secretario del Ex.mo Señor Duque de Alburquerque ... doy de las cantidades que entraron en mi poder en el año de 1716," Madrid, 18 May 1717, AHCDA 463, No. 4.

71 At least the following criados remained in the colony: Secretary Juan de Estacasolo y Otalora; testimonio de ... Estacasolo, Mexico City, 3 September 1715, juicio de residencia ... de Miguel de Luna: AGI, Escribanía 234 A, f. 33; AGN, Bienes Nacionales 813, exp. 5. Treasurer Miguel Munarris and his brother José conducted business with Alburquerque's gentleman-in-waiting Blasco Ruiz de Herrera: AGI, Contratación, 5469, N 1, R 36, 1, ff. 11-15. José Tiburcio, Fernando de Ortega Patiño, and Estéban Rodriguez Santa Cruz, all officials of the royal treasury, also remained: copy of the relación de méritos of Fernando Ortega, Madrid, 9 March 1724, AGI, Indiferente 142, N 10; Güemes to Marquis of la Ensenada, Mexico City, 29 June 1754, AGI, México 516; relación de méritos de D.n Joseph Tiburcio Boet, y Villalon, Madrid, s. n., AGI, Indiferente 152, N 7; Bertrand, *Grandeur et Misères*, 338.

CHAPTER 5 - THE CLASH OVER CONTRABAND COMMERCE AND THE CONSULADO

1 For royal communications issued in the first decade of the eighteenth century that reiterate previous mandates, see *real cédula* prohibiting trade between Mexico and Peru, Madrid, 16 February

1706, AGN, RCO 33, exp. 8; the *real cédula* from 15 March 1710 repeated the ban on trade with foreign nations: Madrid, ibid., 34, exp. 107, ff. 273–77; *real cédula* dated 17 August forbade trade of cacao between Guayaquil and New Spain: Madrid, ibid., 34, exp. 164, f. 2. The *real cédula* issued on 1 March 1702 in Barcelona summarized the Seville *consulado's* complaints: AGI, México 474.

2   See real cédula, Barcelona, 1 March 1702, AGI, México 474; real cédula to Alburquerque, Madrid, 15 February 1708, AGI, México, 403.

3   Pierre Chaunu postulates slow growth of trade between Acapulco and Manila since ca. 1680 to 1691. Trade then levelled off until climbing to new heights in 1726–1745; *Les Philippines et le Pacifique des Ibériques (XVIe, XVIIe, XVIIIe siècles) Introduction méthodologique et indices d'activité* (Paris: SEVPEN, 1960), 256–57.

4   Kenneth J. Andrien, *Crisis and Decline. The Viceroyalty of Peru in the Seventeenth Century* (Albuquerque: University of New Mexico Press, 1985), 29–39.

5   Pérez-Mallaina, *Política naval*, 9–10.

6   Real cédula to Alburquerque, Buen Retiro, 6 June 1703, AGI, México 476.

7   Geoffrey Walker, *Spanish Politics and Imperial Trade, 1700–1789* (Bloomington: Indiana University Press, 1979), 10–15.

8   Ibid., 10–15.

9   David Brading, *Haciendas and Ranchos in the Mexican Bajío, León 1700–1860* (Cambridge: Cambridge University Press, 1978), 23; real cédula to Alburquerque, 9 August 1707, AGI, México, 402. Luis Antonio Sánchez de Tagle became governor of the Marianne islands; AGI, Filipinas, 282 bis, N 9 and nombramiento de gobernador de las Marianas, Madrid, 2 May 1710, AGI, Filipinas, 349, L 7, ff. 155r–157r. Some of the Pérez de Tagle family, closely related to the Sánchez de Tagle family through Luis Sánchez de Tagle's mother María Pérez de la Sierra, also sat in Manila. Pedro Pérez de Tagle, based in Mexico, married the daughter of Pedro Sánchez de Tagle and Luisa, heiress to the title Altamira. María del Carmen Velázquez describes the genealogy of the Marquis of Altamira in *El Marqués de Altamira y las Provincias internas de Nueva España* (Mexico City: El Colegio de México, 1976), 11–17; see also AGI, Contratación, 5540 B, L 5, f. 14v. The Marquis del Villar occasionally joined Don Luis in granting loans to the crown: AGI, Indiferente 136, N 142.

10 Miguel de Ubilla y Estrada and the secretary of the *despacho universal*, Antonio Ubilla y Medina, were related through their great grandfather, Antonio de Ubilla y Alcachoa, see Conde and Sanchiz, *Títulos y dignidades*. The king replaced the secretary on 11 July 1705 and briefly appointed him councillor of the Indies. Philip suspended Ubilla in 1706 under suspicion of conspiring with the Habsburgs. See Mark A. Burkholder, *Biographical Dictionary of Councilors of the Indies, 1717–1808* (New York: Greenwood, 1986), 124–25. Lucas de Careaga confirmed his alliance to Luis Sánchez de Tagle in 1709 when Tagle quarreled with Jerónimo Campo y Marín about preeminence of the *maestres de campo* in the realm: AGI, Escribanía 190 A, f. 100v–108v.

11 Consulado of Seville to Miguel de Ubilla y Estrada, Lucas de Careaga, and Luis Sánchez de Tagle, Seville, 15 March 1702, AGI, Estado, 38 A, N 2. In 1703 Ubilla y Estrada asked the viceroy to implement the *real cédula* from 1 March 1703, enforcing limitations on the Philippine trade: Ubilla to Alburquerque, s.n., AGI, México 474.

12 Confession of Warden José Sebastian Gallo in 1723; Duke of Linares to Gallo, Mexico City, 21 March 1712 and consulta of the Council of the Indies, Madrid, 29 April 1727, AGI, Escribanía 264 A, pza. 5, ff. 2v– 3v.

Luis Sánchez de Tagle himself returned from a voyage to the Philippines in 1700: Robles, *Diario*, 3:134. In a 1721 trial, the *audiencia* of Guatemala also embargoed 349,000 pesos belonging to Pedro Sánchez de Tagle and others for illegal traffic between Callao, Peru, and Realejo (in present Nicaragua). The Council overturned the decision on 4 March 1728: AGI, Escribanía 964. According to rumours, Lucas de Careaga acted for a short period as Alburquerque's business agent in Veracruz, buying illegal merchandise from French traders and shipping it to Mexico City. Testimony of witness Alonso Antonio Fernández de Segade, purveyor of the Inquisition, in favour of Canon Andrés de Costela, Mexico City, 9 October 1708, AGI México 646, expediente without title, ff. 22v–23v.

13 Real decreto to the Marquis of los Vélez, Madrid, 4 January 1686, AGI, Filipinas 04, N 63; real cédula issued by Charles II, Madrid, 31 January 1686, AGI, Contratación 5448, N 149, f. 12. According to William Lytle Schurz, Fausto Cruzat left Acapulco for Manila in 1671 to become governor of the Philippines: *The Manila Galeon* (New York: E. P. Dutton & Co., 1939), 275.

14 In Fausto Cruzat's *residencia*, his enemies in Manila's town hall charged him with breaching royal trade restrictions, a rather conventional claim since most involved parties probably participated in contraband commerce. Further indications of collaboration between the two families include the testimony of the Sánchez de Tagle relative Captain Pedro Pérez de Tagle in May 1702 in favour of Fausto Cruzat's aide, the *Maestre de campo* Tomás de Endaya: juicio de residencia of Fausto Cruzat, Archivo Histórico Nacional (hereinafter AHN), Consejos, leg. 21023. This conflict possibly continued the quarrel between the merchants residing in the Philippines and those based in New Spain to which Schurz refers: *The Manila Galeon*, 363–64, although the boundaries between these groups appear vague like those between peninsulars and Creoles in New Spain.

15 Robles, *Diario*, 3:257.

16 Fray Juan Ibañes, Martín, Fausto, and Juan Cruzat to Alburquerque, AGI, México 642, s.n., f. 913.

17 Luis Sánchez de Tagle to king, Mexico City, 13 October 1704, AGI, México 642, ff. 936–42.

18 Archbishop Ortega to king, Mexico City, 14 December 1703, AGI, México 642, ff. 567–69.

19 Lucas de Careaga testified for Ortega in his *residencia* as interim viceroy in 1704, AGI, Escribanía 233 A, cuaderno 2, ff. 18–22, 205–12.

20 Consulta of the Council of the Indies, Madrid, 20 June 1705, AGI, México 401.

21 The Count of Santiago de Calimaya, *alacalde ordinario* in 1704, vouched for Ortega's integrity; so did *Oidores* Miguel Calderón de la Barca and Francisco Valenzuela Venegas: secret inquiry (sumaria secreta) of Ortega's juicio de residencia, Mexico City, May and June 1704, AGI, Escribanía 233 A, cuaderno 2, ff. 18–48v. The *Enciclopedia de México* reports that Ortega's father held the presidency of the Council of Castile, which would explain his son's rapid rise through the ecclesiastical hierarchy: *Enciclopedia de México. Todo lo Mexicano ordenado alfabéticamente...*, ed. José Rogelio Alvarez (Mexico City: Enciclopedia de México S.A., 1977), 10:15. However, Fayard, *Les membres du Conseil de Castille*, does not corroborate this information.

22 *Familia* refers here to the bishop's entourage. Ortega y Montañés provided his nephew and heir Andrés Patiño Castellanos and his relative Pedro Isidro de Lagos with a captaincy in the palace guard; others received an *alcaldía mayor*: AGI, Escribanía 233 A, ff. 5v–6; Escribanía 192 A and B.

Notes 239

23 King to Ortega, Madrid, 28 August 1705, AGI, México 401.

24 Real cédula to Ortega, Madrid, 28 August 1705, AGI, México, 1079, ff. 371v–373.

25 Alburquerque to king, Mexico City, 22 December 1708, AGI, México 482.

26 AGI, México 642. Records from a civil suit in the *audiencia* in 1718 prove the existence of the offspring of Domingo Ruiz de Tagle and María Bonal de Acuña, the Guadalajaran woman. Manuel Antonio de Tagle and Juan de Tagle demanded in the litigation their share of their father's estate: real provisión, Madrid, 19 February 1718, AGN, Tierras 2985, exp. 38.

27 Declaration of Domingo Ruiz de Tagle, Mexico City, 22 July 1703, ibid., ff. 70v–83.

28 The following *oidores* backed the viceroy's view: Miguel de Calderón, Juan de Escalante, Francisco Valenzuela, Baltasar de Tovar, and José de Uribe: real acuerdo, Mexico City, 24 May 1704; Archbishop Ortega to *Oidor Decano* (senior *oidor*) Miguel de Calderón, 25 May 1704, AGI, México 642, ff. 549–550v.

29 *Oidor* Valenzuela to king, AGI, México 642, ff. 536–39.

30 Ortega to king, Mexico City, 14 December 1703, AGI, México 642, ff. 568v–569v.

31 Declaration of Pedro Sánchez de Tagle, San Martin de Tixtla, 11 August 1703, ibid., ff. 197–204. José Alvarez del Valle was the duke's steward: Mexico City, 23 November 1710, AGI, México 658, f. 32 and certificate by notary José de Neri, Mexico City, 31 December 1710, AGI, México 642, ff. 301–3.

32 Declaration of Pedro Sánchez de Tagle, San Martín de Tixtla, 11 August 1703, AGI, México 642, ff. 204.

33 Ricardo Ortega y Pérez Gallardo, *Historia genealógica de las familias más antiguas de México* (Mexico City: Imprenta de A. Carranzas e hijos, 1908–10), 3:15. See also the duchess's mediating role in Robles, *Diario*, 3:274.

34 Alburquerque to king, Mexico City, 29 November 1703, AGI, México 642, ff. 2–5.

35 Testimony of witnesses, Mexico City, 15 June 1703, AGI, México 657, f. 125.

36 Ibid.

37 Alburquerque to king, Mexico City, 29 November 1703, AGI, México 642, ff. 1–7v. Diligencias executadas en virtud del decreto del … Duque de Alburquerque, Mexico City, 14 June 1703, ibid., 642, ff. 88–97; Robles, *Diario*, 3:272–73. The viceroy deported Don Domingo on 22 October 1703, 3:292.

38 Luis Sánchez de Tagle to king, Mexico City, 13 October 1704, AGI, México 642, f. 942.

39 Will of Ignacia Cruzat y Góngora, Mexico City, 15 August 1704, AGN, Civil 114, ff. 113–16. Robles, *Diario*, 3:276–77.

40 The town, now called Tixtla de Guerrero, lies about 140 km NNE of Acapulco. José de León, one of Alburquerque's legal advisors, conducted the interrogation: Juan de Estrada's testimony in the secret inquiry of Alburquerque's residencia, AGI, México 657, cuaderno 2, f. 42; Mexico 642, ff. 197–201.

41 Robles, *Diario*, 3:292, 296.

42 Ortega to king, Mexico City, AGI, México 642, ff. 567–70; 607–608v; 610–12; 627–29.

43 Luis Sánchez de Tagle to king, Mexico City, 13 October 1704, AGI, México 642, ff. 936–42.

44 The following councillors attended the Council's meeting: Manuel García de Bustamante, Juan de Castro y Gallego, Martín de Solis y Miranda, Mateo Ibañez de Mendoza, Pedro de Gamarra y Arriaga, Diego de Hermoso Romero y Aragón, Juan de Aguilera, José Bolero y Muñoz, Ramón de Portocarrera. In 1706, after the Allies had briefly occupied Madrid, Philip removed all of

these but Solis, Hermoso, and Aguilera: Bernard, *Le secrétariat d'état*, 212–14. The *consulta* executed in a *real cédula* of 1 July 1704 addressed to Alburquerque closely followed the Council's recommendations: AGI, México 1079, f. 22–27v.

45 Parecer of the fiscal, Madrid, 21 April 1705; real cédula, Madrid, 5 August 1705, AGI, México 401.

46 Real cédula, king to Franzisco Lorenzo de San Millán, juez oficial of the casa de la contratación, Madrid, 28 June 1704, AGI, Escribanía 1051 A, legajo 46, No. 16, ff. 1–3. Protocol of Franzisco Lorenzo, Cadiz, 12 August 1704, ibid., ff. 10–11r; see also Escribanía 1053 A.

47 Real cédula, Madrid, 13 October 1704, AGI, México 479. Carta de pago, 19 July 1706, AHAGN, Escribano Diego Antonio Marquina, No. 393, vol. 2614, leg. 6, f. 16.

48 The laws of the Indies stipulate that, at the beginning of each year, the prior and consuls should appoint thirty *electores* (electors) among the merchants who owned a residence within Mexico City. The electors then cast votes for the new prior and the *consul moderno* or incoming junior consul of the year. The merchant receiving the majority of votes won the election. The junior consul of the past year automatically advanced to senior consul. When the prior and the consuls left office, they remained active as *consejeros* (counsellors) advising the incumbents with their expertise. Electors also voted for *diputados* (deputies) who negotiated the *consulado's* commercial interests: *RLRI*, lib. viii, título xlvi, leyes i–xviii. On the elections, see also Bernd Hausberger, "Las elecciones de prior, cónsules y diputados en el Consulado de México en la primera mitad del siglo XVIII: la formación de los partidos de montañeses y vizcaínos," in *Comercio y poder en América colonial: los consulados de comerciantes, siglos XVII–XIX*, ed. Bernd Hausberger and Antonio Ibarra (Madrid, Frankfurt, Mexico City: Iberoamericana, Vervuert, Instituto Mora, 2003), 73–102.

49 Consuls and diputados of the consulado to the king, Mexico City, 22 April 1701, printed in Carmen Yuste, ed., *Comerciantes Mexicanos en el siglo XVIII* (Mexico City: UNAM, 1991), 392.

50 Del Castillo also appeared in a 1721 trial as a partner of Don Pedro in contraband trade. The *audiencia* of Guatemala held them and other merchants guilty of illegally bringing over 300,000 pesos from Callao, Peru, to Realejo (close to León, present Nicaragua), AGI, Escribanía 340. Del Castillo also backed Sánchez de Tagle in the quarrel for preeminence of the *maestres de campo*; AGI, Escribanía 190 A, ff. 100v–108v.

51 Mexican consulado to king, Mexico City, 24 December 1703, AGI, México 474.

52 Archivo Histórico del Distrito Federal (hereinafter AHDF), Actas del Cabildo, vol. 36 A, 1702–1703, f. 78v.

53 Session of the cabildo civil, 5 July 1703, AHDF, Actas del Cabildo, vol. 36 A, ff. 84–85.

54 5 and 7 July 1703, ibid., ff. 84–85; Miguel Diez de la Mora acquired the post of *corregidor* in this period.

55 Alburquerque's decreto, Mexico City, 8 July 1703, AGI, México 474; according to Robles, *Diario*, 3:275, the viceroy published the *bando* on 9 July.

56 Memorial of Juan Miguel de Mayora, Antonio Ramoz de Castilla, José de Urizan, and Juan de Armiaga, "por si y por los demas dueños de tienda de Cacao Canela papel y azafran" to Alburquerque, Mexico City, s.d., AGI, México 474.

57 Mexico City, 5 July 1703, AHDF, actas del cabildo, vol. 36 A, ff. 84–85. Informe of the cabildo civil to Alburquerque, Mexico City, 23 July 1703, AGI, México 474. The Spanish measured paper in one *resma* (ream) that equaled

20 *manos* (hands) of paper; one *mano* = 5 *cuadernillos*; one *cuadernillo* = 5 *pliegos*, a *pliego* being one sheet of paper. The viceregal decree stipulated a price ceiling of 6 pesos for 500 sheets, whereas the municipal council suggested for retailers "el papel quatro pliegos por medio real" ("four sheets for half a real"), ibid., f. 92v. According to that suggestion, 384 *pliegos* should cost 6 pesos. For the measures, see *Diccionario de la lengua castellana*, ed. Real Academia Española (1726: reprint, Madrid: Editorial Gredos, 1963).

58 Alburquerque's orden, Mexico City, 25 July 1703, AGI, México 474.

59 Consulado to king, Mexico City, 24 December 1703, AGI, México 474.

60 Anonymous to king, s.n. AGI, México 377.

61 Alburquerque to king, Mexico City, 3 December 1706, AGI, México 477, exp. 45, ff. 540–44. Junta General, 29 June 1706, ibid., ff. 656–58.

62 The *fiscal* of the Council of the Indies asked the *secretaría del despacho* and *escribanía de cámara* to forward the Sevillian *consulado's* letter from 22 April 1703 and another letter dated 18 December 1703: AGI, México 474. The *consulado's* correspondence could not be located in the AGI.

63 King to Alburquerque, Madrid, 22 June 1709, AGN, RCO 34, exp. 32.

64 Alburquerque to king, Mexico City, 3 December 1706, AGI, México 477, exp. 45, ff. 540–44. Junta General, 29 June 1706, ibid., ff. 656–58.

65 Parecer of the Mexican consulado, 20 March 1706, AGI, México 660.

66 Tutino, "Creole Mexico," 21. On Miravalle's contraband activities, see verdict of the Council of the Indies, Madrid, 27 January 1728, AGI, Escribanía 340 A, ff. 48–52.

67 Session of the ayuntamiento, Mexico City, 1 January 1702, Compendio de los Libros Capitulares de la Muy Noble Insigne, y Muy Leal Ciudad de Mexico (1743–1765), tomo cuatro, AHDF 437, f. 1.

68 Audiencia of Mexico to king, Mexico City, 8 September 1706, AGI, México 642, No. 31, ff. 1004–1005r.

69 Real cédula to Alburquerque, Madrid, 5 August 1705, AGI, México 401. A *marco* corresponded to eight and a half silver pesos. Three hundred and eighty four *tomines* (at 596 mg) equalled one *marco*.

70 Bertrand, *Grandeur et misères*, 346.

71 Pesquisa secreta of the residencia of Oidor José de Luna, Mexico City, 3 September 1715, AGI, Escribanía 234 A, f. 74.

72 Junta de Comercio, 2 December 1706, AGN, AHH 213, exp. 9, f. 200. The crown had granted the viceroy permission to confer three knighthoods on the most generous donors to the monarchy: Alburquerque to king, Mexico City, 1 July 1708, AGI, México 482. De la Canal supported the viceroy in his *juicio de residencia*: testimony, 25 November 1710, ibid., 657, cuaderno 1, f. 452.

73 Consulta of the Council of the Indies, Madrid, 26 September 1707, AGI, México 402.

74 For the relationship to Fausto Cruzat to Garaicoechea, see power of attorney to Garaicoechea by Francisca de Aguirre, Mexico City, 22 November 1706, AGN, Civil 114, ff. 189–189v. Garaicoechea, knight of the order of Santiago, allegedly collaborated with the governor in selling an unusable ship to the crown. He also praised Alburquerque's conduct in the viceroy's *residencia*. Don Juan's brother, Pedro de Garaicoechea received an *encomienda* in the island of Cebu, Philippines, under Fausto Cruzat: real cédula to audiencia of Manila, Madrid, 13 May 1710, AGI, Filipinas, 341, L 8, ff. 298v–301v; real cédula to José de Espinosa, Trujillo, 7 July 1704, AGI Filipinas, 332, L 11, 2, ff. 74v–75v; AGI, México 657, cuaderno 1, f. 253. Real cédula to Fausto Cruzat, Madrid,

27 February 1700, AGI, Filipinas, 349, L 7, ff. 43v–44v.

75   Julián de Osorio, knight of the order of Santiago, blamed the Sánchez de Tagles for the turmoil during the wedding: testimony of witnesses, Mexico City, 15 June 1703, AGI, México 657, f. 119. For his implication in contraband commerce, see king to Alburquerque, Madrid, 25 February 1709, AGI, México 403; anonymous to king, s.n., AGI, México 377; Bernardo de Tinajero to king, Madrid, 5 November 1709, ibid. Osorio's family shared the alliance with the viceroy; for example, Captain Lorenzo Osorio, brother of Don Julián, supported Alburquerque in his *residencia*: AGI, México 657, cuaderno 1, f. 649. For the links among the Osorio family, see Conde and Sanchiz, *Títulos y dignidades*.

76   Testimony of Juan A. Salazar, Mexico City, 11 July 1703, AGI, México 642, ff. 39–42.

77   The Sánchez de Tagle continued to play a key role in Mexico. The fifth Marquis of Altamira, *oidor* of the *audiencia*, became a close ally of the first Count of Revillagigedo: see Velázquez, *El Marqués de Altamira*, 17. For the role of the family during independence, see Doris M. Ladd, *The Mexican Nobility at Independence 1780–1826* (Austin: University of Texas Press, 1976), 121–22.

78   Tribunal de cuentas to king, Mexico City, 8 June 1699, AGI, México 62, R 3, N 29, 3, ff. 1–4v. For the relation of Miguel de Ubilla y Estrada, Marquis of Santa Sabina with the secretary of the *despacho universal*, Antonio de Ubilla y Medina, see Conde and Sanchiz, *Títulos y dignidades*.

79   Ulrich Mücke, *Political Culture in Nineteenth-Century Peru. The Rise of the Partido Civil*, transl. Katya Andrusz (Pittsburgh: University of Pittsburgh Press, 2004), 183–91.

80   Javier Sanchiz, "Lucas de Careaga, Marqués de Santa Fe. La historia fugaz de un noble vasco en la Nueva España. Una biografía en construcción," in *Los vascos en las regiones de Mexico siglos XVI a XX*, ed. Amaya Garritz (Mexico City: UNAM, 1997), 3:203–17.

81   Luis Sánchez de Tagle to the king, Mexico City, 13 October 1704, AGI, México 642, f. 942.

82   Marcello Carmagnani, "Die koloniale Raumordnung: Mutterland, Peripherie und Grenzgebiete," in *Mittel-, Südamerika und die Karibik bis 1760*, 544–46; Walker, *Spanish Politics*, 10.

83   Junta de Comercio, Mexico City, 3 August 1712, AGN, AHH 213, leg. 6, ff. 151–52.

84   John E. Kicza, *Colonial Entrepreneurs. Families and Business in Bourbon Mexico City* (Albuquerque: University of New Mexico, 1983), 52.

85   Careaga replaced his uncle as rector of the *cofradía* Our Lady of Aranzaza in 1702: see Sanchiz, "Lucas de Careaga," 203–17. The following shopkeepers of Careaga vouched for the appointed *alcalde mayor* of Tepeaca: Francisco Gorostia, Juan A. San Martín, Miguel Abajo, Manuel Mascarva, Domingo Mugaguren, Francisco Iramategui Lezinola, Nicolas Quevedo, Pedro Bueno Basori, and José Beazuain. Careaga also put up a deposit for *alcalde mayor* Francisco Diez de Ulzurrun. It is obvious that 6 out of 10 of Careaga's clients had surnames of Basque linguistic origin, with Lezinola and Ulzurrun possibly being of Navarrian stock. Mexico City, 23 March 1708, AGN, MA 50, f. 257; Mexico City, 3 August 1707, AHH 1648, f. 185.

86   7 January 1702, Robles, *Diario*, 3:191.

87   "por los inminentes riesgos que amenazan en lo gen.l por este impensado accidente, y en lo especial entre Montañeses, Vizcaynos y Navarros, maiormente con las experiencias q. se tienen de los lamentables subcesos": Alburquerque's decree, Mexico City, 14 March 1703, AGI, México 642, ff. 95–95v.

88 Santa Sabina was born in 1664, Careaga on 5 October 1671: Conde and Sanchiz, *Títulos y dignidades*.

89 Galicia is located in northwestern Spain. León is east of Galicia.

90 The *calificadores* established which merchant met the legal qualifications to vote in the elections for prior and consuls. In the fight about the *consulado* elections of 1736, the Montañés party argued that many of the Basque merchants had voted without being wholesale traders, thus distorting the results of the elections. The appearance of *Calificador* Francisco Antonio Sánchez de Tagle again underlines the pervasiveness of the Sánchez de Tagle family in merchant circles: testimonio de los auttos de elecciones de Prior.s, Consules, y demas Oficios de el Real tribunal de el Conssulado de Mex.co en la Nueva España hechas en los Años de 1733 y 1735, AGI, Escribanía 205 B, cuaderno 1, pza. 24.

91 Kicza, *Colonial Entrepreneurs*, 52.

92 Ignacio Rubio Mañé, "Gente de España en la ciudad de México, año de 1689. Introducción, recopilación y acotaciones," *Boletín del Archivo General de la Nación* (Mexico City), 2nd series, 7:1–2 (1966), 39–41; Conde and Sanchiz, *Títulos y dignidades*.

93 Lesley Byrd Simpson, *Many Mexicos* (New York: G. P. Putnam's Sons, 1946); Israel, *Race, Class and Politics in Colonial Mexico*.

94 Israel, *Race, Class and Politics*, 267–73.

95 Bertrand, *Grandeur et misères*, 407–9.

CHAPTER 6 - FIGHTING THE FAUX HABSBURG CONSPIRACY, 1706-1708

1 Kamen, *The War of Succession*, 1–24, 87–92.

2 Kamen, *Philip V*, 25–26, 74–75, 98.

3 Analola Borges, *La Casa de Austria en Venezuela durante la Guerra de Sucesión española (1702-1715)* (Salzburg and Tenerifa: University of Salzburg, 1963), 57–120.

4 Real cédula to Alburquerque, Barcelona, 31 March 1702, AGN, Reales Cédulas Duplicadas (hereinafter RCD) 40, 245, ff. 320r–321r. Real cédula to Alburquerque, Buen Retiro, 28 April 1703, AGN, RCO 31, 91, ff. 257–60.

5 Robles, *Diario*, 3:235.

6 Decree of Alburquerque, Mexico City, 17 November 1706, testimony … Antonio Villar, f. 2.

7 Navarro García, *Conspiración*, 91–94. See also idem, "Salvador Mañer, agente carlista en México," *Archivo Hispalense* (Seville) 178 (1975), 1–23.

8 Herzog, *La administración*, 297–308.

9 Deposition of Tovar, Mexico City, 1 November 1706, testimonio de los autos y caussa criminal … contra Benito Cartagena … de orden del Exmo S.r Duque de Alburquerque, AGI, Escribanía 262 B, pza. 20, f. 1v.

10 Alburquerque to king, Mexico City, 17 September 1705, AGI, México 477, ff. 382–85; the two *alcaldes* were Juan Ozaeta y Oro and Manuel Suárez Muñoz.

11 RLRI, libro ii, título xv, ley iii and lxiii; título xvi, ley xxvi and xxviii.

12 Declaración de Gómez Lobato, Mexico City, testimonio de la causa contra Gregorio Gasco, AGI, Escribanía 263 A, f. 8v.

13 Declaración of Antonio Freire, Causa criminal contra Juan López Camaño, 262 A, pza. 3, ff. 7–11; Causa…Gasco, AGI, Escribanía 263 A; autos … Andrés Caballero, 262 B, pza. 9; testimonio … Pedro Collazo, 262 C, pza. 22; testimonio … Puyol, 263 A, pza. 35; autos contra Antonio de Villar, 263 A, pza 38; causa … José Pardo, 263 A, pza. 39, ff. 34–49. The trial against Lorenzo González is in the cuaderno testimonios de los autos criminales que se fulminaron de ofizio por el Ex.mo Señor Juan de Ortega y Montañés, Arzobispo … contra Lorenzo Gonzales de Figueroa, AGI, México 646.

14 AGI, México 657, cuaderno 2; AGI, México 377. In 1701, Lobato acquired a position as accountant in the treasury of Mexico for 8,000 pesos, AGI, Contratación, 5463, N 71, ff. 1r–4v. The satiric Mexican copla also mentioned a person called Lobato, probably a cleric, as having an obligation towards the viceroy, "corresponderá Lobato con su antigua obligacion." Their relation remains unknown: Confession, que haze, en los ultimos dias de Su govierno; el Ex.mo S.r Duque de Alburquerque, s.n., AGN, Inquisición 740, exp. 3, f. 56v. On the Pagabe visita, see Amalia Gómez Gómez, *Las visitas de la Real Hacienda novohispana en el reinado de Felipe V (1710–1733)*, (Seville: Escuela de Estudios Hispano-Americanos, 1979), 7–103.

15 Parecer, Mexico City, 14 August 1707, AGI, Escribanía 263 A, pza 38, f. 74v. Cepeda to king, Mexico City, 20 November 1707, AGI, México 523.

16 *Las Siete Partidas del Rey Don Alfonso el Sabio cotejadas con varios codices antiguos ...*, ed. Real Academia de la Historia (Madrid, Imprenta Real, 1807), séptima partida, título i, ley i.

17 *Las Siete Partidas*, séptima partida, título i, ley vi; segunda partida, título xiii, ley iv. See also Albert du Boys, *Historia del derecho penal de España*, ed. and transl. José Vicente y Caravantes (Madrid: Imprenta de José María Pérez , 1872), 241–52.

18 Francisco Tomás y Valiente, *El derecho penal de la monarquía absoluta (siglos XVI–XVII–XVIII)* (Madrid: Editorial Tecnos, 1969), 241–42.

19 José Vicente y Caravantes and León Galindo y de Vera, eds., *Diccionario razonado de legislacion y jurisprudencia por D. Joaquín Escriche. Nueva edicion reformada y considerablemente aumentada* (Madrid: Imprenta de Eduardo Cuesta, 1874–1876), 3:242–43. Compare also the establishment of the *Giunta d'Infidenza* to "ensure state security" in the kingdom of Naples during Charles's reign from 1734 to 1759: see Stanley and Barbara Stein, *Apogee of Empire*, 6. For crimes against the king, see also José Luis de las Heras Santos, *La justicia penal de los Austrias en la corona de Castilla* (Salamanca: Ediciones Universidad de Salamanca, 1991), 215–17.

20 For the formal procedure of colonial penal trials, see Tamar Herzog, *Upholding Justice. Society, State, and the Penal System in Quito (1650–1750)* (Ann Arbor: University of Michigan Press, 2004), 24–26.

21 Declaracion of General Juan de Garaicoechea, Mexico City, 24 November 1706, AGI, Escribanía 263 A, f. 26.

22 Ibid. Sebastianists believed in the reappearance of the Portuguese king Sebastian (1557–1578), who would establish a powerful empire, a dangerous insinuation at the time when Castile was at war with Portugal. Tomé N. Mbuia João, "Sebastian (Sebastião) of Portugal," in *Encyclopedia of Latin American History and Culture*, ed. Barbara Tenenbaum (New York: Charles Scribner's Sons, 1996), 5:85.

23 AGI, Escribanía 262 A–C, 263 A.

24 Hoberman describes *cargadores* as agents of peninsular traders: *Mexico's Merchant Elite*, 319. The term *cargador de flota* refers to Gasco in the trial documents against his friend Pedro Collazo de Soto. Oidor Tovar confiscated Gasco's property worth about 140,000 pesos attesting to the wealth of the *cargador*: Cepeda to king, Mexico City, 14 April 1708, AGI Escribanía 263 A, pza. 36, ff. 3r–3v.

25 Causa ... Gasco, AGI, Escribanía 263 A, f. 34. Luis Navarro, *Conspiración*, 48, quotes the following passage from the original: "Con mi benida an clavado el pico en este parral todos los opiniones que eran *Coronistas*," and "de mi opinion Y asi tengo ahora muchos amigos Y los *coronistas* se me han echo grandes Amigos por que yo les he descubierto la trampa y al portuges que esta enbargado que sellama, Simoes y sus amigos

se han alegrado mucho de mi benida por saver la verdad" [my inverse] This is in his view another proof of the political activities of Puyol as *coronista*, that is, someone associated in a way with the crown. However, the word in the original reads correctly *cotista*, testimonio ... Puyol, f. 69v. This term is not related to the crown in any sense, yet it could refer to the mentioned commercial competitor of Puyol named "Capitan Juan Cotto Vesino y mercader en esta cuidad": Causa ... Gasco, AGI, Escribanía 263A, f. 34.

26   The *audiencia* also prosecuted other suspects but then dropped the charges, because personal enemies had manufactured the denunciations: Causa ... Alberto Rada, AGI, Escribanía 190 A and 263. *Oidor* Francisco Casa Alvarado prosecuted several individuals in Tochimilco and Guadalcazar and discharged them: AGI, México 660, ff. 1318–1345.

27   Mexico City, 29 July 1707, AGI, Escribanía 263 A, pza. 37, "autos f.hos contra Antonio Cavallero difunto," ff. 33–33v.

28   On Ibáñez's appointment, see Alburquerque to king, Mexico City, 29 March 1706, AGI, México 479. Alburquerque supported senior Accountant Andrés Pardo de Lagos's plea for retirement with full salary: Alburquerque to king, Mexico City, 12 July 1708, AGI, México 479.

29   Andres Pardo de Lagos supported *Oidor* Calderón de la Barca in his *residencia*: AGI, Escribanía 233 A, f. 132.

30   AGI, Escribanía 262 A, pza. 3, ff. 31r–v. Merchant Julián de Osorio had participated actively in the Cruzat-Tagle wedding conflict.

31   *Fiscal del crimen* Cepeda asked for a guilty verdict against Antonio Caballero, Juan López Camaño, José Pardo, and Antonio del Villar Bahamonde: AGI, Escribanía, 263 A, pza. 37, f. 39v; ibid., pza. 39, f. 45v; autos contra Juan López Camaño, f. 38–39. See also parecer of fiscal de lo civil José Antonio Espinosa, demanding the death penalty for Pedro Collazo: AGI, Escribanía 262 C, pza. 22, f. 271v.

32   Parecer, Mexico City, 14 August 1707, AGI, Escribanía 263 A, pza. 38, f. 74v.

33   Herzog, *La administración*, 232.

34   Consulta of the Council of the Indies, Madrid, 10 August 1708, AGI, México 403.

35   Parecer of the fiscal of the Council of the Indies, Madrid, 19 October 1708, AGI, Escribanía 263 A, pza. 36; sentencia of the sala de crimen, Mexico City, 3 October 1708, Causa...Gasco, Escribanía 263 A, ff. 302–3; sentencia of the sala de crimen, Mexico City, 15 November 1708, Escribanía 262 C, pza. 22, ff. 285v–286.

36   Sala de crimen, Mexico City, 3 October 1708, Causa...Gasco, AGI, Escribanía 263 A, ff. 302-3. The *sala* consisted of *Oidor* José de Luna Arias and *Alcaldes de crimen* Juan Ozaeta y Oro and Francisco Casa Alvarado; Navarro, *Conspiración*, 62–63.

37   Causa ... Puyol, f. 194.

38   Tovar to Alburquerque, Mexico City, 2 November 1706, AGI, Escribanía 263 C, pza. 40, f. 21; Ortega to Alburquerque, 3 November 1706, ibid., f. 22.

39   Here, Andres Moreno Bala.

40   The documents for the other trial are lost.

41   Question of the *promotor fiscal*, Mexico City, 14 December 1706, AGI, México 646, "Causa ... Gonzales," f. 47v.

42   Confession of González, ibid., f. 48.

43   See also "confession ... Alburquerque," AGN, Inquisición 740, exp. 3, f. 56v.

44   Sentence, Mexico City, AGI, México 646, "Causa ... Gonzales," f. 94. The doctoral canon, José de Torres, who sentenced González, is already familiar from the Tagle-Cruzat conflict as a client of Archbishop Ortega y Montañés.

45   For sources, see above, note 13.

46 Declaration of Tomás Fernández de Guevara, Mexico City, 1 November 1706, testimonio de los autos y caussa criminal ... contra Benito Cartagena ... de orden del Exmo S.r Duque de Alburquerque, AGI, Escribanía 263A, pza. 40, ff. 6-6v.

47 Declaration of Asinas, Mexico City, 1 November 1706, ibid., f. 7.

48 Cartagena and his wife knew that Asinas stood in favour with the duke: declaration of Cartagena, Mexico City, 1 November 1706, ibid., 262 B, pza. 20, f. 1v. Alburquerque to king, Mexico City, 10 February 1708, AGI, México 1326. Alburquerque applauded Asinas for raising a cavalry company during the turmoil of 1692. The duke procured a salary for Asinas as captain: relación de estado, AGI, México 485, f. 49v. The surname *Duque de Estrada* does not indicate titled nobility.

49 Declaration of Cartagena, Mexico City, 1 November 1706, AGI, Escribanía 262 B, pza. 20, f. 1v. Witnesses from a similar bureaucratic background, such as an assistant to the audiencia chancellor, backed Cartagena: testimonies, Mexico City, 15 January 1707, Escribanía 263A, pza. 40, ff. 56-88v.

50 Sentence by Magistrates José de Luna, Baltasar Tovar, José Uribe, Alonso Abellafuertes, and Juan Ozaeta, Mexico City, 16 February 1707, ibid., f. 99.

51 Ibid., ff. 23-58v.

52 According to Conde and Sanchiz, *Títulos y dignidades*, José de Careaga, *contador de penas de cámara* (accountant of fines and penalties imposed by the *audiencia*) was not related to the merchant Lucas de Careaga. Yet, Nicolas López de Landa acted as guarantor for the *alcalde mayor* of Guanajuato, Fernando Velasco Duque de Estrada, probably a relative of Captain Alsonso Asinas Duque de Estrada. This could also indicate a tie between Don Alonso and the contraband traders: Mexico City, 11 August 1704, AGN, AHH 1648, f. 95v.

53 Causa criminal contra Manuel Sousa y Prado, AGI, Escribanía 262 C, pza. 21, ff. 3v, 17.

54 Declaration of Don Pedro Urtazu, 6 April 1707, Mexico City, ibid., 32v.

55 Declaration, 9 April 1707, ibid., f. 72.

56 Declaration, 25 July 1707, ibid., f. 235.

57 Sentencia, Mexico City, 5 March 1708, f. 284.

58 Benito Ignacio de Oxas, prison notary, Mexico City, 26 December 1708.

59 Declaración of Alférez Juan de Acosta before Oidor Tovar, Mexico City, 22 November 1706, Causa ... Salvador Mañer, AGI, México 661, f. 2. Mañer administered the hacienda San José Comalco in Toluca for its owner, the Cleric Juan Pardo. Two other defendants with that last name, Juan Antonio Pardo and José Pardo, stood trial. If there were a connection, that could further provide evidence for a vendetta against a social network.

60 Confession of Mañer, Mexico City, 20 January 1707, ibid., f. 51v.

61 For the legal background, María Paz Alonso Romero, *El proceso penal en Castilla, siglo XIII-XVIII* (Salamanca: Ediciones Universidad de Salamanca, 1982), 204-5.

62 Sentencia by Uribe, Ozaeta, and Casa Alvarado, Mexico City, AGI, México 661, f. 140.

63 Fiscal of the Casa de Contratación to king, Seville, 1711, AGI, México 661, f. 44-45; confession of Mañer, Córdoba, 15 November 1713, ibid., f. 54-62; sentence of the Council of the Indies, Madrid, ibid., f. 76-77.

64 Navarro García, *Conspiración*, 70-71.

65 Mexico City, 16 April 1708, AGN, MA 50.

66 See the residencia of Joseph de Luna, AGI, Escribanía, 234 A, f. 162 as well as residencia of Miguel de Calderón, ibid., 236 A, pza. 1, ff. 101-102v, 195.

67 AGI, México 658. In the quarrel over the alum monopoly, Ledesma represented Alburquerque's crony Pedro de Escorza Escalante, whereas Hidalgo defended the interests of opponent Augustín López de Valdes. Escorza won the auction for the monopoly after the legal dispute in the *audiencia*: AGI, Escribanía 192 B.

68 Auto of Carlos Navia, Mexico City, 21 January 1711, AGI, México 659, cuaderno 7, exp. 1, labelled "Demanda puesta por D.a Sebastiana Fernandes Nolasco muger lex.ma de D.n Juan Francisco Fernandez Cacho contra el Ex.mo S.or Virrey Duque de Alburquerque," ff. 46–54.

69 RLRI, libro ii, título xv, ley xxxix.

70 RLRI, libro iii, título iii, ley xxv.

71 Alburquerque to king, Mexico City, 26 March 1703, AGI, México 474.

72 Consulta of the Council of the Indies, Madrid, 18 May 1708, AGI, México 403.

73 Juicio de residencia of Calderón, AGI, Escribanía 236 A, B, pza. 1, 5, 6. In 1715 the *audiencia* rejected Uribe's accusations and penalized him to pay half of the *residencia*'s costs. The Council of the Indies upheld the verdict on 11 February 1717, at a time when Calderón had already passed away.

74 Consider the fact that Calderón paid ca. 14,000 pesos for a seat on the Council of the Indies: king to royal officials, s.n., 1702, AGI, México 402.

75 Cepeda was appointed on 20 September 1704: Mark A. Burkholder and Dewitt Samuel Chandler, *Biographical Dictionary of Audiencia Ministers in the Americas, 1687-1821* (Westport, CT: Greenwood, 1982), 370.

76 Cepeda substituted for Uribe's chair in *decretales mayores* (papal decrees): relación de méritos in a consulta of the Council of the Indies, Madrid, 25 November 1702, AGI, México 376.

77 Real acuerdo, Mexico City, 16 December 1706, AGN, Civil 1625, exp. 2.

78 Cepeda to king, Mexico City, 14 April 1708, AGI, Escribanía 263 A, pza. 36, ff. 3r–3v. Testimony of Nuñez de Villavicencia in Alburquerque's residencia, Mexico City, 2 December 1710, AGI, México 657, cuaderno 1, f. 225v.

79 Consulta of the Council of the Indies, Madrid, 10 August 1708, AGI, México 403. Alburquerque to king, Mexico City, 6 December 1707, AGI, México 730; Assistant Notary Diego Antonio Marquina to Secretary Gabriel de Mendieta, Guanajuato, 25 July 1727, AHAGN, Escribano Diego Antonio Marquina, No. 393, vol. 2614, ff. 34–35.

80 Cepeda to king, Mexico City, 20 November 1707, AGI, México 523.

81 Alburquerque to king, Mexico City, 13 October 1707, AGI, México 479; parecer of Fiscal Espinosa, México City, 13 November 1708, AGI, México 479.

82 Consulta of the Council of the Indies, Madrid, 10 August 1708, AGI, México 403.

83 Domínguez Ortiz, *La sociedad española en el siglo XVII*, 200–216.

84 Alburquerque to king, Mexico City, 22 February 1709, AGI, México 1326.

85 Bertrand, *Grandeur et misères*, 342, fn. 52.

86 Uribe married Michaela María de Sandóval y Caballero: Brian Hamnett, *The Mexican Bureaucracy before the Bourbon Reforms, 1700-1770: A Study in the Limitations of Absolutism*, Institute of Latin American Studies, Occasional Papers, vol. 26 (Glasgow: University of Glasgow, 1979), 333–34.

87 Consulta of the Council of the Indies, Madrid, 18 May 1708, AGI, México 403; Real cédula to the Duke of Atrisco, governor of the Council of the Indies, Madrid, 16 April 1708, AGI, México 377.

88 Licence to embark for Cienfuegos, Seville, 23 July 1701, AGI, Contratación, 5460 N 2, R 23; License to embark for Costela, Madrid, 27 May 1702, AGI, México 399. Originally a page of Pope

Innocent XI, Costela became dean of the chapter of Ciudad Rodrigo, Spain. He then advanced to a canonry of the Mexico City cathedral chapter: Robles, *Diario*, 3:236. According to rumours, Costela had already been exiled from his post as dean, and he later participated in a fistfight in the Mexican chapter: Salvador José Mañer to Salvador Mañer, Mexico City, s.n., AGI, México 661, f. 103v.

89   Consulta of the Council of the Indies, Madrid, 18 May 1708, AGI, México 403.

90   Real cédula to the Duke of Linares, Madrid, 21 July 1710, AGI, México 646; Linares to king, Mexico City, 30 October 1711, AGI, México 655; Consulta of the Council of the Indies, Madrid, 22 November 1712, AGI, México 377; King to Frigiliana, Madrid, 12 November 1710, ibid.

91   Manuel de Aperregui, secretary of the Council of the Indies for New Spain, to king, Madrid, 20 January 1706, AGI, México 522; consulta of the Council of the Indies, Madrid, 20 March 1706, AGI, México 402. On Escalante y Mendoza's family connections including the bishop of Michoacán, see Gustavo Rafael Alfaro Ramírez, "Quién encarceló al alguacil mayor de Puebla? La vida, los negocios y el poder de don Pedro de Mendoza y Escalante, 1695–1740," *Estudios de Historia Novohispana* (Mexico City) 17 (1997): 34. On Garzarón's *visita general*, see Bertrand, *Grandeur et misères*, 23, 69.

92   John Frederick Schwaller, "The Secular Clergy in Sixteenth-Century Mexico" (Ph.D. diss., Indiana University, 1978), 78–80.

93   Cathedral chapter to king, Mexico City, 18 February 1709, AGI, México 1326; testimony of witnesses, Mexico City, 4–9 October 1708, exp. without title, AGI, México 646, ff. 14–25v. José de Torres y Vergara and Antonio Aunisbay y Aznaya participated in earlier conflicts as confidants of the archbishop.

94   Testimony of witness Juan Antonio de Santander, Mexico City, 15 June 1703, AGI, México 642, f. 122; Consulta of the Council of the Indies, Madrid, 10 August 1708, AGI, México 403. The satire against Alburquerque "Confession…" also states that the archbishop and Uribe's group exchanged favours: AGN, Inquisición 740, exp. 3, f. 58. The Franciscan provincial and his fellow friars intervened at the Council of the Indies on behalf of the four accused: Mexico City, 30 October 1708, AGI, México 655.

95   Real cédula to the Duke of Linares, Madrid, 21 July 1710, AGI, México 646; Linares to king, Mexico City, 30 October 1711, AGI, México 655; Consulta of the Council of the Indies, Madrid, 22 November 1712, AGI, México 377; King to Frigiliana, Madrid, 12 November 1710, ibid.

96   Alburquerque to king, Mexico City, 2 May 1710, AGI, México 483.

97   Alburquerque to king, ibid. José de Torres, the doctoral canon in charge of the chapter's litigation, wrote the rebuttal against the vice-patron's demands: ibid.

98   Prebendaries Domingo Bayon Vandujo, Miguel González de Valdeosera, Francisco Jiménez Panyagua, and Juan de Castorena vouched for the duke in the *sumaria pesquisa secreta*: residencia of Alburquerque, AGI, México 657, cuaderno 2, f. 118v–351.

99   AGN, Jesuitas 1, leg. 14, exp. 22, ff. 186–96.

100 The duke did not explain how he intended this to work in detail.

101 Guanajuato paid about 693 pesos and Toluca 208: Alburquerque to Minas de Guanajuato, Mexico City, 25 February 1708, AGN, AHH 223, exp. 4, ff. 94–94v; Alburquerque to Toluca, same date, ibid., f. 119.

102 Parecer of the fiscal, Madrid, 21 April 1705; real cédula, Madrid, 5 August 1705, AGI, México 401. The crown

lauded Alburquerque's efforts to raise a loan of one million pesos and sent him six habits of military orders, which the viceroy could confer on the most generous donors at his discretion. One of those went to Alburquerque's ally Domingo de la Canal: king and queen to Alburquerque, Madrid, 6 June 1710, AGI, México 404; king to Alburquerque, Madrid, 20 December 1707, ibid., 479.

103   Ortega to king, Mexico City, 18 November 1700, actas del cabildo, vol. 25, ff. 322–325v, Archivo del Cabildo de la Catedral de México (hereinafter ACCM); archbishop to Viceroy Marquis of Valero, Mexico City, 5 August, 1719, AGN, Bienes Nacionales 867, exp. 5, ff. 1–2v.

104   Alburquerque to Ortega, Mexico City, 21 August 1703, AGN, Bienes Nacionales 574, exp. 4, ff. 2–2v and cathedral chapter, session on 26 September 1703, ibid., exp. 1, ff. 17–19.

105   Declaración of Manuel Sousa y Prada, Mexico City, 9 April 1707, AGI, Escribanía 262 C, f. 72.

CHAPTER 7 - ALBURQUERQUE RESISTS ROYAL REFORMS

1   "Y que este intento de los religiosos era perder el R.l Patronato de V.M. en los Curatos suios": Angel Maldonado to king, Antequera, 13 April 1707, AGI, México 881.

2   The original reads "novedad estraña, y impracticable": Alburquerque to king, Mexico City, 7 January 1709, AGI, México 881.

3   Navarro García, "Los oficios vendibles en Nueva España durante la Guerra de Sucesión," *AEA* 32 (1975): 217.

4   Michel Bertrand, "En torno a una problemática de la administración colonial: la Real Hacienda de Nueva España, 1680–1770," *AEA* 46 (1989): 195–217. The tribunal was restored to fourteen officials.

5   Alburquerque put the accountant of tributes in charge for this task: Alburquerque to king, Mexico City, 10 April 1703, AGI, México 474.

6   The accountants of the Council of the Indies objected to the procedure, and it was revoked in 1732: see Bertrand, "En torno a una problemática," 212–14.

7   Bando by Alburquerque, Mexico City, 10 November 1704, AGN, Indios 97, ff. 23–14. For the organization of the community treasuries in Mexico, see Charles Gibson, *The Aztecs under Spanish Rule. A History of the Indians of the Valley of Mexico 1519–1810* (Stanford: Stanford University Press, 1964), 185–86.

8   Dictamen of Fiscal Espinosa, Mexico, 20 October 1704, AGN, Indios 97, f. 9v.

9   For example, the notary and *regidor* of Malinaltepec, who in somewhat mangled Spanish declared "doy y jusegar sia rixidor" (that is, he swore the accuracy of the contents), claimed that the community gained 26 pesos and spent it all on its fiestas: AGN, Indios 97, f. 25.

10   Cayetana Alvarez de Toledo, *Politics and Reform in Spain and Viceregal Mexico. The Life and Thought of Juan de Palafox, 1600–1659* (Oxford: Clarendon Press, 2004), 48–49.

11   According to Bertrand, *Grandeur et misères*, 333, Veytia Linage's uncle, José de Veytia Linage sat on the Council of the Indies. Lynch mentions in *Spain under the Habsburgs*, 270–72, that José de Veytia Linage became secretary of the *despacho universal* in 1682, but he relinquished the post in 1685 with the resignation of his patron Medinaceli as prime minister. Bernard claims that José de Veytia Linage became councillor in 1711 (*Le secrétariat d´état*, 215), but the historian probably refers to the honorary membership that Juan José obtained in or before 1709; parecer of José de los Ríos, fiscal of the Council of the Indies, Madrid, 28 March 1711, AGI, México 377.

12 Bertrand, *Grandeur et misères*, 333–35.

13 The duke appointed the bishop's brother, Estéban Rodríguez Santa Cruz, official in the viceregal secretariate and in 1705 interim accountant of the tribunal of accounts in Mexico City: Alburquerque to king, 6 June 1706, AGI, México 474, f. 31v. On 21 April 1708, the crown rejected confirming this position; AGS, Hacienda 174–102; Rodríguez Santa Cruz's status as Alburquerque's page indicates that the bishop's family and the duke had some kind of tie before their respective voyages to Mexico.

14 Bertrand, "La contaduría de las alcabalas de Puebla: Un episodio reformador al prinicipio del siglo XVIII," *JbLA* 32 (1995): 321–32.

15 Veytia Linage to king, Puebla, 18 September 1706, AGI, México 479.

16 Bertrand, "La contaduría de las alcabalas," 342, fn. 42.

17 Idem, *Grandeur et misères*, 342, fn. 42.

18 Alburquerque to king, Mexico City, 29 April 1703, AGI, México 473; Alburquerque to king, Mexico City, 5 December 1703, AGI, México 475.

19 Parecer of Fiscal Espinosa, Mexico City, 26 February 1703; consulta of the Council of the Indies, Madrid, 16 January 1705; note by Manuel de Aperregui, secretary of the Council of the Indies for New Spain, Madrid, 7 February 1705; all in AGI, México 474.

20 Veytia Linage to king, Puebla, 18 September 1706, AGI, México 479.

21 Dictamen, fiscal of the Council of the Indies, Madrid, 24 June 1709, AGI, México 481.

22 Bertrand, *Grandeur et misères*, 55–61, 92–93.

23 Alburquerque to king, duplicate, AHCDA, 463, No. 6. Veytia Linage was appointed on 15 January 1709: Antonia Heredia Herrera, *La renta del azogue en Nueva España (1709-1751)* (Seville: Escuela de Estudios Hispano-Americanos, 1978), 181.

24 Junta de Azogues, Madrid, 28 March 1711, AGI, México 377.

25 Representación de la junta general de ministros, Mexico City, 11 November 1709, AHCDA, 463, No. 6; Junta de Azogues, Madrid, 28 March 1711, AGI, México 377.

26 Instruccion delo que hade observar el general D. Andres de Arriola en el viage que ha de hacer con la Armada â conducir los situados de Barlovento este año de 1710, duplicate, Mexico City, 30 April 1710, AHCDA, 463, No. 7.

27 Parecer of the fiscal of the Council of the Indies, José de los Ríos, Madrid, 28 March 1711, AGI, México 377.

28 Bertrand, "La contaduría," 330–31.

29 The original reads "no querer que en su tpo. se diese planta y reglas, a negocio de esta gravedad e importancia, y que no se descubriesen aquellos intereses, que tolerados y consentidos, han resultado en tan grave perjuicio de la R.l hazienda de V.M. para q. concluyendo su Virreynato, quedase la obscuridad de este negozio": junta de azogues, Madrid, 28 March 1711, AGI, México 377.

30 Gibson, *The Aztecs*, 98–99.

31 Lynch, *Spain under the Habsburgs*, 272–73.

32 Stafford Poole, *Pedro Moya de Conteras. Catholic Reform and Royal Power in New Spain, 1571-1591* (Berkeley: University of California Press, 1987), 73.

33 Taylor, *Magistrates of the Sacred. Priests and Parishioners in Eighteenth-Century Mexico* (Stanford: Stanford University Press, 1996), 83–84.

34 Francisco Canterla y Martín de Tovar, *La iglesia de Oaxaca en el siglo XVIII* (Seville: Escuela de Estudios Hispano-Americanos, 1982), 4; *Diccionario Porrúa de Historia, Biografía y Geografía de México*, 6th ed. (Mexico City: Editorial Porrúa, 1995), 3:2087.

35 Poole, *Pedro Moya de Conteras*, 51.

36 Maldonado to king, Antequera, 23 July 1706, AGI, México 881.

37 Real cédula to Alburquerque, Madrid, 4 November 1705, AGN, RCO, 32, 202, ff. 463–463v.

38 Taylor, *Magistrates*, 570.

39 Maldonado to king, Antequera, 13 April 1707, AGI, México 881.

40 Manuel Hidalgo to king, Antequera, 11 September 1704, AGI, México 881.

41 Real cédula to Alburquerque, Madrid, 24 November 1705, AGN, RCO 32, 202, ff. 463–465r. Maldonado had suggested secularizing the following parishes: Santa Cruz, Santa Ana Zagache, Ocotlan, Sachila, Talixtaca, Huizóo, San Francisco Cajonos, San Ildefonso de la Villa Alta, Achutla, and Coixtlahuaca: parecer of Fiscal José de los Ríos, Madrid, 25 September 1707, AGI, México 881.

42 Francisco de Reyna to king, Antequera, s.n., 1706, AGI, 881.

43 Jacinto de Coria to Alburquerque, Antequera, 17 July 1706; Maldonado to Alburquerque, Antequera, 21 July 1706; both in AGI, México 879.

44 Alburquerque's ruego y encargo to the rector of the Jesuit college of Oaxaca, Mexico City, 13 October 1706, AGN, RCD 42, exp. 360, ff. 335v–336r.

45 The viceroy asked the *alcaldes mayores* of Oaxaca, the cuatro villas del marquesado del Valle, Miaquatlan, Villa Alta, Nexapa, and Chichicapa for evaluations. Alburquerque to Angel Maldonado, Mexico City, 25 November 1706, AGN, RCD 42, 363, ff. 339r–341v.

46 See the dictamen of the fiscal of the Council of the Indies, Madrid, 25 September 1707, AGI, México 881, ff. 77–77v.

47 Parecer, Mexico City, 19 November 1706, AGI, México 879; Alburquerque to audiencia, Mexico City, 22 December 1706, ibid.

48 Maldonado to king, Antequera, 31 March 1707, AGI, México 881, ff. 28–28v; Maldonado to king, Antequera, 13 April 1707, ibid., ff. 74–74v.

49 Alburquerque to king, Mexico City, 24 March 1706, AGI, México 881, exp. 35.

50 Procurador general Francisco de Reyna to king, Antequera, s.n., 1706, AGI, 881, f. 68.

51 Miguel de Valverde to Alburquerque, Antequera, 16 August 1707, AGI, México 879.

52 Alburquerque to Dominican provincial of Oaxaca, Mexico City, 13 October 1706, AGN, RCD 42, exp. 359, ff. 335–335v.

53 Canterla, *La iglesia de Oaxaca*, 57–59.

54 Parecer of the fiscal of the Council of the Indies, Madrid, 9 May 1709, AGI, México 881.

55 In the original, Tovar stood in "extraordinario valimiento con el virrey": Maldonado to king, Antequera, 17 April 1708, AGI, México 879.

56 Dictamen, fiscal of the Council of the Indies, Madrid, 9 May 1709, AGI, México 880.

57 Maldonado to king, Antequera, 17 April 1708, AGI, México 879.

58 Ibid.

59 In 1710 Rector Dr. Francisco Oyanguren bought the *fiscalía* of the *audiencia* through *beneficio* only to be removed by *Visitador* Francisco Garzarón for abuses in 1720: Hamnett, *Mexican Bureaucracy*, 17; AGI, México 657, cuaderno 1, f. 56; AGI, Indiferente 135, N 123, 1, f. 1r.

60 "algo confuso y tartamudo": Ortega to king, Mexico City, 31 August 1707, AGI, México 480. Cervantes also held a chair of decrees (*decretos*) at the Mexican university.

61 On León, see AGI, México 657, cuaderno 2, f. 42v; México 642; AGI, Indiferente 134, N 17.

62 Maldonado to king, Antequera, 17 April 1708, AGI, México 879.

63 Ibid. The copla "Confession …" refers to the quarrel as well: "Pues a el otro Guaxaquense/ Obispo de gran Hervor, que vino a esta Corte/ a pleitos muy cargado de razon/ Qual lo trate por lo mucho/ que el fray Angel me cantó/ no obstante de ser su cavesa … del Servicio de Dios. De modo el impertinente Angel, con migo luchó, que quedé mas fatigado/ que con el otro Jacob," AGN, Inquisición 740, exp. 3., f. 58.

64 Maldonado to king, Antequera, 17 April 1708, AGI, México 879.

65 Alburquerque to king, Mexico City, 15 April 1708, AGI, México 879.

66 Canterla, *La iglesia de Oaxaca*, 82–85.

67 Parecer of José de los Ríos, Madrid, 9 May 1709, AGI, México 880.

CHAPTER 8 - REFORM AND REVENGE: THE FALL OF ALBURQUERQUE, 1711–1715

1 Pérez-Mallaina, *Política naval*, 73.

2 Real cédula to Alburquerque, Buen Retiro, 6 June 1703; AGI, México 476. According to Pérez-Mallaina, *Política naval*, 65, three livres corresponded to one Spanish peso, although the exchange rate fluctuated during the War of Succession.

3 The first Count of Revillagigedo also tacitly supported the intercolonial trade. See his relación de Don Francisco de Güemes a Ahumada y Villalón, 8 October 1755, *Instrucciones y Memoriales*, ed. by Torre Villar, 2:811–13.

4 Alburquerque to king, Mexico City, 26 November 1703, AGI, México 475.

5 Informe del estado, Mexico City, 31 March 1703, AGI, México 474.

6 Alan J. Kuethe, "El fin del monopolio: los Borbones y el consulado andaluz," in Enriqueta Vila Vilar and Alan J. Kuethe, eds., *Relaciones de poder y comercio colonial: nuevas perspectivas* (Seville: Escuela de Estudios Hispano-Americanos, 1999), 35–66.

7 Real cédula to Alburquerque, Madrid, 30 December 1705, AGN, RCO 32, exp. 207, ff. 475–76; king to Oidor Juan Mendoza, Madrid, 30 December 1705, AGI, México 401.

8 Andrés de Pez to Gaspar de Pinedo, Veracruz, 23 August 1708, AGI, México 377, ff. 5–6.

9 On Pez's allegiance to the Bourbon cause, see José María Mariluz Urquijo, "Proyectos de Andrés de Pes sobre la organización del Consejo de Indias," in *Actas y estudios del IV congreso del Instituto Internacional de Historia del Derecho Indiano* (Madrid: Instituto de la Historia del Derecho Indiano, 1991), 357–65. Pez also supervised the fortress of San Juan Ulúa as its warden: relación de servicios, Madrid, 16 February 1694, AGI, Indiferente 133, N 100, 1; AGI, Escribanía 1060 B. King to Alburquerque, Madrid, 29 October 1706, AGI, México 402. In 1704, Alburquerque had recommended Pez to the crown, perhaps to promote the official to another post outside of New Spain: Alburquerque to king, Mexico City, 24 September 1704, AGI, México 476.

10 On the cochino, see also Bertrand, *Grandeur et misères*, 35–40.

11 Anonymous to Council of the Indies, s.n., AGI, México 377.

12 Tinajero to king, Madrid, 5 November 1709, AGI, México 377.

13 Testimony of witness Alonso Antonio Fernández de Segade, doorman and purveyor of the Inquisition, in favour of Canon Andrés de Costela, Mexico City, 9 October 1708, AGI, México 646, expediente without title, ff. 22v–23v. The text reads "remitiendo estos la ropa y demas Mercaderias a D.n Lucas de Cariaga, D.n Alonso de Avales y Geronimo Monterde y despues que este quebro con el Duque de Alburquerque … a Julian Osorio." "Este" seems to refer to Monterde, but there is no indication of a falling out between him and the duke. In fact, on 23 October 1710, in his last days in office, Alburquerque

Notes   253

appointed Jerónimo Monterde as administrator of the marquisate of the Valley of Oaxaca, which is certainly an indication of good relationship between the two; AGN, MA 24. Much information, however, indicates a serious conflict between Careaga and Alburquerque.

14 The responsible *oidor*, Miguel Calderón de la Barca, allegedly also collaborated with the Monterde merchant family in the clandestine operation of the Rayas mine in Guanajuato: testimony of witness Alonso Antonio Fernández de Segade, Mexico City, 9 October 1708, AGI, México 646, expediente without title, ff. 22v–23v.

15 Consulta, Madrid, 4 April 1707, AGI, México 402. The Council recommended the duke for the *cordon bleu*, but the Council's governor, the Duke of Atrisco, suggested that the *toison de oro* would be sufficient.

16 Tinajero to king, Madrid, 5 November 1709, AGI, México 377.

17 Consulta, Madrid, 10 December 1708, AGI, México 377.

18 Junta de indultos and parecer of the fiscal, Madrid, 14 November 1711, AGI, México 377.

19 Tinajero to king, Madrid, 5 November 1709, AGI, México 377; González de Agüero to king, Mexico City, 28 December 1710, AGI, México 377.

20 Junta de indultos and parecer of the fiscal, Madrid, 14 November 1711, AGI, México 377.

21 Real cédula, Madrid, 29 June 1710, AGI, México 658, ff. 2v–14v. Alburquerque's friend Miguel Calderón de la Barca, by then councillor of the Indies, signed the *cédula* as well.

22 Instrucción of Fiscal José de los Ríos, Madrid, 30 June 1710, AGI, México 658, ff. 18–21v.

23 Demanda puesta por Don Antonio de la Vega contra … Alburquerque, Mexico City, 4 November 1711 to 16 March 1711, AGI, México 659, cuaderno 7, exp. 2, ff. 1–65v. Alvarez collaborated in the meat scheme with the *regidor*, *maestre del campo*, and knight of the order of Santiago, Pedro de Castro y Cabrera. In the other great quarrel about the meat monopoly, the viceroy adjudicated the monopoly to the municipal council infringing on the rights of merchant Juan Fernández Cacho. This collaboration between the viceroy and the town hall on commerce continued their long-standing alliance.

24 Demanda of Antonio de la Vega, Mexico City, 4 November 1710 and declaración of Juan de Valdés, Mexico City, 2 December 1710, AGI, México 659, cuaderno 7, exp. 2, labelled "Demanda puesta por Don Antonio de la Vega … contra el Ex.mo S.or Virrey Duque de Alburquerque," ff. 1–3r.

25 Demanda puesta por D.a Sebastiana Fernandes Nolasco muger lex.ma de D.n Juan Francisco Fernandez Cacho contra el Ex.mo S.or Virrey Duque de Alburquerque, AGI, México 659, cuaderno 7, exp.1, ff. 11–16v.

26 Auto of Valdés, Mexico City, 16 March 1711, AGI, México 659, cuaderno 7, exp. 1, ff. 80–83; auto of Valdés, Mexico City, 16 March 1711, ibid., exp. 2, ff. 54–59.

27 Consulta of the Council of the Indies, Madrid, 15 August 1710, AGI, México 404.

28 Pesquisa secreta of the residencia, AGI, México 657, cuaderno 1. The *alcalde de crimen*, Marquis of Salvatierra, complained that Alburquerque suspended him from his office for marrying without royal licence. That was more a recommendation for Alburquerque than a critique.

29 Félix Hidalgo and Carlos Bermudes to Valdés, Mexico City, 12 March 1711, AGI, México 659, cuaderno 4, ff. 33–96. Parecer of the Mexican consulado to Alburquerque, Mexico City, 20 March 1706; and extraordinary real acuerdo, Mexico City, 27 March 1706, AGI, México 660.

30 Alburquerque to king, Mexico City, 10 March 1708, AGI, México 481; Hamnett, *Mexican Bureaucracy*, 17; relación de méritos de ... Valdés, AGI, Indiferente 135, N 80.

31 Auto of Valdés, Mexico City, 16 March 1711, AGI, México 659, cuaderno 7, exp. 1, ff. 80-83; auto of Valdés, Mexico City, 16 March 1711, ibid., exp. 2, ff. 54-59. Valdés did not exculpate the duke on the case of the frigate Daubenton, which was pending in Madrid; sentencia, Mexico City, 26 March 1711, AGI, México 660, f. 1403.

32 José María Mariluz Urquijo, *Ensayo sobre los juicios de residencia indianos* (Seville: Escuela de Estudios Hispano-Americanos, 1952), 291-93.

33 Idem, *El agente de la administración pública en Indias* (Buenos Aires: Instituto Internacional de Historia del Derecho Indiano, 1998), 423-24.

34 Clarence H. Haring, *The Spanish Empire in America* (New York: Harcourt Brace, 1975) originally published in 1947, 138-42. See the discussion of the *residencia* and acquittal of the Peruvian Viceroy Count of Castellar (1673-1678) in Schäfer, *El consejo real y supremo*, 2:60-65; see also 2:53, fn. 2.

35 Haring, *The Spanish Empire*, 142.

36 Pietschmann, "Alcaldes Mayores," 204-5, esp. fn. 74.

37 Bertrand, *Grandeur et misères*, 35.

38 Ibid., 23-24.

39 For a discussion of American *visitas*, see also Ismael Sánchez Bella, *Derecho Indiano: Estudios I. Las visitas generales en la América española (siglos XVI-XVII)*, (Pamplona, Spain: Ediciones Universidad de Navarra, 1991), 127-58.

40 Residencia of the Duke of Alburquerque, AGI, México 657-60, and of Juan de Ortega y Montañés, AGI, Escribanía 233 A. The following *residencias* in this footnote are in the same section of the AGI unless otherwise noted: Viceroys Duke of la Conquista (244 A, C), Count of Fuenclara (245 A, B), Count of Revillagigedo (246 A-C) and the *Oidores* José de la Luna (234 A), Miguel Calderón de la Barca (236 A, B) as well as Domingo de Trespalacios and the *Fiscal* Marquis of Aranda, AHN, Consejos, leg. 21461 and 21460, respectively. These are the available *residencias* of viceroys and *oidores* who served in the period from 1700 to 1755.

41 Sentencia of Alonso de Abellafuentes, Mexico City, 6 October 1704, AGI, Escribanía 233 A, pza. 5; sentencia, Council of the Indies, Madrid, 31 March 1705, ibid.; Consulta of the Council of the Indies, Madrid, December 1716, AGI, México 410.

42 "aunque haia querido disfrazarlos el favor, obscurecerlos el poder, o disimularlos la timidez que para deponer en materias graves contra personas elevadas, detiene las mas vezes a los Testigos," consulta of the junta, Madrid, 24 June 1715, AGI, México 1252.

43 Pietschmann, "Alcaldes Mayores," 204-5; Mariluz Urquijo, *El agente*, 418-19.

44 Junta de azogues, Madrid, 28 March 1711, AGI 377.

45 "inobediencia, Contadicion simulada y .. exceso continuado," parecer of the fiscal of the Council of the Indies, ibid.

46 The *fiscal* of the Council of the Indies, José de los Rios was appointed in 1704 and briefly suspended in 1706. He represented the Council in the *junta* of finances in 1713 under Jean Orry's *nueva planta* (the new government structure). Bernardo de Tinajero, an outspoken critic of the *consulado* of Seville, was named councillor in 1706, then promoted to secretary for Peruvian affairs, and secretary of state for navy and Indies in 1714. He fell with Orry in 1715. José Pastor ascended to the Council in 1707, after the dramatic purge of 1706. Ministers Alonso Carnero and Alonso Pérez de Araciel survived politically from the Habsburg period. Carnero joined the Council and the *cámara de Indias* in 1695, and the

crown confirmed him as a minister *de capa y espada* (of cape and sword, that is, a nonlawyer on a Spanish council) in 1717. Araciel became *lugarteniente* (lieutenant) of the viceroy of Naples under Charles II, and he then obtained the seat on the Council on 13 July 1703. Although he became president of the council of Santa Clara in Naples, Araciel participated in Council of the Indies meetings in 1708. He must have been loyal to Orry, because on 10 November 1713, he was chosen to be one of the three presidents of the Council of the Indies under the *nueva planta*. See Kamen, *The War of Succession*, 55, 113; Bernard, *Le Secrétariat d'état*, 211, 213, 214, 227, 229; Burkholder, *Councilors*, 21, 93; consulta of the Council of the Indies, Madrid, 10 August 1708, AGI, México, 403.

47 King to Count of Frigiliana (governor of the Council of the Indies), Corella, 22 June 1711, AGI, México 377.

48 Junta de indultos, Madrid, 14 November 1711, resolved (*acordada*) on 23 October 1711, AGI, México 377.

49 The *junta* consisted of Bernardo de Tinajero, José Pastor, José de los Ríos (*fiscal* of the Council), and Alonso Carnero: ibid.

50 The king ordered the Count of Frigiliana to set up a special *junta*: king to Frigiliana, Corella, 22 June 1711, AGI, México 377.

51 Alonso Carnero voted with Otalora in this case: consulta of the Council of the Indies, Madrid, 22 November 1712, AGI, México 377.

52 Memorial of Francisco de San Millán y Cevallos, Cadiz, 12 April 1755, AGI, México 1505.

53 Alburquerque to king, 1715, AGI, México 1252.

54 Kamen, *The War of Succession*, 233.

55 The financier Juan de Horcasitas y Avellaneda, Count of Moriana, oversaw the *tesoreria mayor de la guerra* under Orry: ibid., 201.

56 Moriana to José Grimaldo (secretary of state for war, finance, and the Indies), Madrid, 27 June 1714, AGI, México 1252.

57 Ibid.

58 Moriana to Grimaldo, ibid.

59 Consulta of the junta, Madrid, 24 June 1715, AGI, Mexico 1252. Juan Antonio de Torres, who convened the *junta*, read law in Alcalá before being named to the Council of State on 27 August 1699. Juan Remírez de Baquedano, Marquis of Andia, taught at Valladolid. Charles II created the title in 1695 and appointed the Marquis of Andia to the Council of Castile on 29 June 1700. García Pérez de Araciel held a chair at Salamanca before ascending to the council on 29 June 1700. His brother Alonso Pérez de Araciel joined the Council of the Indies in the same year. The two following councillors owed their promotion to the Council of Castile to the Bourbon king. Manuel Antonio de Acebedo received the title of Count of Torrehermosa in 1706. Acebedo held the chair of law at Alcalá before rising to the council in 1707. Sebastián García Romero was appointed on 16 December 1714. See Fayard, *Les membres du Conseil de Castille*, 55, esp. fn. 92, 135, esp. fn. 61, 174, 175, 558, 560; Burkholder, *Biographical Dictionary*, 105, 258.

60 Consulta of the junta, Madrid, 24 June 1715, AGI, México 1252.

61 Note with title "Que le Roy peut sans scrupules recevoir de monsieur le Duc d'Alburquerque les septcens milles ecus dont il est question", s.n., 1715, AGI, México 1252.

62 Ibid.

63 Juan Antonio Valenciano to the Marquis of la Ensenada, 23 May 1749, AGI, México 1505.

64 Decreto a favor del Duque, seen by the king on 15 November 1716, AGI, México 1252, No. 5; testimonio de la libranza de pago que dio el conde de

Moriana a favor del Duque de Alburquerque, Madrid, 14 December 1715 (original from 24 September 1715), AHCDA, 463, No. 5; Alburquerque's secretary Francisco Sanz Data affirmed that 700,000 pesos had been disbursed to the king by May 1717: Quentta de data queyo Don Francisco Sanz Daza secretario del Ex.mo Señor Duque de Alburquerque mi s.or: Doy delas cantidades que ymporta el cargo antezedentte yentraron enmi poder, escomo sesigue ..., Madrid, 18 May 1717, ibid., No. 4.

65 Kamen characterizes Orry as such: *War of the Succession*, 165-66.

66 Quoted in van Klaveren, *Europäische Wirtschaftsgeschichte*, 173.

67 Ibid., 172-74. For the return of the *consulado*'s power, see also Pérez-Mallaina, *Política naval*, 202-28; Kuethe, "El fin del monopolio," 38-40.

68 For the complaints, see Tinajero to king, Madrid, 5 November 1709, AGI, México 377.

69 Junta de indultos, Madrid, 14 November 1711, AGI, México 377.

70 Pierce, *Early Bourbon Government*, 27. King Charles II bestowed the title on Monclova's father. The viceroy distinguished himself in a military career and, basking in the king's favour, moved from the viceroyalty of New Spain to Peru in 1688: Rubio Mañé, *Introducción*, 1:156, 256-57. This could explain Monclova's troubled relation to the Bourbons.

71 Rubio Mañé, *Introducción*, 1:137, 153, fn. 61.

72 Alvarez de Toledo, *Politics and Reform*, 172-75, 199.

73 Ibid., viii.

74 For Pagabe's visita, see Bertrand, *Grandeur et misères*, 22.

75 Pietschmann views Linares as such, see "Burocracia y corrupción," 20-21; Bertrand has a more sceptical view, "La contaduría de las alcabalas," 342, fn. 42.

76 Linares to Miguel Gallo, castellan of Acapulco, Mexico City, 21 March 1712, AGI, Escribanía 246 B, pza. 5. The bishop of Oaxaca, Angel de Maldonado, also lambasted corrupt viceroys in 1716, Canterla, *La iglesia de Oaxaca*, 19.

77 Rubio Mañé, *Introducción*, 1:267-70.

78 Kenneth Warren Jones, "New Spain and the Viceregency of the Marqués de Casafuerte, 1722-1723" (Ph.D. diss., University of California, Santa Barbara, 1971). In her thesis "El Marqués de Casafuerte, Virrey de Nueva España, 1722-1734" (Ph.D. diss., University of Seville, Spain, 2002), Ascensión Baeza Martín seconds this view of Casafuerte. Jones and Baeza Martín support the argument of administrative change in the early eighteenth-century empire.

79 Sarrablo Aguareles, *El Conde de Fuenclara*, without pagination, page 1 of the Introduction.

80 Del Valle, *Güemes y Horcasitas*. Lourdes Díaz Trechuelo López-Spínola stresses the viceroy's success in reforming the financial administration and improving the budget of the Mexico City *cabildo*: "El primer conde de Revillagigedo. Virrey de la Nueva España," in *Atti del XL Congresso internazionale degli americanisti, Roma-Genova, 3-10 settembre 1972* (Genua: Tilgher, 1972), 291-94.

81 Fernández de Bethencourt, 298.

82 Marquis of la Paz to Marquis of la Conquista, Madrid, 9 December 1727; certificación of Bernardino Manuel de Spino, Madrid, 22 March 1740, Archivo del Real Palacio, caja 33, exp. 25, no. 1 and 2.

83 Fernández de Bethencourt, 301-2.

CHAPTER 9 - CONCLUSION

1 Israel, *Race, Class and Politics in Colonial Mexico*.

Bibliography

Unpublished Primary Sources

In Mexico

Archivo del Cabildo Catedral Metropolitano de México (ACCM)
Actas del Cabildo Eclesiástico 25–26.

Acervo Histórico del Archivo General de Notarías (AHAGN)
Escribano José de Ledesma, No. 340, vol. 2247; escribano
Diego Antonio Marquina, No. 393, vol. 2614.

Archivo Histórico del Distrito Federal (AHDF)
Actas del Cabildo 36–A, 79–A, 437–A.

Archivo General de la Nación (AGN)
Archivo Histórico de Hacienda (abbreviated as AHH) 213, 223, 931, 1361, 1463, 1466, 1648.
Bienes Nacionales 477, 574, 867, 813, 867.
Civil 114, 455, 1625.
Indios 97.
Inquisición 740.
Media Anata (abbreviated as MA) 24, 27, 34, 42, 50, 65.
Reales Cédulas Duplicadas (abbreviated as RCD) 40–42.
Reales Cédulas Originales (abbreviated as RCO) 31–34, 71, 72, 81.
Subdelegados 34.
Tributos 22.

Biblioteca Nacional (BNM), Fondo Reservado
Manuscritos 439, 1392.
Archivo Franciscano 479.

In the USA

Latin American Library, Tulane University, New Orleans, Louisiana
Viceregal and Ecclesiastical Collection (VEMC) 75.

In Spain

Archivo General de Indias (AGI), Seville
Consulados 376.
Contaduría 643.
Contratación 5448, 5449, 5454, 5456, 5460, 5469, 5540 B.
Escribanía de cámara 188 B, 189 A, 190 A, 192 B, 205 B, 233 A, 234 A, 236 A, B, 239, 244 A, C, 245 A, B, 246, 262–264, 340 A, 964, 969, 1051 A, 1053 A, 1194.
Filipinas 4, 15, 59, 282 bis, 332, 333, 341, 342, 349.
Gobierno
– Audiencia de México 376–377, 399–404, 410, 474–485, 522–523, 601, 610, 642, 645–646, 655, 657–661, 689, 729–730, 741, 804–805, 817, 879–881, 1079, 1252, 1326, 1505, 2501.
– Indiferente General 135–139, 140–142, 145, 152, 157, 214, 215.

Archivo Histórico de la Casa Ducal de Alburquerque (AHCDA), Cuéllar
463, 374, 379.

Archivo Histórico Nacional (AHN), Madrid
Consejos 20718, 21022, 21023, 21460, 21461.
Diversos 33, 36.

Archivo General de Simancas (AGS), Simancas
Hacienda 174-102, 180-136, 182-365.

Archivo del Real Palacio, Madrid
Caja 33.

Real Academia de la Historia (RAH) Madrid
Manuscritos, 9-9-4.

Published Primary Sources

Alburquerque, Francisco Fernández de la Cueva, Duke of. "La memoria de gobierno del virrey duque de Alburquerque, 1710." Edited by Iván Escamilla González. *Estudios de Historia Novohispana*, 25 (2001): 157–78.

Anonymous. *Histoire publique et secrette de la cour de Madrid. Dès l'avènement du Roy Philippe V. a la couronne, avec des considerations sur l'état present de la monarchie espagnole*. Cologne: Pierre le Sincère, 1719.

Bacallar y Sanna, Vicente, Marqués de San Felipe. *Comentarios de la guerra de España e historia de su rey Felipe V, el animoso*. Edited by Carlos Seco Serrano. Biblioteca de Autores Españoles desde la formación del lenguaje hasta nuestros días. Vol. 99. Madrid: Ediciones Atlas, 1957.

Castro Santa-Anna, José Manuel de. *Diario de Sucesos Notables*. Documentos para la historia de Méjico. Vol. iv–vi. Mexico City: Imprenta de Juan R. Navarro, 1854.

Guijo, Gregorio Martín de. *Diario, 1648–64*. Edited by Manuel Romero de Terreros. Mexico City: Editorial Porrúa, 1952.

Recopilación de leyes de los reynos de las Indias mandada imprimir y publicar por la Magestad Católica del Rey Don Carlos II. Nuestro Señor ... [1741] Madrid: Consejo de la Hispanidad, 1953.

Robles, Antonio de. *Diario de sucesos notables (1665–1703)*. Edited by Antonio Castro Leal. 3 vols. 2nd ed. Mexico City: Editorial Porrúa, 1972.

Seijas y Lobera, Francisco de. *Gobierno militar y político del reino imperial de la Nueva España* [1702]. Edited by Pablo Emilio Pérez-Mallaína Bueno. Mexico City: UNAM, 1986.

Las Siete Partidas del Rey Don Alfonso el Sabio cotejadas con varios codices antiguos.... Edited by the Real Academia de la Historia. 3 vols. Madrid: Imprenta Real, 1807.

Solórzano Pereyra, Juan. *Política Indiana*. Edited by Francisco Tomás y Valiente and Ana María Barrero. Madrid: Biblioteca Castro, 1996.

Tobar, Balthasar de. *Compendio Bulario Indico* [1695]. Edited by Manuel Gutiérrez de Arce. Seville: Escuela de Estudios Hispano-Americanos, 1954.

Torre Villar, Ernesto de la, ed. *Instrucciones y memorias de los virreyes novohispanos*. Vol. 2. Mexico City: Editorial Porrúa, 1991.

Secondary Sources

Agueda Méndez, María, ed. *Catálogo de textos marginados novohispános: Inquisición, siglo XVIII y XIX. Archivo General de la Nación*. Mexico City: Archivo General de la Nación et al., 1992.

Alberro, Solange. "Control de la Iglesia y transgresiones eclesiásticas durante el periodo colonial." In *Vicios públicos, virtudes privadas: la corrupción en México*. Edited by Claudio Lomnitz. Mexico City: CIESAS, 2000. 33-47.

Alfaro Ramírez, Gustavo Rafael. "Quién encarceló al alguacil mayor de Puebla? La vida, los negocios y el poder de don Pedro de Mendoza y Escalante, 1695-1740." *Estudios de Historia Novohispana* (Mexico City) 17 (1997): 31-62.

Alonso Romero, María Paz. *El proceso penal en Castilla, siglo XIII-XVIII*. Salamanca: Ediciones Universidad de Salamanca, 1982.

Alvarez de Toledo, Cayetana. *Politics and Reform in Spain and Viceregal Mexico. The Life and Thought of Juan de Palafox 1600-1659*. Oxford: Clarendon Press, 2004.

Ames, Barry. "Approaches to the Study of Institutions in Latin America." *Latin American Research Review* 34:1 (1999): 221-36.

Andrien, Kenneth J. *Crisis and Decline. The Viceroyalty of Peru in the Seventeenth Century*. Albuquerque: University of New Mexico Press, 1985.

Angulo Iñiguez, Diego. *Planos de monumentos arquitectónicos de América y Filipinas existentes en el Archivo de Indias*. 4 vols. Seville: University of Seville, Laboratorio de Arte, 1939.

Archivo Histórico del Distrito Federal. Guia General. Edited by Lina Odena Güemes H. Mexico City: Gobierno del Distrito Federal, 2000.

Archer, Christon I. *The Army in Bourbon Mexico, 1760-1810*. Albuquerque: University of New Mexico Press, 1977.

Arnold, Linda J. *Bureaucracy and Bureaucrats in Mexico City, 1742-1835*. Tucson: University of Arizona Press, 1988.

――――. *Directorio de burócratas en la ciudad de México, 1761-1832*. Mexico City: Archivo General de la Nación, 1980.

Artola, Miguel. *La hacienda del antiguo régimen*. Madrid: Alianza Editorial, 1982.

Autrand, Françoise, ed., *Prosopographie et genèse de l'état moderne. Actes de table ronde*. Paris: École normale superieure de jeunes filles, 1986.

Asch, Ronald G. "Corruption and Punishment? The Rise and Fall of Matthäus Enzlin (1556-1613), Lawyer and Favourite." In *The World of the Favourite*. Edited by J. H. Elliott and L.W.B. Brockliss. New Haven: Yale University Press, 1999. 96-111.

Asch, Ronald G., and Adolf M. Birke, eds. *Princes, Patronage and the Nobility. The Court at the Beginning of the Modern Age, c. 1450-1650*. Oxford: Oxford University Press, 1991.

Baeza Martín, Ascensión. "El Marqués de Casafuerte, Virrey de Nueva España, 1722-1734." Ph.D. diss., University of Seville, Spain, 2002.

Barbier, Jacques. *Reform and Politics in Bourbon Chile, 1755-1796*. Ottawa: University of Ottawa Press, 1980.

Baskes, Jeremy. *Indians, Merchants, and Markets. A Reinterpretation of the Repartimiento and Spanish-Indian Economic Relations in Colonial Oaxaca, 1750-1821*. Stanford: Stanford University Press, 2000.

Baudrillart, Alfred. *Philippe V et la cour de France d'après des documents inédits tirés des archives espagnoles de Simancas et d'Alcala de Hénares, et des archives du ministère des affaires étrangéres a Paris.* 5 vols. Paris: Librairie du Firmin-Didiot et Cie., 1890.

Bernard, Gildas. *Le secrétariat d'état et le conseil espagnol des Indes (1700-1808).* Geneva: Librairie Droz, 1972.

Bertrand, Michel. "Clientélisme et pouvoir en Nouvelle-Espagne." In *Cultures et sociétes, Andes et Méso-Amérique. Mélanges en l'honneur de P. Duviols.* Edited by Raquel Thiercelin. Aix-en-Provence: Publications de l'Université de Provence, 1992. 1:147-59.

———. "La contaduría de las alcabalas de Puebla: Un episodio reformador al principio del siglo XVIII." *Jahrbuch für die Geschichte von Staat, Wirtschaft und Gesellschaft Lateinamerikas* 32 (1995): 321-32.

———. *Grandeur et misères de l'office. Les officiers de finances de Nouvelle-Espagne, XVIIe-XVIIIe siècles.* Paris: Publications de la Sorbonne, 1999.

———. "En torno a una problemática de la administración colonial: la Real Hacienda de Nueva España, 1680-1770." *Anuario de Estudios Americanos* (Seville) 46 (1989): 195-217.

Bethell, Leslie, ed. *The Cambridge History of Latin America.* 11 vols. Cambridge: Cambridge University Press, 1984-95.

Blank, Stephanie. "Patrons, Clients, and Kin in Seventeenth-Century Caracas: A Methodological Essay in Colonial Spanish American Social History." *Hispanic American Historical Review* 54:2 (1974): 260-83.

Bobb, Bernard E. *The Viceregency of Antonio María Bucareli in New Spain, 1771-1779.* Austin: University of Texas Press, 1962.

Borah, Woodrow. *New Spain's Century of Depression.* Berkeley: University of California Press, 1951.

Bouhrass, Asmaa. "La administración virreinal y el comercio en Nueva España (1740-1765)" Ph.D. diss., University of Seville, 1999.

Boyden, James M. *The Courtier and the King. Ruy Gómez de Silva, Philip II, and the Court of Spain.* Berkeley: University of California Press, 1995.

Brading, David. *Haciendas and Ranchos in the Mexican Bajío: León, 1700-1860.* Cambridge: Cambridge University Press, 1978.

———. *Miners and Merchants in Bourbon Mexico, 1763-1810.* Cambridge: Cambridge University Press, 1971.

Brunner, Otto. *Land and Lordship. Structures of Governance in Medieval Austria.* Translated from the 4th, revised edition and introduced by Howard Kaminsky and James van Horn Melton. Philadelphia: University of Pennsylvania Press, 1984. First published as *Land und Herrschaft. Grundfragen der territorialen Verfassungsgeschichte Österreichs im Mittelalter.* Baden, Austria: Rohrer, 1939.

Büschges, Christian, and Bernd Schröter, eds. *Beneméritos, aristócratas y empresarios. Identidades y estructuras sociales de las capas altas urbanas en América hispánica.* Frankfurt am Main: Vervuert, 1999.

Baeza Martín, Ascensión. "El Marqués de Casafuerte, Virrey de Nueva España, 1722-1734." Ph.D. diss., University of Seville, Spain, 2002.

Boys, Albert du. *Historia del derecho penal de España.* Translated and edited by José Vicente y Caravantes. Madrid: Imprenta de J. M. Pérez, 1872.

Burke, Peter. "The Courtier." In *Renaissance Characters.* Edited by Eugenio Garin. Chicago: University of Chicago Press, 1991. 98-123.

Burkholder, Mark A., and Dewitt Samuel Chandler. *Biographical Dictionary of Audiencia Ministers in the Americas, 1687-1821.* Westport, CT: Greenwood, 1982.

———. *From Impotence to Authority: the Spanish Crown and the American Audiencias, 1687-1808.* Columbia: University of Missouri Press, 1977.

Burkholder, Mark A. *Biographical Dictionary of Councilors of the Indies, 1717–1808.* Westport, CT: Greenwood, 1986.

———. "Titled Nobles, Elites, and Independence: Some Comments." *Latin American Research Review* 13:2 (1978): 290–95.

Calderón Quijano, José Antonio, ed. *Los virreyes de Nueva España en el reinado de Carlos III.* Seville: Escuela de Estudios Hispano-Americanos, 1967.

———, ed. *Los virreyes de Nueva España en el reinado de Carlos IV.* 2 vols. Seville: Escuela de Estudios Hispano-Americanos, 1972.

Camp, Roderic Ai. *Mexico's Mandarins: Crafting a Power Elite for the Twenty-First Century.* Berkeley: University of California Press, 2002.

Cañeque, Alejandro. *The King's Living Image. The Culture and Politics of Viceregal Power in Colonial Mexico.* New York: Routledge, 2004.

Carande, Ramón. "Zum Problem einer Wirtschaftsgeschichte Spaniens." *Historische Zeitschrift* 193:1 (1961): 359–65.

Carmagnani, Marcello. "Die koloniale Raumordnung: Mutterland, Peripherie und Grenzgebiete." In *Mittel-, Südamerika und die Karibik bis 1760.* Edited by Horst Pietschmann. Vol. 1 of *Handbuch der Geschichte Lateinamerikas.* Edited by Walther L. Bernecker et al. Stuttgart: Klett-Cotta, 1994. 534–54.

Chaunu, Pierre. *Les Philippines et le Pacifique des Ibériques (XVIe, XVIIe, XVIIIe siècles) Introduction méthodologique et indices d'activité.* Paris: SEVPEN, 1960.

Chaunu, Pierre and Huguette Chaunu. *Séville et l'Atlantique, 1504–1650.* 8 vols. Paris: A. Colin, 1955–59.

Curcio-Nagy, Linda. *The Great Festivals of Colonial Mexico City. Performing Power and Identity.* Albuquerque: University of New Mexico Press, 2004.

Díaz Trechuelo López-Spínola, Lourdes. "El primer conde de Revillagigedo. Virrey de la Nueva España." *Atti del XL Congresso internazionale degli americanisti, Roma-Genova, 3–10 settembre 1972.* Genua: Tilgher, 1972. 291–94.

Diccionario Porrúa de Historia, Biografía y Geografía de México. 6th ed. 4 vols. Mexico City: Editorial Porrúa, 1995.

Domínguez Ortiz, Antonio. *La sociedad española en el siglo XVII.* Madrid: Consejo Superior de Investigaciones Científicas, 1963.

———. *La sociedad española en el siglo XVIII.* Madrid: Consejo Superior de Investigaciones Científicas. 1955.

Dorta, Enrique Marco. "El palacio de los Virreyes a fines del siglo XVIII." *Archivo Español de Arte y Arqueología* (Madrid) 31 (1935): 103–30.

Elias, Norbert. *The Court Society* [1969]. Translated by Edmund Jephcott. Oxford: Basil Blackwell, 1983.

Elliott, John Huxtable. *The Count-Duke of Olivares. The Statesman in an Age of Decline.* New Haven: Yale University Press, 1986.

———. "The Court of the Spanish Habsburgs: A Peculiar Institution?" In *Politics and Culture in Early Modern Europe. Essays in Honor of H. G. Koenigsberger.* Edited by Phyllis Mack and Margaret C. Jacob. Cambridge: Cambridge University Press, 1987.

———. *Richelieu and Olivares.* Cambridge: Cambridge University Press, 1984.

Elton, Geoffrey. "Tudor Government: The Points of Contact: III The Court." *Transactions of the Royal Historical Society,* 5th ser., 26 (1976): 211–28.

Enciclopedia de México. Todo lo Mexicano ordenado alfabéticamente.... Edited by José Rogelio Alvarez. Mexico City: Enciclopedia de México S.A., 1977.

Escamilla Gónzalez, Iván. "La Nueva Alianza: El consulado de México y la monarquía borbónica durante la Guerra de Sucesión." In *Mercaderes, comercio y consulados de Nueva Es-*

paña en el siglo XVIII. Edited by Guillermina de Valle Pavón. Mexico City: Instituto Mora, 2003.

Fayard, Janine. *Les membres du Conseil de Castille a l'époque moderne (1621-1746)*. Geneva: Librairies Droz, 1979.

Flinchpaugh, Steven G. "Economic Aspects of the Viceregal Entrance in Mexico City." *The Americas* 52:3 (1996): 345-65.

Fernández, Martha. *Arquitectura y gobierno virreinal. Los maestros mayores de la ciudad de México, siglo XVII*. Mexico City: UNAM, 1985.

Fernández de Bethencourt, Francisco. *Historia genealógica y heráldica de los grandes de España*. Vol. 10. Madrid: Estab. Tip. de Enríque Teodoro, 1920.

Feros, Antonio. *Kingship and Favoritism in the Spain of Philip III, 1598-1621*. Cambridge: Cambridge University Press, 2000.

Forster, Robert. *The House of Saulx-Tavanes. Versailles and Burgundy 1700-1830*. Baltimore: Johns Hopkins University Press, 1971.

Francis, David. *The First Peninsular War 1702-1713*. New York: St. Martin's Press, 1975.

García Martínez, Bernardo. *El Marquesado del Valle. Tres siglos de régimen señorial en Nueva España*. Mexico City: El Colegio de México, 1969.

Gerhard, Peter. *A Guide to the Historical Geography of New Spain*. Cambridge Latin American Studies. Vol. 14. Cambridge: Cambridge University Press, 1972.

_____. *The North Frontier of New Spain*. Rev. ed. Norman: University of Oklahoma Press, 1993.

Gibson, Charles. *The Aztecs under Spanish Rule. A History of the Indians of the Valley of Mexico, 1519-1810*. Stanford: Stanford University Press, 1964.

Gómez-Centurión Jiménez, Carlos. "Etiqueta y ceremonial palatino durante el reinado de Felipe V: El reglamento de entradas de 1709 y el acceso a la persona del rey." *Hispania* (Madrid) 56:3, 194 (1996): 965-1005.

Gómez Gómez, Amalia. *Las visitas de la Real Hacienda novohispana en el reinado de Felipe V (1710-1733)*. Seville: Escuela de Estudios Hispano-Americanos, 1979.

Griffiths, Ralf A. "The King's Court during the War of the Roses. Continuities in an Age of Discontinuities." In *Princes, Patronage and the Nobility. The Court at the Beginning of the Modern Age, c. 1450-1650*. Edited by Ronald G. Asch and Adolf M. Birke. Oxford: Oxford University Press, 1991. 41-68.

Hamnett, Brian. *The Mexican Bureaucracy before the Bourbon Reforms, 1700-1770: A Study in the Limitations of Absolutism*. Institute of Latin American Studies, Ocasional Papers 26. Glasgow: University of Glasgow, 1979.

Hanke, Lewis, *Spanish Viceroys in America*. The Smith History Lecture 1972. Houston: University of St. Thomas, 1972.

Haring, Clarence Henry. *The Spanish Empire in America*. [1947] New York: Harcourt Brace, 1975.

Hartung, Fritz and Roland Mousnier. "Quelques problèmes concernant la monarchie absolue." In *Relazioni del X Congresso Internazionale di Scienze Storiche*, Rome 1955. Florence: G. C. Sansoni, 1955. 4:1-55.

Hausberger, Bernd. "Las eleciones de prior, cónsules y diputados en el Consulado de México en la primera mitad del siglo XVIII: la formación de los partidos de montañeses y vizcaínos." In *Comercio y poder en América colonial: los consulados de comerciantes, siglos XVII-XIX*. Edited by Bernd Hausberger and Antonio Ibarra. Madrid, Frankfurt, Mexico City: Iberoamericana, Vervuert, Instituto Mora, 2003. 73-102.

Heras Santos, José Luis de las. *La justicia penal de los Austrias en la corona de Castilla*. Salamanca: Ediciones Universidad de Salamanca, 1991.

Hernández Palomo, José Jesús. *El aguardiente de caña en México, 1724-1810*. Seville: Escuela de Estudios Hispano-Americanos, 1974.

Herrera Heredia, Antonia. "México." In *América en el siglo XVIII. Los primeros Borbones*. Edited by Luis Navarro García. Vol. 11-1 of *Historia General de España y América*. Edited by Luis Suárez Fernández et al. Madrid: Ediciones Rialp, 1989. 461-517.

Herzog, Tamar. *La administración como un fenómeno social: La justicia penal de la ciudad de Quito (1650-1750)*. Madrid: Centro de Estudios Constitucionales, 1995.

———. *Upholding Justice. Society, State, and the Penal System in Quito (1650-1750)*. Ann Arbor: University of Michigan Press, 2004.

Hoberman, Louisa Schell. *Mexico's Merchant Elite, 1590-1660. Silver, State, and Society*. Durham: Duke University Press, 1991.

Hofmann, Christina. *Das spanische Hofzeremoniell von 1500-1700*. Frankfurt am Main: Peter Lang, 1985.

Israel, Jonathan. "Mexico and the 'General Crisis' of the Seventeenth Century." *Past and Present* 63 (1974): 33-57.

———. *Race, Class and Politics in Colonial Mexico, 1610-1670*. Oxford: Oxford University Press, 1975.

Jones, Kenneth Warren. "New Spain and the Viceregency of the Marqués de Casafuerte, 1722-1723." Ph.D. diss., University of California, Santa Barbara, 1971.

Kamen, Henry. *Philip V of Spain. The King Who Reigned Twice*. New Haven: Yale University Press, 2001.

———. *Spain in the Later Seventeenth Century, 1665-1700*. London: Longman, 1980.

———. *The War of Succession in Spain 1700-1715*. Bloomington: Indiana University Press, 1969.

Klaveren, Jacob van. *Europäische Wirtschaftsgeschichte Spaniens im 16. und 17. Jahrhundert*. Stuttgart: Gustav Fischer, 1960.

Kettering, Sharon. *Patrons, Brokers, and Clients in Seventeenth-Century France*. Oxford: Oxford University Press, 1986.

Kicza, John E. *Colonial Entrepreneurs. Families and Business in Bourbon Mexico City*. Albuquerque: University of New Mexico, 1983.

Konetzke, Richard. "Grundherrschaftliche Gerichtsbarkeit im spanischen America während des 18. Jahrhunderts." In *Homenaje a Jaime Vicens Vives*. Edited by Juan Maluquer de Motes y Nicolau. Vol. 2. Barcelona: University of Barcelona, 1967. 277-83.

———. "La literatura económica. Así se escribe la historia." *Moneda y Crédito* (Madrid) 81 (1962): 67-77.

Kuethe, Alan J. "El fin del monopolio: los Borbones y el consulado andaluz." In *Relaciones de poder y comercio colonial: nuevas perspectivas*. Edited by Alan J. Kuethe and Enriqueta Vila Vilar. Seville: Escuela de Estudios Hispano-Americanos, 1999. 35-66.

Ladd, Doris M. *The Mexican Nobility at Independence 1780-1826*. Austin: University of Texas Press, 1976.

Latasa Vasallo, Pilar. "La Casa del Obispo-Virrey Palafox: Familia y Patronazgo. Un análisis comparativo con la corte virreinal hispanoamericano." In *Palafox. Iglesia, Cultura y Estado en el Siglo XVII. Congreso Internacional IV Centenario del Nacimiento de Don Juan de Palafox y Mendoza, Universidad de Navarra, Pamplona, 13-15 Abril 2001*. Pamplona: Universidad de Navarra, 2001. 201-28.

Le Roy Ladurie, Emmanuel. *Saint-Simon, and the Court of Louis XIV*. In collaboration with Jean-François Fitou. Translated by Arthur Goldhammer. Chicago: University of Chicago Press, 2001.

Lynch, John. *Bourbon Spain, 1700-1808*. Oxford: Basil Blackwell, 1989.

———. "The Institutional Framework of Colonial Spanish America." *Journal of Latin American Studies* 24 (1992): 69-81.

———. *Spain under the Habsburgs*. Vol. 2. *Spain and America 1598–1700*. 2nd ed. New York: New York University Press, 1984.

McFarlane, Anthony. "Hispanoamerika." In *Mittel-, Südamerika und die Karibik bis 1760*. Edited by Horst Pietschmann. Vol. 1 of *Handbuch der Geschichte Lateinamerikas*. Edited by Walther L. Bernecker et al. Stuttgart: Klett-Cotta, 1994. 751–88.

MacLachlan, Colin M. *Criminal Justice in Eighteenth-Century Mexico: The Tribunal of the Acordada*. Berkeley: University of California Press, 1974.

———. *Spain's Empire in the New World. The Role of Ideas in Institutional and Social Change*. Berkeley: University of California Press, 1988.

MacLachlan, Colin M., and Jaime E. Rodríguez O. *The Forging of the Cosmic Race: A Reinterpretation of Colonial Mexico*. Berkeley: University of California Press, 1980.

Magdaleno, Ricardo, ed. *Títulos de Indias*. Catálogo XX del Archivo General de Simancas. Valladolid: Casa Martín, 1954.

Mariluz Urquijo, José María. *El agente de la administración pública en Indias*. Buenos Aires: Instituto Internacional de Historia del Derecho Indiano, 1998.

———. *Ensayo sobre los juicios de residencia indianos*. Seville: Escuela de Estudios Hispano-Americanos, 1952.

———. "Proyectos de Andrés de Pes sobre la organización del Consejo de Indias." In *Actas y estudios del IV Congreso del Instituto Internacional de Historia del Derecho Indiano*. Madrid: Instituto de la Historia del Derecho Indiano, 1991. 357–65.

Meißner, Jochen. *Eine Elite im Umbruch: Der Stadtrat von Mexiko zwischen kolonialer Ordnung und unabhängigem Staat (1761–1821)*. Stuttgart: Franz Steiner, 1993.

Molas Ribalta, Pere. "Dinastías nobiliarias y guerra de sucesión española." In *El cambio dinástico y sus repercusiones en la España del siglo XVIII*. Edited by José Fernández García, María Antonia Bel Bravo, and José Miguel Delgado Barrado. Jaén: Universidad de Jaén, 2001. 291–305.

Montoro López, José. *Virreyes españoles en América. Relación de virreinatos y biografías de los virreyes*. Barcelona: Editorial Mitre, 1991.

Moraw, Peter. "Personenforschung und deutsches Königtum." In *Über König und Reich. Aufsätze zur deutschen Verfassungsgeschichte des späten Mittelalters. Festschrift Peter Moraw*. Edited by Rainer Christoph Schwinges. Sigmaringen, Germany: Jan Thorbecke, 1995. 1–10. Originally published in *Zeitschrift für historische Forschung* 2 (1975): 7–16.

Mousnier, Roland. *Les institutions de la France sous la monarchie absolue 1598–1789*. Paris: Presses universitaires de France, 1974.

———. *La vénalité des offices sous Henri IV et Louis XIII*. 2nd ed. Paris: Presses universitaires de France, 1971.

Mücke, Ulrich. *Political Culture in Nineteenth-Century Peru. The Rise of the Partido Civil*. Translated by Katya Andrusz. Pittsburgh: University of Pittsburgh Press, 2004.

Navarro García, Luis. "La administración virreinal en México en 1703." *Revista de Indias* (Seville) 115–18 (1969): 360–69.

———. "El cambio de dinastía en Nueva España." *Anuario de Estudios Americanos* (Seville) 36 (1979): 111–68.

———. *Conspiración en México durante el gobierno del Virrey Alburquerque*. Valladolid: Casa-Museo de Colón, 1982.

———. "Los oficios vendibles en Nueva España durante la Guerra de Sucesión." *Anuario de Estudios Americanos* (Seville) 32 (1975): 133–54.

———. "La política Indiana." In *América en el siglo XVIII. Los primeros Borbones*. Edited by Luis Navarro García. Vol. 11-1 of *Historia General de España y América*. Edited by Luis Suárez Fernández et al. Madrid: Ediciones Rialp, 1989. 3–64.

_____. "El real tribunal de cuentas de México a principios del siglo XVIII." *Anuario de Estudios Americanos* (Seville) 34 (1977): 517–35.

_____. "Salvador Mañer, agente carlista en México." *Archivo Hispalense* (Seville) 178 (1975): 1–23.

_____. "El segundo virrey Alburquerque y su memoria de gobierno (México 1710)." In *Reformismo y sociedad en la América borbónica. In memorian Ronald Escobedo*. Edited by Pilar Latasa Vasallo. Barañáin, Spain: Ediciones Universidad de Navarra, 2003. 195–226.

_____. "La secreta condena del virrey Alburquerque." In *Homenaje al Dr. Muro Orejón*. Seville: Facultad de Filosofía y Letras, 1979. 1:201–14.

Nieto Ballester, Emilio. *Breve diccionario de topónimos españoles*. In collaboration with Araceli Striano Corrochano. Madrid: Alianza Editorial, 1997.

Oestreich, Gerhard. "The Constitutional Development of the Early Modern State." In *Neostoicism and the Early Modern State*. Edited by Brigitta Oestreich and H. G. Koenigsberger. Translated by David McLintock. Cambridge: Cambridge University Press, 1982. 258–73. First published as *Geist und Gestalt des frühmodernen Staates. Ausgewählte Aufsätze*. Berlin: Duncker and Humblot, 1969.

Orozco Linares, Fernando. *Gobernantes de México. Desde la época Prehispánica hasta nuestros días*. 3rd ed. Mexico City: Panorama Editorial, 2004.

Ots Capdequí, José María. *El estado español en las Indias*. Mexico City: Fondo de Cultura Económica, 1946.

Ouweneel, Arij. *Shadows over Anáhuac. An Ecological Interpretation of Crisis and Development in Central Mexico, 1730–1830*. Albuquerque: University of New Mexico Press, 1996.

Parry, J. H. *The Sale of Public Office in the Spanish Indies under the Habsburgs*. Berkeley: University of California Press, 1953.

Pérez-Mallaina Bueno, Pablo Emilio. *Política naval española en el Atlántico, 1700–1715*. Seville: Escuela de Estudios Hispano-Americanos, 1982.

Pfandl, Ludwig. *Philip II. Gemälde eines Lebens und einer Zeit*. Munich: Georg D. W. Callwey, 1938.

Phelan, John Leddy. "Authority and Flexibility in the Spanish Imperial Bureaucracy." *Administrative Science Quarterly* 5:1 (1960): 47–65.

_____. *The Kingdom of Quito in the Seventeenth Century. Bureaucratic Politics in the Spanish Empire*. Madison: University of Wisconsin Press, 1967.

Pieper, Renate. "Die demographische Entwicklung." In *Mittel-, Südamerika und die Karibik bis 1760*. Edited by Horst Pietschmann. Vol. 1 of *Handbuch der Geschichte Lateinamerikas*. Edited by Walther L. Bernecker et al. Stuttgart: Klett-Cotta, 1994. 313–28.

_____. *Die Spanischen Kronfinanzen in der zweiten Hälfte des 18. Jahrhunderts (1753–1788). Ökonomische und soziale Auswirkungen*. Beiheft der Vierteljahrsschrift für Sozial- und Wirtschaftsgeschichte. Vol. 85. Stuttgart: Franz Steiner, 1988. Spanish translation: *La Real Hacienda bajo Fernando VI y Carlos III (1753–1788). Repercusiones económicas y sociales*. Madrid: Instituto de Estudios Fiscales, 1992.

Pierce, Adrian John. "Early Bourbon Government in the Viceroyalty of Peru, 1700–1759." Ph.D. diss., University of Liverpool, 1998.

Pietschmann, Horst. "Alcaldes Mayores, Corregidores und Subdelegados. Zum Problem der Distriktsbeamtenschaft im Vizekönigreich Neuspanien." *Jahrbuch für Geschichte von Staat, Wirtschaft und Gesellschaft Lateinamerikas* 81 (1972): 26–220.

_____. "Burocracia y corrupción en Hispanoamérica colonial. Una aproximación tentativa." *Nova Americana* 5 (1983): 11–37.

_____. "Consideraciones en torno al protoliberalismo, reformas borbónicas y revolución. La Nueva España en el último tercio del siglo XVIII." *Historia Mexicana* 41:2 (1991): 167–205.

_____. "La corte virreinal de México en el siglo XVII en sus dimensiones jurídico-institucionales, sociales y culturales: Aproximación al estado de la investigación." In *La creatividad femenina en el mundo barroco hispánico. María de Zayas-Isabel Rebeca Correa-Sor Juana Inés de la Cruz*. Edited by Monika Bosse, Barbara Potthast, and André Stoll. Kassel: Reichenberger, 1999. 2:481–97.

_____. *Die Einführung des Intendantensystems in Neu-Spanien im Rahmen der allgemeinen Verwaltungsreform der spanischen Monarchie im 18. Jahrhundert*. Cologne: Böhlau 1972. Span. translation *La introducción del sistema de intendentes. Un estudio político-institucional*. Mexico City: Fondo de Cultura Económica, 1996.

_____. *Die staatliche Organisation des kolonialen Iberoamerika*. Teilveröffentlichung zum Handbuch der Geschichte Lateinamerikas. Stuttgart: Klett-Cotta, 1980.

_____. *Staat und staatliche Entwicklung am Beginn der spanischen Kolonisation*. Münster, Germany: Aschendorff, 1980. Spanish translation *El estado y su evolución al principio de la colonización española de América*. Mexico City: Fondo de Cultura Económica, 1989.

Poole, Stafford. *Pedro Moya de Conteras. Catholic Reform and Royal Power in New Spain, 1571–1591*. University of California Press: Berkeley, 1987.

Priestley, Herbert Ingram. *José de Gálvez. Visitor-General of New Spain (1765–1771)*. Berkeley: University of California Press, 1916.

Radaelli, Sigfrido Augusto. *La institución virreinal en las Indias; antecedentes históricas*. Buenos Aires: Perrot, 1957.

Real Academia Española, ed. *Diccionario de la lengua castellana en que se explica el verdadero sentido de las voces, su naturaleza y calidad ...* [1726] 3 Vols. Madrid: Editorial Gredos, 1963.

Reinhard, Wolfgang. *Freunde und Kreaturen. "Verflechtung" als Konzept zur Erforschung historischer Führungsgruppen. Römische Oligarchie um 1600*. Munich: Ernst Vögel, 1979.

_____. "Introduction. Power Elites, State Servants, Ruling Classes and the Growth of State Power." In *Power Elites and State Building*. Edited by Wolfgang Reinhard. Oxford: Clarendon Press, 1996. 1–18.

Ringrose, David R. *Madrid and the Spanish Economy, 1560–1850*. Berkeley: University of California Press, 1983.

Rivera, Manuel. *Los Gobernantes de México. Galería de biografías y retratos de los Vireyes, Emperadores, Presidentes y otros gobernantes que ha tenido México, desde Don Hernando Cortes hasta el C. Benito Juarez*. Vol. 1. Mexico City: Imprenta de J. M. Aguilar Ortiz, 1872.

Rosenmüller, Christoph. "Friends, Followers, Countrymen: Viceregal Networking in Mid-Eighteenth Century New Spain." *Estudios de Historia Novohispana* (Mexico City) 34 (2006): 47–72.

Rubio Mañé, Jorge Ignacio. "Gente de España en la ciudad de México, año de 1689. Introducción, recopilación y acotaciones." *Boletín del Archivo General de la Nación* (Mexico City) 7, 2nd series, No. 1–2 (1966): 25–405.

_____. *Introducción al estudio de los virreyes de Nueva España, 1535–1746*. 4 vols. Mexico City: UNAM, 1955–63.

Romano, Ruggiero. *Conjonctures opposées. La "crise" du XVIIe siècle: en Europe et en Amérique ibérique*. Geneva: Librairie Droz, 1992.

Sáez-Arance, Antonio. "La corte de los Habsburgos en Madrid (siglos XVI y XVII): Estado de la cuestión y nuevos planteamientos historiográficos." In *La creatividad femenina en el mundo barroco hispánico. María de Zayas-Isabel Rebeca Correa-Sor Juana Inés de la Cruz*. Edited by Monika Bosse, Barbara Potthast, and André Stoll. Kassel: Reichenberger, 1999. 1:1–16.

Saguier, Eduardo R. "La corrupción administrativa como mecanismo de acumulación y engendrador de una burguesía local." *Anuario de Estudios Americanos* 56 (1989): 269–303.

Sánchez Bella, Ismael. *Derecho Indiano: Estudios I. Las visitas generales en la América española (siglos XVI–XVII)*. Pamplona: Ediciones de la Universidad de Navarra, 1991.

Sanchiz, Javier. "Lucas de Careaga, Marqués de Santa Fe. La historia fugaz de un noble vasco en la Nueva España. Una biografía en construcción." In *Los vascos en las regiones de Mexico siglos XVI a XX*. Edited by Amaya Garritz. Mexico City: UNAM, 1997. 3:203–17.

Sanchiz, Javier and José I. Conde. *Títulos y diginidades nobiliarias en Nueva España*. Mexico City: UNAM, forthcoming.

Sarrablo Aguareles, Eugenio. *El Conde de Fuenclara. Embajador y Virrey 1687–1752*. Seville: G.E.H.A., 1955.

Schäfer, Ernst. *El consejo real y supremo de Indias. Su historia, organización y labor administrativo hasta la terminación de la casa de Austria*. 2 vols. Seville: M. Carmona, 1935–47.

Schmidt, Peer. "Neoestoicismo y disciplinamiento social en Iberoamérica colonial (siglo XVII)." In *Pensamiento europeo y cultura colonial*. Edited by Karl Kohut and Sonia Rose. Frankfurt am Main: Vervuert, 1997. 181–204.

Schmidt, Steffen. *Friends, Followers, and Factions: A Reader in Political Clientelism*. Berkeley: University of California Press, 1977.

Schurz, William Lytle. *The Manila Galeon*. New York: E. P. Dutton, 1939.

Schwaller, John Frederick. "The Secular Clergy in Sixteenth-Century Mexico." Ph.D. diss., Indiana University, 1978.

Simpson, Lesley Byrd. *Many Mexicos*. New York: G. P. Putnam's Sons, 1946.

Slicher van Bath, Bernard Hendrik. *Indianen en Spanjaarden. Een ontmoeting tussen twee werelden, Latijns Amerika 1500–1800*. Amsterdam: B. Bakker, 1989.

Stein, Stanley J., and Barbara H. Stein. *Apogee of Empire. Spain and New Spain in the Age of Charles III, 1759–1789*. Baltimore: Johns Hopkins University Press, 2003.

Taylor, William. *Magistrates of the Sacred. Priests and Parishioners in Eighteenth-Century Mexico*. Stanford: Stanford University Press, 1996.

Tomás y Valiente, Francisco. *El derecho penal de la monarquía absoluta (siglos XVI–XVII–XVIII)*. Madrid: Editorial Tecnos, 1969.

Tutino, John Mark. "Creole Mexico: Spanish Elites, Haciendas, and Indian Towns, 1750–1810." Ph.D. diss., University of Texas at Austin, 1976.

Valle-Arizpe, Artemio de. *Virreyes y virreinas de la Nueva España. Leyendas, tradiciones y sucedios del México virreinal*. Madrid: Biblioteca Nueva, 1938.

Valle Menéndez, Antonio del. *Juan Francisco de Güemes y Horcasitas. Primer Conde de Revillagigedo. Virrey de México. La historia de un soldado (1681–1766)*. In collaboration with Pilar Latasa Vasallo. Santander: Librería Estudios, 1998.

Velázquez, María del Carmen. *El Marqués de Altamira y las provincias internas de Nueva España*. Jornadas 81. Mexico City: El Colegio de México, 1976.

Vicens Vives, Jaime. "The Administrative Structure of the State in the Sixteenth and Seventeenth Centuries." In *The Government of Reformation Europe*. Edited by Henry J. Cohen. London: MacMillan, 1971. 58–87.

Vicente y Caravantes, José, and León Galindo y de Vera, eds. *Diccionario razonado de legislacion y jurisprudencia por D. Joaquín Escriche. Nueva edicion reformada y considerablemente aumentada....* 4 vols. Madrid: Imprenta de Eduardo Cuesta, 1874–1876.

Waldmann, Peter. "Zur Transformation des europäischen Staatsmodells in Lateinamerika." In *Verstaatlichung der Welt? Europäische Staatsmodelle und außereuropäische Machtprozesse*. Edited by Wolfgang Reinhard. Schriften des Historischen Kollegs, Kolloquien. Vol. 47. Munich: Oldenbourg, 1999. 53–66.

Walker, Geoffrey. *Spanish Politics and Imperial Trade, 1700-1789*. Bloomington: Indiana University Press, 1979.

Wasserman, Stanley. *Social Network Analysis: Methods and Applications*. Cambridge: Cambridge University Press, 1994.

Weber, Max. *Politcs as a Vocation*. Translated and edited by H. H. Gerth and C. Wright Mills. Philadelphia: Fortress Press, 1965.

_____. *The Protestant Ethic and the Spirit of Capitalism*. Edited by Anthony Giddens. Translated by Talcott Parsons. New York: Charles Scribner's Sons, 1958.

Weingrod, Alex. "Patrons, Patronage and Political Parties." *Comparative Studies in Society and History* 10:4 (1968): 377-400.

Wolff-Buisson, Inge. *Regierung und Verwaltung der kolonialspanischen Städte in Hochperu, 1538-1650*. Cologne: Böhlau, 1970.

Yuste, Carmen, ed. *Comerciantes mexicanos en el siglo XVIII*. Mexico City: UNAM, 1991.

Zysberg, André. *Les galériens. Vies et destins de 60.000 forçats sur les galères de France, 1640-1748*. Paris: Editions du Seuil, 1987.

Index

A

Abellafuentes, Alonso, 87
Acosta, Juan de, 111
Ajolesa, Martín, 59–60
Alamán, Lucas, 49
Alburquerque, eighth Duke of, 2, 9
Alburquerque, Francisco Férnandez de la Cueva Enríquez, tenth Duke of, vi, 2, 9–10
  allegations against, 145–50, 152–53
  appointment of, 8, 16, 163
  arrival and departure celebrations of, 47–48
  attitude toward *audiencia*, 116–17
  and the Church, 61–62, 127
  corruption of, 104, 115, 166
  crackdown on, 30–31, 134
  death of, 160
  defeat of, 58
  and faux Habsburg conspiracy, 101–25
  impact of fall, 159–61
  journey to Mexico, 17
  legal counsel of, 114
  lineage of, 116
  mercury policy of, 132–35
  opposes the crown, 128
  patronage of, 9, 53–78, 94, 103, 107, 122, 164
  regional background of, 97
  retainers of, 54, 58–59
  return to Spain, 154
  and the Sánchez de Tagle family, 81–92
  and secularization, 138–41
  trade policies of, 79–82, 89–91, 95, 98–99, 143–45
  travels of, 46, 49, 78
  treasury reform of, 128–29
  trial of, 155–57
  vs. Lucas Careaga, 94
alcabala tax, 128–35, 145, 165, 167
alcaldes mayores, 25, 67–68, 129, 131, 151, 152, 163
  role of, 53–54, 65–66
  sale of offices, 31
  under Alburquerque, 55, 59–61, 69–74, 78, 134, 139–40, 148. *See also corregidores*
Alcántara, Order of, 99
Alfonso X, 104
Alvarez de Toledo, Cayetana, 158
Alvarez del Valle, José, 68, 72, 149
Alvarez Osorio, Miguel, 18
Amarillas, Marquis of, 59
Amelot, Michel-Jean, 14–16, 153, 158
Anjou, Duke of, 13, 15, 109
Araciel, Alonso de, 153–54
Aragon, 8
Aranda, Count of, 18–19
Archbishop Juan de Ortega y Montañés. *See* Ortega y Montañés, Juan de
Asch, Ronald, 6

Asinas Duque de Estrada, Alonso de, 103, 111–12
Atrisco, Duke of, 54
audiencia, 5, 20–21, 74, 76
audiencia of Mexico, 8–9, 87, 132, 141, 158–59, 164–65
    and faux-Habsburg conspiracy, 102–3, 108, 113, 118, 120
    offices of, 36
    patio of, 35
    quarrels with viceroy, 34, 116–17
    relationship with archbishop, 84
    role in government, 9, 23–25, 43, 48, 87, 114–15
    sale of offices, 31
    in Sánchez de Tagle-Cruzat controversy, 85–86
    social roles of ministers, 8, 44, 46
Augustinians, 136
Azpilcueta Navarro, Martín de, 17

B

Balthasar Charles, Prince, 123
Baños, Count of, 158
Basques, 11, 95–96, 99, 165
Berri, Duke of, 109
Bertrand, Michel, 5–6, 76, 152
Borah, Woodrow, 11
Borges, Analola, 101
Bourbon (dynasty in Spain), 2, 8, 13, 51, 102, 106, 109, 113, 123–24, 147, 157, 159–60, 163, 165–66
    conflicts with France, 15
    reforms and appointments, 9–10, 20–22, 161, 167
Brading, David, 2, 4
Brunner, Otto, 31
Buenavista, Marquis of, 112
Burke, Peter, 34

C

cabildo civil (municipal council), 7, 21, 48, 56, 84, 86, 88–89, 149
cabildo eclesiástico (ecclesiastical chapter), 120, 122
Calatrava, Order of, 99
Calderón de la Barca, Miguel, 107, 114–15, 147, 152
Campillo y Cossío, José del, 18

Campomanes, Count of, 18
Canal, Domingo de la, 92, 99
Cañeque, Alejandro, 30–31
Cantera, Bernardo de la, 71–72
Capocelato, Bartolomé de, 101
Carande, Ramón, 29
Careaga Sanz de Urrutia, Lucas de, 82, 88–89, 94–96, 112
Careaga, José de, 112
Cartagena, Benito, 110–12
Casafuerte, Marquis of, 22–23, 152, 160
Castile, Admiral of, 13, 101
Castillo, Juan del, 88–89, 99
Castro Santa-Anna, Joaquín, 55–56
Cepeda y Castro Gil de Gibaja, Gaspar Blas, 104–5, 107–8, 115–18, 120
Cerda Morán, José de la, 70
Cerralvo, Marquis of, 130
Chapultepec, 47, 49
Charles II, 12, 14, 16, 116, 124, 131, 155, 164
    appointments in Mexico, 21, 66
Charles III, 2, 22, 167
Charles V, Emperor, 16, 116
Charles, Archduke, 13, 15, 101
Chaunu, Pierre and Huguette, 11
Chinchón, Count of, 151
Church (Roman Catholic), 3–4, 15, 18–19, 24–25, 27, 34, 48, 115, 117, 120–21, 163
    and Alburquerque, 48, 61–62, 78, 109, 124, 164
    and the Enlightenment, 18
    secularization and, 127, 136–42
Cienfuegos, José de, 120–21
Cistercians, 137
compadrazgo, defined, 4–5
Conquest, 3
Conquista, Duke of la, 22–23
consulado, defined, 8
consulado of Mexico, 36, 42–44, 56, 85–91, 94–99, 123, 130, 150, 164–65
consulado of Seville, 10, 21, 81–82, 89, 89–90, 94–99, 105–6, 108, 118, 124, 143–45, 157–58, 164–67
Coria, Jacinto de, 139
corregidores, 2, 19, 20, 53, 67, 113
    under Alburquerque, 59, 65–67, 71–73, 78, 89, 116, 150, 163. *See also alcaldes mayores*

corruption, 2, 9, 19, 21, 29–33, 35, 51, 128, 159–60, 166–67
Cortés, Hernán, 54
Costela, Andrés Pérez de, 117–18, 120–22
Coto, Juan, 106
Council of Castile, 13, 136, 155
Council of the Indies, 13–17, 20, 24–25, 31, 58, 60, 87, 90, 96, 107–8, 113–15, 128, 132–35, 137–39, 141–42, 145, 147–49, 152–55, 158, 165
Council of Trent, 137
Creoles, 2, 55, 76, 96, 98–99, 159, 165
criados (retainers), 10, 35
   in Alburquerque's court, 58–61, 69–74, 76–78
   appointments of, 53, 69, 76
   defined, 7
   role in government, 43
   social roles of, 46
Cruzat family, 83–88, 96, 105, 109, 120–21, 140, 147, 156
Cruzat y Góngora, Fausto, 82–83, 92
Cruzat y Góngora, Ignacia, 83–88, 117, 164

D

Daubenton, Guillaume, 156
despacho universal, 12–14, 77, 82, 94
d'Estrées, Cardinal César, 13
Dominicans, 127, 136–42, 166

E

Elias, Norbert, 6–7, 33, 51
Elton, Geoffrey, 6, 33
Ensenada, Marquis of la, 18–22, 67–68, 128
Escalante y Mendoza, Juan de, 120
Escriche, Joaquín, 105
Espinosa Ocampo y Cornejo, José Antonio, 87, 132, 139
Esquilache, Marquis of, 22, 144, 167
Estacasolo y Otalora, Juan de, 60, 74, 77, 154
Europe, 3, 7

F

Farnese, Elizabeth, 15
Ferdinand, Prince, 160
Fernández Cacho, Juan, 57–58, 149
Fernández de Bethencourt, Francisco, 9

Fernández de Córdoba, Leonor, 59
Fernández de Guevara, Tomás, 111–12
Fernández de la Cueva, Francisco. *See* Alburquerque, tenth Duke of
Fernández de Santa Cruz, Manuel, 131
Fernández de Tubera, Antonio, 96
Fernández Santillán, Diego, 146
Florence, Duke of, 123
Flores Fernández, Juan, 71
France, 5, 13, 15, 18, 27, 91, 95, 145, 157
Franciscans, 136–37, 139
Freire y San Martín, Antonio, 104, 110
Frigiliana, Count of, 15–16
Fuenclara, Viceroy Count of, 46, 160

G

Galve, Count of, 112
Gálvez y Gallardo, José de, 2, 4, 144, 167
   appointment as secretary of state of Indies, 22
   reform program of, 19, 21, 151
Gálvez, Bernardo de, 50
Gama, Antonio de, 57
Garaicoechea, Juan de, 92, 103, 105–7, 110, 150
Garzarón, Francisco, 120, 147–48
Gasco Suárez, Gregorio, 104–8, 116, 124, 165
Gelves, Marquis of, 2, 19, 98, 165
Gerhard, Peter, 70
Giudice, Cardinal Francesco del, appointed, 15
Gómez de Silva, Ruy, 19
Gómez Lobato, Antonio, 103–4, 107, 110, 133, 150
Gómez Lobato, Bernardo, 110
Gómez Lobato, Pedro, 110
González de Agüero, Félix, 67, 147–48, 150, 153, 160
González de Figueroa, Lorenzo, 109
Guadalajara, 21, 25, 73, 84–85, 132, 137
Guevara, Antonio de, 33

H

Habsburg, 2
   monarchy, 8, 12–13, 19, 54, 102, 107, 120, 124–25, 153, 155, 158, 163, 165–66
   sympathizers and conspirators, 9–10, 27, 101, 116, 123, 125, 157

Index   275

Haring, Clarence H., 151
Herrera, Alonso de, 154
Herzog, Tamar, 5
Hidalgo, Félix, 114

I
Ibáñez de Oserin, Luis, 107
Iglesias, Diego de, 73
indemnity junta, 148, 153, 155–58, 160–61, 166
Infantado, Duke of, 160
Innocent XII, Pope, 124
Institutional Revolutionary Party (PRI), 1
Israel, Jonathan, 2, 98

J
Javier de Ayala, Francisco, 123
Jesuits, 139
Joseph, Emperor, 15

K
Kettering, Sharon, 5
Klaveren, Jacob van, 29
Konetzke, Richard, 29

L
Ledesma, José de, 114
León, José de, 141
Lerma, Duke of, 19
Linares, Duke of, 17, 82, 159
López de Landa, Nicolás, 91–92
Louis XIV, King of France, 5–6, 157
  and allies, 13–15
Louis, son of Philip V, 44
Luna Arias, José de, 133
Lynch, John, 2, 3

M
Macanaz, Melchor de, 18
MacLachlan, Colin M., 2
Madrid, 2, 7
Maldonado, Angel de, 61, 127–28, 137–42, 166
Mañer, Salvador, 111, 113–14, 111
Manila galleon, 80, 82–83, 143–44, 146, 160
Manso de Zúñiga, Francisco, 67

Maria Ana, Queen, 123
Maria von Neuburg, Queen, 13
Marie Louise of Savoy, Queen, 15
Mariluz Urquijo, José María, 150–51
Marquina, Diego, 55
Martín de Guijo, Gregorio, 55
Martínez de Aguirre, Jacinto, 47
Medina Picazo, Francisco de, 46
Medinaceli, Duke of, 13, 16–17, 123, 131, 157, 161, 166
  appointed prime minister, 20
  reform program of, 21–22
mercury, 50, 104, 132–35, 153, 156
mercury, accountancy of, 50, 128, 132, 135, 165
mercury junta, 135, 153, 155
mint, Mexico City, 35, 74, 81, 86, 91–92, 99, 164
Miravalle, Alonso de Dávalos Bracamonte, Count of, 91, 93, 146
Moncada, Sancho de, 18
Monclova, Count of, 158–59, 167
Montañeses (Montañés), 95–97, 99, 165
Monteleone, Duke of, 54
Monterrey, Count of, 158
Montezuma, Count of, 55
Morales, Joaquín de, 76
Moriana, Count of, 154
Munarris, José, 59, 77
Munarris, Miguel, 59, 68, 77

N
nao. *See* Manila galleon
Navarrians, 96
Navarro García, Luis, 9, 102, 114, 165
Navia, Carlos de, 114
New Mexico, 8
New Spain, 2, 3, 4, 7, 8, 9
Nuñez de Villavicencio, José, 61

O
Oaxaca, 54, 61, 69–70, 76–77, 127, 136–42, 166
Ocampo, José Antonio Espinosa, 139
Ochoa, Lorenzo, 69
Oestreich, Gerhard, 3, 4
Olivares, Count-Duke of, 19, 21, 31, 98, 128, 130, 166–67

Oropesa, Count of, 3, 12–14, 20–22, 101, 136, 167
Orry, Jean, 15, 154–57
Ortega y Montañés, Archbishop Juan de, 47, 59, 83–85, 87, 96, 99, 109, 112, 121, 124, 152
Ortiz, Luis, 17–18
Osilia y Rayo, Jerónimo de, 152
Osorio, Julián de, 49, 92, 107, 146
Otalora Bravo de Laguna, Juan de, 154

P

Pacheco, Carlos Samaniego, 69
padrinazgo, 4
Pagabe, Francisco de, 104, 152–53, 159
Palafox, Juan de, 19, 159
Palma, Augustín de, 146
Paris, 5
Patiño, José de, 114
patronage, 5, 7–8, 53–78
Pez, Andrés de, 67, 145–46, 155
Phelan, John Leddy, 1, 5, 30
Philip II, 2, 19, 50
Philip IV, 123
Philip V, 8–9, 13, 15–16, 27, 44, 80–81, 101, 107, 112, 123, 128, 137, 153–55, 157, 160, 163–64, 166
  conflicts within government of, 13–14
  policies of, 20, 74, 143, 158
Philippines, the, 18, 25, 80, 82–84, 99, 124, 143, 164
Pietschmann, Horst, 2, 30, 151
Pinedo, Gaspar de, 145
Portocarrero, Cardinal, 12, 14
Puebla, 12, 21, 47, 50, 66, 74, 77, 89, 117, 127–28, 130–36, 165–67
Puyol, Joaquín, 106, 108

Q

Quevedo, Francisco de, 43

R

Ramírez de Arellano, José, 67
Rastatt, treaty of, 15
real acuerdo, 24, 36, 86–87, 115–16, 139–42, 150
Reinhard, Wolfgang, 4

residencia, juicio de, 7, 24, 30, 46, 54, 61, 73, 92, 104, 114, 123, 141, 147–52, 156, 158
Revillagigedo, Countess of, 59
Revillagigedo, first Count of, 22–23, 34, 46, 48–49, 55–56, 59, 160
Revillagigedo, second Count of, 59
Rivera, Manuel, 9
Rivera, Pedro de, 67
Robinet, Jean, 156
Robles, Antonio de, 55
Rodriguez de Santa Cruz, Estéban, 74, 77
Ruano de Arista, Isidro, 75
Ruiz de Tagle, Domingo, 82–87, 93, 99

S

Saint-Simon, Duke of, 45
Salamanca, University of, 115, 155
Salvatierra, Count of, 158–59
Sánchez de Tagle family, 49, 82, 88–94, 96, 99, 105–6, 109, 115, 120–21, 140, 147, 156, 164
Sánchez de Tagle, Luis, 81–92, 95–96, 99, 123, 164–65
Sánchez de Tagle, Pedro, 82, 85–88, 90, 92, 96, 99, 141
Santiago, Order of, 98–99
Schäfer, Ernst, 151
secularization, 127, 136–38
Sevilla, Leonardo de, 114
Seville, viii, 10, 21, 80–82, 89, 94–96, 99, 105–6, 113, 143–45, 157–58, 161, 164–67
silver mining, in New Spain, 11–12
Simpson, Lesley B., 98
Smith, Adam, 19
Sola, Marcos de, 113,
Soto, Domingo de, 17
Sousa y Prado, Manuel de, 111–13, 124, 111
Spain, 4, 7
Spanish Succession, War of, 17, 20–22, 27, 69, 80
Suárez Muñoz, Manuel, 112
superintendent of the *alcabala*, 21, 117, 127–28, 130–34, 165, 167
superintendente general de la real hacienda, 25, 133

Index 277

T

Tagle, Sánchez de. *See* Sánchez de Tagle family
textiles, in New Spain, 12
Toledo, Alvarez de, 159
Torres, José de, 123
Tovar, Baltasar de, 61, 103–5, 107–9, 112–13, 115, 140–41
trade under Alburquerque, 81–82, 91
　illegal, 79–80
　in Mexico, 80–81
　oligopoly, 79–81, 88–91, 95, 103, 106, 131, 144, 146, 148, 158–59, 165
　policies of Spain, 79–81, 143–45
Tutino, John, 2

U

Ubilla y Estrada, Miguel de, 81–82, 94, 96
Ubilla y Medina, Antonio de, 12–13, 82
　removal of, 14
Ulloa, Bernardo de, 18
Union of Arms, 98, 130
Uribe, José Joaquín de, 83, 115–18, 120–21, 154
Ursins, Princess des, 13–15, 153, 155, 157
　dismissal of, 27
　influence at court, 13
Urtazu, Pedro, 111–13
Utrecht, treaty of, 15
Uztariz, Jerónimo de, 18

V

Valdés, Juan de, 148–50
Valero, Marquis of, 76
Valles, Domingo, 74
Valley of Oaxaca, Marquis of the, 54
Velanzuela, Fernando, Marquis of Villa Sierra, 123
Vendôme, Duke of, 15
Vera, Diego de, 111
Veracruz, 86, 90–92, 95, 133–34, 143, 145–48, 151–52, 156, 159
Veytia Linage, Juan José de, 50, 66, 117, 127–28, 130–35, 153, 165–66
viceregal palace, 35, 45, 48, 50, 86, 151

viceroy
　arrival celebrations of, 47
　court of, 33, 42
　defined, 7
　guards of, 42
　legal powers of, 23–25, 33–35, 48–51, 68, 115
　palace of, 35–36, 37, 38, 39, 40, 41, 45
　and religious celebrations, 43–44, 46
　riot in palace, 45
　selection of, 22, 68
　social structure, 43–46
　travels of, 46
Villar, Antonio de, 108
visita, 2, 21, 137, 151–52, 159
visitador, 24, 104, 147, 153
Vitoria, Francisco de, 17
Vizcaínos, 96

W

Ward, Bernardo, 18
Weber, Max, 3